A TREASURY OF

The World's Great Letters

FROM ANCIENT DAYS TO OUR OWN TIME

containing THE CHARACTERISTIC AND CRUCIAL COMMUNICATIONS, AND INTIMATE EXCHANGES AND CYCLES OF CORRESPONDENCE, OF MANY OF THE OUTSTANDING FIGURES OF WORLD HISTORY, AND SOME NOTABLE CONTEMPORARIES, SELECTED, EDITED, AND INTEGRATED WITH BIOGRAPHICAL BACKGROUNDS AND HISTORICAL SETTINGS AND CONSEQUENCES BY M. LINCOLN SCHUSTER

NEW YORK   SIMON AND SCHUSTER   MCMXXXX

Designed by Robert Josephy

MANUFACTURED IN THE UNITED STATES OF AMERICA
BY THE HADDON CRAFTSMEN, INC., CAMDEN, N. J.

TO MY WIFE

In Praise of Letters

The post is the consolation of life. VOLTAIRE

The earth has nothing like a she epistle. BYRON

As long as there are postmen, life will have zest. WILLIAM JAMES

In a man's letters, you know, madam, his soul lies naked.

DR. JOHNSON

The public will always give up its dinner to read love letters.

GEORGE JEAN NATHAN

Letters, such as written by wise men, are, of all the words of men, in my judgment, the best. FRANCIS BACON

I forgot to say that one of the pleasures of reading old letters is the knowledge that they need no answer. BYRON

The need of composing letters was the earliest and most constant incentive to terseness, clarity, and exactitude of statement.

R. L. MÉGROZ

Let those who may complain that it (the Shaw-Ellen Terry "romantic correspondence") was all on paper remember that only on paper has humanity yet achieved glory, beauty, truth, knowledge, virtue, and abiding love. GEORGE BERNARD SHAW

Letters frighten me more than anything else in life. They contain greater possibilities of murder than any poison. I think you ought only to write to a person when you are in the same place and quite certain to see them. When a letter is a continuation of presence it is all right, but when it becomes a codification of absence it is intolerable. . . . Please write to me. . . .

ELIZABETH BIBESCO

Letters make the best anthologies. You remember that enchanting person Pearsall Smith jocularly urging Posterity to "hurry up and get itself born" so that it can have the pleasure of reading Trivia. Similarly there are certain people whom one almost feels inclined to urge to hurry up and die so that their letters can be published. It is chiefly—perhaps only—in letters that one gets the mother-of-pearly shimmer inside the oyster of Fact.

CHRISTOPHER MORLEY

What cannot letters inspire? They have souls; they can speak; they have in them all that force which expresses the transports of the heart; they have all the fire of our passions. They can raise them as much as if the persons themselves were present. They have all the tenderness and the delicacy of speech, and sometimes even a boldness of expression beyond it. Letters were first invented for consoling such solitary wretches as myself! . . . Having lost the substantial pleasures of seeing and possessing you, I shall in some measure compensate this loss by the satisfaction I shall find in your writing. There I shall read your most sacred thoughts.

FROM THE LETTERS OF HELOISE TO ABELARD

Table of Contents

CONTENTS

CONTENTS

xii

CONTENTS

xiv

CONTENTS

CONTENTS

xviii

CONTENTS

xxii

PART III: LETTERS OF YESTERDAY AND TODAY
[from 1898 to 1937]

CONTENTS

xxiv

CONTENTS

xxvi

List of Illustrations

CLASSIFICATION OF LETTERS BY SUBJECT

LOVE LETTERS

xxx

xxxii

ACKNOWLEDGMENTS

A full listing of reprint sanctions for copyrighted letters, and a grateful record of the editor's indebtedness to co-operating authors and publishers, to his research and secretarial staff, friends, and various colleagues and advisers will be found on page 525.

Introduction

I

LETTERS make the most interesting reading in the world—especially other people's.

That, at least, is the conviction that has directed the many years of research and collecting that have gone into the making of this anthology.

Actually, the letters of men have interested me as much and as long as the men of letters. Man and boy, I have been tracking down and hoarding "the great letters of history" since 1915, when I was first enthralled by the rhapsodies that Ludwig van Beethoven poured out on paper to "the immortal beloved." About the same time, I was also thrilled by Captain Robert Falcon Scott's letter from the South Pole, in which he declared that "these rough notes and our dead bodies must tell the tale" of an ill-starred and heroic adventure.

Such letters, together with a number of historic and dramatic communications of Spinoza, Dr. Johnson, Franklin, Lincoln, and Stevenson, which enlivened my youthful explorations in biography, literature, and history, formed the beginning of my collection. From sheer emotional excitement, the hoard grew with the years.

Gradually my accumulation of letters soon began to take more or less systematic form, and in 1923 the first vague pattern of an anthology developed. Since then my collection has grown at a geometric rate. I found myself hunting and saving the famous and durably significant letters of history, annotating, weeding, arranging, appraising, interpreting, and integrating them. Before I realized it, I had amassed many hundreds of letters.

The need for special standards of selection soon became apparent. Intensely interested in biography, and convinced that a man's character was best revealed in his letters, I began to concentrate specifically on the letters reflecting the great personalities, the great events, and the great ideas of history—covering all time and all countries.

Before I realized it, I found I had enough letters to fill many mammoth volumes. My researches became so engrossing that every time I was on the point of going to press, new and apparently irresistible letters came to hand, and I fell into the habit of postponing actual publication year after year. Friends who knew of my craving flooded me with fresh contributions that could not be denied, and I kept on deferring the final deadline, striving constantly and somewhat fastidiously to make my collection historically comprehensive and biographically significant. With fresh letters constantly coming to light, as well as old letters recently discovered and new data on early favorites, it seemed increasingly difficult to close the barriers and publish my collection.

Then I decided to concentrate discriminatingly and ruthlessly on the winnowed best, and in this spirit I began to visualize a single omnibus volume of the world's great letters.

In my first years as a publisher, I accelerated and intensified my researches, for my colleagues indulgently encouraged my interest in great letters, and urged me to compile and edit the pick of my collection for a representative and compact Inner Sanctum anthology. This is it.

II

As I began ransacking the epistolary treasures of the ages, I found that letter sequences could be as exciting as sonnet sequences, and frequently more intense and more revealing. From this rather naïve but exhilarating discovery, I developed for this anthology my own variation on a distinctive quasi-literary form—the amalgam of biography and correspondence, summarized in the standard phrase "life and letters."

Before explaining this phrase in detail, let me first apologize for the use of the rather ambitious adjective "great" in the title of this anthology. I am using the word in a strictly personal sense. I mean to suggest that I have here gathered letters which have had great interest and fascination for me because of their importance in history, their illumination of biography, and their value as a clue to motives. In a sense, then, these letters, taken together, provide an intimate commentary on the story of mankind, a secret casebook of the mainsprings of human behavior. That, at any rate, has been my aim.

Let me be even more personal: with an abiding interest in the turning points of history and the driving forces of homo sapiens and homo stultus, such as love, justice, the struggle for power, self-interest, ambition, and fear, and with a deep devotion to music in general, and with a keen interest in creative genius, it is only natural that my collection should give dominant attention to letters on these subjects and from such personalities. In the main, the authors of the letters included are "the foremost people of history," but there is also a sprinkling of their lesser contemporaries, not to mention some varied voices of our own time.

III

In assembling this anthology of letters, I find myself in illustrious company, for earlier and far more learned collections of famous letters have been edited by George Saintsbury, E. V. Lucas, Lord Birkenhead, and scores of others.

This anthology, however, differs from the others in the following respects:

(1) It provides, in most cases, both sides of the correspondence, or its equivalent, wherever possible.

(2) In time, it ranges from early days of recorded history to our own era, specifically from Alexander the Great to Thomas Mann.

(3) In scope, it covers many of the great civilizations of history, and many cultures and literatures, predominantly, but not entirely, Western.

(4) Each letter is preceded by an introduction, setting the letter in time and space; summarizing the essential biographical information about the person who wrote the letter and, where relevant, about the person to whom it was addressed; explaining the impelling motive for the communication and the pertinent or dramatically significant circumstances.

(5) Each letter is followed by a brief epilogue, giving the result or consequences of the letter, or a summary of the answer to it, when the reply itself is not given.

(6) This anthology does not confine itself merely to one category, such as literary letters or love letters, but covers the wide range of human emotions and human interest, generally, concentrating to a large degree on the outstanding personalities, the crucial events, or the dominant ideas of world history.

(7) In some cases, letters never before published or hitherto restricted to private or limited editions are here made generally available for the first time, as, for example, the letters of Voltaire and Boswell.

(8) In many cases—such as Napoleon, Shelley, Tchaikovsky, Elizabeth Barrett, and Robert Browning, for example—letters only recently made public for the first time are presented here, thus substantially amplifying or drastically changing our knowledge of their lives and characters.

(9) In a number of major instances—such as Alexander the Great, Voltaire, Franklin, Johnson, Napoleon, Shelley, Keats, the Brownings, and Lincoln, among others—there is provided a whole cycle or chronological series of significantly integrated correspondence.

(10) The letters are so arranged and so interrelated as to shed light, from a number of vantage points, on the greatest events, the greatest ideas, and the greatest people of history. Specifically, we see the beginning of Christianity through the eyes and through the letters of not only Saint Paul but also of the Roman emperors; we see the splendors of the Renaissance through the eyes and letters of Leonardo da Vinci and Michelangelo; we witness the French Revolution from the point of view of both Danton and Robespierre, not to mention the background provided by the letters of Voltaire and Madame de Sévigné; we see the American Revolution through the correspondence of George Washington, Thomas Paine, Benjamin Franklin, and Thomas Jefferson; the triumph of the evolutionary theory from the writings of both Darwin and Huxley; the Russian Revolution as observed by the Romanovs, as well as by Lenin and Trotsky. I mention these few representative examples to suggest the integration and total perspective I have tried to achieve by the arrangement of letter sequences, by deadly parallels, and by ironic, tragic, dramatic, and revealing contrasts.

IV

In many biographies, in many other anthologies of letters, I have often wondered in vain as to the cause or the result of a given communication. It seems to me fallacious to assume that great letters can be presented in a vacuum, without background material, biographical notes, and epilogues. It is true that to a large extent some letters tell their own story, but they become much more exciting and much more revealing when we know what has inspired them, and when some of the obscure and cryptic allusions have been explained. For this reason, it has in some cases seemed necessary to provide long introductions for short letters.

V

In most cases I have given the letters in their complete text, but in the instances where there has been some necessary abridgment, that fact is indicated by the use of this symbol: . . .

Some of the longest letters in the book are actually the most dramatic and the most enthralling—like the impassioned love letters of Heloise and Abelard, Spinoza's sublime defense of the faith of a God-intoxicated man, the inspired and unhurried gossip of James Boswell from Voltaire's home, and the fiery indignation of Robert Louis Stevenson in support of Father Damien. Such communications, running on to many pages, are nevertheless given in their entirety.

VI

The noted American historian, Carl Becker, has well put the case for letters as a source of historical illumination: "The record of events, of what men have done, is relatively rich and informing. But a record of the state of mind that conditioned those events, a record that might enable us to analyze the complex of instincts and emotions that lie behind the avowed purpose and the formulated principles of action—such a record is largely wanting. What one requires for such investigation are the more personal writings—memoirs, and, above all, letters—in which individuals consciously or unconsciously reveal the hidden springs of conduct."

Lytton Strachey went even farther, pointing out that letter writers and diarists provide ". . . a badly needed corrective for pompous Clio, the most glorious of the muses, tripping her up, revealing her undergarments in the most indecorous manner."

Like the journals and private papers of the classic gossips and diarists, such as Samuel Pepys, James Boswell, and Saint-Simon, the function of letters is "to reveal to us the littleness underlying great events and to remind us that history was once real life."

Historians may concentrate on coronations and battles, but it is to letter writers we turn when we want to learn—in the words of Sinclair Lewis—"what people ate, with what weapons exactly they killed one another and the precise state of acid pomposity with which a duke or plainsman complains of his breakfast porridge."

Letters give us great lives at their most characteristic, their most glorious, and their most terrible moments. Here history and biography meet, to form the most intimate of all forms of literature—the private letters of the mighty, and their contemporaries.

Here, then, are love letters, taunting letters, shocking letters, letters dipped in honeyed phrases, letters written with words of gall, bombastic letters, letters breathing fire, letters with good news, letters spelling disaster, passionate letters, secret letters, casual letters, gushing letters, impulsive letters, crafty letters, open letters, grandiloquent letters, short letters, voluminous letters, letters of hatred, letters of courage, letters of adoration, letters of fury, letters people forgot to burn, letters people did not dare to mail, letters that glorified literature, thundering letters, tender letters, inspired letters, diabolical letters, letters that made history.

A treasury of such letters is really a treasury of life lived passionately, life disclosed to the uttermost, life set down without fear or inhibition, life brought to a climax, life challenged and critically examined. The dark corridors as well as the loftiest towers in the hall of fame here give up some of their most inviolable secrets. These are the things the foremost men of history fought, bled, and died for—and also the things they lived by.

The word "great," I repeat, is not to be taken too literally. It is at best an elastic term. Not all the letters are of the first importance; not all the people are of the first magnitude. But in the main that is the criterion, with a strong accent on the master spirits of the ages and the sovereigns of the arts, like Leonardo da Vinci, Michelangelo, Baruch Spinoza, Ludwig van Beethoven, Benjamin Franklin, Samuel Johnson, John Keats, Richard Wagner, Charles Darwin, Friedrich Nietzsche, Feodor Dostoevski, D. H. Lawrence, and Thomas Mann . . . on leaders of world history like Paul the Apostle, Christopher Columbus, George Washington, Thomas Jefferson, Napoleon Bonaparte, and Abraham Lincoln . . . and scores of others of almost equal rank.

But, by way of contrast and variety, these titans are accompanied down through the centuries by a few contemporaries and correspondents of less imposing stature and lighter moods, by arch-villains like Nero, royal playboys like Henry VIII, courtesans like Ninon de l'Enclos and Du Barry, actresses like Sarah Bernhardt, and charlatans like P. T. Barnum, finding themselves with such strangely assorted neighbors as George Bernard Shaw, H. L. Mencken, and William Randolph Hearst. . . . What a guest list for a week end on Mount Olympus! After all, even emperors, geniuses, and universe builders, even saints and martyrs, world movers and world forsakers, can't talk shop all the time.

At this point I must also explain that when the letters are over-written or actually dull, as they are in a few exceptional cases, they have been deliberately included, because in the editor's opinion they are significantly so. For example, what would ordinarily be a rather pompous and verbose travel letter is quoted, for many long pages in this book, simply because it was set down by a man named Christopher Columbus after a momentous journey in 1492. The letters in this book are not always the best letters, but simply what to me seemed the most interesting, the most historically important, the most representative, and, in some instances, the most shocking and most surprising.

xlii

VII

I have arranged the letters chronologically, but a glance at the classified Table of Contents on page xix will show the dominant themes or moods represented. Under each basic category of human interest—love, hatred, friendship, courage, despair, death, consolation, religion, philosophy, science, art, history-in-the-making, etc. etc.—the names of the letter writers are listed alphabetically. There is also a general descriptive name index in the back of the book, for the convenience of the reader in referring to all the writers and receivers of the letters, and the persons mentioned in them.

VIII

Leslie Stephen called autobiography the most fascinating branch of literature. It seems to me that private letters constitute the most fascinating branch of autobiography. If the theater is what "literature does at night," then letters tell what the subjects of autobiography do and think behind closed doors. Heinrich Heine declared that "to publish even one line of an author which he himself did not intend for publication—especially letters—is a despicable act," but of such acts the best biographies and histories, from Herodotus to Lytton Strachey, are all compact.

J. Middleton Murry put it well in his preface to the letters of Katherine Mansfield: "Those who hold that human dignity must be protected by veils swathed about the secret beatings of heart are advised not to open such volumes. . . ."

IX

Is there any form of communication more revealing than a letter? Yes, complete candor in conversation, but that is rare. Kipling once spoke of a man with whom he had corresponded, in the most spirited and intimate manner, for many years. The actual meeting some time later proved to be an anticlimax and "a frigid disappointment."

Chesterton described the mailbox as "a sanctuary of human words—the place to which friends and lovers commit their messages, confident that when they have done so they are secret, except to future biographers [and anthologists]—not to be touched by any hands, not even (a religious touch) by time. . . ."

"A letter," Chesterton added, "is one of the few things left entirely romantic, for to be entirely romantic, a thing must be irrevocable. . . ."

X

Many learned authorities have pointed out that the seventeenth and eighteenth centuries produced the world's greatest letters, since it was an age of leisure, of grace, of courtly salons. This, it seems to me, is giving the aristocrats and the ambassadors and the retainers of the overprivileged a monopoly on what is essentially a democratic, if not universal, form of expression.

For myself, I build this anthology of letters on a far broader base. I have included letters from more than twenty centuries of recorded history, and from every class of society, every type of man and woman. I find that where life has been lived intensely, it has almost always been recorded intimately. Great letters are the result.

It is true that in the seventeenth century the "universal craving to give and receive news" became more manifest. But that produced chiefly one type of correspondence—the leisurely newsletter. Of this category I have included in my anthology a notable example by Mme de Sévigné, as well as Boswell's priceless and recently unearthed letter to Temple describing his visit to Voltaire. This has the additional and scandalous interest of intimate autobiographical detail set down by a master.

The tradition of the seventeenth and eighteenth centuries as the

Golden Age of Letter Writing seems to me exaggerated. The letters of Horace Walpole were chiefly the equivalent of our society news and gossip columns de luxe. With a few exceptions, such are not the letters which interest me most, and therefore, despite their "fiddles sighing, wax lights, and glittering coaches . . ." they are not included in this anthology.

Lady Mary Wortley Montagu's fame as a letter writer rests on the fact that in the middle of the eighteenth century she too performed the function of newspapers and telephones. As an ambassador's wife, stationed in Constantinople, she took advantage of the diplomatic pouch and conveyed news wholesale. Though historians have long enshrined her Turkish letters, they find no place in this collection, because they are not as intimate or as dramatic as more urgent candidates for inclusion. I hate to disappoint a lady who so obviously was writing for posterity. The textbooks and more formal anthologies give her adequate representation, however.

XI

The belief that the telegraph and telephone killed the art of letter writing is, in my opinion, without foundation. Every now and then some nostalgic essayist rises up in righteous wrath to deplore its passing. One might as well deplore the passing of great loves, great struggles, great art, great tragedies, great ideas. The eloquent answer is found in the memorable modern letters here presented, the stirring utterances by Émile Zola, Robert Louis Stevenson, Madame Curie, Bartolomeo Vanzetti, D. H. Lawrence, Joseph Conrad, Leon Trotsky, Thomas Mann, and the other moderns and contemporaries represented in this volume.

When any person—humble or great, it matters not—has a soul-shaking experience, he usually can—and frequently must—write a letter about it. The chances are that such a letter written on the

xlv

spur of the moment, hot from the crucible of experience, will be dramatic and memorable.

Learned tomes have been written on the qualifications that make for "effective letter writing." Some favor the compact, some the terse, some the allusive, some the witty, some the gossipy, some the leisurely, some the romantic, some the inspired, some the heroic. I include them all. My main test is simply the life-giving quality—the ability to transfer an experience, an emotion, or an idea.

As on many other subjects, Samuel Johnson had wise things to say about the art of letter writing. Here is what he wrote to Mrs. Thrale on October 27, 1777:

Dearest Madam,

You talk of writing and writing, as if you had all the writing to yourself. If our correspondence were printed, I am sure posterity, for posterity is always the author's favorite, would say that I am a good writer too. To sit down so often with nothing to say: to say something so often, almost without consciousness of saying, and without any remembrance of having said, is a power of which I will not violate my modesty by boasting, but I do not believe everybody has it.

Some, when they write to their friends, are all affection: some wise and contentious: some strain their powers for efforts of gaiety: some write news, and some write secrets: but to make a letter without affection, without wisdom, without gaiety, without news, and without a secret is, doubtless, the great epistolick art.

In a man's letters, you know, Madam, his soul lies naked, his letters are only the mirror of his heart: Whatever passes within him is shown undisguised in its natural process: nothing is inverted, nothing distorted: you see systems in their elements: you discover actions in their motives.

Of this great truth, sounded by the knowing to the ignorant, and so echoed by the ignorant to the knowing, what evidence have you now before you? Is not my soul laid open in these veracious pages? Do you not see me reduced to my first principles? Is not this the pleasure of corresponding with a friend, where doubt and distrust have no place, and everything is said as it is thought? . . . These are the letters by which souls are united, and by which minds naturally in unison move each other as they are moved themselves. I know, dearest Lady, that in the perusal of this, such is the consanguinity of our intellects, you will be touched as I am touched. I have concealed nothing from you, nor do I expect ever to repent of having thus opened my heart. I am, etc.

Samuel Johnson

XII

One of the most discerning critics I know dismisses all love letters as silly. The probable explanation is that he thinks—or thinks he thinks—that love itself is silly.

Silly or not, love letters—or "epistles for two"—represent a large section of this anthology, but probably no more proportionately than the part played by love in the lives of the great men and women of history.

Here, then, are letters set down in the sanctuary of Aphrodite— with all the flutterings, hesitations, and pledges eternal, with all the fleeting interludes, grand passions, petty betrayals, lyrical rhapsodies, romantic marriages, and tear-drenched tragedies inspired by "the very ecstasy of love."

Two strange facts I discovered in this phase of my investigations:

First, that with a few exceptions, geniuses like Beethoven, conquerors like Napoleon, and great creative scientists like Michael Faraday all say pretty much the same romantic, grandiloquent, and sometimes incoherent things when they sit down to write love letters.

xlvii

Second, that in Venezuela the post office permits love letters to go through the mails at half rate, provided they are sent in bright red envelopes.

XIII

After years of postponement, the book has finally and reluctantly gone to press. I say "reluctantly" because irresistible material is still pouring in from many generous and co-operative friends and coworkers.

In conclusion, I quote what the editor of a famous volume of Oriental poetry, Ki no Tsurayuki, wrote about a thousand years ago in the preamble to his anthology:

"So is our task ended, and an anthology compiled plentiful as the floods fed by the unfailing waters of the hills, rich in examples as the seashore in grains of sand; may its reception meet with none of the obstructions that bar the stream of Asuka, and the joys it shall afford accumulate, as dust and pebbles gather together to form a high mountain, into a boulder of delight."

—M. LINCOLN SCHUSTER

Part One

LETTERS OF LONG AGO

[FROM 334 B.C. TO A.D. 1675]

ALEXANDER THE GREAT
AND KING DARIUS III
EXCHANGE DEFIANCE FOR THE
MASTERY OF THE WORLD

[A SERIES OF LETTERS]

THE record of Alexander's life is a tissue of facts difficult to document or corroborate and fables that will not die. Every schoolboy knows the incredible military achievements of the youthful Alexander, his personal prowess and unbridled daring . . . his swift marches across vast stretches of three continents—Europe, Asia, and Africa . . . his surprise attacks and inspired strategy, his refusal to attack at night and "steal a victory" . . . his student days under Aristotle, his constant reading of Homer, his Dionysian orgies, his conquest of Jerusalem, his founding of Alexandria, his Oriental splendor and exquisite cruelty, his cutting of the fatal "Gordian knot," his life like a comet, and his early death, burnt out, at the age of thirty-three.

During the last few years there has been a tendency among historians to correct or at least moderate this earlier legend of Alexander as "a wild

3

youth and drunken barbarian." One outstanding student of Greek history, Professor C. A. Robinson, Jr., goes so far as to say that this "much-exalted and much-maligned conqueror was the first person in history to dream of the brotherhood of man."

Alexander's correspondent in this interchange of letters is not the King Darius the Great who was defeated at Marathon in 491 B.C. and who inherited the Persian Empire of Cyrus, but rather Darius III, known as Codomannus, son of a daughter of Artaxerxes II, who began his reign in the same year as Alexander (336 B.C.).

In the Garden of Purity, by the Moslem historian Mirkhond (1433-1498), we find what is perhaps a semiapocryphal, or at least elaborately romanticized, transcript of this correspondence between Alexander and Darius. During the Middle Ages legendary tales about the glories and grandeurs of Alexander, somewhat comparable to the Arthurian and Carlovingian cycles, were popular. According to such a chronicle set down by Mirkhond, Alexander attained his greatest power by "blending mercy with severity, and promises with threats . . . returning from all his expeditions victorious and exulting."

The youthful monarch of Greece and world conqueror was born at Pella, the Macedonian capital, in 356 B.C., and, after his training by Aristotle in every branch of human learning, became regent when his father, Philip of Macedon, marched against Byzantium.

Alexander was not yet twenty when he ascended the throne. Two years later, in 334 B.C., he crossed the Hellespont with 30,000 foot and 5000 horse, obtaining his first great victory over the Persians at the river Granicus; whereupon most of the cities of Asia Minor opened their gates to him. When "the haughty Darius" heard of Alexander's advances, he became greatly alarmed, says Mirkhond, and wrote to the people of Tehrus as follows:

"A report having come to our exalted hearing of an inroad made by a robber who has collected a multitude of thieves from various quarters, you are hereby enjoined to seize on all his associates, and to hurl them,

4

with their arms and cattle, into the sea; but their chief you are to send, loaded with chains, to our presence. So eminent are you for prudence and bravery that you cannot fail to execute this trifling commission. Besides, as the robber is a contemptible stripling from Room [Rome: that is, Europe], we cannot excuse failure or delay on your side in the accomplishment of this commission."

On Alexander's return from Armenia, he pitched his camp on the banks of the river Astukhus, still further threatening the position of Darius. Whereupon Darius wrote him directly as follows:

". . . the King of Heaven has bestowed on me the dominion of the earth . . ."

[DARIUS TO ALEXANDER]

FROM the capital of the kings of the world: As long as the sun shines on the head of Iskander [Alexander] the robber, etc., etc., let him know that the King of Heaven has bestowed on me the dominion of the earth, and that the Almighty has granted to me the surface of the four quarters. Providence has also eminently distinguished me with glory, exaltation, majesty, and with multitudes of devoted champions and confederates.

A report has reached us that you have gathered to yourself numbers of thieves and reprobates, the multitude of whom has so elated your imagination that you propose through their co-operation to procure the crown and throne, lay waste our kingdom, and destroy our land and people.

Such crude resolves are perfectly consistent with the infatuation

5

of the men of Room. It now behooves you, on reading the contents of this epistle, to return instantly from the place to which you have advanced. As to this criminal movement which has proceeded from you, be under no alarm from our majesty and correction, as you are not yet ranked among the number of those who merit our vengeance and punishment. Behold! I send you a coffer full of gold, and an assload of sesame, to give you by these two objects an idea of the extent of my wealth and powers. I also send you a scourge and a ball: the latter, that you may amuse yourself with a diversion suitable to your age; the former, to serve for your chastisement.

O N RECEIPT of this letter, Alexander ordered the ambassadors who had delivered it to be seized and executed, but the terrified couriers begged for mercy. This Alexander finally granted, and sent back this reply to Darius:

". . . *that you may taste and acknowledge the bitterness of my victory.*"

[ALEXANDER TO DARIUS]

F ROM ZU-UL-KURNAIN [Alexander], to him who pretends to be king of kings; that the very hosts of Heaven stand in awe of him; and that the inhabitants of the world are by him enlightened! How then can it be worthy of such a person to be afraid of a contemptible foe like Iskander?

6

Does not Dárá [Darius] know that the High and Mighty Lord gives power and dominion to whomsoever He wills? And also, whenever a feeble mortal regards himself as a God, and conqueror over the hosts of Heaven, beyond doubt the indignation of the Almighty brings down ruin on his kingdom?

How can the person doomed to death and corruption be a God, he from whom his kingdom is taken away and who leaves the enjoyment of the world to others?

Lo! I have resolved to meet you in battle, and therefore march towards your realms. I profess myself the weak and humble servant of God, to whom I address my prayers and look for victory and triumph, and whom I adore.

Along with the letter in which you make a display of your great power you have sent me a scourge, a ball, a coffer filled with gold, and an assload of sesame; all of which I refer to good fortune and regard as auspicious signs. The scourge portends that I shall be the instrument of your castigation and become your ruler, preceptor, and director. The ball indicates that the surface of the earth and the circumference of the globe shall be under my lieutenants. The coffer of gold, which is part of your treasure, denotes that your riches shall soon be transferred to me. And as to the sesame, although the grains are many in number, it is however soft to the touch and of all kinds of food the least noxious and disagreeable.

In return I send you a kaffis of mustard seed, that you may taste and acknowledge the bitterness of my victory. And whereas through presumption you have exalted yourself, and have become proud through the grandeur of your kingdom, and pretend to be a Divinity on earth, and have even raised to the heavens this standard *I truly am your supreme lord*; and although by the enumeration of your numbers, preparations, and might you have endeavored to alarm me; yet I confidently trust in the interposition of Divine Providence, that it will please the Almighty to make thy boasting

7

attended by the reproach of mankind; and that in the same proportion as you have magnified yourself He may bring on you humiliation and grant me victory over you. My trust and reliance are in the Lord. And so farewell.

BECAUSE of the infirmity of his mother, Alexander was compelled to return to Macedonia, but on her recovery he continued his advance toward Darius in the direction of Faristan, where the armies joined in battle. Mirkhond describes the encounter in these words:

"The two armies began to move like the angry waves of two contending oceans, encountering each other like mountains of iron. The atmosphere over the field of battle was covered with robes of black, from the dust raised by the combatants. Through the alarm excited by the loud kettledrum and the sound of the brazen trumpets, the import of this text Truly the trembling of the great hour is an awful event! removed the veil of skepticism from before the eyes of mortals and revealed to their hearts the truth of this sacred verse The heavens were nearly rent asunder. . . . The blood streamed from the swords of the brave, like rain from the clouds, and the emerald-colored dagger elicited the vermilion gore from the bodies of the slain. . . . The surface of the plain was hid from view by their bodies. . . ."

The victory was Alexander's, and Darius fled across the Euphrates, assembling a still greater army. He offered to negotiate with Alexander, indicating his willingness to offer half his kingdom for peace. But Alexander, against the advice of his generals, preferred to risk his troops in battle and gain the whole of Persia. Here is the reply he flung back to Darius:

8

". . . you shall see I know . . . how to deal honorably with those I conquer."

[ALEXANDER TO DARIUS]

D ARIUS:

Darius* (by whose name you are called), if history tell true, long ago laid waste all the Greek cities on the coast of the Helles-pont; all the Ionian colonies on that side. Neither was he content with this, but passing the sea with a vast army, made a second inva-sion; but being overcome in sea fight, himself retreated; yet let his general Mardonius, who in his absence should spoil all Greece, lay waste the fruitful fields, and raze the flourishing cities.

To this let me add the death of my father Philip, whose mur-derers you basely corrupted and suborned with the promise of a great sum of money.

Thus unjustly do you begin a war, and thus cowardly carry it on, by your endeavors to murder those basely whom you are afraid to encounter in the field; witness the one thousand talents you offered to any that should be my murderer, even when you were leading so great an army against me. The war therefore which at present I am engaged in, is in my own defense; and the gods, by giving success to my arms, in conquering a great part of your em-pire, have manifested the justice of my cause. I have conquered you in the field; and though I am not bound by honor or gratitude, to grant you any request, yet I promise faithfully, if you come to

* Darius the Great, defeated at Marathon.

9

me in the way your condition requires, I will set at liberty your wife and children, even without ransom. As a conqueror you have had experience; you shall see I know as well how to deal honorably with those I conquer. But if you doubt of your safety here I will promise that you shall have an escort to bring you and wait on you back. In the meantime whenever you shall have occasion to write Alexander, remember you write to him not only as a king, but also your king.

FINALLY, on September 21, 331 B.C. (taking advantage of a lunar eclipse) the Macedonian army under Alexander crossed the Tigris, and Greece and Persia again met at Arbela (or Gaugamela), one of the decisive battles of history. Once more victory went to Alexander, and this time it brought him, at the age of twenty-five, the undisputed supremacy over most of the known world of the time. In flight once more, Darius was slain by one of his satraps.

Alexander pushed on into central Asia. The all-conquering youth had only eight more years to complete his work, and into them he crowded imperial consolidations, punitive expeditions, administrative reforms, study and correspondence with philosophers,* exploratory adventures, and countless experiments in Oriental splendor and debauchery. He died at the age of thirty-three, in 323 B.C., and cryptically bequeathed his power "to the strongest." It was divided among three of his surviving generals—Ptolemy, Seleucus, and Antigonus—who established their capitals, in Egypt, Syria, and Macedonia respectively.

* See the following letter he received from Diogenes the Cynic, on page 11.

DIOGENES DECLINES TO RENDER A COMMAND PERFORMANCE FOR ALEXANDER THE GREAT

[A LETTER TO ARISTIPPUS]

DIOGENES, the "ragged cynic," was born at Sinope, in Asia Minor, in 412 B.C. and died at Corinth in 323 B.C. Exiled with his father from their native city, he turned to Athens. In his early manhood he evidenced a keen interest in matters philosophical and soon became famous for his preference for extreme poverty, his masterly self-control, his encounter with pirates at sea, and his ceaseless search for an honest man—"poking in dark corners illumined only by a little lantern and a great self-possession." This letter shows how a man who had conquered the world, Alexander the Great,* could be quietly defied by one who had conquered himself:

"... let him come hither ..."

ARISTIPPUS:
You send me word that Alexander, King of Macedonia, has a great desire to see me. You did well to give him that title, for whatever the Macedonians may be, you know I am subject to nobody. If that prince has a mind to be acquainted with me, and

* See the series of letters between Alexander the Great and Darius III, pages 3-10.

my manner of life, let him come hither, for I shall always think Athens as far distant from Macedon as Macedon is from Athens.

Farewell

THE only record of a meeting between Alexander and Diogenes is the historic episode which took place in Athens, when the Emperor, encountering Diogenes by chance, asked how he could serve him. "You can stand out of my light," Diogenes answered. The reply so impressed the conqueror with the contentment of Diogenes that he walked away exclaiming to himself that if he were not Alexander, he would like to be Diogenes.

Commenting on this, Plutarch adds: "And what did this virtually mean? That Alexander was vexed with his own high fortune, splendor, and power, because they were an obstacle to virtue for which he could find no time, and that he envied the cloak and wallet, which made Diogenes as invincible and unassailable as he himself was made by armor and horses and spears. And yet by the practice of philosophy he might have secured the moral character of a Diogenes while retaining the position of an Alexander. Nay, he should have become all the more a Diogenes for being an Alexander, since his high fortune, so liable to be tossed by stormy winds, required ample ballast and a master hand at the helm."

PAUL THE APOSTLE EXHORTS THE CORINTHIANS WITH THE TONGUES OF MEN AND OF ANGELS

[EXTRACTS FROM I CORINTHIANS 1, 2, 7, 13, 16]

THESE are the impassioned words of a Christ-intoxicated man. He was a roving tentmaker of the first century, a Jew, a Greek, a zealot who spent his early years persecuting the first Christians and his later ones organizing them for perhaps the greatest spiritual victory in the history of Western religion.

On his way to Damascus to suppress some of the early Christian sects, Paul—then known as Saul—experienced the famous "vision of Christ glorified," when Jesus challenged him with the direct question, "Why persecutest thou me?"

Paul's answer was a mystical conversion that literally changed the course of world history. Henceforward, he was truly a Roman citizen, an Apostle of Christ, and one of the greatest missionary geniuses of all time.*

Professor Irwin Edman has described Paul's vision as "immediate, intuitive, passionate, and absolute . . . an enraptured indistinction between himself and divine being, out of his sense of Christ's indwelling presence."

The letters of Paul, of which this is among the most famous, constitute the first record of Christ prior to the Gospels. Wandering through the Mediterranean lands, preaching in synagogues and market places,

* See the correspondence between the younger Pliny and the Emperor Trajan regarding the early Christians, on page 23.

Paul literally laid the foundations of the Christian faith. He has been described as "a supreme artist in propaganda and doctrinal synthesis."

Sir Arthur Quiller-Couch has said that the secrets of Paul's "unparalleled success" as preacher, theologian, reformer, organizer, and martyr were "burning zeal, absolute self-sacrifice, undaunted courage, and a strong conviction that he was fulfilling a ministry which he had received directly from God." Neither disasters at sea, hardships at home, nor floggings in prison could dismay him.

When some of the perplexed members of the Church in Corinth sent Paul a list of detailed questions about dogma, church administration, marriage, ethics, social obligations, and conduct generally, this "practical mystic," living hopefully in a despairing and pagan world, wrote, in A.D. 56 from Philippi, what we now know as the First Epistle to the Corinthians.

This letter contains his historic utterance on marriage and his famous words on "faith, hope, and charity." In Paul's mind, of course, "charity" was not to be construed as mere mercy, benevolence, or almsgiving, but as "divine love to man, human love to God and one's neighbors, and, above all, Christian love to one's fellow man."

Professor Edgar J. Goodspeed has pointed out that these Epistles of Paul were not "open letters" dealing officially with administrative problems of the Church but actual private communications addressed to his friends, and written without thought of publication.

According to Ernest Sutherland Bates, whose arrangement of the letters as given in The Bible Designed to Be Read as Living Literature is followed here, Paul's literary style is marked by "a great variety of moods, ranging through emotional tenderness, passionate invective, eloquent persuasion, and logical reasoning." In all these forms of expression he had undergone an intensive rabbinical training, and he employed them with consummate genius as "the hope of the second coming became more and more transmuted into the almost equally consolatory doctrine of personal immortality":

14

"... but the greatest of these is charity."

Unto the Church of God which is at Corinth, to them that are sanctified in Christ Jesus, called to be saints, with all that in every place call upon the name of Jesus Christ our Lord, both theirs and ours:

Grace be unto you, and peace, from God our Father, and from the Lord Jesus Christ. I thank my God always on your behalf, for the grace of God which is given you by Jesus Christ; that in every thing ye are enriched by him, in all utterance, and in all knowledge; even as the testimony of Christ was confirmed in you: so that ye come behind in no gift; waiting for the coming of our Lord Jesus Christ: who shall also confirm you unto the end, that ye may be blameless in the day of our Lord Jesus Christ. God is faithful, by whom ye were called unto the fellowship of his Son Jesus Christ our Lord.

Now I beseech you, brethren, by the name of our Lord Jesus Christ, that ye all speak the same thing, and that there be no divisions among you; but that ye be perfectly joined together in the same mind and in the same judgment. For it hath been declared unto me of you, my bretheren, by them which are of the house of Chloe, that there are contentions among you. Now this I say, that every one of you saith, "I am of Paul"; and "I of Apollos"; and "I of Cephas"; and "I of Christ." Is Christ divided? was Paul crucified for you? or were ye baptized in the name of Paul? I thank God that I baptized none of you, but Crispus and

Gaius; lest any should say that I had baptized in mine own name. And I baptized also the household of Stephanas: besides, I know not whether I baptized any other. For Christ sent me not to baptize, but to preach the gospel: not with wisdom of words, lest the cross of Christ should be made of none effect.

For the preaching of the cross is to them that perish foolishness; but unto us which are saved it is the power of God. For it is written,

"I will destroy the wisdom of the wise,

And will bring to nothing the understanding of the prudent."

Where is the wise? where is the scribe? where is the disputer of this world? hath not God made foolish the wisdom of this world? For after that in the wisdom of God the world by wisdom knew not God, it pleased God by the foolishness of preaching to save them that believe. For the Jews require a sign, and the Greeks seek after wisdom: but we preach Christ crucified, unto the Jews a stumblingblock, and unto the Greeks foolishness; but unto them which are called, both Jews and Greeks, Christ the power of God, and the wisdom of God. Because the foolishness of God is wiser than men; and the weakness of God is stronger than men.

For ye see your calling, brethren, how that not many wise men after the flesh, not many mighty, not many noble, are called: but God hath chosen the foolish things of the world to confound the wise; and God hath chosen the weak things of the world to confound the things which are mighty. And base things of the world, and things which are despised, hath God chosen, yea, and things which are not, to bring to nought things that are: that no flesh should glory in his presence. But of him are ye in Christ Jesus, who of God is made unto us wisdom, and righteousness, and sanctification, and redemption: that, according as it is written, "He that glorieth, let him glory in the Lord." . . .

Therefore let no man glory in men. For all things are yours;

16

whether Paul, or Apollos, or Cephas, or the world, or life, or death, or things present, or things to come; all are yours; and ye are Christ's; and Christ is God's.

Now concerning the things whereof ye wrote unto me: it is good for a man not to touch a woman. Nevertheless, to avoid fornication, let every man have his own wife, and let every woman have her own husband. Let the husband render unto the wife due benevolence: and likewise also the wife unto the husband. The wife hath not power of her own body, but the husband: and likewise also the husband hath not power of his own body, but the wife. Defraud ye not one the other, except it be with consent for a time, that ye may give yourselves to fasting and prayer; and come together again, that Satan tempt you not for your incontinency.

But I speak this by permission, and not of commandment. For I would that all men were even as I myself. But every man hath his proper gift of God, one after this manner, and another after that.

I say therefore to the unmarried and widows, it is good for them if they abide even as I. But if they cannot contain, let them marry: for it is better to marry than to burn.

And unto the married I command, yet not I, but the Lord, let not the wife depart from her husband: but and if she depart, let her remain unmarried, or be reconciled to l r husband; and let not the husband put away his wife. . . .

Though I speak with the tongues of men and of angels, and have not charity, I am become as sounding brass, or a tinkling cymbal. And though I have the gift of prophecy, and understand all mysteries, and all knowledge; and though I have all faith, so that I could remove mountains, and have not charity, I am nothing. And though I bestow all my goods to feed the poor, and though I give my body to be burned, and have not charity, it profiteth me nothing.

Charity suffereth long, and is kind; charity envieth not; charity vaunteth not itself, is not puffed up, doth not behave itself unseemly, seeketh not her own, is not easily provoked, thinketh no evil; rejoiceth not in iniquity, but rejoiceth in the truth; beareth all things, believeth all things, hopeth all things, endureth all things.

Charity never faileth: but whether there be prophecies, they shall fail; whether there be tongues, they shall cease; whether there be knowledge, it shall vanish away. For we know in part, and we prophesy in part. But when that which is perfect is come, then that which is in part shall be done away.

When I was a child, I spoke as a child, I understood as a child, I thought as a child: but when I became a man, I put away childish things.

For now we see through a glass, darkly; but then face to face: now I know in part; but then shall I know even as also I am known. And now abideth faith, hope, charity, these three; but the greatest of these is charity. . . .

The churches of Asia salute you. Aquila and Priscilla salute you much in the Lord, with the church that is in their house. All the brethren greet you. Greet ye one another with a holy kiss.

The salutation of me Paul with mine own hand. If any man love not the Lord Jesus Christ, let him be Anathema Maran-atha. The grace of our Lord Jesus Christ be with you. My love be with you all in Christ Jesus. Amen.

PAUL, CALLED TO BE AN APOSTLE OF JESUS CHRIST THROUGH THE WILL OF GOD, AND SOSTHENES OUR BROTHER

PHILIPPI, 56 A.D.

IN HIS last missionary letters, written just before his death in A.D. 67, Paul wrote, "I have fought a good fight, I have finished my course, I have kept the faith." His final monument was the establishment of Christianity throughout the Roman Empire and his reward the influence of his doctrine and inspiration of his faith throughout the centuries. When he was finally sentenced and imprisoned for his "disturbances" he appealed to Caesar, was sent to Rome, and, after two years of captivity, was executed in the reign of Nero.*

* See the following letter to Nero, from his mother, on page 20.

AGRIPPINA, NERO'S MOTHER, PLEADS TO HER EM-
PEROR-SON FOR HER OWN LIFE

IT WAS through the help of his mother Agrippina, wife of the Emperor Claudius, that Nero instead of Britannicus, the rightful heir, succeeded to the throne in A.D. 54. He was a contemporary of Jesus Christ and Saint Paul. Described as "bowlegged, thick-necked, potbellied," Nero fancied himself a veritable Apollo and made a practice of walking around completely nude. When he was bored with one of his friends or statesmen, he would dispatch a brief note, tactfully suggesting that the victim's suicide would not be unwelcome to him and to the state. The hint was usually taken. The Emperor's philosopher-tutor, Seneca, stoically took his own life by the sword when he received such a suggestion from Nero. Engrossed in an elaborate plan for the history of Rome, which was eventually to consist of four hundred books of verse, Nero loved to declaim from these manuscripts.

Once Emperor, Nero needed little help to bring about the murder of numerous persons who stood in his way. His mistress, Poppaea Sabina, wife of Otho, afterwards Emperor, influenced Nero to bring false charges of treason against his own mother. She was basely accused of plotting against her son, and it is against this accusation that Agrippina defends herself in the letter that follows.

Agrippina herself has been called "one of the vilest of women." Intriguing to win the throne for her own son, she had poisoned all his rivals and enemies, including her third husband, the Emperor Claudius, who was also her uncle. There is some question in the minds of scholars as to the authenticity of this text, but regardless of the precise accuracy of this version, it brings out in colorful detail the debauchery and wanton cruelty of Imperial Rome in the first century of the Christian era.

". . . I carried you in my womb and nourished you with my blood."

I DO not wonder that barren Silana has no sense of maternal affection. One who has never borne a son naturally would not know how to bear the loss of one. Nature renders either hateful or indifferent those objects that we do not ourselves experience. . . . I am amazed that even the most skillful sorcery of words could make you pay the least attention to such barbarous inhumanity. . . .

Don't you know, my son, the affection all mothers naturally bear their children? Our love is unbounded, incessantly fed by that tenderness unknown to all but ourselves. Nothing should be more dear to us than what we have bought with the risk of our lives; nothing more precious than what we have endured such grief and pain to procure. These are so acute and unbearable that if it were not for the vision of a successful birth, which makes us forget our agonies, generation would soon cease.

Do you forget that nine full months I carried you in my womb and nourished you with my blood? How likely is it, then, that I would destroy the dear child who cost me so much anguish to bring into the world? It may be that the just gods were angry at my excessive love of you, and used this way to punish me.

Unhappy Agrippina! You are suspected of a crime of which nobody could really think you guilty. . . . What does the title of empress mean to me, if I am accused of a crime that even the basest of women would abhor? Unhappy are those who breathe the air of the court. The wisest of people are not secure from storms in that harbor. There even a calm is dangerous. But why blame the court? Can that be the cause of my being suspected of parricide? . . .

Tell me, why should I plot against your life? To plunge myself into a worse fate? That's not likely. What hopes could induce me to build upon your downfall? I know that the lust for empire often corrupts the laws of nature; that justice has no sword to punish those who offend in this way; and that ambition disregards wrong so long as it succeeds in its aim. . . . Nay, to what deity could I turn for absolution after I had committed so black a deed? . . .

What difficulties have I not surmounted to crown your brow with laurels? But I insult your gratitude by reminding you of my services. My innocence ought not to defend itself but to rely wholly on your justice.

Farewell

NERO was apparently neither moved nor convinced by his mother's plea for her own life. He ordered her executed, and she was strangled to death in 59 A.D. In an outburst of imperial wrath, he then ungallantly kicked his mistress Poppaea, who had helped engineer Agrippina's death. His mistress was pregnant at the time, and died from the blow.

After a sinister reign of fourteen years, Nero was rather belatedly condemned to death by the Roman Senate. He managed, however, to deprive the authorities of such retribution, by taking his own life by the sword. According to legend, his last words were: "What a pity for such an artist to die!" It is recorded that only Petronius had the courage to tell this blackest of all emperors the truth. He actually wrote a letter to Nero calling him "the worst singer of all time," and then, anticipating the Emperor's punishment, opened his veins.

THE YOUNGER PLINY ASKS THE EMPEROR TRAJAN HOW TO ARREST AND PUNISH "THE DEPRAVED AND EXCESSIVE SUPERSTITION" OF THE EARLY CHRISTIANS

SHOLOM ASCH, author of The Nazarene, says this letter marks a milestone in the history of the world. It shows us graphically how the power of the Roman Empire was challenged by the rise of the Christian faith at the end of the first century.

The younger Pliny, adopted at the age of seventeen by his uncle, the elder Pliny, was governor of Bithynia, a province in Asia Minor, about A.D. 104, when he sent this communication to one of the greatest of the Roman emperors, asking for advice on the treatment of the first Christian sects.

Until after the fall of Jerusalem (A.D. 70) these Christians had been regarded as members of the Jewish faith. They were thus tolerated by Rome. Toward the end of the century, however, they were first deemed to be a menace—small but insidious—to the imperial sovereignty. Most provincial governors wanted to deal strictly with this "contagious superstition," but the younger Pliny, trained for a legal career in Rome, proceeded with caution and sought imperial sanction. The Biblical record of the clash between the first Christian missionaries and the authorities of Rome is found in the Book of Revelation.

Pliny's historic letter to the Emperor is given in the following pages, together with a summary of the Emperor's reply.

". . . if they still persevered, I ordered them
to be executed . . ."

IT IS a rule, Sire, which I inviolably observe, to refer myself to you in all my doubts; for who is more capable of removing my scruples, or of guiding my uncertainty? having never been present at any trials of the Christians, I am unacquainted as to the method and limits to be observed in examining and punishing them. Whether, therefore, any difference is to be made with respect to age, or no distinction is to be observed between the young and adult; whether repentance admits to a pardon; or if a man has been once a Christian, it avails him nothing to recant; whether the mere profession of Christianity, albeit without any criminal act, or only the crimes associated therewith are punishable; in all these points I am greatly doubtful.

In the meanwhile the method I have observed towards those who have been denounced to me as Christians, is this: I interrogated them whether they were Christians; if they confessed I repeated the question twice again, adding a threat of capital punishment; if they still persevered, I ordered them to be executed; for I was persuaded, that whatever the nature of their creed, a contumacious and inflexible obstinacy certainly deserved chastisement. There were others also brought before me possessed with the same infatuation: but being citizens of Rome, I directed them to be carried thither.

These accusations, from the mere fact that the matter was being investigated, began to spread, and several forms of the mischief came to light. A placard was posted up without any signature, accusing a number of people by name. Those who denied that they were Christians, or had ever been so, who repeated after me an invocation to the gods, and offered religious rites with wine and frankincense to your statue (which I had ordered to be brought for the purpose, together with those of the gods), and finally cursed the name of Christ (none of which, it is said, those who are really Christians can be forced into performing), I thought proper to discharge. Others who were named by the informer at first confessed themselves Christians, and then denied it; true, they had been of that persuasion formerly, but had now quitted it (some three years, others many years, and a few as much as twenty-five years ago). They all worshipped your statue, and the images of the gods, and cursed the name of Christ.

They affirmed, however, that the whole of their guilt or their error was, that they met on a certain fixed day before it was light and sang an antiphonal chant to Christ, as to a god, binding themselves by a solemn oath, not to any wicked deeds, but never to commit any fraud, theft or adultery, never to falsify their word, nor deny a trust when they should be called upon to deliver it up; after which it was their custom to separate, and then reassemble to partake of food—food of an ordinary innocent kind.* Even this practice, however, they had abandoned after the publication of my edict, by which, according to your orders, I had forbidden political associations. I judged it so much the more necessary to extract the real truth, with the assistance of torture, from two female slaves, called deaconesses. But I could discover nothing but depraved and excessive superstition.

I therefore thought it proper to adjourn all further proceedings in this affair, in order to consult with you. For the matter is well worth referring to you, especially considering the numbers

* Jews in the Middle Ages were accused of eating children.

endangered: persons of all ranks and ages, and of both sexes, are and will be involved in the prosecution. For this contagious superstition is not confined to the cities only, but has spread through the villages and the countryside. Nevertheless it seems still possible to check and cure it. The temples, at least, which were once almost deserted, begin now to be frequented, and the sacred solemnities, after a long intermission, are again revived; while there is a general demand for sacrificial animals which for some time past have met with but few purchasers. From hence it is easy to imagine, what numbers might be reclaimed from this error, if the door is left open to repentance.

THE Emperor's reply characterized Pliny's proceedings "as extremely proper." Pointing out that no general rule would be applied to all cases, Trajan said, "No search is to be made for these people. When they are denounced, and found guilty, they must be punished, with the restriction, however, that where the party denies himself to be a Christian, and shall give proof that he is not, by invoking our gods, let him (notwithstanding any former suspicion) be pardoned upon his repentance."

Historians of Christianity have laid great stress on the importance of this correspondence. Allusions to it are found in the works of Tertullian, Saint Jerome,* and Eusebius. A particularly dramatic passage is found in the writings of the first named, who lived from 155 to 222. In a long manifesto addressed to the persecutors of the first Christians Tertullian indicated how the hand of history was writing its own answer to the younger Pliny's letter of inquiry, and why it was becoming increasingly difficult "to check and cure" the new faith:

"And now, O worshipful judges, go on with your show of justice, and

* See Saint Jerome's letter on the decline and fall of Rome, on page 31.

believe me, you will be juster and juster still in the opinion of the people the oftener you make them a sacrifice of Christians: Crucify, torture, condemn, grind us all to powder if you can; your injustice is an illustrious proof of our innocence, for the proof of this is that God permits us to suffer; and by your late condemnation of a Christian woman to the lust of a pander, rather than the rage of a lion, you notoriously confess that such a pollution is more abhorred by a Christian than all the torments and deaths you heap upon her. But do your worst, and rack your invention for tortures for Christians; it is all to no purpose. You do but attract the world and make it fall more in love with our religion; the more you mow us down the quicker we rise; the Christian blood you shed is the seed you sow; it springs from the earth again and fructifies the more."

AURELIAN, EMPEROR OF ROME, ORDERS ZENOBIA, QUEEN OF PALMYRA, TO SURRENDER, AND SHE DEFIES HIM

[AN EXCHANGE OF LETTERS]

Lucius Domitius Aurelianus, *"Restorer of the Roman Empire" in the third century after Christ, began his military career as a common soldier. After attaining the highest command in the army, he was elected Emperor in 270. A sweep of continued conquests, almost world-wide in scope, was temporarily halted when Zenobia, Queen of Palmyra, held Syria, Asia Minor, and Egypt against him. In the following letter, the Emperor lays down his terms:*

"I command you to surrender the city . . ."

What I now require you ought to have done long since of your own accord. I command you to surrender the city, and thereupon promise both you and yours your lives, but not your liberty. You, Zenobia, and your children must be content to go, where I and the most august Senate of Rome think fit to place you. Your jewels, gold, silver, and other riches must all be confiscated to the Roman treasury. Your subjects alone will be freed from captivity, and have their privileges assured them.

28

THE Queen, however, was not afraid to hurl back her own defiance. She had helped her late husband in a victorious war against Persia and had inherited and effectively exercised a virtual sovereignty over the Near East. Moreover, she was a learned woman, instructed by the great Longinus in the arts and sciences, and a master of Latin, Greek, Coptic, and Syrian. Her reply to Aurelian follows:

"You will surely change your tone . . ."

NO MAN ever yet presumed to command me as you have done. Bravery alone, Aurelian, will accomplish your ends in war. You demand that I surrender my city of Palmyra as if you did not know that my ancestress, Cleopatra, preferred to die a queen than live a slave, of however great position, to your predecessor Augustus.

We await help from the Persians. The Saracens arm for us; the Armenians have declared in our favor; a band of highwaymen has defeated your army in Syria. Then judge what is in store for you when all these forces arrive. You will surely change your tone then, and not command me so imperiously to give up my birthright, as if you were the absolute disposer of the universe.

AURELIAN's troops defeated Zenobia's at Antioch, and finally the ancient and beautiful city of Palmyra was besieged and destroyed. In flight with her children, Zenobia was captured. She saved her life by blaming the war on her instructor and secretary, the learned Longinus, who was promptly beheaded. Zenobia herself was brought back to grace Aurelian's triumphal procession in Rome. He graciously allowed his former enemy to live in splendor the life of an honorable Roman matron. Her daughters married into the nobility and her son received the governorship of a small principality in Asia Minor. Aurelian was assassinated near Byzantium during a campaign against the Persians in the year 275.

SAINT JEROME BEHOLDS THE DECLINE AND FALL
OF ROME BEFORE HIS EYES

[A LETTER TO A FRIEND]

HERE is a vivid account of the sack of Rome and the dissolution of the world's greatest empire. Saint Jerome, or Eusebius Sophronius Hieronymus, who wrote it in the form of a private message to a friend, was born in 340 and died in 420. He won his place in history, not only by this account of one of the greatest events of all time, but also by his translation of the Bible, generally known as the Vulgate—hailed by Quiller-Couch as "one of the most important intellectual legacies ever left to the Western church . . . by which he lived and reigned for a thousand years." Erasmus called Jerome the Christian Cicero.

Until the fifth century, the Old Testament, written in Hebrew, was a locked book to all except scholars and priests of advanced erudition. Latin was then the language of the common people, and it was Saint Jerome who by his monumental achievement made it available to them by translating it from Hebrew into Latin.

Jerome's parents were Christians, citizens of Dalmatia, who sent their young son to Rome to study. Thus he fell under the spell of the great pagan masterpieces of Roman literature, subsequently became a devout Christian, and was distressed by this early heretical adoration. When his friend Innocentius died on a trip through the East, and he himself miraculously recovered, he vowed to devote his "entire life to teaching and writing in the service of God." The Vulgate was his consecration and his triumph—a labor that changed the course of world history.

Alaric swooped down from the north and sacked Rome in 410. To

Eusebius Sophronius Hieronymus, then seventy years old and living in retirement at Bethlehem, dire news came ceaselessly that must have made it seem as though the world was coming to an end. The Eternal City was in ruins. Such was the death agony of an empire that one of the greatest of the Latin Fathers describes in this historic letter:

". . . the wolves of the North have been let loose . . ."

I SHUDDER when I think of the calamities of our time. For twenty years the blood of Romans has been shed daily between Constantinople and the Alps. Scythia, Thrace, Macedon, Thessaly, Dacia, Achaea, Epirus—all these regions have been sacked and pillaged by Goths and Alans, Huns and Vandals. How many noble and virtuous women have been made the sport of these beasts! Churches have been overthrown, horses stalled in the holy places, the bones of the saints dug up and scattered.

Indeed, the Roman world is falling; yet we still hold up our heads instead of bowing them. The East, indeed, seemed to be free from these perils; but now, in the year just past, the wolves of the North have been let loose from their remotest fastnesses, and have overrun great provinces. They have laid siege to Antioch, and invested cities that were once the capitals of no mean states.

> *Non mihi si linguae centum sint oraque centum,*
> *Ferrea vox, omnes scelerum comprendere formas,*
> *Omnia poenarum percurrere nomine possim.**

Well may we be unhappy, for it is our sins that have made the

* *Had I a hundred tongues, a hundred mouths,*
  A voice of iron, I could not compass all
  Their crimes, nor tell their penalties by name.
  —Virgil, Aeneid VI, 625-627

barbarians strong; as in the days of Hezekiah, so today is God using the fury of the barbarian to execute His fierce anger. Rome's army, once the lord of the world, trembles today at sight of the foe.

Who will hereafter believe that Rome has to fight now within her own borders, not for glory but for life? and, as the poet Lucan says, "If Rome be weak, where shall strength be found?"

And now a dreadful rumor has come to hand. Rome has been besieged, and its citizens have been forced to buy off their lives with gold. My voice cleaves to my throat; sobs choke my utterance. The city which had taken the whole world captive is itself taken. Famine too has done its awful work.

The world sinks into ruin; all things are perishing save our sins; these alone flourish. The great city is swallowed up in one vast conflagration; everywhere Romans are in exile.

Who could believe it? who could believe that Rome, built up through the ages by the conquest of the world, had fallen; that the mother of nations had become their tomb? who could imagine that the proud city, with its careless security and its boundless wealth, is brought so low that her children are outcasts and beggars? We cannot indeed help them; all we can do is sympathize with them, and mingle our tears with theirs.

WHEN this missive was dispatched by Saint Jerome to his friends, fresh hordes of barbarians were waiting to overwhelm the remains of the capital of the Roman Empire. The second sack of Rome by Genseric was even more ruthless, more barbarous than the first. The work of the Caesars was to crumble more and more, and only many years later was the splendor of the Popes to rise from these ruins. "Tell this tale to those that come after," wrote Saint Jerome in The Story of Melchus, "so that they may know that even in the midst of swords and deserts and wild beasts virtue is never made a captive, and that he who has surrendered himself to Christ may be slain but cannot be conquered."

33

HELOISE AND ABELARD
IMMORTALIZE, IN THEIR LEARNED
AND PASSIONATE LETTERS,
ONE OF HISTORY'S ENDURING
LOVE STORIES

[AN EXCHANGE OF LETTERS]

AT THE age of thirty-seven, in the year 1116, Peter Abelard, the son of noble and wealthy Breton parents, had attained the highest academic honor in medieval France, the chair of logic in the University of Paris, and a canonship of the cathedral of Notre-Dame. Students from all parts of Europe crowded to hear the brilliant heresies of his discourse. He was the leader of the nominalists, pitted in violent dialectic against the more orthodox realists.

Heloise, then nineteen, came from a convent school to the home of her uncle Fulbert, in a Paris aglow with praise of Abelard. Hearing of her intellect and beauty, Abelard contrived successfully to be engaged as her teacher in philosophy. Their love was inevitable. In his famous letter to Philintus, known as *A History of the Calamities*, Abelard recounts to his friend the ecstasies and sorrows that marked his love for Heloise:

34

"It is vain to try to avoid it [love]. I was a philosopher, yet this tyrant of the mind triumphed over all my wisdom; his darts were of greater force than all my reasoning, and with a sweet constraint he led me wherever he pleased. . . . . Her wit and her beauty would have stirred the dullest and most insensible heart, and her education was equally admirable. . . . I saw her, I loved her, I resolved to make her love me. . . . I thought of nothing but Heloise; everything brought her image to my mind. . . . I flattered myself already with the most bewitching hopes. My reputation had spread itself everywhere, and could a virtuous lady resist a man who had confounded all the learned of the age? I was young . . . my person was advantageous enough, and by my dress no one would have suspected me for a doctor; and dress, you know, is not a little engaging with women. . . . I saw Heloise, I spoke to her. . . . The same house, the same love, united our persons and our desires. How many soft moments did we pass together!"

But, as Abelard goes on to say in his letter, their love could not long be secret. Passion had fled from his teaching into his love. He could concentrate on no writing save poetry for his beloved. In his own words, he "quitted Aristotle and his dry maxims to practice the precepts of the more ingenious Ovid." Lovers everywhere took these songs to their hearts. All Paris knew of their attachment. Uncle Fulbert alone remained ignorant. At last, however, he too found out and, incensed, sent Abelard from the house.

"It being impossible," Abelard wrote, "that I could live without seeing Heloise," he continued to see her in secret. He smuggled her to Brittany where their son was born. Repeatedly he urged her to marry him; but she refused to take a step which would ruin his career in the church. To deflect his will, she employed every argument her brilliant mind could devise. "Will not love have more power than marriage," she argued, "to keep our hearts firmly united?"

But he prevailed upon her at last, and they returned to Paris together, hoping to keep their marriage secret. But Fulbert heard of it and took

35

barbaric revenge upon Abelard. At his instigation, a band of ruffians entered Abelard's house one night, attacked, and mutilated him. In disgrace and despair, Abelard fled from Paris. At his insistence, Heloise entered a nunnery. Subsequently she became the abbess of her convent. Abelard, hounded and pursued by enemies, outraged at the debauched and depraved life of the monks with whom his lot was cast, wandered from monastery to monastery, seeking in vain for peace of body and spirit. Yet through all this, he wrote, "I have not triumphed over that unhappy passion. In the midst of my retirement I sigh, I weep, I pine, I speak the dear name of Heloise, and delight to hear the sound." Their letters were his sole earthly comfort. The two that are reprinted here (with some minor excisions) are taken from the text of an anonymous translation published in London in 1722.

The authenticity of these letters has often been challenged, but never their fascination. They record one of the most moving tragedies of all time—one which has been celebrated by poets and dramatists down through the centuries—from Alexander Pope to Ralph Adams Cram, George Moore, and Helen Waddell. Controversy has long raged about the text and interpretation of these letters. Some editions print five letters, some six, some as many as eight in the entire interchange. George Moore declared that the first letter, known as A History of the Calamities of Abelard, and written not to Heloise, but his friend Philintus, was actually a literary forgery, "designed to create a background and a justification for the rest of the letters," from the pen of Jean de Meung, one of the authors of the Roman de la Rose.

In the traditional cycle of this correspondence, Abelard's preliminary "letter to a friend" is followed by the first letter from Heloise to Abelard:

36

HELOISE FINDS HER PASSION STRONGER THAN HER SACRED OBLIGATION AND BLOTS HER LETTERS WITH HER TEARS

'Veiled as I am, behold in what a disorder
you have plunged me!"

[HELOISE TO ABELARD]

To her Lord, her Father, her Husband, her Brother; his Servant, his Child, his Wife, his Sister, and to express all that is humble, respectful and loving to her Abelard, Heloise writes this.

A CONSOLATORY letter of yours to a friend happened some days since to fall into my hands; my knowledge of the writing and my love of the hand gave me the curiosity to open it. In justification of the liberty I took, I flattered myself I might claim a sovereign privilege over everything which came from you. Nor was I scrupulous to break through the rules of good breeding when I was to hear news of Abelard. But how dear did my curiosity cost me! What disturbance did it occasion, and how surprised I was to find the whole letter filled with a particular and melancholy account of our misfortunes! I met with my name a hundred times; I never saw it without fear—some heavy calamity always followed it. I saw yours too, equally unhappy.

These mournful but dear remembrances put my heart into such violent motion that I thought it was too much to offer comfort

37

to a friend for a few slight disgraces, but such extraordinary means as the representation of our sufferings and revolutions. What reflections did I not make! I began to consider the whole afresh, and perceived myself pressed with the same weight of grief as when we first began to be miserable. Though length of time ought to have closed up my wounds, yet the seeing them described by your hand was sufficient to make them all open and bleed afresh. . . .

My tears, which I could not restrain, have blotted half your letter; I wish they had effaced the whole, and that I had returned it to you in that condition; I should then have been satisfied with the little time I kept it; but it was demanded of me too soon.

I must confess I was much easier in my mind before I read your letter. Surely all the misfortunes of lovers are conveyed to them through the eyes: upon reading your letter I feel all mine renewed. I reproached myself for having been so long without venting my sorrows, when the rage of our unrelenting enemies still burns with the same fury. Since length of time, which disarms the strongest hatred, seems but to aggravate theirs; since it is decreed that your virtue shall be persecuted till it takes refuge in the grave—and even then, perhaps, your ashes will not be allowed to rest in peace!—let me always meditate on your calamities, let me publish them through all the world, if possible, to shame an age that has not known how to value you. . . .

Let me have a faithful account of all that concerns you; I would know everything, be it ever so unfortunate. Perhaps by mingling my sighs with yours I may make your sufferings less, for it is said that all sorrows divided are made lighter.

Tell me not by way of excuse you will spare me tears; the tears of women shut up in a melancholy place and devoted to penitence are not to be spared. And if you wait for an opportunity to write pleasant and agreeable things to us, you will delay writing too long. Prosperity seldom chooses the side of the virtuous, and

38

fortune is so blind that in a crowd in which there is perhaps but one wise and brave man it is not to be expected that she should single him out. Write to me then immediately and wait not for miracles; they are too scarce, and we too much accustomed to misfortunes to expect a happy turn. I shall always have this, if you please, and this will always be agreeable to me, that when I receive any letter from you I shall know you still remember me. . . .

I have your picture in my room; I never pass it without stopping to look at it; and yet when you are present with me I scarce ever cast my eyes on it. If a picture, which is but a mute representation of an object, can give such pleasure, what cannot letters inspire? They have souls; they can speak; they have in them all that force which expresses the transports of the heart; they have all the fire of our passions, they can raise them as much as if the persons themselves were present; they have all the tenderness and the delicacy of speech, and sometimes even a boldness of expression beyond it.

We may write to each other; so innocent a pleasure is not denied us. Let us not lose through negligence the only happiness which is left us, and the only one perhaps which the malice of our enemies can never ravish from us. I shall read that you are my husband and you shall see me sign myself your wife. In spite of all our misfortunes you may be what you please in your letter. Letters were first invented for consoling such solitary wretches as myself. Having lost the substantial pleasures of seeing and possessing you, I shall in some measure compensate this loss by the satisfaction I shall find in your writing. There I shall read your most sacred thoughts; I shall carry them always about with me, I shall kiss them every moment; if you can be capable of any jealousy let it be for the fond caresses I shall bestow upon your letters, and envy only the happiness of those rivals.

That writing may be no trouble to you, write always to me

39

carelessly and without study; I had rather read the dictates of the heart than of the brain. I cannot live if you will not tell me that you still love me; but that language ought to be so natural to you, that I believe you cannot speak otherwise to me without violence to yourself. And since by this melancholy relation to your friend you have awakened all my sorrows, 'tis but reasonable you should allay them by some tokens of your unchanging love. . . .

You cannot but remember (for lovers cannot forget) with what pleasure I have passed whole days in hearing your discourse. How when you were absent I shut myself from everyone to write to you; how uneasy I was till my letter had come to your hands; what artful management it required to engage messengers. This detail perhaps surprises you, and you are in pain for what may follow. But I am no longer ashamed that my passion had no bounds for you, for I have done more than all this. I have hated myself that I might love you. I came hither to ruin myself in a perpetual imprisonment that I might make you live quietly and at ease.

Nothing but virtue, joined to a love perfectly disengaged from the senses, could have produced such effects. Vice never inspires anything like this: it is too much enslaved to the body. When we love pleasures we love the living and not the dead. We leave off burning with desire for those who can no longer burn for us. This was my cruel uncle's notion; he measured my virtue by the frailty of my sex, and thought it was the man and not the person I loved. But he has been guilty to no purpose. I love you more than ever; and so revenge myself on him. I will still love you with all the tenderness of my soul till the last moment of my life. If, formerly, my affection for you was not so pure, if in those days both mind and body loved you, I often told you even then that I was more pleased with possessing your heart than with any other happiness, and the man was the thing I least valued in you.

40

You cannot but be entirely persuaded of this by the extreme unwillingness I showed to marry you, though I knew that the name of wife was honorable in the world and holy in religion; yet the name of your mistress had greater charms because it was more free. The bonds of matrimony, however honorable, still bear with them a necessary engagement, and I was very unwilling to be necessitated to love always a man who would perhaps not always love me. I despised the name of wife that I might live happy with that of mistress; and I find by your letter to your friend you have not forgot that delicacy of passion which loved you always with the utmost tenderness—and yet wished to love you more!

You have very justly observed in your letter that I esteemed those public engagements insipid which form alliances only to be dissolved by death, and which put life and love under the same unhappy necessity. But you have not added how often I have protested that it was infinitely preferable to me to live with Abelard as his mistress than with any other as Empress of the World. I was more happy in obeying you than I should have been as lawful spouse of the King of the Earth. Riches and pomp are not the charm of love. True tenderness makes us separate the lover from all that is external to him, and setting aside his position, fortune, or employments, consider him merely as himself. . . .

It is not love, but the desire of riches and position which makes a woman run into the embraces of an indolent husband. Ambition, and not affection, forms such marriages. I believe indeed they may be followed with some honors and advantages, but I can never think that this is the way to experience the pleasures of affectionate union, nor to feel those subtle and charming joys when hearts long parted are at last united. These martyrs of marriage pine always for larger fortunes which they think they have missed. The wife sees husbands richer than her own, and the husband wives better portioned than his. Their mercenary vows occasion regret, and regret produces hatred. Soon they part—or else desire to. This restless and tormenting passion for gold punishes them for aiming at other advantages by love than love itself.

If there is anything that may properly be called happiness here below, I am persuaded it is the union of two persons who love each other with perfect liberty, who are united by a secret inclination, and satisfied with each other's merits. Their hearts are full and leave no vacancy for any other passion; they enjoy perpetual tranquillity because they enjoy content. . . .

What rivalries did your gallantries of this kind occasion me! How many ladies lay claim to them? 'Twas a tribute their self-love paid to their beauty. How many have I seen with sighs declare their passion for you when, after some common visit you had made them, they chanced to be complimented for the Sylvia of your poems. Others in despair and envy have reproached me that I had no charms but what your wit bestowed on me, nor in anything the advantage over them but in being beloved by you. Can you believe me if I tell you, that notwithstanding my sex, I thought myself peculiarly happy in having a lover to whom I was obliged for my charms; and took a secret pleasure in being admired by a man who, when he pleased, could raise his mistress to the character of a goddess. Pleased with your glory only, I read with delight all those praises you offered me, and without reflecting how little I deserved, I believed myself such as you described, that I might be more certain that I pleased you.

But oh! where is that happy time? I now lament my lover, and of all my joys have nothing but the painful memory that they are past. Now learn, all you my rivals who once viewed my happiness with jealous eyes, that he you once envied me can never more be mine. I loved him; my love was his crime and the cause of his punishment. My beauty once charmed him; pleased with each other, we passed our brightest days in tranquillity and happiness. If that were a crime, 'tis a crime I am yet fond of, and I have no other regret save that against my will I must now be innocent.

But what do I say? My misfortune was to have cruel relatives whose malice destroyed the calm we enjoyed; had they been reasonable I had now been happy in the enjoyment of my dear husband. Oh! how cruel were they when their blind fury urged a villain to surprise you in your sleep! Where was I—where was your Heloise then? What joy should I have had in defending my lover; I would have guarded you from violence at the expense of my life. Oh! whither does this excess of passion hurry me? Here love is shocked and modesty deprives me of words.

But tell me whence proceeds your neglect of me since my being professed? You know nothing moved me to it but your disgrace, nor did I give my consent, but yours. Let me hear what is the occasion of your coldness, or give me leave to tell you now my opinion. Was it not the sole thought of pleasure which engaged you to me? And has not my tenderness, by leaving you nothing to wish for, extinguished your desires?

Wretched Heloise! you could please when you wished to avoid it; you merited incense when you could remove to a distance the hand that offered it: but since your heart has been softened and has yielded, since you have devoted and sacrificed yourself, you are deserted and forgotten!

I am convinced by a sad experience that it is natural to avoid those to whom we have been too much obliged, and that uncommon generosity causes neglect rather than gratitude. My heart surrendered too soon to gain the esteem of the conqueror; you took it without difficulty and threw it aside with ease. But ungrateful as you are I am no consenting party to this, and though I ought not to retain a wish of my own, yet I still preserve secretly the desire to be loved by you.

43

When I pronounced my sad vow I then had about me your last letters in which you protested your whole being wholly mine, and would never live but to love me. It is to you therefore I have offered myself; you had my heart and I had yours; do not demand anything back. You must bear with my passion as a thing which of right belongs to you, and from which you can be no ways disengaged.

Alas! what folly it is to talk in this way! I see nothing here but marks of the Deity, and I speak of nothing but man! You have been the cruel occasion of this by your conduct, unfaithful one! Ought you at once to break off loving me! Why did you not deceive me for a while rather than immediately abandon me? If you had given me at least some faint signs of a dying passion I would have favored the deception. But in vain do I flatter myself that you could be constant; you have left no vestige of an excuse for you. I am earnestly desirous to see you, but if that be impossible I will content myself with a few lines from your hand.

Is it so hard for one who loves to write? I ask for none of your letters filled with learning and writ for your reputation; all I desire is such letters as the heart dictates, and which the hand cannot transcribe fast enough. How did I deceive myself with hopes that you would be wholly mine when I took the veil, and engaged myself to live forever under your laws? For in being professed I vowed no more than to be yours only, and I forced myself voluntarily to a confinement which you desired for me. Death only then can make me leave the cloister where you have placed me; and then my ashes shall rest here and wait for yours in order to show to the very last my obedience and devotion to you.

Why should I conceal from you the secret of my call? You know it was neither zeal nor devotion that brought me here. Your conscience is too faithful a witness to permit you to disown it. Yet here I am, and here I will remain; to this place an unfortunate love and a cruel relation have condemned me. But if you do not continue your concern for me, if I lose your affection, what have I gained by my imprisonment? What recompense can I hope for? The unhappy consequences of our love and your disgrace have made me put on the habit of chastity, but I am not penitent of the past. Thus I strive and labor in vain. Among those who are wedded to God I am wedded to a man; among the heroic supporters of the Cross I am the slave of a human desire; at the head of a religious community I am devoted to Abelard alone.

What a monster am I! Enlighten me, O Lord, for I know not if my despair of Thy grace draws these words from me! I am, I confess, a sinner, but one who, far from weeping for her sins, weeps only for her lover; far from abhorring her crimes, longs only to add to them; and who, with a weakness unbecoming my state, please myself continually with the remembrance of past delights when it is impossible to renew them.

Good God! What is all this? I reproach myself for my own faults, I accuse you for yours, and to what purpose? Veiled as I am, behold in what a disorder you have plunged me! How difficult it is to fight for duty against inclination. I know what obligations this veil lays upon me, but I feel more strongly what power an old passion has over my heart. . . .

Oh, for pity's sake help a wretch to renounce her desires—her self—and if possible even to renounce you! If you are a lover—a father, help a mistress, comfort a child! These tender names must surely move you; yield either to pity or to love. If you gratify my request I shall continue a religious, and without longer profaning my calling.

I am ready to humble myself with you to the wonderful goodness of God, who does all things for our sanctification, who by His grace purifies all that is vicious and corrupt, and by the great riches of His mercy draws us against our wishes, and by degrees opens our eyes to behold His bounty which at first we could not perceive. . . .

A heart which has loved as mine cannot soon be indifferent. We

fluctuate long between love and hatred before we can arrive at
tranquillity, and we always flatter ourselves with some forlorn hope
that we shall not be utterly forgotten.

Yes, Abelard, I conjure you by the chains I bear here to ease
the weight of them, and make them as agreeable as I would they
were to me. Teach me the maxims of Divine Love; since you have
forsaken me I would glory in being wedded to Heaven. My heart
adores that title and disdains any other; tell me how this Divine
Love is nourished, how it works, how it purifies.

When we were tossed on the ocean of the world we could hear
of nothing but your verses, which published everywhere our joys
and pleasures. Now we are in the haven of grace is it not fit you
should discourse to me of this new happiness, and teach me everything that might heighten or improve it? Show me the same com-
plaisance in my present condition as you did when we were in the
world. Without changing the ardor of our affections let us change
their objects; let us leave our songs and sing hymns; let us lift up
our hearts to God and have no transports but for His glory!

I expect this from you as a thing you cannot refuse me. God has
a peculiar right over the hearts of great men He has created. When
He pleases to touch them He ravishes them, and lets them not
speak nor breathe but for His glory. Till that moment of grace
arrives, O think of me—do not forget me—remember my love and
fidelity and constancy: love me as your mistress, cherish me as your
child, your sister, your wife! Remember I still love you, and yet
strive to avoid loving you. What a terrible saying is this! I shake
with horror, and my heart revolts against what I say. I shall blot
all my paper with tears. I end my long letter wishing you, if you
desire it (would to Heaven I could!), forever adieu!

To THIS letter from Heloise, Abelard replied in the letter which
follows:

46

ABELARD, FROM HIS MONASTIC SOLITUDE, LIVING IN A HUT OF REEDS, YIELDS HIMSELF AND HELOISE TO GOD

". . . I purpose now to dry up those tears . . ."

[ABELARD TO HELOISE]

COULD I have imagined that a letter not written to yourself would fall into your hands, I had been more cautious not to have inserted anything in it which might awaken the memory of our past misfortunes. I described with boldness the series of my disgraces to a friend, in order to make him less sensible to a loss he had sustained.

If by this well-meaning device I have disturbed you, I purpose now to dry up those tears which the sad description occasioned you to shed; I intend to mix my grief with yours, and pour out my heart before you: in short, to lay open before your eyes all my trouble, and the secret of my soul, which my vanity has hitherto made me conceal from the rest of the world, and which you now force from me, in spite of my resolutions to the contrary.

It is true, that in a sense of the afflictions which have befallen us, and observing that no change of our condition could be expected; that those prosperous days which had seduced us were now past, and there remained nothing but to erase from our minds, by painful endeavors, all marks and remembrances of them. I had wished to find in philosophy and religion a remedy for my disgrace; I searched out an asylum to secure me from love. I was

47

come to the sad experiment of making vows to harden my heart.

But what have I gained by this? If my passion has been put under a restraint my thoughts yet run free. I promise myself that I will forget you, and yet cannot think of it without loving you. My love is not at all lessened by those reflections I make in order to free myself. The silence I am surrounded by makes me more sensible to its impressions, and while I am unemployed with any other things, this makes itself the business of my whole vocation. Till after a multitude of useless endeavors I begin to persuade myself that it is a superfluous trouble to strive to free myself; and that it is sufficient wisdom to conceal from all but you how confused and weak I am.

I remove to a distance from your person with an intention of avoiding you as an enemy; and yet I incessantly seek for you in my mind; I recall your image in my memory, and in different disquietudes I betray and contradict myself. I hate you! I love you! Shame presses me on all sides.

I am at this moment afraid I should seem more indifferent than you fare, and yet I am ashamed to discover my trouble. How weak are we in ourselves if we do not support ourselves on the Cross of Christ. Shall we have so little courage, and shall that uncertainty of serving two masters which afflicts your heart affect mine too? You see the confusion I am in, how I blame myself and how I suffer.

Religion commands me to pursue virtue since I have nothing to hope for from love. But love still preserves its dominion over my fancies and entertains itself with past pleasures. Memory supplies the place of a mistress. Piety and duty are not always the fruits of retirement; even in deserts, when the dew of heaven falls not on us, we love what we ought no longer to love.

The passions, stirred up by solitude, fill these regions of death

48

and silence; it is very seldom that what ought to be is truly followed here and that God only is loved and served. Had I known this before I had instructed you better. You call me your master; it is true you were entrusted to my care. I saw you, I was earnest to teach you vain sciences; it cost you your innocence and me my liberty.

Your uncle, who was fond of you, became my enemy and revenged himself on me. If now having lost the power of satisfying my passion I had also lost that of loving you, I should have some consolation. My enemies would have given me that tranquillity which Origen purchased with a crime. How miserable am I! I find myself much more guilty in my thoughts of you, even amidst my tears, than in possessing you when I was in full liberty. I continually think of you; I continually call to mind your tenderness.

In this condition, O Lord! if I run to prostrate myself before your altar, if I beseech you to pity me, why does not the pure flame of the Spirit consume the sacrifice that is offered? Cannot this habit of penitence which I wear interest Heaven to treat me more favorably? But Heaven is still inexorable, because my passion still lives in me; the fire is only covered over with deceitful ashes, and cannot be extinguished but by extraordinary grace. We deceive men, but nothing is hid from God.

You tell me that it is for me you live under that veil which covers you; why do you profane your vocation with such words? Why provoke a jealous God with a blasphemy? I hoped after our separation you would have changed your sentiments; I hoped too that God would have delivered me from the tumult of my senses. We commonly die to the affections of those we see no more, and they to ours; absence is the tomb of love. But to me absence is an unquiet remembrance of what I once loved which continually torments me. I flattered myself that when I should see you no more you would rest in my memory without troubling my mind; that

49

Brittany and the sea would suggest other thoughts; that my fasts and studies would by degrees delete you from my heart. But in spite of severe fasts and redoubled studies, in spite of the distance of three hundred miles which separates us, your image, as you describe yourself in your veil, appears to me and confounds all my resolutions.

What means have I not used! I have armed my hands against myself; I have exhausted my strength in constant exercises; I comment upon Saint Paul; I contend with Aristotle: in short, I do all I used to do before I loved you, but all in vain; nothing can be successful that opposes you. Oh! do not add to my miseries by your constancy. . . . Why use your eloquence to reproach me for my flight and for my silence? Spare the recital of our assignations and your constant exactness to them; without calling up such disturbing thoughts I have enough to suffer. What great advantages would philosophy give us over other men, if by studying it we could learn to govern our passions? What efforts, what relapses, what agitations do we undergo! And how long are we lost in this confusion, unable to exert our reason, to possess our souls, or to rule our affections? . . .

How can I separate from the person I love the passion I should detest? Will the tears I shed be sufficient to render it odious to me? I know not how it happens, there is always a pleasure in weeping for a beloved object. It is difficult in our sorrow to distinguish penitence from love. The memory of the crime and the memory of the object which has charmed us are too nearly related to be immediately separated. And the love of God in its beginning does not wholly annihilate the love of the creature.

But what excuses could I not find in you if the crime were excusable? Unprofitable honor, troublesome riches, could never tempt me: but those charms, that beauty, that air, which I yet behold at this instant, have occasioned my fall. Your looks were the beginning of my guilt; your eyes, your discourse, pierced my heart; and in spite of that ambition and glory which tried to make a defense, love was soon the master.

God, in order to punish me, forsook me. You are no longer of the world; you have renounced it: I am a religious devoted to solitude; shall we not take advantage of our condition? Would you destroy my piety in its infant state? Would you have me forsake the abbey into which I am but newly entered? Must I renounce my vows? I have made them in the presence of God; whither shall I fly from His wrath should I violate them? Suffer me to seek ease in my duty. . . .

Regard me no more, I entreat you, as a founder or any great personage; your praises ill agree with my many weaknesses. I am a miserable sinner, prostrate before my Judge, and with my face pressed to the earth I mix my tears with the earth. Can you see me in this posture and solicit me to love you? Come, if you think fit, and in your holy habit thrust yourself between my God and me, and be a wall of separation. Come and force from me those sighs and thoughts and vows I owe to Him alone. Assist the evil spirits and be the instrument of their malice. What cannot you induce a heart to do whose weakness you so perfectly know?

Nay, withdraw yourself and contribute to my salvation. Suffer me to avoid destruction, I entreat you by our former tender affection and by our now common misfortune. It will always be the highest love to show none; I here release you from all your oaths and engagements. Be God's wholly, to whom you are appropriated; I will never oppose so pious a design. How happy shall I be if I thus lose you! Then shall I indeed be a religious and you a perfect example of an abbess.

Make yourself amends by so glorious a choice; make your virtue a spectacle worthy of men and angels. Be humble among your children, assiduous in your choir, exact in your discipline, diligent in your reading; make even your recreations useful.

Have you purchased your vocation at so light a rate that you should not turn it to the best advantage? Since you have permitted yourself to be abused by false doctrine and criminal instruction, resist not those good counsels which grace and religion inspire me with.

I will confess to you I have thought myself hitherto an abler master to instill vice than to teach virtue. My false eloquence has only set off false good. My heart, drunk with voluptuousness, could only suggest terms proper and moving to recommend that. The cup of sinners overflows with so enchanting a sweetness, and we are naturally so much inclined to taste it, that it needs only to be offered to us.

On the other hand the chalice of saints is filled with a bitter draught and nature starts from it. And yet you reproach me with cowardice for giving it to you first. I willingly submit to these accusations. I cannot enough admire the readiness you showed to accept the religious habit; bear therefore with courage the Cross you so resolutely took up. Drink of the chalice of saints, even to the bottom, without turning your eyes with uncertainty upon me; let me remove far from you and obey the Apostle who hath said "Fly!"

You entreat me to return under a pretense of devotion. Your earnestness in this point creates a suspicion in me and makes me doubtful how to answer you. Should I commit an error here my words would blush, if I may say so, after the history of our misfortunes. The Church is jealous of its honor, and commands that her children should be induced to the practice of virtue by virtuous means. When we approach God in a blameless manner then we may with boldness invite others to Him.

But to forget Heloise, to see her no more, is what Heaven demands of Abelard; and to expect nothing from Abelard, to forget him even as an idea, is what Heaven enjoins on Heloise. To forget, in the case of love, is the most necessary penance, and the most difficult. It is easy to recount our faults; how many, through indiscretion, have made themselves a second pleasure of this instead of confessing them with humility. The only way to return to God is by neglecting the creature we have adored, and adoring the God whom we have neglected. This may appear harsh, but it must be done if we would be saved.

To make it more easy consider why I pressed you to your vow before I took mine; and pardon my sincerity and the design I have of meriting your neglect and hatred if I conceal nothing from you. When I saw myself oppressed by my misfortune I was furiously jealous, and regarded all men as my rivals. Love has more of distrust than assurance. I was apprehensive of many things because of my many defects, and being tormented with fear because of my own example I imagined your heart so accustomed to love that it could not be long without entering on a new engagement. Jealousy can easily believe the most terrible things.

I was desirous to make it impossible for me to doubt you. I was very urgent to persuade you that propriety demanded your withdrawal from the eyes of the world; that modesty and our friendship required it; and that your own safety obliged it. After such a revenge taken on me you could expect to be secure nowhere but in a convent.

I will do you justice, you were very easily persuaded. My jealousy secretly rejoiced in your innocent compliance; and yet, triumphant as I was, I yielded you up to God with an unwilling heart. I still kept my gift as much as was possible, and only parted with it in order to keep it out of the power of other men. I did not persuade you to religion out of any regard to your happiness, but condemned you to it like an enemy who destroys what he cannot carry off. And

53

yet you heard my discourses with kindness, you sometimes interrupted me with tears, and pressed me to acquaint you with those convents I held in the highest esteem. What a comfort I felt in seeing you shut up. I was now at ease and took a satisfaction in considering that you continued no longer in the world after my disgrace, and that you would return to it no more.

But still I was doubtful. I imagined women were incapable of steadfast resolutions unless they were forced by the necessity of vows. I wanted those vows, and Heaven itself for your security, that I might no longer distrust you. Ye holy mansions and impenetrable retreats! from what innumerable apprehensions have ye freed me? Religion and piety keep a strict guard around your grates and walls. What a haven of rest this is to a jealous mind! And with what impatience did I endeavor after it!

I went every day trembling to exhort you to this sacrifice; I admired, without daring to mention it then, a brightness in your beauty which I had never observed before. Whether it was the bloom of a rising virtue, or an anticipation of the great loss I was to suffer, I was not curious in examining the cause, but only hastened your being professed. I engaged your prioress in my guilt by a criminal bribe with which I purchased the right of burying you. The professed of the house were alike bribed and concealed from you, at my directions, all their scruples and disgusts. I omitted nothing, either little or great; and if you had escaped my snares I myself would not have retired; I was resolved to follow you everywhere. The shadow of myself would always have pursued your steps and continually have occasioned either your confusion or your fear, which would have been a sensible gratification to me.

But, thanks to Heaven, you resolved to take the vows. I accompanied you to the foot of the altar, and while you stretched out your hand to touch the sacred cloth I heard you distinctly pronounce those fatal words that forever separated you from man.

Till then I thought your youth and beauty would foil my design and force your return to the world. Might not a small temptation have changed you? Is it possible to renounce oneself entirely at the age of two-and-twenty? At an age which claims the utmost liberty could you think the world no longer worth your regard? How much did I wrong you, and what weakness did I impute to you? You were in my imagination both light and inconstant. Would not a woman at the noise of the flames and the fall of Sodom involuntarily look back in pity on some person? I watched your eyes, your every movement, your air; I trembled at everything. You may call such self-interested conduct treachery, perfidy, murder. A love so like to hatred should provoke the utmost contempt and anger.

It is fit you should know that the very moment when I was convinced of your being entirely devoted to me, when I saw you were infinitely worthy of all my love, I imagined I could love you no more. I thought it time to leave off giving you marks of my affection, and I considered that by your Holy Espousals you were now the peculiar care of Heaven, and no longer a charge on me as my wife. My jealousy seemed to be extinguished. When God only is our rival we have nothing to fear; and being in greater tranquillity than ever before I even dared to pray to Him to take you away from my eyes.

But it was not a time to make rash prayers, and my faith did not warrant them being heard. Necessity and despair were at the root of my proceedings, and thus I offered an insult to Heaven rather than a sacrifice. God rejected my offering and my prayer, and continued my punishment by suffering me to continue my love. Thus I bear alike the guilt of your vows and of the passion that preceded them, and must be tormented all the days of my life.

If God spoke to your heart as to that of a religious whose innocence had first asked Him for favors, I should have matter of comfort; but to see both of us the victims of a guilty love, to see this

55

love insult us in our very habits and spoil our devotions, fills me
with horror and trembling. Is this a state of reprobation? Or are
these the consequences of a long drunkenness in profane love?

We cannot say love is a poison and a drunkenness till we are
illuminated by grace; in the meantime it is an evil we dote on.
When we are under such a mistake, the knowledge of our misery
is the first step towards amendment. Who does not know that 'tis
for the glory of God to find no other reason in man for His mercy
than man's very weakness? When He has shown us this weakness
and we have bewailed it, He is ready to put forth His omnipotence
and assist us. Let us say for our comfort that what we suffer is one
of those terrible temptations which have sometimes disturbed the
vocations of the most holy.

God can grant His presence to men in order to soften their
calamities whenever He shall think fit. It was His pleasure when
you took the veil to draw you to Him by His grace. I saw your
eyes, when you spoke your last farewell, fixed upon the Cross. It
was more than six months before you wrote me a letter, nor during
all that time did I receive a message from you. I admired this
silence, which I durst not blame, but could not imitate. I wrote to
you, and you returned me no answer: your heart was then shut,
but this garden of the spouse is now opened; He is withdrawn from
it and has left you alone.

By removing from you He has made trial of you; call Him back
and strive to regain Him. We must have the assistance of God,
that we may break our chains; we are too deeply in love to free
ourselves.

Our follies have penetrated into the sacred places; our amours
have been a scandal to the whole kingdom. They are read and
admired; love which produced them has caused them to be described. We shall be a consolation to the failings of youth forever;
those who offend after us will think themselves less guilty. We are

criminals whose repentance is late; oh, let it be sincere! Let us repair as far as is possible the evils we have done, and let France, which has been the witness of our crimes, be amazed at our repentance. Let us confound all who would imitate our guilt; let us take the side of God against ourselves, and by so doing prevent His judgment.

Our former lapses require tears, shame, and sorrow to expiate them. Let us offer up these sacrifices from our hearts, let us blush and let us weep. If in these feeble beginnings, O Lord, our hearts are not entirely Thine, let them at least feel that they ought to be so.

Deliver yourself, Heloise, from the shameful remains of a passion which has taken too deep root. Remember that the least thought for any other than God is an adultery. If you could see me here with my meager face and melancholy air, surrounded with numbers of persecuting monks, who are alarmed at my reputation for learning and offended at my lean visage, as if I threatened them with a reformation, what would you say of my base sighs and of those unprofitable tears which deceive these credulous men? Alas! I am humbled under love, and not under the Cross. Pity me and free yourself. If your vocation be, as you say, my work, deprive me not of the merit of it by your continual inquietudes.

Tell me you will be true to the habit which covers you by an inward retirement. Fear God, that you may be delivered from your frailties; love Him that you may advance in virtue. Be not restless in the cloister, for it is the peace of saints. Embrace your bands, they are the chains of Christ Jesus; He will lighten them and bear them with you, if you will but accept them with humility.

Without growing severe to a passion that still possesses you, learn from your misery to succor your weak sisters; pity them upon consideration of your own faults. And if any thoughts too natural should importune you, fly to the foot of the Cross and there beg for mercy—there are wounds open for healing; lament them before the dying Deity.

At the head of a religious society be not a slave. and having rule over queens, begin to govern yourself. Blush at the least revolt of your senses. Remember that even at the foot of the altar we often sacrifice to lying spirits, and that no incense can be more agreeable to them than the earthly passion that still burns in the heart of a religious.

If during your abode in the world your soul has acquired a habit of loving, feel it now no more save for Jesus Christ. Repent of all the moments of your life which you have wasted in the world and on pleasure; demand them of me, 'tis a robbery of which I am guilty; take courage and boldly reproach me with it.

I have been indeed your master, but it was only to teach sin. You call me your father; before I had any claim to the title, I deserved that of parricide. I am your brother, but it is the affinity of sin that brings me that distinction. I am called your husband, but it is after a public scandal.

If you have abused the sanctity of so many holy terms in the superscription of your letter to do me honor and flatter your own passion, blot them out and replace them with those of murderer, villain, and enemy, who has conspired against your honor, troubled your quiet, and betrayed your innocence. You would have perished through my means but for an extraordinary act of grace, which, that you might be saved, has thrown me down in the middle of my course.

This is the thought you ought to have of a fugitive who desires to deprive you of the hope of ever seeing him again. But when love has once been sincere how difficult it is to determine to love no more! 'Tis a thousand times more easy to renounce the world than love. I hate this deceitful, faithless world; I think no more of it; but my wandering heart still eternally seeks you, and is filled with anguish at having lost you, in spite of all the powers of my reason. In the meantime, though I should be so cowardly as to retract what you have read, do not suffer me to offer myself to your thoughts save in this last fashion.

Remember my last worldly endeavors were to seduce your heart; you perished by my means and I with you: the same waves swallowed us up. We waited for death with indifference, and the same death had carried us headlong to the same punishments. But Providence warded off the blow, and our shipwreck has thrown us into a haven.

There are some whom God saves by suffering. Let my salvation be the fruit of your prayers; let me owe it to your tears and your exemplary holiness. Though my heart, Lord, be filled with the love of Thy creature, Thy hand can, when it pleases, empty me of all love save for Thee.

To love Heloise truly is to leave her to that quiet which retirement and virtue afford. I have resolved it: this letter shall be my last fault. Adieu.

If I die here I will give orders that my body be carried to the house of the Paraclete. You shall see me in that condition, not to demand tears from you, for it will be too late; weep rather for me now and extinguish the fire which burns me.

You shall see me in order that your piety may be strengthened by horror of this carcase, and my death be eloquent to tell you what you brave when you love a man. I hope you will be willing, when you have finished this mortal life, to be buried near me. Your cold ashes need then fear nothing, and my tomb shall be the more rich and renowned.

IN THE letters that followed this initial exchange of letters, both Heloise and Abelard gradually began to devote more and more attention to philosophical and ecclesiastical matters. Abelard apologized for not having written sooner, attributing the delay not to any lack of interest but to his having "such confidence in her prudence, learning, piety, and devotion that he did not imagine that she required either exhortation or comfort. . . ." Following this classic of Jesuitical extenuation, Abelard's subsequent letters revealed what Scott-Moncrieff called "growing irritation and boredom." In his last letters he incorporated long quotations and passages copied from earlier letters of Heloise. He extolled "the wisdom and clemency of God" and offered up many prayers.

In reply, Heloise asked Abelard to "promulgate some rules for the guidance of nuns, to prescribe a way of life which should apply to women only—a thing never done before by any of the Holy Fathers." Then came long inquiries, and longer answers, on details of doctrine. In the final letter of the whole series Abelard virtually set down a treatise on the sacred orders, on continence, voluntary poverty, and silence.

At the age of sixty-three, friendless and persecuted, Abelard died. His body was given to Heloise for burial. Twenty-two years later, Heloise was buried beside him. To this day they lie side by side in the cemetery of Père-Lachaise in Paris. On the tombstone of these world-renowned lovers this inscription has been immortalized:

"Here, under the same stone, repose, of this monastery the founder, Peter Abelard, and the first abbess, Heloise, heretofore in study, genius, love, inauspicious marriage, and repentance, now, as we hope, in eternal happiness united. Peter died April 21, 1142. Heloise May 17, 1164."

CHRISTOPHER COLUMBUS REPORTS HIS FIRST IMPRESSIONS OF AMERICA

[A LETTER TO GABRIEL SANCHEZ, TREASURER OF KING FERDINAND OF SPAIN]

ON FEBRUARY 14, 1493, says Dr. A. S. W. Rosenbach in Books and Bidders, Christopher Columbus "carefully prepared as complete an account of his marvelous voyage as was possible under the circumstances. He wrote the details of his journey on a stout piece of parchment, wrapped it carefully in a piece of waterproof cloth, then placed it in an iron-bound barrel and threw it into the raging ocean. . . . And if I thought there were one chance in a million of finding it I would take my power boat, the First Folio, and cruise in the neighborhood of the Azores forever!"

The Columbus letter here printed is the next best thing, being the account by Columbus himself of the discovery of America, which he dispatched to "the magnificent lord Raphael Sanxis [Gabriel Sanchez] treasurer of the same most illustrious king [Ferdinand], and which the noble and learned man Leander de Cosco has translated from the Spanish language into Latin, on the third of the kalends of May [April 29th], 1493, the first year of the pontificate of Alexander the Sixth."

Without the signature of Christopher Columbus, and without the date line marking one of the turning points of world history, this would probably be an ordinary, if somewhat grandiloquent and overwritten, travel letter.

In the words of President Lowell of Harvard: "when Columbus set out he did not know where he was going; when he arrived he did not know where he was; when he returned he did not know where he had been, but all the same he discovered America."

61

According to the latest researches, Columbus was by blood a Spanish Jew whose forebears had sought safety in Genoa from the Inquisition in Spain.

A Harvard University expedition recently retraced the routes of the Columbus voyages to answer the question of "whether Christopher Columbus was really a sailor, or only a landlubber with a big idea that something besides horrible monsters filled the space beyond the Atlantic horizon."

This expedition, directed by Dr. Samuel Eliot Morison, employed two schooners under the direction of eight experienced navigators, and checked the accounts of the Columbus voyages against their own observations. After sailing the route from Cadiz to Madeira, the Canaries, and Trinidad and along the shores of Central American countries for more than four months, identifying and following most of the courses and landfalls in the logs of Columbus and notes left by him and his son, Dr. Morison announced that the reputation of Columbus as a seaman and navigator was strongly confirmed. He declared that Columbus was "a master navigator and a shrewd and accurate observer with a keen sense of beauty."

In the opinion of some historians, Bjarni Herjulfsson of Iceland actually discovered America in the year 987, more than four hundred and fifty years before Columbus was born. Leif Ericsson, also of Icelandic birth, may have set foot on the mainland of America in A.D. 1000. Columbus himself actually never set foot on the mainland of North or South America, and he died without knowing that he had discovered a new world. His name, moreover, was not Columbus but Cristóbal Colón.

What follows is the document in which the discoverer of America (until the experts definitely prove Leif's claim) reports to "the most invincible Ferdinand," King of Spain, concerning the islands recently discovered in what Columbus believed to be "the Indian Sea, beyond the Ganges." Here is a fresh and firsthand picture of prehistoric America —our continent "as God made it."

According to Wilberforce Eames, who edited the letter for the Lenox Library of New York in 1893, it was first printed in Spanish at Barcelona, in April, 1493. In it is recounted the earliest information of an event that literally opened up a new world.

The voyage itself lasted two hundred and twenty-four days, from August 3, 1492, when Columbus sailed from the harbor of Palos on the southern coast of Spain, in his forty-first year, with three small ships, the Santa Maria, the Pinta, and the Nina, to March 15, 1493, when he returned in a single vessel to the same port. Traditional historians still tell us that when Columbus landed at Watling Island in the Bahamas group, on October 12, 1492, he thought he was near Cipango, or Japan. But according to the latest biography of Columbus, a brilliant and searching study by Salvadore de Madariaga, his plan when he left Spain was "merely to up anchor and sail due west until he hit something, whether what he hit was Cipango or Cathay or some of the myriads of islands with which, like other men of his time, he believed the unknown West was jammed."

In any event, the letter that follows gives a detailed firsthand account of what Columbus found when he came ashore on October 12, 1492:

"These things that have been done are thus briefly related."

BECAUSE my undertakings have attained success, I know that it will be pleasing to you: these I have determined to relate, so that you may be made acquainted with everything done and

63

discovered in this our voyage. On the thirty-third day after I departed from Cadiz, I came to the Indian sea, where I found many islands inhabited by men without number, of all which I took possession for our most fortunate king, with proclaiming heralds and flying standards, no one objecting.

To the first of these I gave the name of the blessed Saviour,[1] on whose aid relying I had reached this as well as the other islands. But the Indians called it Guanahany. I also called each one of the others by a new name. For I ordered one island to be called Santa Maria of the Conception,[2] another Fernandina,[3] another Isabella,[4] another Juana,[5] and so on with the rest.

As soon as we had arrived at that island which I have just now said was called Juana, I proceeded along its coast towards the west for some distance; I found it so large and without perceptible end, that I believed it to be not an island, but the continental country of Cathay;[6] seeing, however, no towns or cities situated on the seacoast, but only some villages and rude farms, with whose inhabitants I was unable to converse, because as soon as they saw us they took flight.

I proceeded farther, thinking that I would discover some city or large residences. At length, perceiving that we had gone far enough, that nothing new appeared, and that this way was leading us to the north, which I wished to avoid, because it was winter on the land, and it was my intention to go to the south, moreover the winds were becoming violent, I therefore determined that no other plans were practicable, and so, going back, I returned to a certain bay

---

[1] In Spanish, San Salvador, one of the Bahama Islands. It has been variously identified with Grand Turk, Cat, Watling, Mariguana, Samana, and Acklin islands. Watling's Island seems to have much in its favor.

[2] Perhaps Crooked Island or, according to others, North Caico.

[3] Identified by some with Long Island; by others with Little Inagua.

[4] Identified variously with Fortune Island and Great Inagua.

[5] The island of Cuba.

[6] China.

that I had noticed, from which I sent two of our men to the land, that they might find out whether there was a king in this country, or any cities. These men traveled for three days, and they found people and houses without number, but they were small and without any government, therefore they returned. . . .

This island is surrounded by many very safe and wide harbors, not excelled by any others that I have ever seen. Many great and salubrious rivers flow through it. There are also many very high mountains there. All these islands are very beautiful, and distinguished by various qualities; they are accessible, and full of a great variety of trees stretching up to the stars; the leaves of which I believe are never shed, for I saw them as green and flourishing as they are usually in Spain in the month of May; some of them were blossoming, some were bearing fruit, some were in other conditions; each one was thriving in its own way. The nightingale and various other birds without number were singing, in the month of November, when I was exploring them.

There are besides in the said island Juana seven or eight kinds of palm trees, which far excel ours in height and beauty, just as all the other trees, herbs, and fruits do. There are also excellent pine trees, vast plains and meadows, a variety of birds, a variety of honey, and a variety of metals, excepting iron. In the one which was called Hispana, as we said above, there are great and beautiful mountains, vast fields, groves, fertile plains, very suitable for planting and cultivating, and for the building of houses.

The convenience of the harbors in this island, and the remarkable number of rivers contributing to the healthfulness of man, exceed belief, unless one has seen them. The trees, pasturage, and fruits of this island differ greatly from those of Juana. This Hispana, moreover, abounds in different kinds of spices, in gold, and in metals.

On this island, indeed, and on all the others which I have seen,

65

and of which I have knowledge, the inhabitants of both sexes go always naked, just as they came into the world, except some of the women, who use a covering of a leaf or some foliage, or a cotton cloth, which they make themselves for that purpose.

All these people lack, as I said above, every kind of iron; they are also without weapons, which indeed are unknown; nor are they competent to use them, not on account of deformity of body, for they are well formed, but because they are timid and full of fear. They carry for weapons, however, reeds baked in the sun, on the lower ends of which they fasten some shafts of dried wood rubbed down to a point; and indeed they do not venture to use these always; for it frequently happened when I sent two or three of my men to some of the villages, that they might speak with the natives, a compact troop of the Indians would march out, and as soon as they saw our men approaching, they would quickly take flight, children being pushed aside by their fathers, and fathers by their children. And this was not because any hurt or injury had been inflicted on any one of them, for to every one whom I visited and with whom I was able to converse, I distributed whatever I had, cloth and many other things, no return being made to me; but they are by nature fearful and timid.

Yet when they perceive that they are safe, putting aside all fear, they are of simple manners and trustworthy, and very liberal with everything they have, refusing no one who asks for anything they may possess, and even themselves inviting us to ask for things. They show greater love for all others than for themselves; they give valuable things for trifles, being satisfied even with a very small return, or with nothing; however, I forbade that things so small and of no value should be given to them, such as pieces of plate, dishes and glass, likewise keys and shoestraps; although if they were able to obtain these, it seemed to them like getting the most beautiful jewels in the world. . . .

66

In all these islands there is no difference in the appearance of the people, nor in the manners and language, but all understand each other mutually; a fact that is very important for the end which I suppose to be earnestly desired by our most illustrious king, that is, their conversion to the holy religion of Christ, to which in truth, as far as I can perceive, they are very ready and favorably inclined. . . .

In all these islands, as I have understood, each man is content with only one wife, except the princes or kings, who are permitted to have twenty. The women appear to work more than the men. I was not able to find out surely whether they have individual property, for I saw that one man had the duty of distributing to the others, especially refreshments, food, and things of that kind. . . .

Truly great and wonderful is this, and not corresponding to our merits, but to the holy Christian religion, and to the piety and religion of our sovereigns, because what the human understanding could not attain, that the divine will has granted to human efforts. For God is wont to listen to his servants who love his precepts, even in impossibilities, as has happened to us on the present occasion, who have attained that which hitherto mortal men have never reached.

For if anyone has written or said anything about these islands, it was all with obscurities and conjectures; no one claims that he had seen them; from which they seemed like fables. Therefore let the king and queen, the princes and their most fortunate kingdoms, and all other countries of Christendom give thanks to our Lord and Saviour Jesus Christ, who has bestowed upon us so great a victory and gift. Let religious processions be solemnized; let sacred festivals be given; let the churches be covered with festive garlands. Let Christ rejoice on earth, as he rejoices in heaven, when he foresees coming to salvation so many souls of people hitherto lost. Let us be glad also, as well on account of the exaltation of our faith, as on account of the increase of our temporal affairs, of which not only Spain, but universal Christendom will be partaker. These things that have been done are thus briefly related. Farewell. Lisbon, the day before the ides of March.[7]

Christopher Columbus, admiral of the Ocean fleet

SUBSEQUENTLY Columbus made three other voyages to America, the last in 1503, still seeking (according to the older view of traditional historians) the westward route to the fabulous islands of Asia. He was a poor colonial administrator, and his last years were marked by tragedy and failure.

From his second voyage to the new world Columbus returned to Spain in sackcloth and ashes; from his third, in chains. He was a quixotic discoverer, dreaming great dreams and validating them by a blind courage, guided by "mythical charts and apocryphal fables"; but as a governor of men in a new island empire he was a dismal failure; and he paid the price for both his triumphs and his failures. George Santayana put it compactly in a celebrated sonnet which ends with these lines:

> Columbus found a world and had no chart,
> Save one that faith deciphered in the skies;
> To trust the soul's invincible surmise
> Was all his science and his only art.

[7] March 14, 1493.

LEONARDO DA VINCI ASKS THE DUKE OF MILAN FOR A JOB

Perhaps the most resplendent figure in the human race," Thomas Craven called Leonardo. Certainly it is an amazing catalogue of accomplishments that Leonardo himself sets forth with such modest assurance in this straightforward letter of application. He might correctly have added that he was a geologist, a botanist, a biologist, and master of many other arts and sciences.

Born in 1452 a few miles from Florence, Leonardo made "his life an epoch—and his epoch the Renaissance." In the latest and one of the most authoritative biographical studies of the great Florentine, Antonina Vallentin has deflated "the legend of a man who soared like a rocket amidst his contemporaries" and has portrayed him instead "as a human painfully groping his way out of darkness, struggling for light and life, dreaming vast dreams and seeing them one after another shattered. . . . Fame did not come to him until he was past forty, and it came too late to alleviate his loneliness or to mitigate his contempt for mankind. . . ."

In accordance with the most modern scientific discoveries, Leonardo believed that all things were made of the same basic substance. He thought flying within the realm of human achievement and built a model of a flying machine. The perfection of his paintings, the vitality of his merest sketches, the range of his interests, the copiousness of his writings, the balance and profundity of his thought, all have made him one of the legendary titans of all time. His lifelong motto—and his daily practice—was "obstinate rigor."

Leonardo was thirty years old when, bored and in search of new fields to conquer, he quit his native Florence, decadent now under the Medici, for Milan, flourishing under the rule of Lodovico Sforza. It was to him that Leonardo addressed this letter seeking employment:

69

". . . certain of my secrets."

HAVING, most illustrious lord, seen and considered the experiments of all those who pose as masters in the art of inventing instruments of war, and finding that their inventions differ in no way from those in common use, I am emboldened, without prejudice to anyone, to solicit an appointment of acquainting your Excellency with certain of my secrets.

1. I can construct bridges which are very light and strong and very portable, with which to pursue and defeat the enemy; and others more solid, which resist fire or assault, yet are easily removed and placed in position; and I can also burn and destroy those of the enemy.

2. In case of a siege I can cut off water from the trenches and make pontoons and scaling ladders and other similar contrivances.

3. If by reason of the elevation or the strength of its position a place cannot be bombarded, I can demolish every fortress if its foundations have not been set on stone.

4. I can also make a kind of cannon which is light and easy of transport, with which to hurl small stones like hail, and of which the smoke causes great terror to the enemy, so that they suffer heavy loss and confusion.

5. I can noiselessly construct to any prescribed point subterranean passages either straight or winding, passing if necessary underneath trenches or a river.

6. I can make armoured wagons carrying artillery, which shall break through the most serried ranks of the enemy, and so open a safe passage for his infantry.

70

7. If occasion should arise, I can construct cannon and mortars and light ordnance in shape both ornamental and useful and different from those in common use.

8. When it is impossible to use cannon I can supply in their stead catapults, mangonels, *trabocchi*, and other instruments of admirable efficiency not in general use— In short, as the occasion requires I can supply infinite means of attack and defense.

9. And if the fight should take place upon the sea I can construct many engines most suitable either for attack or defense and ships which can resist the fire of the heaviest cannon, and powders or weapons.

10. In time of peace, I believe that I can give you as complete satisfaction as anyone else in the construction of buildings both public and private, and in conducting water from one place to another.

I can further execute sculpture in marble, bronze or clay, also in painting I can do as much as anyone else, whoever he may be.

Moreover, I would undertake the commission of the bronze horse, which shall endue with immortal glory and eternal honour the auspicious memory of your father and of the illustrious house of Sforza. ——

And if any of the aforesaid things should seem to anyone impossible or impracticable, I offer myself as ready to make trial of them in your park or in whatever place shall please your Excellency, to whom I commend myself with all possible humility.

P. s. *He got the job, and kept it for sixteen years, until the French invaded the city and captured his employer. . . . Leonardo da Vinci died in France, prematurely old, at the age of sixty-seven, in 1519. Though hailed by the later centuries as "a universal genius," he felt that his "greatest schemes in science remained unrealized" and that "his quest for perfection in art" was unsuccessful.*

MICHELANGELO NEGOTIATES TERMS WITH HIS HOLINESS THE POPE

[A LETTER TO MAESTRO GIULIANO, ARCHITECT OF THE VATICAN]

BORN in 1475, Michelangelo Buonarroti won fame at twenty-one by the daring originality and flawless technique of both his painting and his sculpture. When he was summoned to Rome by Julius II, the Pope, ruthless and politically ambitious, knew little about art, but he knew what he demanded. This time it was a tomb for himself, suitable to one of his exalted rank. The plan that Michelangelo submitted led to "The Tragedy of that Tomb," lasting forty years. The specifications were on gigantic scale, calling for a main edifice three stories high and forty major statues in bronze relief and marble.

It was said that the Pope had the Basilica of St. Peter's razed in order to house this mammoth structure. However, things did not go smoothly. Bramante, the Pope's head architect, wishing to substitute for Michelangelo his own young nephew, Raphael of Urbino, poisoned the papal mind with accusations against the Florentine. At last Michelangelo, whose pride and insolence were equaled only by the Pope's, fled in anger to Florence. The following letter to Giuliano da San Gallo, another of the papal architects, was written by Michelangelo in answer to the Pope's summons to return and complete the tomb.

*". . . it will be a work without equal
in all the world . . ."*

Florence, May 2, 1506

MAESTRO GIULIANO, *Architect to the Pope*
Giuliano, I learn from a letter sent by you that the Pope
was angry at my departure, that he is willing to place the money at
my disposal and to carry out what was agreed upon between us;
also, that I am to come back and fear nothing.

As far as my departure is concerned, the truth is that on Holy
Saturday I heard the Pope, speaking at table with a jeweler and the
Master of the Ceremonies, say that he did not want to spend
another *baiocco* on stones, whether small or large, which surprised
me very much. However, before I set out I asked him for some of
the money required for the continuance of my work. His Holiness
replied that I was to come back again on Monday: and I went on
Monday, and on Tuesday, and on Wednesday, and on Thursday—
as His Holiness saw. At last, on the Friday morning, I was turned
out, that is to say, I was driven away: and the person who turned
me away said he knew who I was, but that such were his orders.
Thereupon, having heard those words on the Saturday and seeing
them afterwards put into execution, I lost all hope. But this alone
was not the whole reason of my departure. There was also another
cause, but I do not wish to write about it; enough that it made me
think that, if I were to remain in Rome, my own tomb would be
prepared before that of the Pope. This is the reason for my sudden
departure.

73

Now you write to me on behalf of the Pope, and in similar manner you will read this letter to the Pope. Give His Holiness to understand . . . that if he really wishes to have this tomb erected it would be well for him not to vex me as to where the work is to be done, provided that within the agreed period of five years it be erected in St. Peter's, on the site he shall choose, and that it be a beautiful work, as I have promised: for I am persuaded that it will be a work without equal in all the world if it be carried out.

If His Holiness wishes to proceed, let him deposit the said money here in Florence with a person whose name I will communicate to you. . . . With regard to the aforesaid money and work, I will bind myself in any way His Holiness may direct, and I will furnish whatever security here in Florence he may require. Let it be what it may, I will give him full security, even though it be the whole of Florence. There is yet one thing I have to add: it is this, that the said work could not possibly be done for the price in Rome, but it could be done here because of the many conveniences which are available, such as could not be had in Rome. . . . I beg of you to let me have an answer, and quickly. I have nothing further to add.

Your Michelangelo,

Sculptor, in Florence

IT TOOK *three papal bulls and a threat of war against the Florentine Republic to get Michelangelo back to Rome. Once there, however, he was not permitted to resume work on the tomb. Instead, after a few trifling commissions, he was ordered to decorate the ceiling of the Sistine Chapel. For four years, a virtual prisoner, he heroically slaved on this colossal task, perched aloft on a high scaffold, lying on his back as he labored "in a tumult of humanity" to depict the creation and fall of man.*

A year later, Julius II died. At the mercy of his niggling heirs and the succeeding popes, Michelangelo was forced to change the plans five times. The heroic statue of Moses is the only visible result of forty years of effort to fulfill his contract; Thomas Craven has said that into this creation went "the compacted fury of the twoscore years in which the artist's vision clashed and compromised with the world of fact." Eventually, the contract itself was destroyed by Pope Paul III, at whose order Michelangelo painted The Last Judgment on the wall of the Sistine Chapel—by many critics called "the greatest singlehanded work of art that man has ever produced."

HENRY VIII AND ANNE BOLEYN EXCHANGE EN-DEARMENTS AND ENTREATIES

[AN EXCHANGE OF LETTERS]

AFTER he had been married for thirteen years to Catherine of Aragon, Henry VIII fell in love with the beautiful Anne Boleyn, one of his Queen's fairest ladies in waiting. For eleven years he tried every means in and out of his power to divorce his wife and marry his "own sweetheart." In a final effort that wrested England completely from the Pope's sway in 1533, he disposed of Catherine and married Anne, "whose ambition took her all the way to the throne of England but could not keep her from the executioner's block."

According to Katharine Anthony, Anne Boleyn was a "spoiled girl . . . like Marie Antoinette the victim of an impotent man. During the six years in which she imagined she was holding Henry off, she was abetted by his secret infirmity. Her egoistic and evasive lover showered her with jewels, titles, honors, riches, a marriage under the rose, a solo coronation, everything in fact except the simple wifely and matronly position she coveted. . . ." She was also loved by the poet Thomas Wyatt. Here is one of the love letters the much-married monarch addressed to Anne Boleyn:

"... my Fervence of Love ..."

MYNE awne Sweetheart, this shall be to advertise you of the great ellingness* that I find here since your departing, for I ensure you, me thinketh the Tyme longer since your departing now last than I was wont to do a whole Fortnight; I think your Kindness and my Fervence of Love causeth it, for otherwise I wolde not thought it possible, that for so little a while it should have grieved me, but now that I am comeing toward you, me thinketh my Pains by half released, and also I am right well comforted, insomuch that my Book maketh substantially for my Matter, in writing whereof I have spent above IIII Hours this Day, which caused me now write the shorter Letter to you at this Tyme, because of some Payne in my Head, wishing my self (specially an Evening) in my Sweethearts Armes whose pritty Duckyst† I trust shortly to kysse. Writne with the Hand of him that was, is, and shall be yours by his will,

H. R.

THREE years later, tired of this love, Henry VIII trumped up charges against Anne Boleyn and had her imprisoned in the Tower, where shortly after her thirtieth year, she was to sacrifice her youth to a middle-aged, jaded royal lover. In the following piteous letter written during her imprisonment she tried to "erase a foul blot on a most dutiful wife. ..."

* Loneliness.
† Breasts.

"... never Prince had Wife more Loyal ..."

SIR, Your Grace's Displeasure, and my Imprisonment, are Things so strange unto me, as what to Write, or what to Excuse, I am altogether ignorant. Whereas you send unto me (willing me to confess a Truth, and to obtain your Favour) by such an one whom you know to be mine ancient professed Enemy; I no sooner received this Message by him, than I rightly conceived your Meaning; and if, as you say, confessing a Truth indeed may procure my safety, I shall with all Willingness and Duty perform your Command.

But let not your Grace ever imagine that your poor Wife will ever be brought to acknowledge a Fault, where not so much as a Thought thereof proceeded. And to speak a truth, never Prince had Wife more Loyal in all Duty, and in all true Affection, than you have ever found in *Anne Boleyn*, with which Name and Place I could willingly have contented my self, if God, and your Grace's Pleasure had been so pleased. Neither did I at any time so far forget my self in my Exaltation, or received Queenship, but that I always looked for such an Alteration as now I find; for the ground of my Preferment being on no surer Foundation than your Grace's Fancy, the least Alteration, I knew, was fit and sufficient to draw that Fancy to some other Subject. You have chosen me, from a low Estate, to be your Queen and Companion, far beyond my Desert or Desire. If then you found me worthy of such Honour, Good your Grace let not any light Fancy, or bad Councel of mine Enemies, withdraw your Princely Favour from me; neither let that Stain, that unworthy Stain of a Disloyal Heart towards your good

78

Grace, ever cast so foul a Blot on your most Dutiful Wife, and the Infant Princess your Daughter:

Try me good King, but let me have a Lawful Trial, and let not my sworn Enemies sit as my Accusers and Judges; yea, let me receive an open Trial, for my Truth shall fear no open shame; then shall you see, either mine Innocency cleared, your Suspicion and Conscience satisfied, the Ignominy and Slander of the World stopped, or my Guilt openly declared. So that whatsoever God or you may determine of me, your Grace may be freed from an open Censure; and mine Offence being so lawfully proved, your Grace is at liberty, both before God and Man, not only to execute worthy Punishment on me as an unlawful Wife, but to follow your Affection already settled on that Party, for whose sake I am now as I am, whose Name I could some good while since have pointed unto: Your Grace being not ignorant of my Suspicion therein.

But if you have already determined of me, and that not only my Death, but an Infamous Slander must bring you the enjoying of your desired Happiness; then I desire of God, that he will pardon your great Sin therein, and likewise mine Enemies, the Instruments thereof; and that he will not call you to a strict Account for your unprincely and cruel usage of me, at his General Judgment-Seat, where both you and my self must shortly appear, and in whose Judgment, I doubt not, (whatsoever the World may think of me) mine Innocence shall be openly known, and sufficiently cleared.

My last and only Request shall be, That my self may only bear the Burthen of your Grace's Displeasure, and that it may not touch the Innocent Souls of those poor Gentlemen, who (as I understand) are likewise in strait Imprisonment for my sake. If ever I have found favour in your Sight; if ever the Name of *Anne Boleyn* hath been pleasing in your Ears, then let me obtain this

Request; and I will so leave to trouble your Grace any further, with mine earnest Prayers to the Trinity to have your Grace in his good keeping, and to direct you in all your Actions. From my doleful Prison in the *Tower*, this 6th of *May*.

Your most Loyal and ever Faithful Wife,

Ann Boleyn

T*HE piteous appeal was futile. While the King made preparations to marry Jane Seymour, her successor, Anne Boleyn was beheaded. Anne's daughter was later to become Queen Elizabeth of England. As for Jane Seymour, she died giving birth to a son, the future Edward VI, but almost immediately her husband found fleeting solace in the arms of Anne of Cleves, closely followed by Catherine Howard, and finally by the already twice-married Catherine Parr, the wife of Henry's old age, who survived him and married again.*

SIR WALTER RALEIGH BIDS FAREWELL TO HIS WIFE A FEW HOURS BEFORE HE EXPECTS TO BE EXECUTED

M ANY critics have pointed out that this dramatic letter is marked by a "Shakespearian eloquence." It was written with what Raleigh believed was his dying hand, as he expected to be executed the following morning.

Born in 1552, Walter Raleigh achieved early fame as a favorite of Queen Elizabeth, as the classic type of courtier, as historian, explorer, and foreign adventurer. He is known partly in legend and partly in history for his gallantry and for his colonial exploits, which led to the introduction of tobacco to the civilized world. He was supplanted in the Queen's favor by the Earl of Essex, went to Ireland, and was finally restored to favor until the Queen discovered his intrigue with Elizabeth Throgmorton. After his rise and fall, his many powerful enemies at court took advantage of one of his unsuccessful colonial expeditions to South America and had him brought to trial at Winchester, on a charge of conspiring against the crown. On his conviction, he was sent to the Tower of London in 1603, under James I. During his stay there, he wrote the famous History of the World, which contains his oft-quoted apostrophe to death. It is quoted here because it is relevant to the theme of his letter:

"It is therefore death alone that can suddenly make man to know himself. He tells the proud and insolent, that they are but abjects, and humbles them at the instant; makes them cry, complain, and repent; yea, even to hate their fore-passed happiness.

"He takes the account of the rich, and proves him a beggar; a naked beggar, which hath interest in nothing, but in the gravel that fills his mouth. *He holds a glass before the eyes of the most beautiful, and makes them see therein their deformity and rottenness; and they acknowledge it.*

"O eloquent, just, and mighty death! whom none could advise, thou hast persuaded; what none hath dared thou has done; and whom all the world hath flattered, thou only hast cast out of the world and despised: thou hast drawn together all the farstretched greatness, all the pride, cruelty, and ambition of man, and covered it all over with these two narrow words, Hic jacet."

" . . . I am but dust."

[1603]

YOU shall now receive (my deare wife) my last words in these my last lines. My love I send you that you may keep it when I am dead, and my councell that you may remember it when I am no more. I would not by my will present you with sorrowes (dear Besse) let them go to the grave with me and be buried in the dust. And seeing that it is not Gods will that I should see you any more in this life, beare it patiently, and with a heart like thy selfe.

First, I send you all the thankes which my heart can conceive, or my words can reherse for your many travailes, and care taken for me, which though they have not taken effect as you wished, yet my debt to you is not the lesse: but pay it I never shall in this world.

Secondly, I beseech you for the love you beare me living, do not hide your selfe many dayes, but by your travailes seeke to helpe your miserable fortunes and the right of your poor childe. Thy mourning cannot availe me, I am but dust.

82

Thirdly, you shall understand, that my land was conveyed *bona fide* to my childe: the writings were drawne at midsummer was twelve months, my honest cosen Brett can testify so much, and Dolberry too, can remember somewhat therein. And I trust my blood will quench their malice that have cruelly murthered me: and that they will not seek also to kill thee and thine with extreame poverty.

To what friend to direct thee I know not, for all mine have left me in the true time of tryall. And I perceive that my death was determined from the first day. Most sorry I am God knowes that being thus surprised with death I can leave you in no better estate. God is my witnesse I meant you all my office of wines or all that I could have purchased by selling it, halfe of my stuffe, and all my jewels, but some one for the boy, but God hath prevented all my resolutions. That great God that ruleth all in all, but if you live free from want, care for no more, for the rest is but vanity. Love God, and begin betimes to repose your selfe upon him, and therein shall you finde true and lasting riches, and endlesse comfort: for the rest when you have travailed and wearied your thoughts over all sorts of worldly cogitations, you shall but sit downe by sorrowe in the end.

Teach your son also to love and feare God whilst he is yet young, that the feare of God may grow with him, and then God will be a husband to you, and a father to him; a husband and a father which cannot be taken from you.

Baily oweth me 200 pounds, and Adrian Gilbert 600. In Jersey I also have much owing me besides. The arrearages of the wines will pay my debts. And howsoever you do, for my soules sake, pay all poore men. When I am gone, no doubt you shall be sought for by many, for the world thinkes that I was very rich. But take heed of the pretences of men, and their affections, for they last not but in honest and worthy men, and no greater misery can befall you in

83

this life, than to become a prey, and afterwards to be despised. I speake not this (God knowes) to dissuade you from marriage, for it will be best for you, both in respect of the world and of God. As for me, I am no more yours, nor you mine, death hath cut us asunder: and God hath divided me from the world, and you from me.

Remember your poor childe for his father's sake, who chose you, and loved you in his happiest times. Get those letters (if it be possible) which I writ to the Lords, wherein I sued for my life: God is my witnesse it was for you and yours that I desired life, but it is true that I disdained my self for begging of it: for know it (my deare wife) that your son is the son of a true man, and one who in his owne respect despiseth death and all his misshapen & ugly formes.

I cannot write much, God he knows how hardly I steale this time while others sleep, and it is also time that I should separate my thoughts from the world. Begg my dead body which living was denied thee; and either lay it at Sherburne (and if the land continue) or in Exeter-Church, by my Father and Mother; I can say no more, time and death call me away.

The everlasting God, powerfull, infinite, and omnipotent God, That Almighty God, who is goodnesse it selfe, the true life and true light keep thee and thine: have mercy on me, and teach me to forgive my persecutors and false accusers, and send us to meet in his glorious Kingdome. My deare wife farewell. Blesse my poore boy. Pray for me, and let my good God hold you both in his armes.

Written with the dying hand of sometimes thy Husband, but now alasse overthrowne.

Yours that was, but now not my own.

Walter Rawleigh

ACTUALLY, Sir Walter Raleigh was not executed the following morning, but was confined in the Tower of London with his wife until 1616, when he was allowed to undertake an expedition to the Orinoco in search of gold. But this proved only a reprieve, and he was finally executed in 1618, in the same courtyard of the Tower where he had once witnessed the execution of his bitter and far more popular rival, Robert Devereux, Earl of Essex.

FRANCIS BACON FROM THE TOWER OF LONDON
PLEADS FOR MERCY WITH KING JAMES I

BARON VERULAM and Viscount St. Albans, better known as Francis Bacon, has been called "the most powerful mind of modern times." He came perilously close to realizing the Platonic ideal of the "philosopher-king," by becoming the guide and counselor of two successive monarchs. He "rang the bell that called the wits together," and "announced that Europe had become of age."

The scion of an old and distinguished family, lawyer, philosopher, and statesman, he became the crafty adviser of Queen Elizabeth, and in succession solicitor general, attorney general, lord keeper, and lord chancellor under her successor, James I. He seems to have merited the words carved under his statue in his native village: "Of Science the Light and of Eloquence the Law."

Francis Bacon was born in 1561 and died in 1626. Charged before the House of Lords with accepting bribes while sitting in judgment on important cases, he confessed to "corruption and neglect," but denied that he had ever "perverted justice." The deep wisdom and worldly common sense of his prolific writings, their pithy and witty expression, and their profound philosophical content make them today as illuminating and as instructive as they were three hundred years ago. Yet their writer was a spendthrift, twice arrested for debt; and a scheming and ambitious political opportunist who turned faithlessly, and with diabolical erudition, upon his friend and benefactor, the Earl of Essex, and caused his execution. For this masterpiece of treachery he received £1200 from Queen Elizabeth, thereby relieving his own financial desperation caused by opulent extravagances and beginning his spectacular climb to power. Pope called Bacon "the wisest, brightest, and meanest of mankind." He thirsted for the advancement of learning but never neglected the advancement of Bacon.

When in his fiftieth year, at the height of his fame and glory, he was convicted of bribery, fined £40,000, deprived of the great seal, relieved of public office, and sentenced to the Tower of London to be released at the King's pleasure. It was here that this "wise, sinuous, dangerous creature," whom, for all his philosophical and courtly splendors, as a true child of the Renaissance, Lytton Strachey called "a glittering serpent, swaying in ecstasy," wrote this appeal for mercy to his sovereign:

"... this theme of my misery ..."

MAY it please your most excellent Majesty,
    In the midst of my misery, which is rather assuaged by remembrance than by hope, my chiefest worldly comfort is to think, That . . . I was evermore so happy as to have my poor services graciously accepted by your Majesty. . . . For as I have often said to your Majesty, I was towards you but as a bucket, and a cistern; to draw forth and conserve; whereas yourself was the fountain. Unto this comfort of nineteen years' prosperity, there succeeded a comfort even in my greatest adversity, somewhat of the same nature; which is, That in those offences wherewith I was charged, there was not any one that had special relation to your Majesty. . . . I have an assured belief that there is in your Majesty's own princely thoughts a great deal of serenity and clearness towards me your Majesty's now prostrate and cast down servant. . . .

And indeed, if it may please your Majesty, this theme of my misery is so plentiful, as it need not be coupled with any thing else. I have been somebody by your Majesty's singular and undeserved favour: even the prime officer of your kingdom. Your Majesty's arm hath been over mine in council, when you presided at the table; so near I was: I have borne your Majesty's image in metal; much more in heart; I was never in nineteen years' service chidden by your Majesty. . . . But why should I speak of these things which are now vanished? but only the better to express my downfall.

For now it is thus with me: I am a year and a half old in misery: though I must ever acknowledge your Majesty's grace and mercy, for I do not think it possible, that any one that you once loved should be totally miserable. Mine own means, through mine own improvidence, are poor and weak, little better than my father left me. . . .

. . . I have (most gracious Sovereign) faith enough for a miracle, and much more for a grace, that your Majesty will not suffer your poor creature to be utterly defaced, nor blot the name quite out of your book, upon which your sacred hand hath been so oft for new ornaments and additions.

Unto this degree of compassion, I hope God above (of whose mercies towards me, both in my prosperity and my adversity, I have had great testimonies and pledges, though mine own manifold and wretched unthankfulness might have averted them) will dispose your princely heart, already prepared to all piety. . . . I most humbly beseech your Majesty to give me leave to conclude with those words which Necessity speaketh: Help me (dear sovereign lord and master) and pity me so far, as I that have borne a bag be not now in my age forced in effect to bear a wallet; nor I that desire to live to study, may not study to live. . . . God of heaven ever bless, preserve, and prosper your Majesty.

Your Majesty's poor ancient servant and beadsman,

Fr. St. Alban

ALTHOUGH there is some doubt as to this letter ever having been sent, it was certainly calculated (like many of Bacon's writings) to persuade. In any event, whether the letter came to him or not, the King took pity on his "poor ancient servant and beadsman," permitting him to be released after only four days in the Tower. James even mitigated his fine. Bacon's most important philosophical writing was done in those last five years, after his disgrace and retirement from public life. He "took all knowledge as his province" and made enduring contributions to science, metaphysics, and literature, writing—"for greater permanence," as he said—in Latin. His chief titles to fame are the brief and pungent essays—published in his thirty-sixth year—and the vast Novum Organum, which proved of fundamental value in the history of philosophy, after the repudiation of scholasticism. .

NINON DE L'ENCLOS TELLS THE MARQUIS DE SÉVIGNÉ WHAT MAKES LOVE SO DANGEROUS

SOME scholars may question the authenticity of this letter, but even if it be spurious, it epitomizes the sophistication of the Paris salons of the seventeenth century. Moreover, it provides a clue to the "philosophy of love" of one of the most celebrated hetairai of history, famed as "a Venus for her beauty and a Minerva for her wit . . ." called by Horace Walpole "a veritable Notre-Dame des Amours." Her drawing room was renowned throughout Europe.

Born Anne Lenclos in May, 1616, Ninon lived to the age of ninety and numbered among her lovers such eminent men as Condé, La Rochefoucauld, Saint-Évremond, and the Marquis to whom the letter that follows was addressed. Her group of admirers was dominated by literary people. Voltaire himself met her when he was still a boy. In her will she left him a legacy with which to buy books.

Sainte-Beuve himself paid tribute to "the naturalness, originality, and simplicity" of Ninon's letters but declared that he has found in the entire canon only twelve of absolute authenticity. All of these were written to Saint-Evremond.

Ninon's father was a nobleman, a bon vivant, a dueler, a freethinker; her mother was stern and respectable. When Anne or Ninon found herself an orphan at the age of fifteen, she was naturally disposed, in the words of Sainte-Beuve, "to enjoy her liberty with a boldness seasoned with wit and tempered with good taste which was to recall the existence of the hetairai of Greece."

Before her death, Ninon became almost a legendary figure. Voltaire himself declared that there were so many biographies of Ninon that "if this fashion continues, there will soon be as many Histories of Ninon as there are of Louis XIV." Scholars have laboriously compiled chronological tables and histories of her lovers "almost as precise as those of the Assyrian and Egyptian kings."

Of Ninon the great Saint-Simon remarked, "She had illustrious friends of all sorts, and had so much wit that she kept them all, and kept them in harmony together, or at least without the least disturbance. Everything went off in her house with a respect and an external decency which the highest princesses rarely keep up with their frailties."

Mlle de l'Enclos drank nothing but water, but it was said she was "intoxicated with the soup." Her repartee was celebrated for its brilliance, and her conversation was always light and piquant. The famed epicure La Fare wrote of her: "I did not see this Ninon in the days of her beauty; but at the age of fifty, and even after she was sixty, she had lovers who were very fond of her, and the most honorable men in France for her friends. Until ninety she was still sought after by the best society of her time. She died with all reason, and even with all the charm of her wit, which was the best and the most amiable that I have known in any woman."

Ninon's noted correspondent, Saint-Évremond, wrote to her in the twilight of her years:

"With all respect to that old dreamer (Solon) who held that nobody was happy before his death, I consider you, in full life as you are, the happiest creature that ever was. You have been loved by the most honorable men in the world, and have loved often enough to leave nothing untasted in pleasures, and as wisely as it was needful to anticipate the disgusts of a languishing passion. . . ."

One of the many remarkable things about Mlle de l'Enclos was that she won her renown with the most distinguished men of her time and yet did not suffer "the usual accompaniment of unpopularity among the celebrated ladies." Mothers tried to get their sons introduced at her salon. Mme de Sévigné,* who had so much reason to complain of Ninon on account of her husband and her son, saw without dread her grandson, the Marquis de Grignan, pay his respects to her. The letter that follows is addressed to the Marquis de Sévigné and is doubly interesting because of this background:

". . . this charming passion . . ."

YES, Marquis, I will keep my word with you, and upon all occasions shall speak the truth, though I sometimes tell it at my own expense. I have more firmness of mind than perhaps you may imagine, and 'tis very probable that in the course of this correspondence, you will think I push this quality too far, even to severity. But then, please to remember that I have only the outside of a woman, and that my heart and mind are wholly masculine. . . .

Shall I tell you what makes love so dangerous? 'Tis the too high idea we are apt to form of it. But to speak the truth, love, considered as a passion, is merely a blind instinct, that we should rate accordingly. It is an appetite, which inclines us to one object, rather than another, without our being able to account for our taste. Considered as a bond of friendship, where reason presides, it is no longer a passion and loses the very name of love. It becomes esteem: which is indeed a very pleasing appetite, but too tranquil; and therefore incapable of rousing you from your present supineness.

If you madly trace the footsteps of our ancient heroes of ro-

* See Mme de Sévigné's letter, describing a royal supper at Chantilly, to her daughter, Mme de Grignan, on page 100.

mance, adopting their extravagant sentiments, you will soon experience, that such false chivalry metamorphoses this charming passion into a melancholy folly; nay, often a tragical one: a perfect frenzy! but divest it of all the borrowed pomp of opinion, and you will then perceive how much it will contribute both to your happiness and pleasure. Be assured that if either reason or knight errantry should be permitted to form the union of our hearts, love would become a state of apathy and madness.

The only way to avoid these extremes, is to pursue the course I pointed out to you. At present you have no occasion for any thing more than mere amusement, and believe me, you will not meet it except among women of the character I speak of. Your heart wants occupation; and they are framed to supply the void. At least, give my prescription a fair trial, and I will be answerable for the success.

I promised to reason with you, and I think I have kept my word. Farewell. . . .

Tomorrow the Abbé Chateauneuf, and perhaps Molière are to be with me. We are to read over the Tartuffe together, in order to make some necessary alterations. Depend upon it, Marquis, that whoever denies the maxims I have here laid down, partakes a little of that character in his play.

THE Marquis de Sévigné is known in history only as the husband of the noted letter writer* and salonnière, who was eighteen when she married him. He was killed in a duel in 1651.

* See page 100 for a characteristic letter by Mme de Sévigné.

BLAISE PASCAL ASKS A COLLEAGUE TO CONFIRM
A SCIENTIFIC PREDICTION

[A LETTER TO PÉRIER]

THIS brief communication, dealing with a simple matter of measurement of mercurial pressure, may seem drab and routine, but it is included here because it indicates the true spirit of scientific inquiry. The noted French mystic, philosopher, and mathematician shows in this note how he "subjected his thoughts to rigorous investigation and empirical collaboration."

Born in June, 1623, Pascal is most famous for his Pensées, known in English as Thoughts on Religion and Evidences of Christianity, translated in 1850. But in the world of science, he is equally noted as the founder of the modern theory of probabilities, inventor of Pascal's triangle, and contributor to the advance of the differential calculus. His scientific work was also important in the field of barometric measurements. His experiments increased knowledge of the pressure of the atmosphere and the equilibrium of fluids.

After he had predicted "the simple and common fact that air pressure at the summit of a mountain would be less than that in the valley below," he realized that only by experiment could his predictions be confirmed or refuted. He therefore dispatched to his brother-in-law, Florin Périer, the following letter:

94

"... bothering you with questions of physics ..."

November 15, 1647

I AM taking the liberty of interrupting you in your daily professional labors, and of bothering you with questions of physics, because I know that they provide rest and recreation for your moments of leisure. . . . The question concerns the well-known experiment carried out with a tube containing mercury, first at the foot and then at the top of a mountain, and repeated several times on the same day, in order to ascertain whether the height of the column of mercury is the same or differs in the two cases. . . . For it is certain that at the foot of the mountain the air is much heavier than at the top.

ALMOST a year later, on September 22, 1648, Pascal received this reply from Périer:

"I have at last carried out the experiment which you have so long desired. . . . On top of the Puy-de-Dôme . . . we found that there were 23.2 inches of mercury in the tube, whereas in the cloister gardens the tube showed 26.35 inches. There was thus a difference of 3.15 inches between the levels of the mercury in the tube in the two cases. This filled us with wonder and admiration."

Pascal died in August, 1662.

95

AURANGZEB, EMPEROR OF HINDUSTAN, REBUKES A FORMER TEACHER FOR INFLICTING UPON HIM "THINGS . . . HARD TO UNDERSTAND AND VERY EASY TO FORGET"

[A LETTER TO MULLAH SAHE]

I N 1658, Aurangzeb, after a series of conflicts with his father and brothers over the succession to the throne, was crowned Emperor of Hindustan, which for almost fifty years he ruled with conscientiousness, dignity, and military glory. That he did not attribute his success as a monarch to his early teaching is evinced in this scathing reply (an intensely personal dissertation on education) to a boyhood tutor, probably Mullah Sahe, who came before him craving a sinecure and a reward:

". . . a multitude of barbarous and dark words . . ."

W HAT is it you would have of me, Doctor? Can you reasonably desire that I should make you one of the chief omrahs of my court? Let me tell you, if you had instructed me as you should have done, nothing would be more just; for I am of this persuasion, that a child well educated and instructed is as much, at least, obliged to his master as to his father.

But where are those good documents [instructions] you have

96

given me? In the first place you have taught me that all Frangistan (so it seems they call Europe) was nothing but I know not what little island, of which the greatest king was he of Portugal, and next to him he of Holland, and after him he of England: and as to the other kings, as those of France and Andalusia, you have represented them to me as our petty rajas, telling me that the kings of Indostan were far above them altogether, that they [the kings of Indostan] were . . . the great ones, the conquerors and kings of the world; and those of Persia and Usbec, Kashgar, Tartary and Cathay, Pegu, China and Matchina did tremble at the name of the kings of Indostan. Admirable geography! You should rather have taught me exactly to distinguish all those states of the world, and well to understand their strength, their way of fighting, their customs, religions, governments, and interests; and by the pursual of solid history, to observe their rise, progress, decay; and whence, how, and by what accidents and errors those great changes and revolutions of empires and kingdoms have happened.

I have scarce learned of you the name of my grandsires, the famous founders of this empire; so far were you from having taught me the history of their life, and what course they took to make such great conquest.

You had a mind to teach me the Arabian tongue, to read and to write. I am much obliged, forsooth, for having made me lose so much time upon a language that requires ten or twelve years to attain to its perfection; as if the son of a king should think it to be an honor to him to be a grammarian or some doctor of the law, and to learn other languages than of his neighbors when he can well be without them; he, to whom time is so precious for so many weighty things, which he ought by times to learn. As if there were any spirit that did not with some reluctancy, and even with a kind of debasement, employ itself in so sad and dry an exercise, so longsome and tedious as is that of learning words.*

Know you not that childhood well governed, being a state which is ordinarily accompanied with a happy memory, is capable of thousands of good precepts and instructions, which remain deeply impressed the whole remainder of a man's life, and keep the mind always raised for great actions? The law, prayers, and sciences, may they not as well be learned in our mother tongue as in Arabick? You told my father Shah Jehan that you would teach me philosophy. 'Tis true, I remember very well, that you have entertained me for many years with airy questions of things that afford no satisfaction at all to the mind and are of no use in humane society, empty notions and mere fancies, that have only this in them, that they are very hard to understand and very easy to forget. . . .

I still remember that after you had thus amused me, I know not how long, with your fine philosophy, all I retained of it was a multitude of barbarous and dark words, proper to bewilder, perplex, and tire out the best wits, and only invented the better to cover the vanity and ignorance of men like yourself, that would make us believe that they know all, and that under those obscure and ambiguous words are hid great mysteries which they alone are capable to understand.

If you had seasoned me with that philosophy which formeth the mind to ratiocination, and insensibly accustoms it to be satisfied with nothing but solid reasons; if you had given me those excellent precepts and doctrines which raise the soul above the assaults of fortune, and reduce her to an unshakable and always equal temper, and permit her not to be lifted up by prosperity nor

* We cannot tell how much of the following (and perhaps of the preceding) quotation is Bernier's, and how much Aurangzeb's; we only know that it bears reprinting.—Note by Will Durant in his *Our Oriental Heritage* (Part I of *The Story of Civilization*).

debased by adversity; if you had taken care to give me the knowledge of what we are and what are the first principles of things, and had assisted me in forming in my mind a fit idea of the greatness of the universe, and of the admirable order and motion of the parts thereof; if, I say, you had instilled into me this kind of philosophy, I should think myself incomparably more obliged to you than Alexander was to his Aristotle, and believe it my duty to recompense you otherwise than he did him.

Should you not, instead of your flattery, have taught me somewhat of that point so important to a king, which is, what the reciprocal duties are of a sovereign to his subjects and those of subjects to their sovereigns; and ought not you to have considered that one day I should be obliged with the sword to dispute my life and my crown with my brothers? . . .

Have you ever taken any care to make me learn what 'tis to besiege a town, or to set an army in array? For these things I am obliged to others, not at all to you. Go, and return to the village whence you are come, and let nobody know who you are or what is become of you.

THERE is nothing in the records to indicate whether or not the Emperor's boyhood tutor obeyed his former pupil's orders, as given in the last sentence of the letter. At any rate, he succeeded in achieving abysmal obscurity, and he is unknown to fame except as the recipient of this letter.

MME DE SÉVIGNÉ TELLS THE TALE OF A ROYAL SUPPER AT CHANTILLY

TOWARD the end of the seventeenth century," wrote Professor Copeland of Harvard, a "wealthy, witty, and aristocratic lady— companion of royalty, intimate of Madame La Fayette, contemporary of Corneille, Pascal, Descartes, and La Rochefoucauld, retired twice a year from the gaiety and opulence of the court of Louis XIV to find peace and serenity at her country estate. Most of her time she spent enjoying the beauties of nature or writing incessantly to her beloved daughter."

The letters won her immortality, for in the histories and encyclopedias to this day Mme de Sévigné is listed simply as "a letter writer." Critics have called her "the most competent woman writer that ever lived," and have generally agreed that her gaiety, her unfailing savor and piquancy, her genius for observing the trivial and the ludicrous, and for expressing vividly the domestic affections have all contributed to the glory of French literature.

"She made phrases," says Lyn Irvine, "with the swiftness and dexterity and coolness of an accomplished modiste twisting a bow of ribbon or placing a flower. . . . Her style is one of the mysteries of literature, for while it possesses the greatest refinement and sophistication, polish and wit, its basis is simply that of a nursery rhyme, the adding of statement to statement, the stringing together of large bright beads of fact. . . ."

Marie de Rabutin-Chantal, Marquise de Sévigné, was born in Paris in 1626, of a Burgundian family of noble rank. She was beautiful in a slightly irregular way, was admirably educated, and inherited a fortune of 100,000 crowns. Her husband, a Breton nobleman, wasted his money and hers on a grand scale. Among his inamoratas was none other than Ninon de l'Enclos.* In a duel over a love affair, he was fatally wounded, and Mme de Sévigné found herself a widow at twenty-five. She never remarried, and she never stopped writing letters. Her salon, particularly when she was holding court at the Hôtel Carnavalet, was celebrated, but her letters were even more famous. She could make a blank sheet of note paper a living drawing room of the Grand Monarch. Kings and wits came to life from her restless pen, gossiping divinely. On December 15, 1670, for example, Mme de Sévigné wrote to M. de Coulanges a letter with this irresistible opening paragraph:

"I am going to tell you a thing the most astonishing, the most surprising, the most marvelous, the most miraculous, the most magnificent, the most confounding, the most unheard of, the most singular, the most extraordinary, the most incredible, the most unforeseen, the greatest, the least, the rarest, the most common, the most public, the most private till today, the most brilliant, the most enviable; in short, a thing of which there is but one example in past ages, and that not an exact one neither; a thing that we cannot believe at Paris; how then will it gain credit at Lyons? a thing which makes everybody cry, 'Lord, have mercy upon us!' a thing which causes the greatest joy to Mme de Rohan and Mme de Hauterive; a thing, in fine, which is to happen on Sunday next, when those who are present will doubt the evidence of their senses; a thing which, though it is to be done on Sunday, yet perhaps will not be finished on Monday. I cannot bring myself to tell you: guess what it is. I give you three times to do it in. What, not a word to throw at a dog? Well then, I find I must tell you."

After thus building up the proper degree of anticipation in this intriguing manner, Mme de Sévigné would then retell the latest tidbit of court scandal.

* See page 90 for a letter of Ninon on the philosophy of love.

". . . all was enchantment."

Paris, Sunday, April 26, 1671

THIS is Sunday, April 26th, and this letter will not go out till Wednesday; but it is not so much a letter as a narrative that I have just learned from Moreuil, of what passed at Chantilly with regard to poor Vatel. I wrote to you last Friday that he had stabbed himself—these are the particulars of the affair: the King arrived there on Thursday night; the walk, and the collation, which was served in a place set apart for the purpose, and strewed with jonquils, were just as they should be.

Supper was served, but there was no roast meat at one or two of the tables, on account of Vatel's having been obliged to provide several dinners more than were expected. This affected his spirits, and he was heard to say, several times, "I have lost my honor! I cannot bear this disgrace!" "My head is quite bewildered," said he to Gourville. "I have not had a wink of sleep these twelve nights; I wish you would assist me in giving orders." Gourville did all he could to comfort and assist him; but the failure of the roast meat (which, however, did not happen at the King's table, but at some of the other twenty-five), was always uppermost with him.

Gourville mentioned it to the Prince, who went directly to Vatel's apartment, and said to him: "Everything is extremely well conducted, Vatel; nothing could be more admirable than his majesty's supper." "Your highness's goodness," replied he, "overwhelms me; I am sensible that there was a deficiency of roast meat at two tables." "Not at all," said the Prince; "do not perplex yourself, and all will go well."

Midnight came; the fireworks did not succeed, they were covered with a thick cloud; they cost sixteen thousand francs. At four o'clock in the morning Vatel went round and found everybody asleep; he met one of the underpurveyors, who had just come in with only two loads of fish. "What!" said he, "is this all?" "Yes, sir," said the man, not knowing that Vatel had dispatched other people to all the seaports around.

Vatel waited for some time; the other purveyors did not arrive; his head grew distracted; he thought there was no more fish to be had. He flew to Gourville: "Sir," said he, "I cannot outlive this disgrace." Gourville laughed at him. Vatel, however, went to his apartment, and setting the hilt of his sword against the door, after two ineffectual attempts, succeeded in the third, in forcing his sword through his heart.

At that instant the carriers arrived with the fish; Vatel was inquired after to distribute it. They ran to his apartment, knocked at the door, but received no answer, upon which they broke it open, and found him lying in a sea of blood.

A messenger was immediately dispatched to acquaint the Prince with what had happened, who was like a man in despair. The Duke wept, for his Burgundy journey depended upon Vatel. The Prince related the whole affair to his majesty with great concern; it was considered as a consequence of too nice a sense of honor; some blamed, others praised him for his courage.

The King said he had put off this excursion for more than five years because he was aware it would be attended with infinite trouble. He told the Prince that he ought to have had but two tables, and not have been at the expense of so many, and declared that he would never suffer him to do so again; but all this was too late for poor Vatel. However, Gourville attempted to supply the loss of Vatel, which he did in great measure. The dinner was elegant, the collation the same. They supped, they walked, they hunted; all was perfumed with jonquils, all was enchantment. . . .

MME DE SÉVIGNÉ's daughter, the recipient of a veritable hoard of such letters, year after year, almost up to her mother's dying day in 1696, and the recipient of a huge dowry, to boot, was ungrateful for both. She even refused to attend her mother during her last illness, but a few years later she, too, like her mother, died of the smallpox, and is known today only because of her mother's voluminous and brilliant correspondence.

BARUCH SPINOZA, CHALLENGED BY A FORMER PUPIL TO PROVE THAT HIS PHILOSOPHY IS NOT "A MERE ILLUSION AND A CHIMERA," DEFENDS THE FAITH OF A "GOD-INTOXI-CATED MAN"

[AN EXCHANGE OF LETTERS WITH ALBERT BURGH]

G OETHE himself declared that Spinoza's correspondence with his friends and disciples was "the most interesting book one could read in the world of uprightness and humanity." These letters provide a living record of his serene and lofty contemplations, illumined by flashes of fire that the unimaginative reader would scarcely expect from a philosopher frequently described as "a reasoning machine."

Born on November 24, 1632, Spinoza lived most of his life at The Hague, earning a bare subsistence as a lens grinder.

Spinoza's pantheistic philosophy—his conception of God-in-everything that was exalted to a form of intellectual adoration—has enriched and colored the world of philosophy for almost three centuries. The development of this doctrine, and the incorruptible integrity with which he proclaimed and defended it, are brought out clearly in many of Spinoza's letters. We see him trying to "discover and attain the faculty of enjoying throughout eternity continual supreme happiness." We see him critically examining, and finally rejecting, one by one, honor, riches, pleasure, fame . . . and seeking out for himself "the love towards a thing eternal and infinite . . . a love that alone feeds the mind with a pleasure secure from all pain. . . ." For him the indestructible and highest good was "the knowledge of the Union which the mind has with the whole of nature. . . ."

When a prince, the Elector Palatine, offered Spinoza a professorship in philosophy at the University of Heidelberg and thus promised him freedom from financial cares, Spinoza, unwilling to make any promise to refrain from "disturbing the publicly established religion," graciously but firmly refused. When Louis XIV of France offered him a pension, in return for the dedication of his next book, he again refused. Obstinately, but quietly, serenely, even graciously and elegantly, Spinoza rejected the advice of "worldlings and careerists" and spurned "the spurious immortality of popular acclamation." The easy security of a comfortable post offered by His Electoral Highness or His Imperial Majesty could not lure him. The truth Spinoza sought would be found only in solitude —and besides he needed every year, every day, every precious hour to finish his Ethics, undistracted by fame, free from royal favor.

Spinoza's integrity met the supreme test when he was cast out from the Jewish religion and reviled by the synagogue of his forefathers for heresies springing from his thirst for truth. His denial of immortality won him the hatred alike of Jews and Christians.

The only books published by Spinoza in his lifetime were The Principles of the Cartesian Philosophy (1663) and A Treatise on Religion and the State (Tractatus Theologico-Politicus), which appeared anonymously in 1670. This was promptly honored with a place in the Index Expurgatorius.

Spinoza had many friends among the influential governing classes at The Hague. Among them was Conrad Burgh, one of the wealthiest citizens of Amsterdam, who in 1666 held office as Treasurer General of the United Netherlands. His son, Albert Burgh, was a pupil of Spinoza. Young Burgh continued his study of philosophy in Italy, and finally turned to the Catholic faith with the fanatical zeal of a convert. Burgh's family was disturbed by this and persuaded Spinoza to write to Albert. But it was to no avail. The youth joined the Franciscan order.

106

When Spinoza's books were banned by the civic authorities, many of his friends and disciples carried on the resulting theological controversy both in person and by correspondence. Spinoza received many letters "intended to reform him." Typical of them was the following letter from young Albert Burgh, his old friend and former pupil—a letter that some students of church history believe was officially prompted or at least actively encouraged by the ecclesiastical authorities of the time:

". . . you wretched little man, vile worm of the earth, ay, ashes, food for worms . . ."

TO THE Very Learned and Acute Baruch Spinoza:
Many greetings.

When leaving my country, I promised to write to you if anything noteworthy occurred during my journey. Since, now, an occasion has presented itself, and one, indeed, of the greatest importance, I discharge my debt, and write to inform you that, through the infinite Mercy of God, I have been restored to the Catholic Church, and have been made a member thereof. How this came to pass you will be able to learn in greater detail from the letter that I wrote to the most illustrious and experienced Mr. D. Craenen, Professor at Leyden. I will, therefore, now only add some brief remarks, which concern your own advantage.

The more I formerly admired you for your penetration and acuteness of mind, the more do I now weep for you and deplore you; for although you are a very talented man, and have received a mind adorned by God with brilliant gifts, and are a lover of truth, indeed eager for it, yet you suffer yourself to be led astray

107

and deceived by the wretched and most haughty Prince of evil Spirits. For, all your philosophy, what is it but a mere illusion and a Chimera? Yet you stake on it not only your peace of mind in this life, but also the eternal salvation of your soul. See on what a miserable foundation all your interests rest.

You presume to have at length discovered the true philosophy. How do you know that your Philosophy is the best among all those which have ever been taught in the world, or are actually taught now, or ever will be taught in the future? And, to say nothing about the thought of the future, have you examined all those philosophies, ancient as well as modern, which are taught here and in India and everywhere throughout the world? And, even if you have duly examined them, how do you know that you have chosen the best? You will say: my philosophy is in accord with right reason, the others are opposed to it. But all the other philosophers except your disciples differ from you, and, with the same right, they declare each about himself and his philosophy what you do about yours, and they accuse you, as you accuse them, of falsity and error. It is clear, therefore, that, in order that the truth of your philosophy may become manifest, you must put forward arguments which are not common to the other philosophies, but which can be applied to yours alone. Otherwise it must be confessed that your philosophy is as uncertain and as worthless as the rest.

However, confining myself now to your book, to which you have given that impious title, and taking your Philosophy together with your Theology, for you yourself really blend them, although, with diabolical cunning, you pretend to show that the one is distinct from the other, and that they have different principles, I proceed thus ——

Perhaps you will say: others have not read Holy Scripture as frequently as I have, and it is from Holy Scripture itself, the recognition of whose authority constitutes the difference between Christians and the remaining peoples of the whole world, that I prove my views. But how? I explain Holy Scripture by applying the clear texts to the more obscure, and from this interpretation of mine I form my Doctrines, or confirm those which are already produced in my brain.

But I adjure you seriously to consider what you say. For how do you know that you make the said application correctly, and, next, that the application, even if made correctly, is sufficient for the interpretation of Holy Scripture, and that you are thus putting the interpretation of Holy Scripture on a sound basis? Especially since Catholics say, and it is very true, that the whole Word of God is not given in writing, so that Holy Scripture cannot be explained through Holy Scripture alone, I will not say, by one man but not even by the Church itself, which is the sole interpreter of Holy Scripture. For the Apostolic traditions must also be consulted. This is proved from Holy Scripture itself, and by the testimony of the Holy Fathers, and it is in accord not only with right reason but also with experience. Since, therefore, your principle is most false, and leads to perdition, where will your whole teaching remain, which is founded and built upon this false foundation?

So then, if you believe in Christ crucified, acknowledge your most evil heresy, recover from the perversion of your nature, and be reconciled with the Church.

For do you prove your views in a way which is different from that in which all the Heretics who have left God's Church in the past, or are leaving it now, or will leave it in the future, have done, do, or will do? For they all employ the same principle as you do, that is, they make use of Holy Scripture alone for the formation and confirmation of their dogmas.

Do not flatter yourself because, perhaps, the Calvinists or the so-called Reformers, or the Lutherans, or the Mennonites, or the Socinians, etc., cannot refute your doctrine: for all these, as has already been said, are as wretched as you are, and, like you, sit in the shadow of death.

If, however, you do not believe in Christ, you are more wretched than I can say. But the remedy is easy: return from your sins, and realize the fatal arrogance of your wretched and insane reasoning. You do not believe in Christ. Why? You will say: because the teaching and life of Christ are not consistent with my principles, nor is the doctrine of Christians about Christ consistent with my doctrine. But I repeat, do you then dare to think yourself greater than all those who have ever arisen in the State or Church of God, than the Patriarchs, Prophets, Apostles, Martyrs, Doctors, Confessors and Virgins, Saints without number, and, in your blasphemy, even than Our Lord Jesus Christ Himself? Do you alone surpass these in doctrine, in your manner of life, and in every other respect? Will you, you wretched little man, vile worm of the earth, ay, ashes, food for worms, dare, in your unspeakable blasphemy, to put yourself above the Incarnate, Infinite Wisdom of the Eternal Father? Will you alone consider yourself wiser, and greater than all those who, from the beginning of the world, have belonged to the Church of God, and have believed or still believe that Christ will come, or already has come? On what foundation does your bold, mad, pitiable, and execrable arrogance rest?

You deny that Christ is the son of the living God, the Word of the eternal wisdom of the Father, made manifest in the flesh, who suffered and was crucified for the human race. Why? Because all this does not correspond to your principles. But, besides the fact that it has now been proved that you have not the true principles but false, rash, and absurd ones, I will now say more, namely, that, even if you had relied on true principles, and based

110

all your views on them, you would not be more able to explain, by means of them, all things which exist, or have happened, or happen in the world, nor ought you to assert boldly that something is really impossible, or false, when it seems to be opposed to these principles.

For there are very many, indeed innumerable, things which you will not be able to explain, even if there is some sure knowledge of natural things; you will not even be able to remove the manifest contradiction between such phenomena and your explanations of the rest, which are regarded by you as quite certain. From your principles you will not explain thoroughly even one of those things which are achieved in witchcraft and in enchantments by the mere pronunciation of certain words, or simply by carrying about the words, or characters, traced on some material, nor will you be able to explain any of the stupendous phenomena among those who are possessed by demons, of all of which I have myself seen various instances, and I have heard most certain evidence of innumerable happenings of the kind from very many most trustworthy persons, who spoke with one voice.

How will you be able to judge of the essences of all things, even if it be granted that certain ideas which you have in your mind, adequately conform to the essences of those things of which they are the ideas? For you can never be sure whether the ideas of all created things exist naturally in the human mind, or whether many, if not all, can be produced in it, and actually are produced in it, by external objects, and even through the suggestion of good or evil spirits, and through a clear divine revelation. How, then, without considering the testimony of other men, and experience of things, to say nothing now of submitting your judgment to the Divine omnipotence, will you be able, from your principles, to define precisely and to establish for certain the actual existence, or nonexistence, the possibility, or the impossibility, of the existence of, for instance, the following things (that is, whether they actually exist, or do not exist, or can exist, or cannot exist, in Nature), such as divining rods for detecting metal and underground waters; the stone which the Alchemists seek, the power of words and characters; the apparitions of various spirits both good and evil, and their power, knowledge, and occupation; the restoration of plants and flowers in a glass phial after they have been burnt; Sirens; pygmies very frequently showing themselves, according to report, in mines; the Antipathies and Sympathies of very many things; the impenetrability of the human body, etc.?

Even if you were possessed of a mind a thousand times more subtle and more acute than you do possess, you would not be able, my Philosopher, to determine even one of the said things. If in judging these and similar matters you put your trust in your understanding alone, you no doubt already think in this way about things of which you have no knowledge and no experience, and which you, therefore, consider impossible, but which in reality should seem only uncertain until you have been convinced by the testimony of very many trustworthy witnesses. Thus, I imagine, would Julius Caesar have thought, if someone had told him that a certain powder could be made up, and would become common in subsequent ages, the strength of which would be so effective that it would blow up into the air castles, whole cities, even the very mountains, and such too that wherever it is confined, when ignited, it would expand suddenly to a surprising extent, and shatter everything that impeded its action. Julius Caesar would in no wise have believed this; but he would have derided this man with loud jeers as one who wanted to persuade him of something contrary to his own judgment and experience and the highest military knowledge.

But let us return to the point. If you do not know the aforementioned things, and are unable to pronounce on them, why

112

will you, unhappy man swollen with diabolical pride, rashly judge
of the awful mysteries of the life and Passion of Christ, which
Catholic teachers themselves pronounce incomprehensible? Why,
moreover, will you rave, chattering foolishly and idly about the
innumerable miracles, and signs, which, after Christ, his Apostles
and Disciples and later many thousands of Saints performed in
evidence and confirmation of the truth of the Catholic Faith,
through the omnipotent power of God, and innumerable instances of which, through the same omnipotent Mercy and loving-
kindness of God, are happening even now in our days, throughout
the whole world? If you cannot contradict these, as you certainly
cannot, why do you object any longer? Give in, turn away from
your errors and your sins; put on humility and be born again.

But let us also descend to truth of fact, as it really is the foundation of the Christian religion. How, if you give the matter due
consideration, will you dare to deny the efficacy of the consensus
of so many myriads of men, of whom some thousands have been,
and are, many miles ahead of you in doctrine, in learning, in true
and rare importance, and in perfection of life? All these unani-
mously and with one voice declare that Christ, the incarnate son
of the living God, suffered, and was crucified, and died for the
sins of the human race, and rose again, was transfigured, and reigns
in heaven as God, together with the eternal Father in the Unity of
the Holy Spirit, and the remaining doctrines which belong here;
and also that through the Divine power and omnipotence there
were performed in the Church of God by this same Lord Jesus,
and afterwards, in his name, by the Apostles and the other Saints,
innumerable miracles, which not only exceeded human comprehension but were even opposed to common sense (and of these
there remain even to this day countless material indications, and
visible signs scattered far and wide throughout the world) and
that such miracles still happen.

113

Might I not in like manner deny that the ancient Romans ever existed in the world, or that the Emperor Julius Caesar, having suppressed the Liberty of the Republic, changed their form of government to a monarchy, if I disregarded the many monuments evident to all, which time has left us of the power of the Romans; if I disregarded the testimony of the most weighty authors who have ever written the histories of the Roman Republic and Monarchy, wherein they particularly treat of Julius Caesar; and if I disregarded the judgment of so many thousands of men who have either themselves seen the said monuments, or have put, and still put, their trust in them (seeing that their existence is confirmed by countless witnesses) as well as in the said histories, on the ground that I dreamed last night that the monuments, which have come down from the Romans, are not real things, but mere illusions; and similarly, that those stories which are told of the Romans are just like the stories which the books called Romances relate, puerile stories about Amadis of Gaul and similar Heroes; also that Julius Caesar either never existed in the world, or if he existed was a melancholic man, who did not really crush the Liberty of the Romans, and raise himself to the Throne of the Imperial Power, but was induced to believe that he had performed these achievements, either by his own foolish imagination or by the persuasion of friends who flattered him. . . .

Lastly, reflect on the very wretched and restless life of Atheists, although they sometimes make a display of great cheerfulness of mind, and wish to seem to spend their life joyfully, and with the greatest internal peace of mind. More especially consider their most unhappy and horrible death, of which I have myself seen some instances and know with equal certainty of many more, or rather of countless cases, from the report of others, and from History. Learn from their example to be wise in time.

Thus you see, or at least I hope you see, how rashly you entrust

114

yourself to the opinions of your brain; (for if Christ is the true God, and at the same time man, as is most certain, see to what you are reduced; for by persevering in your abominable errors, and most grave sins, what else can you expect but eternal damnation? How horrible this is, you may ponder for yourself) how little reason you have for laughing at the whole world with the exception of your wretched adorers; how foolishly proud and puffed up you become with the knowledge of the excellence of your talents, and with admiration for your very vain, indeed quite false, and impious doctrine; how shamefully you make yourself more wretched than the very beasts, by depriving yourself of the freedom of the will; nevertheless, even if you do not actually experience and recognize this, how can you deceive yourself by thinking that your works are worthy of the highest praise, and even of the closest imitation?

If you do not wish (which I will not think) that God or your neighbor should have pity on you, do you yourself at least take pity on your own misery, whereby you endeavor to make yourself more unhappy than you are now, or less unhappy than you· will be, if you continue in this manner.

Come to your senses, you Philosopher, and realize the folly of your wisdom, the madness of your wisdom; put aside your pride and become humble, and you will be healed. Pray to Christ in the Most Holy Trinity, that he may deign to commiserate your misery, and receive you. Read the Holy Fathers, and the Doctors of the Church, and let them instruct you in what you must do that you may not perish, but have eternal life. Consult Catholics profoundly learned in their faith and living a good life, and they will tell you many things which you have never known and whereat you will be amazed.

I, for my part, have written this letter to you with truly Christian intention, first that you may know the great love that I bear you although a Gentile; and secondly to beg you not to continue to pervert others also.

I will therefore conclude thus: God is willing to snatch your soul from eternal damnation, if only you are willing. Do not hesitate to obey the Lord, who has so often called you through others, and now calls you again, and perhaps for the last time, through me, who, having obtained this grace through the ineffable Mercy of God Himself, pray for the same for you with my whole heart. Do not refuse: for if you will not hear God now when He calls you, the anger of the Lord Himself will be kindled against you, and there is the danger that you may be abandoned by His Infinite Mercy, and become the unhappy victim of the divine Justice which consumes all things in its anger. May the omnipotent God avert this fate to the greater glory of His name, and to the salvation of your soul, and also as a salutary and imitable example for your most unfortunate Idolaters, through our Lord and Saviour, Jesus Christ, who with the Eternal Father lives and reigns in the Unity of the Holy Ghost as God for all eternity. Amen.

Albert Burgh

Florence, September 3, 1675

GRIEVED *though he must have been by this violent outburst from an old friend and former pupil, Spinoza calmly waited four months before replying. This is what he wrote in a letter dated December, 1675:*

". . . how do you know that you have chosen the best?"

December, 1675

BARUCH SPINOZA Sends Greetings
To the Very Noble Young Man Albert Burgh:

What I could scarcely believe when it was related to me by others, I at last understand from your letter; that is, that not only have you become a member of the Roman Church, as you say, but that you are a very keen champion of it and have already learned to curse and rage petulantly against your opponents. I had not intended to reply to your letter, being sure that what you need is time rather than argument, to be restored to yourself, and to your family, to say nothing of other grounds which you once approved when we spoke of Stenonius (in whose footsteps you are now following). But certain friends who with me had formed great hopes for you from your excellent natural talent, earnestly prayed me not to fail in the duty of a friend, and to think of what you recently were rather than of what you now are, and similar things. I have been induced by these arguments to write to you these few words, earnestly begging you to be kind enough to read them with a calm mind.

I will not here recount the vices of Priests and Popes in order to turn you away from them, as the opponents of the Roman Church are wont to do. For they are wont to publish these things from ill-feeling, and to adduce them in order to annoy rather than to instruct. Indeed, I will admit that there are found more men of great learning, and of an upright life, in the Roman than in any

117

other Christian Church; for since there are more men who are members of this Church, there will also be found within it more men of every condition. You will, however, be unable to deny, unless perhaps you have lost your memory together with your reason, that in every Church there are many very honest men who worship God with justice and charity; for we have known many men of this kind among the Lutherans, the Reformers, the Mennonites, and the Enthusiasts, and to say nothing of others, you know of your own ancestors who in the time of the Duke of Alva suffered for the sake of their Religion every kind of torture with both firmness and freedom of mind. Therefore you must allow that holiness of life is not peculiar to the Roman Church, but is common to all.

And since we know through this (to speak with the Apostle John, The First Epistle, Chapter 4, verse 13) that we dwell in God and God dwells in us, it follows that whatever it is that distinguishes the Roman Church from the others, it is something superfluous, and therefore based merely on superstition.

For, as I said with John, justice and charity are the only and the surest sign of the true Catholic faith, and the true fruits of the Holy Spirit, and wherever these are found, there Christ really is, and where they are lacking, there Christ also is not. For by the Spirit of Christ alone can we be led to the love of justice and of charity. If you had been willing duly to ponder these facts within yourself, you would not have been lost, nor would you have caused bitter sorrow to your parents who sorrowfully lament your lot.

But I return to your letter in which you first bewail the fact that I suffer myself to be deceived by the Prince of evil Spirits. But I beg you to be of good cheer, and to come to yourself. When you were sane, if I am not mistaken, you used to worship an infinite God, by whose power all things absolutely come into being, and are preserved: but now you dream of a Prince, an enemy of

118

God, who, against the will of God, misleads and deceives most men (for good men are rare), whom God consequently delivers up to this master of vices to be tortured for all eternity. Thus divine justice permits the Devil to deceive men with impunity, but does not permit the men who have been miserably deceived and misled by this same Devil to go unpunished.

These absurdities might still be tolerated if you worshipped a God infinite and eternal, and not one whom Chastillon in the town of Tienen, as it is called by the Dutch, gave with impunity to the horses to eat. And do you, unhappy one, weep for me? And do you call my Philosophy, which you have never seen, a Chimera? O brainless youth, who has bewitched you, so that you believe that you swallow the highest and the eternal, and that you hold it in your intestines?

Yet you seem to want to use your reason, and you ask me, *how I know that my philosophy is the best among all those which have ever been taught in the world, or are taught now, or will be taught in the future?* This, indeed, I can ask you with far better right. For I do not presume that I have found the best Philosophy, but I know that I think the true one. If you ask me how I know this, I shall answer, in the same way that you know that the three angles of a triangle are equal to two right angles. That this is enough no one will deny whose brain is sound, and who does not dream of unclean spirits who inspire us with false ideas which are like true ones: for the truth reveals itself and the false.

But you who presume that you have at last found the best religion, or rather the best men, to whom you have given over your credulity, *how do you know that they are the best among all those who have taught other Religions, or are teaching them now, or will teach them in the future? Have you examined all those religions, both ancient and modern, which are taught here and in India and everywhere throughout the world? And even if you have duly ex-*

119

amined *them, how do you know that you have chosen the best?*
For you can give no reason for your faith. But you will say that you
assent to the inward testimony of the Spirit of God, while the
others are cheated and misled by the Prince of evil Spirits. But all
those outside the Roman Church make the same claims with the
same right for their Churches as you do for yours.

As to what you add about the common consent of myriads of
men, and of the uninterrupted succession of the Church, etc., this
is the same old song of the Pharisees. For these also, with no less
confidence than the adherents of the Roman Church, produce their
myriads of witnesses, who relate what they have heard about, with
as much pertinacity as do the witnesses of the Romans, just as if
they themselves had experienced it.

They trace back their lineage to Adam. They boast with equal
arrogance that their Church maintains its growth, stability, and
solidity to this very day, in spite of the hostility of the Heathen
and the Christians. Most of all do they take their stand on their
antiquity. They declare with one voice that they have received
their traditions from God Himself, and that they alone preserve
the written and unwritten word of God.

No one can deny that all heresies have left them, but that they
have remained constant for some thousands of years, without any
imperial compulsion, but through the mere power of superstition.
The miracles they relate are enough to weary a thousand gossips.
But what they chiefly pride themselves on is that they number far
more martyrs than any other nation and daily increase the number
of those who with extraordinary constancy of mind have suffered
for the faith that they profess. And this is not untrue. I myself
know, among others, of a certain Judah, whom they call the Faithful, who in the midst of the flames, when he was believed to be
dead already, began to sing the hymn which begins *To Thee, O*
God, I commit my soul, and died in the middle of the hymn.

The order of the Roman Church, which you so greatly praise, I
...ss, is politic and lucrative to many. I should think that there
...ne more suited to deceive the people and to constrain the
... men, were there not the order of the Mohammedan
... far surpasses it. For from the time that this super-
... ve arisen no schisms in their Church.

... ulate correctly, you will see that only what
you r... ...ce is in favor of the Christians, namely,
that un... ...n men were able to convert almost the
whole w... ...Christ. But this argument militates not
only for t... ..., but for all who acknowledge the
name of Chr...

But suppose ... ...guments which you adduce are in
favor of the Rom... ...church alone. Do you think that you can
thereby mathematically prove the authority of the Church? Since
this is far from being the case, why then do you want me to believe
that my proofs are inspired by the Prince of evil Spirits, but yours
of God? Especially so, as I see and your letter clearly shows that
you have become a slave of this Church, under the influence not
so much of the love of God as of the fear of hell, which is the sole
cause of superstition. Is this your humility, to put no faith in yourself, but only in others, who are condemned by very many? Do you
regard it as arrogance and pride because I use my reason, and
acquiesce in that true Word of God which is in the mind and can
never be depraved or corrupted? Away with this deadly superstition, acknowledge the reason God has given you, and cultivate it,
if you would not be numbered among the brutes. Cease, I say, to
call absurd errors mysteries, and do not shamefully confuse those
things which are unknown to us, or as yet undiscovered, with those
which are shown to be absurd, as are the horrible secrets of this
Church, which, the more they oppose right reason, the more you
believe they transcend the understanding.

For the rest, the basis of the *Tractatus Theologico-Politicus*, namely, that Scripture must only be explained through Scripture, which you so boldly and without any reason proclaim to be false, is not merely assumed, but apodictically proved to be true or well established, chiefly in Chapter 7, where the opinions of opponents are also refuted. Add to this what is proved at the end of Chapter 15.

If you will consider these carefully, and also examine the Histories of the Church (of which I see you are most ignorant), in order to see how false are many of the Pontifical traditions, and by what fate and with what arts the Roman Pontiff, six hundred years after the birth of Christ, obtained sovereignty over the Church, I doubt not that you will at last come to your senses. That this may be so, I wish you from my heart. Farewell, etc.

B. d. Spinoza

[The Hague, December, 1675.]

SPINOZA's hopes for his former disciple proved too sanguine. The records show that "young Burgh somehow grew into old Burgh." He died in a monastery in Rome.

Spinoza died two years later, in 1677, at the age of forty-five. At the unveiling of a statue of Spinoza at The Hague in 1882, Ernest Renan concluded his address with this famous tribute to "the greatest Jew of modern times":

"Woe to him who in passing should hurl an insult at this gentle and pensive head. He would be punished, as all vulgar souls are punished, by his very vulgarity, and by his incapacity to conceive what is divine. This man, from his granite pedestal, will point out to all men the way of blessedness that he found; and ages hence, the cultivated traveler, passing by this spot, will say in his heart, 'The truest vision ever had of God came, perhaps, here.'"

Part Two

LETTERS OF NOT SO LONG AGO

[FROM 1747 TO 1896]

LORD CHESTERFIELD LAYS DOWN SOME PRE-CEPTS FOR HIS NATURAL SON

T HIS is a characteristic letter from the courtly pen of one who was described by Dr. Johnson as having "the morals of a whore and the manners of a dancing master."*

The illegitimate son to whom Philip Dormer Stanhope, Fourth Earl of Chesterfield, diplomat, statesman, and maxim maker, addressed these admonitions was born of a liaison between Lord Chesterfield and a French governess while he was serving as ambassador to The Hague. These letters provide a good example of "the dextrous interplay of wit and elegance" for which eighteenth-century correspondence was noted. Lofty sentiments and bombastic ways of expressing them were the fashion of the period. Lord Chesterfield, the undisputed social arbiter of his time, was the past master of this type of letter writing.

". . . even polished brass will pass upon more people than rough gold."

London, March 6, O.S. 1747.

D EAR BOY,
Whatever you do, will always affect me, very sensibly, one way or another; and I am now most agreeably affected by two letters, which I have lately seen from Lausanne, upon your subject; the one was from Madame St. Germain, the other from

* See the following letter, on page 128, from Dr. Johnson to Lord Chesterfield.

Monsieur Pampigny: they both give so good an account of you, that I thought myself obliged, in justice both to them and to you, to let you know it.

Those who deserve a good character, ought to have the satisfaction of knowing that they have it, both as a reward and as an encouragement. They write, that you are not only *décrotté*, but tolerably well-bred; and that the English crust of awkward bashfulness, shyness, and roughness, (of which, by the bye, you had your share,) is pretty well rubbed off. I am most heartily glad of it; for, as I have often told you, those lesser talents, of an engaging, insinuating manner, an easy good-breeding, a genteel behaviour and address, are of infinitely more advantage than they are generally thought to be, especially here in England.

Virtue and learning, like gold, have their intrinsic value; but if they are not polished, they certainly lose a great deal of their lustre: and even polished brass will pass upon more people than rough gold.

What a number of sins does the cheerful, easy good-breeding of the French frequently cover! Many of them want common sense, many more common learning; but, in general, they make up so much, by their manner, for those defects, that, frequently, they pass undiscovered.

I have often said, and do think, that a Frenchman, who, with a fund of virtue, learning, and good-sense, has the manners and good-breeding of his country, is the perfection of human nature. This perfection you may, if you please, and I hope you will, arrive at.

You know what virtue is: you may have it if you will; it is in every man's power; and miserable is the man who has it not. Good-sense God has given you. Learning you already possess enough of, to have, in a reasonable time, all that a man need have. With this, you are thrown out early into the world, where it will be your own fault if you do not acquire all the other accomplishments necessary to complete and adorn your character.

You will do well to make your compliments to Madame St. Germain and Monsieur Pampigny; and tell them how sensible you are of their partiality to you, in the advantageous testimonies which, you are informed, they have given of you here.

Adieu! Continue to deserve such testimonies; and then you will not only deserve, but enjoy, my truest affection.

THE natural son of Lord Chesterfield was not greatly impressed by his father's famous letters. He died at the age of thirty-six, a mediocre person, immemorable save for the mass of worldly wisdom, wit, and moral precepts he received from his lordly father for twenty-one years— and completely disregarded. He even kept his marriage a secret from his father. The son's widow, Eugenia, cruelly flouted all the lofty canons elaborately promulgated by her father-in-law, and published Lord Chesterfield's letters (not written for publication) while he was still alive. On his death she sold copies of them for £1500.

SAMUEL JOHNSON SPURNS THE PROFFERED HELP

OF THE EARL OF CHESTERFIELD

A<small>LL</small> his life," wrote Augustine Birrell, "Dr. Johnson was an old struggler, struggling against scrofula, against semi-blindness, against poverty, against neglect." In the preface to his English Dictionary, Johnson himself referred to these struggles:

"In this work, when it shall be found that much is omitted, let it not be forgotten that much likewise is performed; and though no book was ever spared out of tenderness to the authour, and the world is little solicitous to know whence proceeded the faults of that which it condemns; yet it may gratify curiosity to inform it, that the English Dictionary was written with little assistance of the learned, and without any patronage of the great; not in the soft obscurities of retirement, or under the shelter of academick bowers, but amidst inconvenience and distraction, in sickness and in sorrow.* It may repress the triumph of malignant criticism to observe, that if our language is not here fully displayed, I have only failed in an attempt which no human powers have hitherto completed."

In the Dictionary itself, Johnson defined a "patron" as "one who countenances, supports, and protects—usually a writer; who supports with insolence and is repaid with flattery." The experience which doubtless suggested this definition also instigated perhaps the most famous single letter in the history of English literature.

In 1747, when he was still struggling against obscurity in Grub Street, Johnson planned his great Dictionary as the first definitive, authoritative work of its kind in English. With the sanction of Dodsley, the bookseller who sponsored the publication, Johnson sent a prospectus to the Earl of Chesterfield, who was then Secretary of State. The Earl acknowl-

* See Dr. Johnson's letter to Mrs. Thrale on page 132.

128

edged this with a gift of £10 but was "not at home" when Johnson called. (The legend of Johnson's being kept waiting in the great Lord's antechamber while Colley Cibber was admitted without delay was later denied by Johnson himself.) For seven years Johnson slaved on the Dictionary, meanwhile winning some measure of fame by his brilliant literary criticism. Aside from rare hunting trips, his only form of exercise was battering down "defenseless bores and jostling the celebrities."

When the Dictionary was virtually completed, Chesterfield "heard mention" of its renown and, "seeking to merit the dedication of the work," wrote two essays in commendation of it—distinguished only for their condescending tone. By that time Lord Chesterfield's "honeyed words" and "courtly devices" (as Boswell described them) proved of no avail—and produced the opposite of their intended effect on one who would ordinarily have been gratified by praise "from a man of rank and elegant accomplishments." Dr. Johnson had now proved to the world that he was a one-man equivalent of the entire French Academy. He was "an oracle of literature, a pensioner of the crown, the court of appeals of morality." He had, in fact, reached the stage where—in the words of Sir Arthur Quiller-Couch—"he could and did knock down insolent publishers," and he forthwith rejected the belated patronage of Lord Chesterfield in a letter that Carlyle called "that far-famed Blast of Doom proclaiming that patronage should be no more."

"... no man is well pleased to have his all neglected ..."

February 7, 1755.

MY LORD,
I have been lately informed, by the proprietor of the World, that two papers, in which my Dictionary is recommended

to the publick, were written by your Lordship. To be so distinguished, is an honour, which, being very little accustomed to favours from the great, I know not well how to receive, or in what terms to acknowledge.

When, upon some slight encouragement, I first visited your Lordship, I was overpowered, like the rest of mankind, by the enchantment of your address; and could not forbear to wish that I might boast myself *Le vainqueur du vainqueur de la terre;*—that I might obtain that regard for which I saw the world contending; but I found my attendance so little encouraged, that neither pride nor modesty would suffer me to continue it. When I had once addressed your Lordship in publick, I had exhausted all the art of pleasing which a retired and uncourtly scholar can possess. I had done all that I could; and no man is well pleased to have his all neglected, be it ever so little.

Seven years, my Lord, have now past, since I waited in your outward rooms, or was repulsed from your door; during which time I have been pushing on my work through difficulties, of which it is useless to complain, and have brought it, at last, to the verge of publication, without one act of assistance, one word of encouragement, or one smile of favour. Such treatment I did not expect, for I never had a Patron before.

The shepherd in Virgil grew at last acquainted with Love, and found him a native of the rocks.

Is not a Patron, my Lord, one who looks with unconcern on a man struggling for life in the water, and, when he has reached ground, encumbers him with help? The notice which you have been pleased to take of my labours, had it been early, had been kind; but it has been delayed till I am indifferent, and cannot enjoy it; till I am solitary, and cannot impart it; till I am known, and do not want it. I hope it is no very cynical asperity not to confess obligations where no benefit has been received, or to be unwilling that the Publick should consider me as owing that to a Patron, which Providence has enabled me to do for myself.

Having carried on my work thus far with so little obligation to any favourer of learning, I shall not be disappointed though I should conclude it, if less be possible, with less; for I have been long wakened from that dream of hope, in which I once boasted myself with so much exultation,

My Lord,
Your Lordship's most humble,
Most obedient servant,
Sam. Johnson

THE Dictionary was of course not dedicated to Lord Chesterfield. In keeping with the tradition of his class, his Lordship retained his equanimity and attempted no reply. When asked what he thought of Dr. Johnson's celebrated letter, he conceded that it was "very well written."

SAMUEL JOHNSON CONGRATULATES AN OLD FRIEND ON AN IGNOMINIOUS MARRIAGE

[A LETTER TO HESTER LYNCH THRALE]

THIS brief communication is a triumph of Johnsonian irony in the grand manner. Hester Lynch Thrale, to whom it was addressed, was the unloved and unloving wife of a rich brewer and the mother of twelve children—eight living—when she became the chief comfort of Johnson's later years. It was to her home that he turned when he was ill and lonely. She saw to it that a room was always ready for the famous lexicographer and critic, either at her country seat or in her town house in Brighton, where he found his chief relaxation in the twilight of his life.

Mrs. Thrale's friendship with Johnson lasted for more than sixteen years. It became ardent when she was twenty-four and he fifty-five. He was accustomed to address her with mock gallantry as "My Mistress." The "Great Bear of English Letters" was also a friend of Mrs. Thrale's husband. Indeed, Johnson "ghosted" Thrale's speeches when the Hon. Gentleman was a candidate for Parliament. Furthermore, the learned doctor served as a volunteer consultant on problems of brewery administration.

Peter Quennell has brilliantly described this strange relationship between Dr. Johnson and Mrs. Thrale: "With Dr. Johnson in tow, she became a personage. It was she who had had the credit of domesticating that magnificent, if uncouth, and at times, decidedly repulsive figure; she who helped to raise him from the depths of melancholy, where he wallowed among the lost souls, to her Streatham drawing rooms, where he was well-fed, well looked after, well flattered and could meet such company as he chose, on his own terms. It was she who had taken him

132

to Paris and Brighton and Bath. . . . Unfortunately a woman—even a woman as frivolous and shallow, in many respects, as Hester Lynch Thrale—may develop, quite unexpectedly and disconcertingly, far more fundamental needs. The feminine forties are always dangerous; and it was during the fourth decade of this busy life that Aphrodite swept down, attaching herself entire to Mrs. Thrale's protesting and hitherto utterly irreproachable person, charging her helpless heart with erotic frenzy . . ."

Thus it came to pass that "when the novelty of being Johnson's admirer and confidante had worn off," Mrs. Thrale became impatient with "the erratic, pedantic, and melancholy old man," then himself a widower. Doubtless he would have married her, after her husband's death, if she would have had him, but, against his wishes, she instead secretly married Gabriel Piozzi, a handsome Italian singer, whom she first met in 1780.

Perplexed as to how to break the news of her marriage to her old hero and protégé—her "dearest friend and mentor," then 73—she finally decided to send him a "circular letter." As an afterthought, no doubt, she added a few handwritten notations on the formal announcement. Dr. Johnson replied as follows:

"... God forgive your wickedness ..."

MADAM,
If I interpret your letter right, you are ignominiously married; if it is yet undone, let us at once more talk together. If you have abandoned your children and your religion, God forgive your wickedness; if you have forfeited your fame and your country, may your folly do no further mischief.

If the last act is yet to do, I, who have loved you, esteemed you, reverenced you, and served you, I who long thought you the first of womankind, entreat that, before your fate is irrevocable, I may once more see you.

I was, I once was,

Madam, most truly yours,

Sam: Johnson

I T WAS to no avail. Mrs. Thrale married her musical cavalier, and the friendship which had "soothed twenty years of life radically wretched" came to an end.

After Johnson's death and well before the appearance of Boswell's immortal biography, Mrs. Thrale published her Anecdotes, covering the last twenty years of Johnson's life. The book was an immediate success. The first edition completely sold out on the day of issue. It was in this book that Mrs. Thrale referred to her association with Dr. Johnson as "the yoke my husband first put upon me."

DU BARRY MAKES A BUSINESS PROPOSITION TO AN ADMIRER

[A LETTER TO M. DUVAL]

Du Barry lived from 1746 to 1793. After her resplendent triumphs as one of the leading ornaments of the ancien régime, she achieved mortality as one of the first victims of the French Revolution and the Terror. She was clearly a great lady of considerable attainments, famed in song and story for her allure. Her real name was Jeanne Bécu, being the natural daughter of Anne Bécu and a monk known (ironically enough) as Frère Ange. After various minor preliminary seductions, she found her first real opportunity as a salesgirl in LaBille's millinery shop off the Rue Saint-Honoré, where her blonde and piquant charms soon made her famous among the smart young bloods of Paris. For business reasons, she assumed the surname of the man whom her mother (eventually) married, Rançon. That her rise in the world was due in great part to a truly Gallic business sense is shown in this letter to one of her early admirers.

"I don't want to remain a shopgirl . . ."

April 6th, 1761.

Yes, my dear friend, I have told you, and repeat it: I love you dearly. You certainly said the same thing to me, but on your side it is only impetuosity; directly after the first enjoyment, you

135

would think of me no more. I begin to know the world. I will tell you what I suggest, now: pay attention. I don't want to remain a shopgirl, but a little more my own mistress, and would therefore like to find someone to keep me. If I did not love you, I would try to get money from you; I would say to you, You shall begin by renting a room for me and furnishing it; only as you told me that you were not rich, you can take me to your own place. It will not cost you any more rent, not more for your table and the rest of your housekeeping. To keep me and my headdress will be the only expense, and for those give me one hundred livres a month, and that will include everything. Thus we could both live happily, and you would never again have to complain about my refusal. If you love me, accept this proposal; but if you do not love me, then let each of us try his luck elsewhere. Good-by, I embrace you heartily.

Rançon

WHETHER or not M. Duval's ardor was dampened by this letter, we have no way of knowing. But we do know that before many months had passed, Jeanne was installed in the household of Count Du Barry, a fine gentleman whose wealth accrued from "unmentionable sources." It is believed that Du Barry acted as his decoy for a gambling establishment. With his help, she advanced rapidly to the boudoir of Louis XV. The story of her rise to power in the court, her flight from France, and her execution by the Terror forms one of the most dramatic episodes in modern history. She was guillotined at the age of forty-seven, on December 7, 1793.

JAMES BOSWELL TOUCHES THE KEYS IN UNISON
WITH VOLTAIRE

[A LETTER TO HIS FRIEND WILLIAM JOHNSON TEMPLE]

TEMPLE," wrote Boswell himself, "this is a noble letter!"
The same qualities which make Boswell's Life of Johnson the
most famous biography in English literature make this one of the great
intimate letters of history. It overflows with self-revelation, teeming with
luscious gossip. Its uninhibited, unhurried pages provide an appropriate
setting for the reigning princes and philosophers of the time, and their
dominant ideas.

Although Dr. Johnson said of Boswell that "he lived among the sav-
ages and rakes in London," a letter like this reveals that, on the Continent
as well as in England, he actually traveled with the monarchs of his generation. Immortals like Rousseau and Voltaire, as well as the Johnson
group, people his journals and storm through his letters. In his travels
and interviews Boswell also made it a point to keep his eyes open for the
most beautiful ladies.

Walpole's historic charge that Boswell was the "ape of most of
Johnson's faults without a grain of his sense" is thus somewhat in-
validated.

When he called The Life of Johnson the "story of a mountebank
and his zany," he was not familiar with the secret diaries and letters of
James Boswell, which were not brought to light until 1927.

This letter, for example, quoted here in its entirety, was excavated
after a century and a half from the dark recesses of Malahide Castle—
the twelfth-century ancestral country seat of the Talbots, near Dublin.
The Boswell line, which connected with the Talbots in the nineteenth

century, was traced back to the Norman Conquest with such pride that young James Boswell was even held in disrepute for fraternizing with his hero, Dr. Johnson, "the recognized despot of English literature."

The nineteenth-century Lord Talbot de Malahide married a Miss Boswell, great-granddaughter of James Boswell. In 1925, the noted eighteenth-century scholar, Prof. Chauncey Tinker, heard for the first time that some of the original Boswell papers were still at Malahide. Two years later, Lt. Col. Ralph H. Isham acquired them by purchase, after Lady Talbot had gone over them with paint and ink. Fortunately, Lt. Col. Isham was able to restore most of the censored passages. One of these censored items recounted an interview with Johnson in which he was asked, "What is the greatest pleasure of life?"—a question that the lexicographer answered briefly and unblushingly. The Private Papers were known to contain many such interviews, in which Johnson's blunt and devastating answers were matched and immortalized by Boswell's accurate and uncensored reporting.

In his loose-leaf journal, for example, Boswell described a journey to London in which he had gallantly escorted Rousseau's inamorata from Paris and "at every stop of the diligence on the road to Calais, had collected his fee." In an interview with Lt. Col. Isham, Lady Talbot, shocked by such disclosures from the family archives, consigned most of the leaves about this episode to the fire. But fortunately most of the letters and diaries were saved. The hoard discovered at Malahide far exceeded the dreams of the most erudite and avaricious collector. Rosenbachs have swooned with ecstasy at the mere thought of such discoveries. The Private Papers of James Boswell were found to contain numerous journals, manuscripts of the highest literary and historical importance, and letters to and from Voltaire, Burns, Goldsmith, and other giants of the time.

In the letter that follows, printed here (with the original spellings) by the sanction of Lt. Col. Isham, as prepared by him and Geoffrey Scott for its first publication in the Limited Edition of the Private Papers, Boswell recounts for his friend in England one of the most memorable conversations in literary history. Boswell, then 24 years of

He has left the letter open for me to read, altho' it
contains his most important concerns and the kindest
effusions of his heart. Is not this treating me with a
regard which my Soul must be proud of I must
give you a sentence of this letter.

; Je suis bien aise que M. Boswell et vous fassiez
connoissance. Dans la première lettre qu'il m'écrivoit
il me marqua qu'il étoit un Homme d'un merite singulier.
J'eus la curiosité de voir celui qui parloit ainsi de
luimème, et Je trouvois qu'il m'avoit dit vrai.

And whence do I now write to you, My Freind?
From the Chateau of M. de Voltaire. I had a letter
for him from a Swiss Colonel at the Hague. I came
hither Monday and was presented to him. He received
me with dignity and that air of a man who has been
much in the world which a Frenchman acquires
in perfection. I saw him for about half an hour before
dinner. He was not in spirits. yet he gave me
some brilliant Sallies. He did not dine with us, and
I was obliged to post away immediatly after
dinner, because the Gates of Geneva shut
before five, and Ferney is a good hour from
Town. I was by no means satisfyd to have been so
little time with the monarch of French Literature.
A happy scheme sprung up in my adventurous
mind. Madame Denis the niece of M. de Voltaire
had been extremely good to me. She is fond of
our language. I wrote her a letter in English
begging her interest to obtain for me the Privilege of lodging a night under the roof of M.
de Voltaire who in opposition to our Sun, rises in
the evening. I was in the finest humour and my
letter was full of wit. I told her I am a hardy
and a vigourous Scot. You may mount me to
the highest and coldest Garret. I shall not even
refuse to sleep upon two chairs in the Bedchamber
of your maid. I saw her pass thro' the room where
we sat before dinner. I sent my letter on Tuesday
by an Express. It was shewn to M. de Voltaire who
with his own hand wrote this answer in the Character
of Madam Denis. You will do us much honour and
pleasure. We have few beds; But you will [not] shall not sleep
on two chairs. My Uncle tho' very sick hath giv[e] a special
mark — I know it better, for, I have been you
longer. Temple, I am your most obedient. How do
you

age and relatively unknown (he had just met Johnson the year before and had been "severely buffeted by him"), had visited the Château de Ferney on the night of December 27, 1764.

Voltaire was in his seventy-second year and the most famous man of letters of his time. The principal topic of conversation was "the argument of Religion." As Colonel Isham has expressed it, "Not Voltaire's fame, age, or infirmity was proof against Boswell's inquisition."

The letter recounts many other adventures and experiences, including Boswell's numerous romantic attachments, his travels, his secret hopes and fears, but the historic interview with Voltaire is the climax:

"I wish you had heard the Music."*

Chateau de Ferney.
28 Decr. 1764.

MY DEAR TEMPLE;
Think not that I insult you, when you read the full tale of my supreme Felicity. After thanking you for your two letters of the month of October, I must pour forth the Exultation of a heart swelling with Joy. Call me Bombast. Call me what you please. Thus will I talk. No other stile can give the most distant expression of the feelings of Boswell. If I appear ridiculous, it is because our Language is deficient.

I compleated my Tour thro' the German Courts. At all of them I found state and Politeness. At Baaden Durlach I found Worth, Learning and Philosophy united in the Reigning Marggrave. He is a Prince whose character deserves to be known over Europe. He is the best Sovereign, the best Father, the most amiable Man. He has

travelled a great deal. He has been in England and he speaks the
language in amazing Perfection.

During the time that I stayed at his Court, I had many, many
conversations with him. He shewed me the greatest distinction.
The Inspector of his Cabinet, His Library-keeper, and the Officers
of his court had orders to do every thing in their power to render
my stay agreable. Madame La Marggrave, who paints in perfection and has a general taste for the fine arts, treated me in the
most gracious manner.

The Marggrave told me how happy he was to have me with him.
I asked him if I could do any thing that might shew my gratitude.
He replied, "I shall write to you sometimes. I shall be very happy
to receive your letters." He was in earnest. I have allready been
honoured with a letter from His Most Serene Highness. I have
promised to return and pass some weeks at his court. He is not far
from France.

I have been with Rousseau. He lives in the Village of Môtiers
Travers in a beautifull Valley surrounded with immense mountains. I went thither from Neufchatel. I determined to put my real
merit to the severest test, by presenting myself without any recommendation before the Wild, illustrious Philosopher.

I wrote him a letter in which I told him all my worth, and
claimed his regard as what I had a title to. "*Ouvrez donc votre
Porte, Monsieur, à un Homme qui ose vous assurer qu'il merite d'y
entrer.*" Such was my bold and manly stile. He received me, altho'
he was very ill. "*Je suis malade, souffrant, hors d'etat de recevoir
des visites. Cependant Je ne puis me refuser à celle de Monsieur
Boswell pourvu que par égard pour mon etat il veuille bien la faire
courte.*"

I found him very easy and unaffected. At first he complained and
lamented the state of humanity. But I had address enough to bring
him upon Subjects which pleased him, and he grew very animated,

140

quite the amiable St. Preux at fifty. He is a genteel man, has a fine countenance and a charming voice.

You may beleive I had a difficult task enough to come up to the Idea which I had given him of myself. I had said all that my honest Pride beleived. My letter was a piece of true Oratory. You shall see it when we meet. No other man in Europe could have written such a letter, and appeared equal to all it's praise.

I stayed at this time three days in the Village, and was with M. Rousseau every day. A week after, I returned and stayed two days. He is extremely busy. The Corsicans have actually applied to him to give them a set of Laws. What glory for him. He said, "C'est au dessus de mes forces; mais pas au dessus de mon Zèle."

He is preparing to give a compleat and splendid Edition of all his works. When I was sure of his good opinion on my own merit, I shewd him a Recommendation which My Lord Marischal had given me. I talked to him with undisguised confidence. I gave him a written sketch of my life. He studied it, and he loved me with all my failings. He gave me some Advices which will influence the rest of my existence. He is to corespond with me while he lives. When I took leave of him, he embraced me with an elegant cordiality and said, "Souvenez vous toujours de moi. Il y a des points ou nos Ames sont liés."

On my arrival at Geneva I received a letter from him, with a letter of Recommendation to an intimate freind of his at the Court of Parma, a man of uncommon value. He has left the letter open for me to read, altho' it contains his most important concerns and the kindest effusions of his heart. Is not this treating me with a regard which my Soul must be proud of? I must give you a sentence of this letter.

"Je suis bien aise que M. Boswell et vous fassiez connoissance. Je crois que vous m'en saurrez gré tous deux. Dans la première lettre qu'il m'écrivit il me marqua qu'il etoit un Homme d'un *merite singuliere. J'eus la curiosite de voir celui qui parloit ainsi de luimeme, et Je trouvois qu'il m'avoit dit vrai."*

And whence do I now write to you, My Freind? From the Chateau of M. de Voltaire. I had a letter for him from a Suiss Colonel at the Hague. I came hither Monday and was presented to him. He received me with dignity and that air of a man who has been much in the world, which a Frenchman acquires in perfection. I saw him for about half an hour before dinner. He was not in spirits. Yet he gave me some brilliant Sallies. He did not dine with us, and I was obliged to post away immediatly after dinner, because the Gates of Geneva shut before five, and Ferney is a good hour from Town.

I was by no means satisfy'd to have been so little time with the Monarch of French Literature. A happy scheme sprung up in my adventurous mind. Madame Denis, the niece of M. de Voltaire, had been extremely good to me. She is fond of our language. I wrote her a letter in English begging her interest to obtain for me the Privilege of lodging a night under the roof of M. de Voltaire who, in opposition to our Sun, rises in the evening. I was in the finest humour and my letter was full of wit. I told her, "I am a hardy and a vigourous Scot. You may mount me to the highest and coldest Garret. I shall not even refuse to sleep upon two chairs in the Bedchamber of your maid. I saw her pass thro' the room where we sat before dinner."

I sent my letter on Tuesday by an Express. It was shewn to M. de Voltaire who with his own hand wrote this answer in the Character of Madam Denis. "You will do us much honour and pleasure. We have few beds; But you will (*shall*) not sleep on two chairs. My uncle, tho' very sick, hath guessed at your merit. I know it better; for I have seen you longer."

Temple, I am your most Obedient. How do you find yourself?

142

Have you got such a thing as an old freind in this world? Is he to be valued or is he not?

I returned yesterday to this enchanted castle. The Magician appeared a very little before dinner. But in the evening he came into the drawing room in great spirits. I placed myself by him. I touched the keys in unison with his Imagination. I wish you had heard the Music. He was all Brilliance. He gave me continued flashes of Wit. I got him to speak english which he does in a degree that made me, now and then, start up and cry, "Upon my soul this is astonishing."

When he talked our language He was animated with the Soul of a Briton. He had bold flights. He had humour. He had an extravagance; he had a forcible oddity of stile that the most comical of our *dramatis Personæ* could not have exceeded. He swore bloodily as was the fashion when he was in England. He hum'd a Ballad; He repeated nonsense.

Then he talked of our Constitution with a noble enthusiasm. I was proud to hear this from the mouth of an illustrious Frenchman.

At last we came upon Religion. Then did he rage. The Company went to Supper. M. de Voltaire and I remained in the drawing room with a great Bible before us; and if ever two mortal men disputed with vehemence we did. Yes, upon that occasion He was one Individual and I another. For a certain portion of time there was a fair opposition between Voltaire and Boswell. The daring bursts of his Ridicule confounded my understanding. He stood like an Orator of ancient Rome. Tully was never more agitated than he was. He went too far. His aged frame trembled beneath him. He cried, "O I am very sick; My head turns round," and he let himself gently fall upon an easy chair. He recovered.

I resumed our Conversation, but changed the tone. I talked to him serious and earnest. I demanded of him an honest confession

143

of his real sentiments. He gave it me with candour and with a mild eloquence which touched my heart. I did not beleive him capable of thinking in the manner that he declared to me was "from the bottom of his heart." He exprest his veneration—his love— of the Supreme Being, and his entire resignation to the will of Him who is Allwise. He exprest his desire to resemble the Authour of Goodness, by being good himself. His sentiments go no farther. He does not inflame his mind with grand hopes of the immortality of the Soul. He says it may be; but he knows nothing of it. And his mind is in perfect tranquillity.

I was moved; I was sorry. I doubted his Sincerity. I called to him with emotion, "Are you sincere? are you realy sincere?" He answered, "Before God I am."

Then with the fire of him whose Tragedies have so often shone on the Theatre of Paris, he said, "I suffer much. But I suffer with Patience and Resignation; not as a Christian—But as a Man."

Temple, was not this an interesting Scene? Would a Journey from Scotland to Ferney have been too much to obtain such a remarkable Interview? I have given you the great lines. The whole Conversation of the evening is fully recorded, and I look upon it as an invaluable Treasure. One day the Public shall have it. It is a Present highly worthy of their Attention. I told M. de Voltaire that I had written eight quarto Pages of what he had said. He smiled and seemed pleased.

Our important Scene must not appear till after his death. But I have a great mind to send over to London a little Sketch of my Reception at Ferney, of the splendid manner in which M. de Voltaire lives and of the brilliant conversation of this celebrated Authour at the age of Seventy-two. The Sketch would be a letter, addressed to you, full of gayety and full of freindship. I would send it to one of the best Public Papers or Magazines. But this is probably a flight of my overheated mind. I shall not send the Sketch unless you approve of my doing so.

Before I left Britain, I was idle, dissipated, ridiculous and regardless of Reputation. Often was I unworthy to be the freind of Mr. Temple. Now I am a very different Man. I have got a character which I am proud of. Speak thou who hast known me from my earliest years, couldst thou have imagined eight years ago that thy Companion in the Studies of Antiquity who was debased by an unhappy education in the smoak of Edinburgh, couldst thou have imagined him to turn out the Man that he now is?

We are now, my freind, united in the strictest manner. Let us do nothing of any consequence without the consent of each other.

And must I then marry a Dutchwoman? Is it allready marked in the rolls of Heaven? Must the proud Boswell yeild to a tender inclination? Must he in the strength and vigour of his youth resign his liberty for life to one Woman? Rather (say you) shall not my freind embrace the happiness which Fortune presents to him? Will not his Pride be gratified by the Attachment of a Lady who has refused many advantageous offers? Must he not marry to continue his ancient family? and where shall he find a more amiable wife? Is he not a man of a most singular character? and would not an ordinary woman be insupportable to him?

Should he not thank the Powers above for having shewn him Zélide, a young Lady free from all the faults of her sex, with Genius, with good humour, with elegant accomplishments? But, My Dear Temple, she is not by half so rich as I thought. She has only £400 a year.

Besides, I am not pleased with her conduct. We had agreed to corespond, and she directed me to send my letters to the care of her Bookseller. I wrote to her from Berlin a long letter. She did not answer it. I was apprehensive that I had talked too severely of her faults, and wrote her from Anhalt-Dessau begging pardon for my too great freedom. Still I remain unanswer'd.

Her father is a very worthy Man. He and I corespond and we write to each other of his Daughter in a strange mysterious manner. I have trusted him upon honour with a letter to her. So I shall be sure that she receives it and shall see how she behaves. After all, when I consider my unhappy constitution, I think I should not marry, at least for some time, and when I do, should chuse a healthy, chearfull woman of rank and fortune. I am now well because I am agitated by a variety of new scenes. But when I shall return to the uniformity of Scotland, I dread much a relapse into the gloomy distemper. I must endeavour by some scheme of ambition, by elegant Study and by rural occupations to preserve my mind. Yet I own that both of us are sadly undetermin'd. However, I hope the best.

My worthy Father has consented that I shall go to Italy. O my freind what a rich Prospect spreads before me. My letter is allready so long that I shall restrain my enthusiastic sallies. Imagine my Joy. On Tuesday morning I set out for Turin. I shall pass the rigourous Alps with the resolution of Hannibal. I shall be four months in Italy and then return thro' France. I expect to pass some time at Paris.

Forgive me, Temple, for having delayed to mention your concerns till allmost at the end of my letter. You are sure how much I suffer from your uneasiness. I wish I could be as sure of releiving you. I know well the great, and can have no confidence in them. Lord Eglintoune would forget to do anything. I have written to Lady Northumberland begging she may get Bob put upon whole Pay. Lord Warkworth was in General Craufurd's Regiment and

146

both my Lord and My Lady had a great esteem of the General. I have told her Ladyship that the General had promised to take care of the young Lieutenant and that if her Ladyship puts him again in Commission "in so doing you will fullfill the intentions of Him who is no more, whose memory you must ever regard. May I add that your Ladyship will give me a pleasure—a comfort—which I can hardly express. Were I at present as rich as I shall probably be, the Brother of my freind should not depend for a Commission on the uncertain favour of any Great Person alive."

She may be angry at this last period. It ought to please, it ought to rouse her. "O Madam! be truly great. Be generous to the unfortunate. If your Ladyship will befreind the Young Man sincerely, I beg to be honoured with a line," etc. I own to you I have but little hopes from her Ladyship. We shall see. I have not been mean enough to flatter her. That I am determined never to practice.

I have also written to Mr. Mitchell, late envoy at the Court of Berlin, who is just recalled. He is an old freind of my Father's, and a man of the strictest Probity and the warmest Generosity. I have told him your Story as I did to Lady Northumberland.

O my Temple! how do I glory in displaying the conduct of my freind. If Mr. Mitchell can aid Us, he will. I would hope he may serve either your Father or Brother. I have sollicited him for Both. Why am I not in power? I may be so perhaps, yet, before I die.

Temple, I am again as loyal as ever. I abhorr a despotic Tyrant. But I revere a limited Monarch. Shall I be a British Courtier? Am I worthy of the Confidence of my King? May George the Third chuse that the most honest and most amiable of his Subjects should stand continually in his Royal Presence? I will if he says, "You shall be independent." Churchill's death is awefull. The

147

lines which Characterise him are excellent. Temple, this is a noble letter. Fare you well, My ever Dear Freind.

James Boswell

To
William Johnson Temple Esq:
at the Reverend Mr. Stockdale's
Berwic upon Tweed,
Great Britain

Boswell's reference to his romantic attachment for Zélide and his hopes for an ambitious marriage are all the more interesting in the light of the fact that five years after this letter to Temple was written, he married his cousin, Margaret Montgomerie. . . . "The argument of Religion" is further illuminated by Voltaire himself in a letter he wrote shortly afterward to Boswell. This communication, one of the treasured "association items" in the history of letters, is printed on the pages immediately following. . . .

Deeming himself a failure, unaware of the fame that lay ahead, Boswell died in 1795, at the age of fifty-five, eleven years after his hero, Dr. Johnson, and six years after his wife, who left him five children. According to Boswell's non-Boswellian biographer, Thomas Seccombe, "she had been an excellent mother and a good wife, despite the infidelities and drunkenness of her husband, and from her death Boswell relapsed into worse excesses, grievously aggravated by hypochondria."

TWO LETTERS OF VOLTAIRE
WRITTEN FIFTY YEARS APART

[ADDRESSED TO JAMES BOSWELL AND OLYMPE DUNOYER]

D RAMATIST, poet, philosopher, historian, and crusader for the enlightenment, François Marie Arouet was the spokesman for the eighteenth century, the undisputed ruler of European letters for more than fifty years. He lived from 1694 to 1778, wrote seventy-seven volumes of prose and poetry, and cleared the ground for the French Revolution by his indefatigable and inspired campaign to crush the infamy of "the persecuting and privileged orthodoxy."

He adopted the pseudonym "Voltaire," which was an anagram of his own name. Educated in a Jesuit college, he was exiled frequently, lived in many courts and capitals of Europe, where he regarded himself not as the equal of kings, but their superior, and returned in triumph to his beloved Paris at the age of eighty-four. Bigots and tyrants were his sworn enemies.

The grimacing and chattering "Prince of Scoffers" was delineated by Macaulay as the supreme virtuoso of "the unlawful weapon of ridicule," described by Lord Brougham as the "withered Pontiff of Encyclopedism," and hailed by Addison as "the uncompromising fighter for the rights of human intelligence," as " the man who recovered for mankind its lost title-deeds. . . ." In these two letters, the one written with the romantic ardor of his first love, the other, fifty years later, in the full perspective of his ripened wisdom, he stands revealed for us as he lived and breathed.

11: fevrier 1765 · au Chateau de ferney (par genêve).

My distempers and my bad eyes do not permit me
to answer with that celerity and exactness that my
duty and my heart require. you seem sollicitous
about that pretty thing call'd Soul. j do protest
you j know nothing of it. nor wether it is, nor
what it is, nor what it shall be. young scolars, and
priests know all that perfectly. for my part j am
but a very ignorant fellow.
Let it be what it will, j assure you my soul has
a great regard for your own. when you will
make a turn into our deserts, you shall find me
(if a live) ready to show you my respect and
obsequiousness.
                    V.

VOLTAIRE TO JAMES BOSWELL
"...that pretty thing call'd Soul."

VOLTAIRE CONCEDES THAT HE IS BUT A VERY IGNORANT FELLOW

[A LETTER TO JAMES BOSWELL]

THIS brief letter is actually an epilogue to the interview between Voltaire and Boswell on the evening of December 27, 1764, described in full detail in the previously quoted letter which Boswell himself wrote to Temple.* As Boswell said in that letter written from the Château de Ferney: "M. Voltaire and I remained in the drawing room with a great Bible between us, and if ever two mortal men disputed with vehemence, we did. . . . For a certain portion of the time there was a fair opposition between Voltaire and Boswell. . . . I have given you the great lines. The whole conversation . . . is an invaluable Treasure."

"Conversation was not enough," Lieutenant Colonel Isham has said, in describing the background of this letter. "After leaving Ferney, Boswell conceived that a letter questioning Voltaire might procure him a written record, a confirmation, a trophy to display. He wrote accordingly." . . . After one hundred and fifty years, Voltaire's reply was found among Boswell's private papers at Malahide Castle and, like the earlier letter from Boswell to Temple, is printed here with the generous permission of The Viking Press.

* See page 137.

*" . . . that pretty thing call'd Soul."** *

11ᵉ. fevrier 1765. au Chauteau de Ferney par Genève.

MY DISTEMPERS and my bad eyes do not permit me to answer with that celerity and exactness that my duty and my heart require. You seem sollicitous about that pretty thing call'd Soul. I do protest you I know nothing of it: nor wether it is, nor what it is, nor what it shall be. Young scolars, and priests know all that perfectly. For my part I am but a very ignorant fellow.

Let it be what it will, I assure you my soul has a great regard for your own. When you will make a turn into our deserts, you shall find me (if alive) ready to show you my respect and obsequiousness.

V.

A Monsieur,
Monsieur Bossvell,
Chez Messieurs Paul et Pierre,
Torraz,
A Turin.

THIS *is not a translation. Voltaire composed it in English. Hence the original misspellings have been retained. This letter written in the last decade of Voltaire's life was taken out of its chronological order so* as to place it in juxtaposition to Boswell's earlier letter to Temple, which also relates in part to "the argument of Religion."

In interpreting Voltaire's views on this subject, it is interesting to recall that in later years he was fond of quoting—in letters and in conversation—his memorable utterance to the effect that "if there were no God it would be necessary to invent one. . . . All nature cries out aloud that He does exist. . . ." Voltaire expressed this view in a letter he wrote to Frederick William, heir to the Prussian throne, after his visit to the court at Potsdam. On his deathbed Voltaire is reputed to have declared: "I die adoring God, loving my friends, not hating my enemies, and detesting superstition. . . ."

VOLTAIRE ARRANGES A TRYST WITH HIS BE-LOVED

[A LETTER TO OLYMPE DUNOYER]

WE NOW turn back to Voltaire's youth. When he was nineteen years old, he was sent to The Hague as attaché to the French ambassador to the Netherlands. There he fell in love with Mlle Dunoyer, the daughter of a poor and very déclassée mother, who, together with the ambassador, heartily disapproved of the match. Voltaire was imprisoned by the ambassador, escaped by climbing out of the window, and fled "like the wind" with his love (nicknamed "Pimpette") to Scheveningen, five miles away, to arrange their flight to Paris. Attached is one of the letters he wrote while a prisoner:

". . . they can take my life, but not the love that I feel for you."

The Hague, 1713.

I AM a prisoner here in the name of the King; they can take my life, but not the love that I feel for you. Yes, my adorable mistress, tonight I shall see you, and if I had to put my head on the block to do it. For Heaven's sake, do not speak to me in such disastrous terms as you write; you must live and be cautious; beware of madame your mother as of your worst enemy. What do I say?

154

Beware of everybody, trust no one; keep yourself in readiness, as soon as the moon is visible; I shall leave the hotel incognito, take a carriage or a chaise, we shall drive like the wind to Scheveningen; I shall take paper and ink with me; we shall write our letters.

If you love me, reassure yourself, and call all your strength and presence of mind to your aid; do not let your mother notice anything, try to have your picture, and be assured that the menace of the greatest tortures will not prevent me to serve you.

No, nothing has the power to part me from you; our love is based upon virtue, and will last as long as our lives. Adieu, there is nothing that I will not brave for your sake; you deserve much more than that. Adieu, my dear heart!

Arouet

BUT it all came to nothing. The lovers were intercepted, Voltaire was sent to Paris to work in a lawyer's office. Pimpette married someone else and became the Countess of Winterfield. Her mother, some years later, published several of the Voltaire letters, to help pay off her debts.

As for Voltaire, he quickly forsook the law for literature and through the success of his play Oedipe was admitted to the famous coterie of the fair and aristocratic Duchesse du Maine at Sceaux. After he became one of the foremost men of letters in Europe, following his youthful escapades and fleeting imprisonments in the Bastille and his three-year visit to England, he formed his great friendship with Gabrielle-Émilie Le Tonnelier de Breteuil, Marquise du Châtelet—an amateur philosopher, musician, linguist, and mathematician of distinguished attainments. This intimacy lasted to her death in 1749, when she was forty-three and Voltaire was fifty-five.

THE LOVES, THE LETTERS,
THE WIT AND WISDOM
OF BENJAMIN FRANKLIN

[A SERIES]

As in the case of almost all other men of the first magnitude we are embarrassed by riches when we come to examine the accumulated horde of Benjamin Franklin's letters. The "first civilized American" was a prodigious correspondent, and his communications reflect every mood of his vast and multifarious activities—as statesman, scientist, philosopher, editor, printer, inventor, raconteur, bon vivant, and man of the world.

The printer's devil who became perhaps America's greatest genius in the art of versatility lived a long life and a full one. The basic facts of that life, from his birth in Boston in 1706 to his death in 1790, are too well known to require summary here.

Ever since he wrote his own classic life story, there has been a constant stream of new critical interpretations of Franklin. Carl

156

Van Doren has written the latest and doubtless the best and most definitive biography.

"The chief aim of the book," according to Van Doren, "has been to restore to Franklin, so often remembered piecemeal in this or that of his diverse aspects, his magnificent central unity as a great and wise man moving through great and troubling events. No effort has been made to cut his nature to fit any simple scheme of what a good man ought to be.

"Here, as truly as it has been possible to find out, is what Franklin did, said, thought, and felt. Perhaps these things may help to rescue him from the dry, prim people who have claimed him as one of them. They praise his thrift. But he himself admitted that he could never learn frugality, and he practiced it no longer than his poverty forced him to.* They praise his prudence. But at seventy he became a leader of a revolution, and throughout his life he ran bold risks. They praise him for being a plain man. Hardly another man of affairs has ever been more devoted than Franklin to the pleasant graces. The dry, prim people seem to regard him as a treasure shut up in a savings bank to which they have the lawful key. I herewith give him back, in his grand dimensions, to his nation and the world."

One of Franklin's best-known letters—that to Madame Brillon, written in Passy, November 10, 1779, is not quoted here, because it is actually more of a Poor Richard dissertation than a private communication. This is the famous letter in which Franklin wrote, "In short, I conceive that great part of the miseries of mankind are brought upon them by the false estimates they have made of the value of things, and by their giving too much for their whistles." Instead, the editor of this anthology, taking his inspiration from Van Doren's masterly portrait, presents a series of typical Franklin

---

* It was discovered in 1940, from the early ledgers of the Bank of North America in Philadelphia, that Franklin was overdrawn at least three times a week.

letters, representing three totally different moods and phases—
first, Rabelaisian exuberance tempered by cynical sophistication,
second, compassionate consolation in the face of death, and lastly,
fiery controversy in the heat of politics and revolution.

BENJAMIN FRANKLIN URGES A YOUNG FRIEND
TO TAKE AN OLD MISTRESS

THE identity of Franklin's young correspondent has never been clearly established. Apparently he had sought advice on amatory matters from the "all-embracing Doctor Franklin." In his classic reply, the "First American" proved again not only his lack of prudery in an age of artifice but also his true stature as a man of the world.

Of this letter, Dr. A. S. W. Rosenbach has said: "Franklin was a real master of the double meaning. In fact, it was not double, but really quadruple allusion that must be read into his literary works. His celebrated treatise of Wives and Old Mistresses has been quoted from time immemorial. It used to be considered quite naughty, but now, in our own enlightened times, when children know more than their grandmothers, and flappers take to bed with them the Life and Loves of Frank Harris, this old treatise would be relegated to the family album.

"The original manuscript came to me in a curious way. It was thought immoral in the chaste city of Chicago to which it had been bequeathed by the will of a discriminating citizen. Chicago being known for its purity, and not tolerating anything that is even slightly indelicate, offered it to me—at a price of course, for it did not hesitate to profit, like a frail sister, from its shame. I would sooner have this precious document written entirely by the hand of Franklin, than many of the public monuments of that great western city."

"... the sin is less."

June 25, 1745.

MY DEAR FRIEND:—
I know of no Medicine fit to diminish the violent natural inclination you mention; and if I did, I think I should not communicate it to you. Marriage is the proper Remedy. It is the most natural State of Man, and therefore the State in which you will find solid Happiness. Your Reason against entering into it at present appears to be not well founded. The Circumstantial Advantages you have in View by Postponing it, are not only uncertain, but they are small in comparison with the Thing itself, *the being married and settled*. It is the Man and Woman united that makes the complete human Being. Separate she wants his force of Body and Strength of Reason; he her Softness, Sensibility and acute Discernment. Together they are most likely to succeed in the World. A single Man has not nearly the Value he would have in that State of Union. He is an incomplete Animal. He resembles the odd Half of a Pair of Scissors.

If you get a prudent, healthy wife, your Industry in your Profession, with her good Economy, will be a Fortune sufficient.

But if you will not take this Counsel, and persist in thinking a Commerce with the Sex is inevitable, then I repeat my former Advice that in your Amours you should *prefer old Women to young ones*. This you call a Paradox, and demand my reasons. They are these:

1 Because they have more Knowledge of the world, and their

160

Minds are better stored with Observations; their Conversation is more improving, and more lastingly agreeable.

2   Because when Women cease to be handsome, they study to be good. To maintain their Influence over Man, they supply the Diminution of Beauty by an Augmentation of Utility. They learn to do a thousand Services, small and great, and are the most tender and useful of all Friends when you are sick. Thus they continue amiable. And hence there is hardly such a thing to be found as an old Woman who is not a good Woman.

3   Because there is no hazard of children, which irregularly produced may be attended with much inconvenience.

4   Because through more Experience they are more prudent and discreet in conducting an Intrigue to prevent Suspicion. The Commerce with them is therefore safer with regard to your reputation; and regard to theirs, if the Affair should happen to be known, considerate People might be inclined to excuse an old Woman, who would kindly take care of a young Man, form his manners by her good Councils, and prevent his ruining his Health and Fortune among mercenary Prostitutes.

5   Because in every Animal that walks upright, the Deficiency of the Fluids that fill the Muscles appears first in the highest Part. The Face first grows lank and wrinkled; then the Neck; then the Breast and Arms; the lower parts continuing to the last as plump as ever; so that covering all above with a Basket, and regarding only what is below the Girdle, it is impossible of two Women to know an old from a young one. And as in the Dark all Cats are grey, the Pleasure of Corporal Enjoyment with an old Woman is at least equal and frequently superior; every Knack being by Practice capable by improvement.

6   Because the sin is less. The Debauching of a Virgin may be her Ruin, and make her for Life unhappy.

7   Because the Compunction is less. The having made a young

Girl *miserable* may give you frequent bitter Reflections; none of which can attend making an old Woman *happy.*

8th & lastly. They are so grateful!!!

Thus much for my Paradox. But still I advise you to **marry** immediately; being sincerely

Your Affectionate Friend,

Benj. Franklin

WHETHER the unknown friend acted on this advice is not known, but we have every reason to believe that Franklin practiced what he preached—especially in France, where his ambassadorial privileges gave him ample opportunity.

BENJAMIN FRANKLIN CONSOLES A RELATIVE ON THE DEATH OF HIS BROTHER

THIS letter was prompted by the death of Franklin's brother John, and was sent to Miss E. Hubbard, daughter (by another marriage) of the second wife of John Franklin. It is another "classic of compassion," and reflects a mood not generally associated with the fame of Benjamin Franklin.

". . . we are soon to follow . . ."

Philadelphia, February 23, 1756.

I CONDOLE with you. We have lost a most dear and valuable relation. But it is the will of God and nature, that these mortal bodies be laid aside, when the soul is to enter into real life. This is rather an embryo state, a preparation for living.

A man is not completely born until he is dead. Why then should we grieve, that a new child is born among the immortals, a new member added to their happy society? We are spirits. That bodies should be lent us, while they can afford us pleasure, assist us in acquiring knowledge, or in doing good to our fellow creatures, is a kind and benevolent act of God. When they become unfit for these purposes, and afford us pain instead of pleasure, instead of an aid become an encumbrance, and answer none of the intentions for which they were given, it is equally kind and benevolent, that a way is provided by which we may get rid of them. Death is

163

that way. We ourselves, in some cases, prudently choose a partial death. A mangled painful limb, which cannot be restored, we willingly cut off. He who plucks out a tooth, parts with it freely, since the pain goes with it; and he, who quits the whole body, parts at once with all pains and possibilities of pains and diseases which it was liable to, or capable of making him suffer.

Our friend and we were invited abroad on a party of pleasure, which is to last for ever. His chair was ready first, and he is gone before us. We could not all conveniently start together; and why should you and I be grieved at this, since we are soon to follow, and know where to find him?

Adieu,

B. Franklin

BENJAMIN FRANKLIN HURLS HIS DEFIANCE AT AN OLD COMRADE

[A LETTER TO WILLIAM STRAHAN]

WILLIAM STRAHAN, the member of British Parliament to whom this letter was addressed, was an old and intimate friend of Benjamin Franklin. Before being elected to the House, Strahan had established himself as the printer of Samuel Johnson's Dictionary and had published the first volumes of Hume's history. Later he published Adam Smith, Gibbon, and Blackstone.

The warm friendship and active transatlantic correspondence between Franklin and Strahan continued for about fourteen years. They regularly sent each other family news. When Franklin's daughter was six or seven, he had humorously planned a marriage between her and Strahan's son, William, then three years older. Franklin usually signed his letters "Your affectionate friend and humble servant." Franklin had visited Strahan frequently in London.

It will be remembered that Franklin did pioneer work in the preliminary stages of the American Revolution as the director of the Committee on Secret Correspondence.* When on the eve of the actual Revolution, his old friend Strahan became a member of Parliament, the letter that follows was written by Franklin in white-heat indignation. As Carl Van Doren says: "Some time during the long day at the Committee of Safety or in Congress, or earlier or later, the thought of Lexington and Bunker Hill came to him, and of his friend who had voted for the measures which led to the battle, and the thought became a letter as in another

* See Thomas Jefferson's letter regarding the Declaration of Independence, on page 167.

man it might have become a lyric. One plain sentence of statement, another of hard accusation, then the third and fourth suddenly throbbed with strong feeling and a bitter image. But the moment of lyric anger passed, and Franklin tempered his sixth and last sentence with his deft conclusion."

"Look upon your hands . . . "

Philad^a July 5, 1775

MR. STRAHAN,
You are a Member of Parliament, and one of that Majority which has doomed my Country to Destruction.—You have begun to burn our Towns and murder our People.—Look upon your hands!—They are stained with the Blood of your Relations!— You and I were long Friends:—You are now my Enemy,—and
I am
Yours,
B. Franklin

ACTUALLY Franklin never mailed the letter to Strahan. Instead, a few days later, Franklin wrote him a friendly letter, and received a cordial answer. Despite the American Revolution, Strahan and his fiery colonial correspondent became boon companions again.

THOMAS JEFFERSON PREPARES TO WRITE THE
DECLARATION OF INDEPENDENCE

[A LETTER TO HIS FRIEND WILLIAM FLEMING]

MANY historians believe that Thomas Jefferson was the greatest mind ever to occupy the White House. For his own epitaph he simply wrote the words: "Author of the Declaration of American Independence, of the Statute of Virginia for Religious Freedom, and Father of the University of Virginia." He completely disregarded his presidential and diplomatic achievements, his democratic struggles with the Federalist group headed by Hamilton, his purchase of Louisiana, and his accomplishments in music, architecture, science, law, medicine, engineering, astronomy, horticulture, mathematics, and literature. He was "a whole man" in addition to being a great one.

In June of the fateful year 1776, Jefferson made the three-hundred-mile journey from his home in Virginia to attend the Continental Congress in Philadelphia. It was an expedition that in those days required ten days of plodding travel through a struggling agricultural countryside. The battles of Lexington, Concord, and Bunker Hill had already been fought. On June 7, 1776, another delegate from Virginia, Richard Henry Lee, introduced his historic resolution, "That these United Colonies are, and of right ought to be, free and independent States." Four days later Thomas Jefferson, John Adams, Benjamin Franklin, Roger Sherman, and Robert R. Livingston were appointed to draft a Declaration based on Lee's resolution. It was Jefferson who did the actual writing—four pages in four days. They changed the course of world history.

In the letter that follows Jefferson describes the military position of

167

the Colonies at the time, and indicates the spirit with which he went about the task of composing the Declaration of Independence*:

"... an effectual stand may be made ..."

Philadelphia, July 1, 1776

DEAR FLEMING
Yours of the 22d June came to hand this morning and gratified me much as this with your former contain interesting intelligence.

Our affairs in Canada go still retrograde, but I hope they are now nearly at their worst. the fatal source of these misfortunes have been want of hard money with which to procure provisions, the ravages of the small pox with which one half of our army is still down, and an unlucky choice of some officers. by our last letters, Genl. Sullivan was retired as far as Isle au noix with his dispirited army and Burgoyne pursuing him with one of double or treble his numbers. it gives much concern that he had determined to make a stand then as it exposes to great danger of losing him & his army; & it was the universal sense of his officers that he ought to retire. Genl. Schuyler has sent him position orders to retire to Crown point but whether they will reach him time enough to withdraw him from danger is questionable. here it seems to be the opinion of all the General officers that an effectual stand may be made & the enemy not only prevented access into New York, but by preserving a superiority on all the lakes we may renew our attacks on them to advantage as soon as our army is recovered from the

* See the biographical note on Thomas Paine, and his influence on Jefferson in the writing of the Declaration, on page 177.

small pox & recruited. but recruits, tho long ordered, are very difficult to be procured on account of that dreadful disorder.

The Conspiracy at New York is not yet thoroughly developed, nor has any thing transpired, the whole being kept secret till the whole is got through. one fact is known of necessity, that one of the General's lifeguard being thoroughly convicted was to be shot last Saturday. General Howe with some ships (we know not how many) is arrived at the Hook, & as is said, has landed some horse on the Jersy shore. the famous major Rogers is in custody on violent suspicion of being concerned in the conspiracy.

I am glad to hear of the Highlanders carried into Virginia. it does not appear certainly how many of these people we have but I imagine at least six or eight hundred. great efforts should be made to keep up the spirits of the people the succeeding three months: which in the universal opinion will be the only ones in which our trial can be severe.

I wish you had depended on yourself rather than others for giving me an account of the late nomination of delegates. I have no other state of it but the number of votes for each person. the omission of Harrison & Braxton & my being next to the lag give me some alarm. it is a painful situation to be 300 miles from one's country, & thereby open to secret assassination without a possibility of self-defence. I am willing to hope nothing of this kind has been done in my case, & yet I cannot be easy. if any doubt has arisen as to me, my country will have my political creed in the form of a 'Declaration' which I was lately directed to draw. this will give decisive proof that my own sentiment concurred with the vote they instructed us to give. had the post been to go a day later we might have been at liberty to communicate this whole matter.

July 2. I have kept open my letter till this morning but nothing more new. Adieu.

Th. Jefferson

169

JEFFERSON's draft of the Declaration of Independence was edited and corrected to some extent by Benjamin Franklin and John Adams. Where Jefferson had written, "We hold these truths to be sacred and undeniable," Franklin substituted "self-evident" for "sacred and undeniable." In the famous opening sentence Jefferson had written, "When in the course of human events it becomes necessary for a people"; Franklin changed the word "a" to "one."

The moment the draft of the Declaration was submitted to the Continental Congress for approval, Benjamin Harrison rose to his feet and said: "There is but one word in this paper which I approve, and that is the word Congress."

After a great deal of spirited discussion pro and con, four hundred words were cut from the first draft. In some cases strong words were changed to weak ones. By the third day, Jefferson, who was somewhat sensitive, said he was "writhing." Benjamin Franklin came to his aid, not only with editorial advice, but with full moral and parliamentary support. Thus the basic structure of the document was retained and its integrity preserved.

On July 4, 1776, the motion for independence was carried and preparations made for the formal signing of the Declaration. Actually, this did not take place until August 2. And so there came into being the "birth certificate of the American nation."

When Jefferson was seventy-three, in the year 1816, he wrote to a friend: "Some men look at constitutions with sanctimonious reverence and deem them like the Ark of the Covenant, too sacred to be touched. They ascribe to the men of the preceding age a wisdom more than human, and suppose what they did to be beyond amendment. I knew that age well; I belonged to it and labored with it. It deserved well of its country. It was very like the present; and forty years of experience in government is worth a century of book reading; and this they would

170

Dear Fleming

Philadelphia July 1. 1776.

THOMAS JEFFERSON TO WILLIAM FLEMING

"... an effectual stand may be made..."

To

Mr William Fleming

free
Th:Jefferson   Williamsburgh.

Th: Jefferson

themselves say, were they to rise from the dead. . . . Laws and institutions must go hand in hand with the progress of the human mind."

On another occasion Jefferson said: "I like a little rebellion now and then. It is like a storm in the atmosphere."

GEORGE WASHINGTON ANSWERS HIS CRITICS IN CONGRESS AND FROM A COLD, BLEAK HILL AT VALLEY FORGE DEFENDS HIS NAKED AND DISTRESSED TROOPS

WHEN the Commander in Chief of the American Revolutionary armies wrote this letter to the Continental Congress just before the fateful Christmas of 1777, he was forty-five years old. The youthful surveyor of Virginia, after his early military triumphs in the French and Indian Wars, threw himself into the struggle of the Colonies with the mother country, and was elected to the First Continental Congress in 1774. The following year he took charge of the colonial forces in the field and guided them through victory in Boston and defeat in New York.

Toward the end of 1776 and early in 1777, Washington achieved his great victories at Trenton and Princeton. Then came the dark and harrowing days, when, after his defeat at the Brandywine, he established winter headquarters at Valley Forge. The camp was "a pesthole of disease, prostitution, and complete demoralization." Most of the soldiers were in rags, and during those terrible months Washington saw all about him "sickness, madness, starvation, and attempted desertion."

At this time the criticism of Washington's leadership grew louder and more clamorous, not only in military circles, but among the populace generally, and in the Continental Congress. It is this "detraction and calumny" which inspired the following letter from General Washington to the assembled delegates back home in Philadelphia:

"... miseries which it is neither in my power to relieve or prevent."

Valley Forge, December 23, 1777.

SIR:

. . . Though I have been tender heretofore of giving any opinion, or lodging complaints, as the change in that department took place contrary to my judgment, and the consequences thereof were predicted; yet, finding that the inactivity of the army, whether for want of provisions, clothes, or other essentials, is charged to my account, not only by the common vulgar but by those in power, it is time to speak plain in exculpation of myself. With truth, then, I can declare that no man in my opinion ever had his measures more impeded than I have, by every department of the army.

. . . As a proof of the little benefit received from a clothier-general, and as a further proof of the inability of an army, under the circumstances of this, to perform the common duties of soldiers . . . we have, by a field-return this day made, no less than two thousand eight hundred and ninety-eight men now in camp unfit for duty, because they are barefoot and otherwise naked. . . . Since the 4th instant, our numbers fit for duty, from the hardships and exposures they have undergone, particularly on account of blankets (numbers having been obliged, and still are, to sit up all night by fires, instead of taking comfortable rest in a natural and common way), have decreased near two thousand men.

We find gentlemen, without knowing whether the army was really going into winter-quarters or not . . . reprobating the measure as much as if they thought the soldiers were made of stocks or stones, and equally insensible of frost and snow. . . .

But what makes this matter still more extraordinary in my eye is, that these very gentlemen,—who were well apprized of the nakedness of the troops from ocular demonstration . . . should think a winter's campaign, and the covering of these States [New Jersey and Pennsylvania] from the invasion of an enemy, so easy and practicable a business. I can assure those gentlemen, that it is a much easier and less distressing thing to draw remonstrances in a comfortable room by a good fireside, than to occupy a cold, bleak hill, and sleep under frost and snow, without clothes or blankets. However, although they seem to have little feeling for the naked and distressed soldiers, I feel superabundantly for them, and, from my soul, I pity those miseries, which it is neither in my power to relieve or prevent.

It is for these reasons, therefore, that I have dwelt upon the subject; and it adds not a little to my other difficulties and distress to find, that much more is expected of me than is possible to be performed, and that upon the ground of safety and policy I am obliged to conceal the true state of the army from public view, and thereby expose myself to detraction and calumny. . . .

George Washington

ON THE Memorial Arch at Valley Forge is this inscription composed by Henry Armitt Brown:

". . . And here in this place of sacrifice, in this vale of humiliation, in this valley of the shadow of that death out of which the life of America rose regenerate and free, let us resolve with an abiding faith that to them Union will seem as dear, and liberty as sweet, and progress as glorious, as they were to our Fathers and are to you and me, and that the Institutions which have made us happy, preserved by the virtue of our children shall bless the remotest generation of the time to come."

GEORGE WASHINGTON SPURNS THE SUBTLE OFFER OF A CROWN

[A LETTER TO COLONEL NICHOLA]

WITHIN four years after Valley Forge, George Washington had led his ragged and untrained troops to victory over the fresh waves of British reinforcements. In 1781 he forced the surrender of General Cornwallis at Yorktown. The "Cincinnatus of the West," the Father of his Country, became "first in war, first in peace, and first in the hearts of his countrymen."

Not long after this epochal triumph, an officer of the Revolutionary Army, one Colonel Nichola, whose first name is not recorded, wrote to his commander in chief, suggesting that the Thirteen Colonies, just consolidated by their successful revolution against the British, could "never become a nation under a Republican form of government," and proposed "the establishment of a kingdom with Washington at the head." Immediately upon receipt of this letter at his headquarters in Newburgh, Washington called his secretary, Jonathan Trumbull, and dictated this reply:

". . . I must view with abhorrence . . ."

Newburgh May 22ᵈ '82

SIR,
    With a mixture of great surprise & astonishment I have read with attention the Sentiments you have submitted to my perusal.— Be assured Sir, no occurrence in the course of the War, has given

175

me more painful sensations than your information of there being such ideas existing in the Army as you have expressed, & I must view with abhorrence, and reprehend with severety—For the present, the communication of them will rest in my own bosom, unless some further agitation of the matter shall make a disclosure necessary.—

I am much at a loss to conceive what part of my conduct could have given encouragement to an address which to me seems big with the greatest mischiefs that can befall my Country.—If I am not deceived in the knowledge of myself, you could not have found a person to whom your schemes are more disagreeable—at the same time in justice to my own feeling I must add, that no man possesses a more sincere wish to see ample justice done to the Army than I do, and as far as my powers & influence, in a constitution, may extend, they shall be employed to the utmost of my abilities to effect it, should there be any occasion—Let me conjure you then, if you have any regard for your Country—concern for yourself or posterity—or respect for me, to banish these thoughts from your mind, & never communicate, as from yourself, or any one else, a sentiment of the like nature.—

> With esteem I am Sir
> Yr Most Obed Ser
> G. Washington

Col Nichola,

A FTER presiding, as a delegate from Virginia, at the Constitutional Convention in 1787, Washington was elected first President of the United States in 1789, and was re-elected, against his will, in 1792. He retired to his estates in 1797 and died there in 1799, leaving no children.

176

THOMAS PAINE BRANDS GEORGE WASHINGTON
AS TREACHEROUS IN PRIVATE FRIENDSHIP
AND A HYPOCRITE IN PUBLIC LIFE

B ENJAMIN FRANKLIN declared, "Where Liberty is, there is my country." To this, Thomas Paine replied, "Where Liberty isn't, there is
mine."

Paine was a born liberator, to his dying day an implacable enemy of
tyranny. He carried on his inspired pamphleteering so courageously, so
uncompromisingly, so brilliantly, both in America and in France, that he
became literally the revolutionary "hero of two worlds." He was "the
North Star" of the new American republic, actually one of the Founding
Fathers, and indeed the author of the phrase "The United States of
America."

Born in England in 1737, he met Benjamin Franklin in London when
the visiting Philadelphian was "taken with those wonderful eyes of his."
In his youth Paine had run away to sea, and in early manhood had
gone bankrupt as a tobacco merchant. Franklin persuaded him to
come to America, then seething with revolutionary conspiracies and
aspirations.

Paine arrived in 1775, during a period he described in the immortal
phrase "the times that try men's souls." A year later he was in the fore-
front of the fight. He wrote a classic manifesto, Common Sense, which
became a truly epochal best-seller, with half a million copies distributed
in short order. Jefferson, Washington, and John Adams read this pamphlet; Congress voted him $3000 for his pamphleteering services, and
the state of New York awarded him three hundred acres of land. The
propaganda caught fire throughout the land; the militant phrases did

their work, and were reflected almost immediately in the Declaration of Independence.*

In 1787, a few years after the Colonies had won their fight, Paine went to England as a bridge designer. The French Revolution drew him like a magnet. When Edmund Burke viewed the Terror with alarm, Paine answered him boldly with another classic of pamphleteering, The Rights of Man. For this ringing declaration he had to flee England but was rewarded with honorary membership in the French Assembly, together with Washington, Priestley, and Kosciusko.

When Paine wrote The Age of Reason, Robespierre had him thrown into the Luxembourg (which was temporarily serving as a prison), largely because it was a plea for a "reasoned religion." The orthodox, however, deemed the pamphlet heretical, and a hundred years later Theodore Roosevelt denounced Paine as "a filthy little atheist." The American minister to France, Gouverneur Morris, an aristocrat of the old school who feared and hated radicals like Paine, refused to help him. He languished in prison for ten months. For what he regarded as deliberate treachery and ingratitude on the part of the republic he helped to establish, Paine held not merely Morris, but George Washington himself, directly responsible, and he therefore addressed the following masterpiece of vituperation directly to his erstwhile friend, then serving his second term as President:

"... deceitful, if not even perfidious."

Paris, July 30th, 1796.

AS CENSURE is but awkwardly softened by apology, I shall offer you no apology for this letter. The eventful crisis to

* See Thomas Jefferson's letter on the writing of the Declaration, on page 167.

178

which your double politics have conducted the affairs of your country, requires an investigation uncramped by ceremony.

There was a time when the fame of America, moral and political, stood fair and high in the world. The lustre of her revolution extended itself to every individual, and to be a citizen of America gave a title to respect in Europe. . . . The Washington of politics had not then appeared. . . . I declare myself opposed to several matters in the constitution, particularly to the manner in which, what is called the Executive, is formed. . . . I also declare myself opposed to almost the whole of your administration; for I know it to have been deceitful, if not even perfidious. . . .

It was very well said . . . that "thirteen staves and never a hoop will not make a barrel," and as any kind of hooping the barrel, however defectively executed, would be better than none, it was scarcely possible but that considerable advantages must arise from the federal hooping of the States. It was with pleasure that every sincere friend to America beheld as the natural effect of union, her rising prosperity, and it was with grief they saw that prosperity mixed, even in blossom, with the germ of corruption. Monopolies of every kind marked your administration almost in the moment of its commencement. The lands obtained by the revolution were lavished upon partizans; injustice was acted under pretence of faith; and the chief of the army became the patron of the fraud. From such a beginning what else could be expected, than what has happened? A mean and servile submission to the insults of one nation; treachery and ingratitude to another. The fugitives have found protection in you. . . .

As the federal constitution is a copy, though not quite so base as the original, of the form of the British Government, an imitation of its vices was naturally to be expected.

The part I acted in the American revolution is well known; I shall not here repeat it. I know also that had it not been for the aid received from France in men, money and ships, that your cold and unmilitary conduct, as I shall show in the course of this letter, would, in all probability have lost America; at least she would not have been the independent nation she now is. You slept away your time in the field till the finances of the country were exhausted, and you have but little share in the glory of the final event. It is time, sir, to speak the undisguised language of historical truth.

Elevated to the Presidency you assumed the merit of every thing to yourself, and the natural ingratitude of your constitution began to appear. You commenced your Presidential career by encouraging and swallowing the grossest adulation, and you travelled America from one end to the other, to put yourself in the way of receiving it. You have as many addresses in your chest as James the II. As to what were your views, for if you are not great enough to have ambition you are little enough to have vanity, they cannot be directly inferred from expressions of your own; but the partizans of your politics have divulged the secret.

John Adams has said, (and John it is known was always a speller after places and offices, and never thought his little services were highly enough paid)—John has said, that as Mr. Washington had no child, the Presidency should be made hereditary in the family of Lund Washington. John might then have counted upon some sinecure for himself, and a provision for his descendants. He did not go so far as to say, also, that the Vice Presidency should be made hereditary in the family of John Adams. He prudently left that to stand, on the ground that one good turn deserves another. . . . The right to set up and establish hereditary government . . . is of a degree beyond treason; it is a sin against nature. The equal rights of every generation is a fixed right in the nature of things; it belongs to the son when of age, as it belonged to the father before him. . . .

John Jay has said, (and this John was always the sycophant of every thing in power, from Mr. Girard in America to Grenville in

England)—John Jay has said, that the Senate should have been appointed for life. He would then have been sure of never wanting a lucrative appointment for himself, and have had no fears about impeachment. . . .

I began to find that I was not the only one who had conceived an unfavorable opinion of Mr. Washington; it was evident that his character was on the decline as well among Americans, as among foreigners of different nations. From being the chief of the government, he had made himself the chief of a party. . . . The mission of Mr. Jay to London . . . was beginning to be talked of. . . .

In the year 1790, or about that time, Mr. Washington, as President, had sent Gouverneur Morris to London, as his secret agent. . . . If, while Morris was minister in France, he was not an emissary of the British ministry and the coalesced powers, he gave strong reason to suspect him of it. . . . Morris still loiters in Europe, chiefly in England; and Mr. Washington is still in correspondence with him. Mr. Washington ought, therefore, to expect, especially since his conduct in the affairs of Jay's treaty, that France must consider Morris and Washington as men of the same description. The chief difference, however, between the two is, (for in politics there is none) that one is profligate enough to profess an indifference about moral principles, and the other is prudent enough to conceal the want of them. . . . Errors, or caprices of the temper, can be pardoned and forgotten; but a cold, deliberate crime of the heart, such as Mr. Washington is capable of acting, is not to be washed away. . . .

The character which Mr. Washington has attempted to act in this world, is a sort of non-describable, camelion-colored thing, called prudence. It is, in many cases, a substitute for principle, and is so nearly allied to hypocrisy, that it easily slides into it. . . .

The first account that arrived in Paris of a treaty being negotiated by Mr. Jay, (for nobody suspected any) came in an English news-paper, which announced that a treaty, *offensive* and *defensive* had been concluded between the United States of America and England. This was immediately denied . . . but at length the treaty itself arrived. . . . The party papers of that imbecile administration were on this occasion filled with paragraphs about sovereignty. A paltroon may boast of his sovereign right to let another kick him, and this is the only kind of sovereignty shown in the treaty with England. . . .

The Washington administration shows great desire that the treaty between France and the United States be preserved. Nobody can doubt its sincerity upon this matter. There is not a British minister, a British merchant, or a British agent, or factor, in America, that does not anxiously wish the same thing. The treaty with France serves now as a passport to supply England with naval stores, and other articles of American produce; whilst the same articles, when coming to France, are made contraband, or seizable, by Jay's treaty with England. . . . It is too paltry to talk of faith, of national honor, and of the preservation of treaties, whilst such a barefaced treachery as this stares the world in the face.

The Washington administration may save itself the trouble of proving to the French government its most *faithful* intentions of preserving the treaty with France; for France has now no desire that it should be preserved; she had nominated an envoy extraordinary to America, to make Mr. Washington and his government a present of the treaty, and to have no more to do with *that*, or with *him*. It was at the same time officially declared to the American minister at Paris, *that the French Republic had rather have the American government for an open enemy than a treacherous friend.* This, sir, with the internal distractions caused in America, and the loss of character in the world, is the *eventful crisis* alluded to in the begin-ning of this letter. . . .

182

A stranger might be led to suppose, from the egotism with which Mr. Washington speaks, that himself, and himself only, had generated, conducted, completed, established, the revolution. In fine, that it was all his own doing. . . . Mr. Washington's merit consisted in constancy. . . .

But when we speak of military character, something more is to be understood than constancy; and something more ought to be understood than the Fabian system of doing nothing.—The nothing part can be done by any body. Old Mrs. Thompson, the house-keeper of head quarters (who threatened to make the sun and the wind shine through Rivington of New York) could have done as well as Mr. Washington. Deborah would have been as good as Barak.

Mr. Washington had the nominal rank of Commander in Chief; but he was not so in fact. . . . He had no control over, or direction of, the army to the northward, under Gates, that captured Burgoyne, nor of that of the south, under Green, that recovered the southern States. The nominal rank, however, of Commander in Chief, served to throw upon him the lustre of those actions, and to make him appear as the soul and centre of all the military operations in America. . . .

When the revolution of America was finally established . . . the minister *penitentiary*, (as some of the British prints called him) Mr. Jay, was sent on a pilgrimage to London, to make all up by penance and petition. . . . The commerce of America, so far as it had been established, by all the treaties that had been formed prior to that by Jay, was free. . . . The commerce of America is, by Jay's treaty, put under foreign dominion. There never was such a base and servile treaty of surrender, since treaties began to exist. . . .

And as to you, sir, treacherous to private friendship (for so you have been to me, and that in the day of danger) and a hypocrite in public life, the world will be puzzled to decide whether you are an apostate or an impostor, whether you have abandoned good principles, or whether you ever had any?

Thomas Paine

P‍AINE'S release from prison was effected finally through the good offices of the new American minister, James Monroe. In 1802, with his friend Jefferson as President, Paine's attitude toward the new American nation changed, and he returned to the United States. But the patriots denounced him for denouncing orthodoxy, the politicians for denouncing Washington. In New Rochelle, where he made his home, he was even denied the right to vote. Lonely, forsaken, burdened with debts, he died in 1809 at the age of seventy-two.

ROBESPIERRE PROMISES DANTON DEVOTION
UNTO DEATH

THOSE two bloodstained friends and enemies, Robespierre and Danton, were lawyers by training, revolutionary leaders by profession, and both heroes and victims of the Reign of Terror. They were born a year apart and died within a few months of each other—both on the guillotine.

When the French Revolution began in 1789, Maximilien François Marie Isidore de Robespierre, then thirty-one years old, was a deputy to the Estates-General, and Georges Jacques Danton, thirty, was a high officer in the National Guard. They were intimate and loyal companions, comrades-in-arms of the Revolution. Danton became administrator of Paris, then minister of justice; his rival organized and directed the Terror and became dictator of the young republic.

When Danton's wife died, leaving her husband the prey of grief "as excessive as were all his other emotions," Robespierre was still his loyal friend. It was on this occasion that he sent him this tender expression of sympathy and undying devotion:

"Let us weep together . . ."

MY DEAR DANTON,
If, in the only sorrow that can overwhelm a spirit like yours, the knowledge that you have the devotion and tender sympathy of a friend affords you any consolation, I offer you mine. I

185

love you more than ever and until death. At this moment I am one with you. Do not shut your heart to the voice of a friendship which shares all your grief. Let us weep together for our friends and let us before long demonstrate the effects of our sorrow to the tyrants who are the cause of our public ills and private woes. My friend, I have written these words that spring from my heart to you from Belgium. I should already have come to see you except that I respected the first moments of your great affliction.

Your friend,

Robespierre

L ESS than a year after this affectionate letter, the friends became enemies, fighting ruthlessly for control of the Committee of Public Safety, established by the incorruptible Robespierre. Danton, the idol of the people, though serving on the Revolutionary Tribunal and voting for the King's death, refused to go all the way with Robespierre. It was Danton, the warmhearted, violent extremist, whose phrase "de l'audace, encore de l'audace, toujours de l'audace" became the inflammatory catchword of the Revolution; and it was Danton, the posturing hero, who was sent to the guillotine on April 6, 1794, by the express command of his old comrade Robespierre, who had but recently written his friend a compassionate letter of grief and devotion.

Danton's death warrant proved to be Robespierre's own undoing. Four short and terrible months later the incorruptible Robespierre, accused of acquiring too much power for himself, was executed in his thirty-sixth year by order of his own Committee of Public Safety.

JOSEPH PRIESTLEY RETURNS BLESSINGS FOR CURSES IN A LETTER TO HIS NEIGHBORS OF BIRMINGHAM

Nonconformist minister, scientist, and politician, Joseph Priestley was an uncompromising dissenter both in chemical research and religion. The world-famous chemist and discoverer of oxygen, nitric oxide, and sulphur dioxide always made things hard for himself not only by his unorthodox views, but by his bold way of proclaiming them.

He was born in 1733 and lived in Birmingham. When Edmund Burke denounced the Terror in his Reflections on the French Revolution, Priestley opposed him so vehemently that he was made a citizen of the French Republic. Incensed at his heresy, the jingoes of eighteenth-century Birmingham burned Priestley's house and chapel to the ground. His laboratory was demolished, his library was sacked, and many priceless and irreplaceable manuscripts were destroyed. Immediately after this shocking act of vandalism, Priestley addressed this letter to his fellow citizens of Birmingham:

"... we are the sheep and you the wolves."

London, July 19, 1791.

My LATE Townsmen and Neighbours,
After living with you eleven years, in which you had uniform experience of my peaceful behaviour, in my attention to the quiet duties of my profession, and those of philosophy, I was far

187

from expecting the injuries which I and my friends have lately received from you. But you have been misled. By hearing the Dissenters, and particularly the Unitarian Dissenters, continually railed at, as enemies to the present government, in church and state, you have been led to consider any injury done to us as a meritorious thing; and not having been better informed, the means were not attended to.

When the *object* was right, you thought the *means* could not be wrong. By the discourses of your teachers, and the exclamations of your superiors in general, drinking confusion and damnation to us (which is well known to have been their frequent practice) your bigotry has been excited to the highest pitch, and nothing having been said to you to moderate your passions, but every thing to inflame them; hence, without any consideration on your part, or on theirs, who ought to have known, and taught you better, you were prepared for every species of outrage; thinking that whatever you could do to spite and injure us, was for the support of government, and especially the church. In *destroying* us, you have been led to think, you *did God* and your country the most substantial *service*.

Happily, the minds of Englishmen have an horror of *murder*, and therefore you did not, I hope, think of *that*. . . . But what is the value of life, when every thing is done to make it wretched? . . .

You have destroyed the most truly valuable and useful apparatus of philosophical instruments that perhaps any individual, in this or any other country, was ever possessed of, in my use of which I annually spent large sums, with no pecuniary view whatever, but only in the advancement of science, for the benefit of my country and of mankind. You have destroyed a library corresponding to that apparatus, which no money can re-purchase, except in a long course of time. But what I feel far more, you have destroyed *manuscripts*, which have been the result of the laborious study of many years, and which I shall never be able to re-compose;

and this has been done to one who never did, or imagined, you any harm. . . .

You are still more mistaken, if you imagine that this conduct of yours has any tendency to serve your cause, or to prejudice ours. It is nothing but *reason* and *argument* that can ever support any system of religion. Answer our arguments, and your business is done; but your having recourse to *violence*, is only a proof that you have nothing better to produce. Should you destroy myself, as well as my house, library, and apparatus, ten more persons, of equal or superior spirit and ability, would instantly rise up. If those ten were destroyed, an hundred would appear. . . .

. . . In this business we are the sheep and you the wolves. We will preserve our character, and hope you will change yours. At all events, we return you blessings for curses; and pray that you may soon return to that industry, and those sober manners, for which the inhabitants of Birmingham were formerly distinguished.

I am, your sincere well-wisher,

J. Priestley

Because of this catastrophe, Priestley quit Birmingham for London. He stayed there for three years and then sailed for America. On his arrival in New York, he was enthusiastically acclaimed. Priestley spent the remainder of his life writing a church history and carrying on chemical experiments in Northumberland, Pennsylvania, dying there in 1804. Few Englishmen did more for the advancement of science in the eighteenth century.

THE LOVES AND LETTERS
OF NAPOLEON BONAPARTE

[A CYCLE OF CORRESPONDENCE, CHIEFLY WITH
THE EMPRESS JOSEPHINE, THE COUNTESS MARIE
WALEWSKA, AND THE EMPRESS MARIE LOUISE,
FROM 1796 TO 1814]

THE "Napoleon industry" rivals, perhaps even exceeds, the research and literature devoted to Shakespeare. In range and intensity it is outranked only by the study and criticism devoted to the life and teachings of Jesus.

Approximately 30,000 books about Napoleon are actually indexed in the libraries of the world—and this is a conservative estimate. The Corsican is reputed to have written or dictated somewhere between 55,000 and 75,000 letters and dispatches. Many of these were burned in Russia, but altogether 41,000 have been printed. New ones are always coming to light. Fresh interpretations and new books are constantly pouring from the presses.

In this anthology only a few representative or significant samples can be given. It would require a battalion of encyclopedic volumes, rank on rank deployed, to chronicle the whole cycle of Napoleonic correspond-ence. The love letters to Josephine alone would make a bulky series of books, ranging from the first note "offering friendship" to the last one telling Josephine that he hears she "is getting fat as a Norman farmer's good wife." Laurence Stallings has observed that "somewhere between that first faltering letter from a little sawed-off subordinate general of the Republican army and that last disdainful note from the Emperor of the French lie sixty pitched battles, millions of screaming men, and an incredible human folly."

Through the dangers of military campaigns and the hazards of passing amours, Napoleon remained the lover of Josephine. From the first mo-ment he met her, when he was an unknown penniless subaltern, and she a widow of thirty-two, not beautiful, but of elegant and distinguished bearing, his emotional life was more or less dominated by his love for her. Neither perils of war nor affairs of state affected the frequency of his letters. Even after his divorce from Josephine, necessitated by his desire for an heir to the throne, a tender affection remained. In his letters to Josephine, we find the great conqueror exulting in his conquest of "an incomparable treasure." His love letters to Josephine have been described by Hendrik Willem van Loon as "boyish shouts from a love-sick youngster who simply could not believe his own luck in having captured such a prize."

These, then, are the amatory footnotes to the thirty thousand books written about the "world's greatest traveling man of slaughter."

NAPOLEON CELEBRATES THE CONQUEST OF JOSEPHINE BY SETTING FORTH ON THE CONQUEST OF ITALY

IN MARCH, 1796, Marie Rose Josephine Tascher de la Pagerie, the thirty-three-year-old daughter of a lieutenant of artillery, consented to marry "a thin, impecunious, and irrepressible suitor" from Corsica, named Napoleon Bonaparte. He was then a rising young officer of the French Army, who had won recognition from the Revolutionary Convention by effectively dispersing the malcontents of the French capital on the famous day of 13 Vendémiaire—October 5, 1795. She was "a languid Creole beauty," born in Martinique, and the widow of an ex-noble, the Vicomte de Beauharnais, who had been executed by the Jacobins. At the time of her marriage to Napoleon, she was not only one of the queens of Parisian society—vivacious, extravagant, pleasure loving—but also an intimate friend of the powerful Barras.

This was the woman who, in Napoleon's own words, inspired him "with a love that has taken away my reason—I can't eat. I can't sleep. I don't care for my friends. I don't care for glory. I value victory only because it pleases you. . . . You have filled me with a limitless love . . . an intoxicating frenzy. . . ."

Shortly thereafter, in his twenty-seventh year, Napoleon was designated by the Directory as general in chief of the Army of Italy, a capacity in which he was to liberate that unhappy country from the Austrian yoke. Two days after the marriage, Napoleon set out for his Italian command. Josephine remained behind to enjoy the pleasures of Paris. Time after time, Napoleon, full of longing of his adored wife, sent for her to come to him, but she chose to abide by the order of the Directory that she should not distract General Bonaparte from his duties. In fact, she rarely answered her husband's letters. When he reached Milan, however, the ban was lifted, and she joined him there.

"I hope before long to crush you in my arms . . ."

Verona, November 13th, 1796

I DON'T love you, not at all; on the contrary, I detest you— You're a naughty, gawky, foolish Cinderella. You never write me; you don't love your husband; you know what pleasure your letters give him, and yet you haven't written him six lines, dashed off casually!

What do you do all day, Madam? What is the affair so important as to leave you no time to write to your devoted lover? What affection stifles and puts to one side the love, the tender and constant love you promised him? Of what sort can be that marvelous being, that new lover who absorbs every moment, tyrannizes over your days, and prevents your giving any attention to your husband? Josephine, take care! Some fine night, the doors will be broken open, and there I'll be.

Indeed, I am very uneasy, my love, at receiving no news of you; write me quickly four pages, pages full of agreeable things which shall fill my heart with the pleasantest feelings.

I hope before long to crush you in my arms and cover you with a million kisses burning as though beneath the equator.

Bonaparte

NAPOLEON TELLS JOSEPHINE OF HIS LONELINESS

O<small>N HIS</small> Italian campaign Napoleon began to realize Josephine's essential "shallowness and frivolity." Though the passion cooled, an affectionate regard remained, and the more or less one-sided correspondence continued unabated. Before he returned from his Egyptian campaign he became suspicious of Josephine's friendship with an officer, M. Charles, and began thinking of a divorce. But "tears and entreaties brought a reconciliation," and biographers are agreed that up to the year 1804 "their relations were on the whole happy." With respect to their disagreements and quarrels, Napoleon said in later years, "Generally I had to give in." In a typical letter from Verona in 1797, Napoleon wrote, ". . . I give you a thousand kisses; I am very well. We have had only ten men killed and a hundred wounded.—Bonaparte."

". . . your husband alone is very, very unhappy."

Milan, November 27th, 1796, three o'clock afternoon.

I ARRIVE at Milan, I rush to your apartment, I have left everything to see you, to press you in my arms . . . You were not there: you run from town to town after the fêtes; you leave as I am about to arrive; you do not concern yourself about your dear Napoleon any more. It was a caprice that caused you to love him; inconstancy makes him indifferent to you. Accustomed to dangers, I know the remedy for the ennuis and evils of life. The ill-fortune I experience is beyond reckoning; I should have been exempt.

195

I shall be here until the evening of the 9th. Do not put yourself out; run the round of pleasures; happiness is made for you. The whole world is too happy if it can please you, and your husband alone is very, very unhappy.

Bonaparte

NAPOLEON CLAMORS FOR MAIL FROM JOSEPHINE

Fɪʀsᴛ Consul of France for life and now elevated to Emperor, Napoleon acceded to Josephine's wish and was remarried to her with due religious pomp and full splendor on December 1, 1804, at the height of his glory. With a calculating eye to the future, the canny Napoleon outwitted his vigilant wife and deliberately left out one formality from the ceremony. No parish priest was present. Six years later this technicality made a divorce possible. But in her moment of "radiant triumph," on the eve of the historic coronation at Notre-Dame, Josephine was blissfully unaware of this detail. She was exulting triumphantly over a host of envious relatives. At this time he intensified his victorious campaigning against the coalition of European nations. The battles of Trafalgar and Austerlitz were behind him; Jena was yet to come. Deeply involved in foreign wars and malice domestic, intriguing for the control of Europe, he somehow found time for this sort of epistolary dalliance with Josephine. From Malmaison he wrote in June, 1803, ". . . the weather is very fine. I beg you to believe that nothing is more genuine than the feelings I have for my little Josephine. All thine—B."

"Deign, from the height of your grandeur ..."

Brünn
December 19th, 1805.

GREAT EMPRESS, not a letter from you since your departure from Strassburg. You have been to Baden, to Stuttgart, to Munich, without writing us one word. That is not very amiable nor very tender. I am still at Brünn. The Russians have gone; I have made a truce. In a few days I shall see what I am going to be. Deign, from the height of your grandeur, to trouble yourself a little about your slaves.

Napoleon

NAPOLEON TELLS JOSEPHINE WHY HE HATES INTRIGUING WOMEN

AFTER the decisive battle of Jena and the temporary capitulation of western Europe, Napoleon was planning new conquests in the East. The Russian Empire was a challenge that he had to answer. Josephine, perhaps feeling a slight coolness on Napoleon's part, begged to join him, but now he did not want her. Nevertheless, he continued to write with amazing frequency and surprising ardor.

197

". . . I love good, ingenuous, and sweet women;
but it is because they resemble you."

Berlin
November 6th, 1806, 9 o'clock in the evening.

I HAVE received your letter in which you show yourself vexed at certain hard things I say about women*; it is true that beyond all I hate intriguing women. I am accustomed to good, sweet and conciliatory women; they are the ones I love. If they have spoiled me, it is not my fault; but yours. Besides, you will see that I have been very good to one woman who showed herself sensible and good, Madame d'Hatzfeld. When I showed her the letter of her husband, she said to me, sobbing with profound emotion and ingenuously, "Ah, that is indeed his writing!" When she read it, her tone went to my soul; she made me suffer. I said to her: "Ah! well, Madame, throw that letter into the fire; I shall never now be able to order your husband to be punished!" She burned the letter and seemed to me very happy. Her husband is now freed of anxiety. Had the above meeting occurred two hours later it would have been too late. You see that I love good, ingenuous, and sweet women; but it is because they resemble you.

Adieu, my love; I am well.

Napoleon

* The Empress had shown herself pained because the Queen of Prussia was treated without consideration in the *Bulletin of the Grand Army*.

NAPOLEON IMPLORES THE COUNTESS MARIE WALEWSKA TO HAVE COMPASSION ON HIS HEART

[A SERIES OF THREE NOTES SENT BY COURIER]

ABOUT this time Napoleon began thinking more and more of the East. The idea of "conquering England in India" began to obsess him, and the union of "world dominion hovered before his eyes." To achieve this dream, he realized the necessity of winning Russia's friendship, and for this in turn he needed Poland "as a fulcrum."*

Hence his journey to Warsaw in 1806. Napoleon now began complaining that he was "a lonely man." During the cold winter nights, he wrote passionate and homesick letters to Josephine, assuring her that she was the only woman in his life. About this time he received news that a trifling amatory interlude of the previous winter had given him a bastard son. On this expedition to Poland he first realized that his dynastic hopes were not futile. And here, "in the old palace of Poland's kings . . . ravished by eyes which were pools of Slavic melancholy . . ." he fell in love with Marie Walewska, then eighteen years of age, the daughter of an ancient Polish line so poor that she had been married off to a wealthy old count. At an imperial ball on "the evening of evenings," Napoleon had chosen her as his first and favorite partner in a contradance. He was instantly smitten by her blue eyes, her broken French, her easy grace, her dainty figure, her fair complexion.

The next morning Napoleon wrote her the first of the three brief notes printed in this section and sent it to her by his friend Duroc. There was

* An interesting parallel to the European events of September, 1939.

199

no answer, and as Emil Ludwig remarks, the Emperor, unaccustomed to rebuffs from even princesses and actresses, found "this virginal shrinking the more enchanting." But after two more notes dispatched during the next three days, the young Countess became his devoted mistress, and Napoleon lingered in Poland as one bewitched.

In the words of Emil Ludwig: ". . . the palace, the army, Paris, Europe—let them wait. He, more a slave than any other, refuses today to obey the nature of things; a man of thirty-seven whose wife, well past forty, no longer stirs his passion. Profoundly moved by a girl, twice rebuffed, he must devise lures from his other realms, must tempt her with the freedom of her country, in order that, after nearly a decade of quiescent feeling, he may spread upon the shoulders of a young woman the mantle of his yearning for tranquillity." The Countess Walewska became "his angel . . . the quiet and loving companion whom Napoleon's young soul had sought."

She bore him a son, born in a lonely castle near Warsaw on May 4, 1810. Later he was to become a noted French politician and diplomat under Louis Philippe and a minister of state and senator during the Second Empire. Two years before his death in 1868 he was created a duke, elected to the Academy of Fine Arts, and awarded the Grand Cross of the Legion of Honor. The Countess herself lived to see the Second Empire, and in her later years married a French nobleman. The three Napoleon notes to Marie Walewska follow:

"... I desire only you."

Jan. 1807 [?]

I HAVE seen only you, I have admired only you, I desire only you. A very prompt reply to calm the impatient ardor of

N.

HAVE I displeased you? I hoped the opposite. Or has your first feeling vanished? My passion grows. You rob me of my rest. Vouchsafe a little joy, a little happiness, to the poor heart that would fain worship you! Is it so hard to give me an answer? You now owe me two.

[unsigned]

THERE are moments in life when high position is a heavy burden. That is borne in on me at this moment ... If only you would! None but you can overcome the obstacles which separate us. My friend Duroc will do what he can to make it easy for you. Oh, come, come! All your wishes shall be fulfilled! Your country will even be dearer to me, if you have compassion on my heart.

N.

NAPOLEON TELLS JOSEPHINE NOT TO TRIFLE WITH GLORY

PERHAPS the querulous note in this letter to Josephine is the natural result of Napoleon's romantic attachment to Marie Walewska during his Polish campaign, while he was marking time to have his try at Russia. There is perhaps some psychological significance in his reference to children.

". . . your heart is excellent, and your reason weak . . ."

[1807]

MY LOVE, your letter of January 20th disturbed me; it is too sad. Now see, how unfortunate it is not to be a little pious. You tell me that your happiness stands to you in place of glory: that is not magnanimous: you ought to say, the happiness of others stands to me in place of glory. It is not being a good wife. You should say: "The happiness of my husband constitutes my glory." It is not maternal; you should say, the happiness of my children constitutes my glory; seeing that the people, your husband, your children, cannot be happy without a trifle of glory, why flout it so? Josephine, your heart is excellent, and your reason weak; you feel wonderfully, but you don't reason well.

Enough of quarrelling. I want you to be gay, contented with your lot, and obedient, not grumbling and weeping, but gay at heart, and with a spice of good-nature. Adieu, my love; I am leaving to inspect my advance-posts.

Napoleon

NAPOLEON REPRIMANDS AND REASSURES HIS
DISCARDED WIFE

THE Bonaparte family had long been intriguing to bring about Napoleon's divorce from Josephine. It will be recalled that he himself had arranged the formalities of his wedding so that the possibility was always left open. About 1809 his decision to bring about a break became more and more definite. He hungered for a legitimate heir, and his Polish interlude convinced him that he could have one. The fault was clearly Josephine's, as the fair Polish Countess had proved.

Staps' attempted assassination of the Emperor made his eagerness to found a dynasty all the more pronounced. Josephine's continued extravagance, after the "august marriages" of her relatives, aggravated the situation. She complained of the Emperor's "infidelities and growing callousness."

Finally, after the military campaign of 1809, Napoleon announced that "for reasons of state" he was compelled to divorce her. Josephine pleaded in vain. At a "most affecting scene" on the evening of November 30, 1809, the Emperor sternly "held to his resolve." The old marriage of December 1, 1804—at which the parish priest was conveniently absent— was simply and with full technical legality declared null and void in January, 1810. Josephine spent her twilight years "in dignified retirement" at Malmaison, her château near Paris. She died on May 24, 1814.

Meantime Napoleon, with an eye to consolidating his imperial conquests and assuring his dynasty, had, after some hesitation between Vienna and St. Petersburg, chosen the Grand Duchess Marie Louise of Austria. Thus the Emperor Francis saved the tottering Austrian Empire, and the crafty Metternich weakened the Franco-Russian alliance. The marriage ceremony took place at Notre-Dame on April 2, 1810. A son, to become the King of Rome, was born on March 20, 1811.

Although the discarded wife, Josephine, lived to see Napoleon abdicate the throne of France, she never completely lost her affection for him. And he in turn continued to correspond with her, as is proved by this letter written less than three weeks after he had married her successor.

". . . persons like me never change."

Compiègne, April 21, 1810.

MY LOVE, I have received your letter of April 19—it is in a bad style. I am always the same; persons like me never change. I do not know what Eugène has told you. I had not written you because you had not written and because I wished only what should be agreeable to you.

I note with pleasure that you are going to Malmaison and that you are content. I shall be happy to receive news of you, and to give you news of myself. I say no more till you have compared this letter with yours; after that, I shall leave you to judge which is the better or the greater friend, you or I.

Adieu, my love; keep well and be just to yourself and to me.

Napoleon

NAPOLEON LEARNS FROM JOSEPHINE THAT SHE HAS RECOVERED HER HEART

To this letter Josephine replied by reiterating her abiding affection for her ex-husband and Emperor. For the four remaining years of her life, the discarded wife maintained a serene dignity, at times an affectionate and tender gratitude. Many years later he was to return the compliment from his deathbed in St. Helena.

". . . it is my whole heart that speaks."

Navarre, April, 1810.

A THOUSAND, thousand tender thanks for not having forgotten me. My son has just brought me your letter. With what ardor I read it and yet it has taken a deal of time, because there is not a word which has not made me weep; but those tears were very sweet! I have recovered my heart entirely, and such as it will always be; there are feelings which are life itself, and which may not end but with life.

I am in despair that my letter of the 19th should have displeased you; I do not entirely recall the wording; but I know what very painful feeling had dictated it, it was grief at not having a word from you.

I wrote you on leaving Malmaison; and how many times thereafter did I wish to write! But I felt the reasons for your silence, and I feared to seem importunate, by writing. Your letter has been a

205

balm to me. Be happy; be as happy as you deserve; it is my whole heart that speaks. You have given me my share, too, of happiness, and a share very keenly felt; nothing else can have for me the value of a token of remembrance.

Adieu, my friend; I thank you as tenderly as I shall love you always.

Josephine

NAPOLEON DIVULGES A SECRET TO HIS EMPRESS, MARIE LOUISE

SHORTLY after his marriage to Marie Louise in 1810, Napoleon told Metternich that he "was now beginning to live, that he always longed for a home, and now at last had one."

The character of the relationship between Napoleon and his second wife is most graphically revealed by his letters to her. In 1935, three hundred and eighteen of these letters—which for more than a century had been kept secret by the Austrian relatives of Marie Louise—were sold to the French government, and finally released for publication.

Charles de la Roncière, chief custodian of the Bibliothèque Nationale at Paris, has described the story of Napoleon and Marie Louise as that "of a middle-aged man married to a young woman, a dynamic and ego-centric man trying to create from an unformed and naïve girl the figure of an empress. He trusted her with state secrets, even with the regency, and, in the manner of a good bourgeois husband, expected her to be both loyal and clever. She was too weak to be either."

From the mass of letters Napoleon wrote Marie Louise from the battle-fields of Russia, Germany, and France, the editor of this anthology has selected a crucial note that Napoleon wrote to her on a fateful day, March 23, 1814. It was written, like many of his letters, in his tent.

"Adieu, mon amie. A kiss to my son."

March 23, 1814

MON AMIE, I have been in the saddle all the last few days. On the 20th I took Arcis-sur-Aube. The enemy attacked me there at 6* o'clock in the evening; I beat him the same day, killing 400(o). I took 2 of his guns, he took 2 of mine, which leaves us quits. On the 21st, the enemy army formed up in battle array for the purpose of covering the advance of his convoys towards Brienne and Bar-sur-Aube. I decided to make for the Marne and his line of communications, in order to push him back farther from Paris and draw nearer to his fortress. I shall be at Saint-Dizier this afternoon. Adieu, mon amie. A kiss to my son.

Nap

THIS is the famous intercepted letter which led to Napoleon's defeat in the campaign of 1814 and his exile to Elba, costing him the throne of France and the mastery of Europe. For the note, telling of Napoleon's plans to march toward the Marne in order to drive the Allies away from Paris, told Blücher exactly what he needed to know.

When Marie Louise learned that the letter had been intercepted, she wrote to the Duchesse de Montebello: "I have just heard that the courier of the 23rd was captured. What a misadventure! It angers me!" And well

* This has 2 written over it.

it might! The courier was the bearer of extremely important news. Apologizing with ironical politeness for having opened the letter, General Blücher forwarded it to its destination, "laying it at the feet of the August daughter of His Majesty the Emperor of Austria." As de la Roncière says: "The Allies were now fully informed. Napoleon was turning his back to the capital. The road to Paris was free. The tide of invasion promptly swept along it. Minister of Police Savary, to whom Marie Louise related the mishap, failed to discern its frightful consequences; he did not warn the Emperor, but allowed him to be overwhelmed by fatality."

This cycle of letters to Marie Louise closes with a note from Elba apologizing for his exile and both begging and commanding her to join him there—an appeal that was never answered. He threatened her with forcible abduction if she did not obey. She still refused—and the alienation was complete. During the Hundred Days, Marie Louise remained in Vienna and did nothing to help Napoleon in France. She became the mistress, and eventually the morganatic wife, of Count von Neïpperg, who helped her escape from France to Austria with her son at the time of Napoleon's first abdication. Toward the end she "shook off all association with Napoleon." He spoke of her in his will "with marked tenderness" and both "excused and forgave her infidelity." She outlived him by twenty-six years and died in Vienna in 1847.

As for Napoleon, at the time of this intercepted letter, Elba, Waterloo, St. Helena were just ahead. . . . The last words he uttered were "France! . . . Armée! . . . Tête d'armée . . . Joséphine!"

THE DEVOTIONS AND DESPAIRS
OF LUDWIG VAN BEETHOVEN

[A SERIES OF LETTERS TO HIS "IMMORTAL BE-
LOVED" AND HIS BROTHERS KARL AND JOHANN]

How Ludwig van Beethoven could possibly have found time to write any letters at all is one of the mysteries of his genius. It would seem that the creation of his nine symphonies, his thirty-two sonatas, his violin and piano concertos, his Masses, his grand opera, and his cycles of songs and chamber music could not have left free hours for anything else. But by some miracle he managed to find time for the more human and more tragic necessities—such as loneliness, despair, and love—and when he did he poured out his heart in letters.

In his music Beethoven showed an exacting discipline, a rigorous economy of means. But in his private correspondence he simply babbled. His anguish was not hammered out like a symphony. It gushed.

These wild and tempestuous letters, interpreted in the light of the masterpieces he was creating at the time, unlock his secret. Reading them and reliving this music, we can begin to appreciate how Beethoven triumphed over massed battalions of sufferings and misfortunes. We begin to realize how he could at long last attain (as in his last quartets and in the "Choral" Symphony) a world-embracing and yea-saying serenity. In the continuous, organic, and gloriously ascending spiritual development of Beethoven's life, his letters and his conversation books offer a mass of relevant testimony. His greatest biographers—especially Newman, Thayer, and Sullivan—have all remarked on this. Only with this evidence can we fully understand Beethoven's growth from youthful genius through mature heroism to ultimate synthesis.

Against such a background the bare facts of Beethoven's life fall into perspective. He was born in 1770; he studied under Haydn; he conquered Vienna and the world of music in his early manhood; he struggled with sorrows and maladies most of his years; he brought the symphony to its supreme perfection; he died in 1827.

Wallace Brockway and Herbert Weinstock have put it succinctly and eloquently in Men of Music: "Beethoven could not be content merely to write music: unrest was in his soul, and doubt which in its savage intensity made the polite skepticism of the eighteenth century seem puny. Thought pursued him like a nemesis—he could not get away from it. His wrestling with destiny, not only his own but that of mankind, is one of the great epics of the modern world: he told it in a succession of mighty works which, in their boundless humanity and immediacy of appeal, have never been equaled.

"By his struggles, Beethoven became one of the heroes of mankind; by his triumphs, he has become one of its prophets. He was born at one of those strange moments of history when nature spews forth genius with an inexplicable lavishness. The time was, for better or worse, fateful for the shaping of life and art. . . . Beethoven alone had the strength and integrity to die as he had lived—faithful to the daemon that had moved him. His life has been painted as a tragedy, but he had the only kind of success that could really have mattered to him."

LUDWIG VAN BEETHOVEN PLEDGES HIS HEART
TO THE "IMMORTAL BELOVED"

T HESE outpourings of a tortured and romantic spirit were found in a
cashbox, together with some bonds, after Beethoven's death. They
form a series of three letters that were never actually sent.

Short, massive, uncouth, outwardly misanthropic, racked by suffering
and handicapped by a growing deafness, Beethoven was nevertheless
idealistic in his adoration of women, a romantic dreamer of dreams, and
deeply passionate by nature. Many of the ladies returned the compliment.
His improvisations were not confined to the piano.

The exact identity of the "Immortal Beloved" to whom these letters
were addressed is still a matter of conjecture. Precise proof is impossible,
but the choice narrows down to three candidates: the Countess Giulietta
Guicciardi, to whom the "Moonlight" Sonata was dedicated; her cousin,
Therese von Brunswick, and Bettina Brentano von Arnim. Some biographers hold that she may have been any one of a dozen others. No less
an authority than Vincent d'Indy favored Giulietta Guicciardi.

At any rate, we have reason to believe that Giulietta, "the little minx
of seventeen," was an inspiration to Beethoven, in a vague romantic sort
of way, for a large part of his life, even after they had ceased to meet. To
him, "She epitomized all that was denied to him forever—beauty, charm,
social security, and poise."

Beethoven's romantic attachments have been summed up graphically:
Beethoven believed passionately in marriage and longed for the comfort
and companionship of his own home. Whether he remained unmarried
because no woman of the type he cared for would consider the stormy,
self-willed boor that he outwardly seemed to be; or because he was frustrated by some deep-rooted maladjustment; or because his deafness and

his genius set him apart from the conventional way of life—that is one of the mysteries always associated with one of the supreme geniuses of all time.

Regardless of the identity of the "Immortal Beloved," the letters here quoted obviously spring from a full heart—and one that had known joy.

At the age of twenty-two, in 1792, Beethoven went to Vienna to study under "Papa" Haydn. The following eight years were perhaps the happiest in his life. He was a favorite in aristocratic society, a lover of nature, good food, and companionable drinking, an all-conquering virtuoso, and a growing young composer.

Toward the turn of the century, first slight signs of deafness appeared. The dark years, the solitary years, the titanic symphonies, the hammer-blows of fate were still ahead—but there were signs and portents. About this time, in his thirty-first year, not long after his first public concert, featuring the First Symphony and the Septet for Strings and Wind Instruments, he put down on paper, but for some reason apparently never mailed, these three love letters to an unidentified inamorata:

"... ever thine, ever mine, ever for each other."

July 6, in the morning [1801]

MY ANGEL, my all, my very self—only a few words today and at that with pencil (with yours)—not till tomorrow will my lodgings be definitively determined upon—what a useless waste of time. Why this deep sorrow where necessity speaks—can our love endure except through sacrifices—except through not demanding everything—can you change it that you are not wholly mine, I not wholly thine.

212

Oh, God! look out into the beauties of nature and comfort your-self with that which must be—love demands everything and that very justly—*thus it is with me so far as you are concerned, and you with me.* If we were wholly united you would feel the pain of it as little as I. My journey was a fearful one; I did not reach here until 4 o'clock yesterday morning; lacking horses the post coach chose another route—but what an awful one.

At the stage before the last I was warned not to travel at night—made fearful of a forest, but that only made me the more eager and I was wrong; the coach must needs break down on the wretched road, a bottomless mud road—without such postilions as I had with me I should have stuck in the road. Esterhazy, traveling the usual road hitherward, had the same fate with eight horses that I had with four—yet I got some pleasure out of it, as I always do when I successfully overcome difficulties.

Now a quick change to things internal from things external. We shall soon surely see each other; moreover, I cannot communicate to you the observations I have made during the last few days touching my own life—if our hearts were always close together I would make none of the kind. My heart is full of many things to say to you—Ah!—there are moments when I feel that speech is nothing after all—cheer up—remain my true, my only treasure, my all as I am yours; the gods must send us the rest that which shall be best for us.

Your faithful Ludwig

Evening, Monday, July 6

YOU are suffering, my dearest creature—only now have I learned that letters must be posted very early in the morn-ing. Mondays, Thursdays—the only days on which the mail coach goes from here to K. You are suffering—Ah! wherever I am there you are also. I shall arrange affairs between us so that I shall live and live with you, what a life!!!! thus!!!! thus without you—pursued by the goodness of mankind hither and thither—which I as little try to deserve as I deserve it.

Humility of man toward man—it pains me—and when I consider myself in connection with the universe, what am I and what is he whom we call the greatest—and yet—herein lies the divine in man. I weep when I reflect that you will probably not receive the first intelligence from me until Saturday—much as you love me, I love you more—but do not ever conceal your thoughts from me—good night—as I am taking the baths I must go to bed. Oh, God! so near so far! Is our love not truly a celestial edifice—firm as Heaven's vault.

Good morning, on July 7

THOUGH still in bed my thoughts go out to you, my Immortal Beloved, now and then joyfully, then sadly, waiting to learn whether or not fate will hear us. I can live only wholly with you or not at all—yes, I am resolved to wander so long away from you until I can fly to your arms and say that I am really at home, send my soul enwrapped in you into the land of spirits.—Yes, unhappily it must be so—you will be the more resolved since you know my fidelity—to you, no one can ever again possess my heart—none—never—Oh, God! why is it necessary to part from one whom one so loves and yet my life in W. [Vienna] is now a wretched life—your love makes me at once the happiest and the unhappiest of men—at my age, I need a steady, quiet life—can that be under our conditions? My angel, I have just been told that the mail coach goes every day—and I must close at once so that you may receive the L. at once. Be calm, only by a calm consideration of our existence can we achieve our purpose to live together—be calm—love me—today—yesterday—what tearful longings for you—you—you

214

—my life—my all—farewell—Oh continue to love me—never misjudge the most faithful heart of your beloved L.

ever thine

ever mine

ever for each other

THE fair Giulietta spurned Beethoven and married Count Gallenberg. It was a "crushing blow" to the young composer. . . . Beethoven never married.

The following note by Sir George Grove regarding the Fourth Symphony is significant: "In May of the year in which Beethoven was occupied over this symphony (1806—five years after writing the three letters to his "Immortal Beloved") he became engaged to Countess Thérèse, sister of his intimate friend, Franz von Brunswick. . . . Although Beethoven had often been involved in love affairs, none of them had yet been permanent; certainly he had never before gone so far as an engagement; and when writing the Symphony his heart must have been swelling with his new happiness. It is, in fact, the paean which he sings over his first conquest."

LUDWIG VAN BEETHOVEN PREPARES TO MEET HIS FATE

[THE HEILIGENSTADT TESTAMENT]

Like the letter to his "Immortal Beloved," this moving document known as the "Heiligenstadt Testament" was not found until a year after Beethoven's death. It has been well described as "his tortured hysterical farewell" and like his love letters it was never dispatched but was written to enable Beethoven to unburden his heart. He set it down in 1802, in his thirty-second year, while he was relaxing in the rustic quietude of Heiligenstadt, a village near Vienna. Signs of deafness had first appeared between 1799 and 1800. The first symptom was a slight humming in his ears.

In the "Heiligenstadt Testament," two years later, following futile visits to many doctors, we find him for the time resigned to an acceptance of his affliction as "inevitable and necessary," and his unconquerable spirit soaring on wings of music to things higher than bodily suffering. "He always held his head high even when in pain."

As the calamity of increasing deafness grew nearer and nearer, Beethoven's uneasiness became alarm, then frenzy, then despair, then defiance. But Beethoven was not to stop there. He was not content to exert his heroic will and "clutch fate by the throat." That was "the old morality of power, the language of pride." As J. W. N. Sullivan put it in his masterly study of Beethoven: His Spiritual Development:

". . . Only when the consciously defiant Beethoven has succumbed, only when his pride and strength had been so reduced that he was willing to die and abandon the struggle, did he find that his creative power was indeed indestructible and that it was its deathless energy that made it impossible for him to die. . . . By the end of this summer, he found that his genius, that he had felt called upon to cherish and protect, was really a mighty force using him as a channel or servant. . . ."

At the same time, another element was involved in this strange and tragic letter. According to recent biographies of Beethoven, he went through one dark Aeschylean phase when he believed his deafness was a form of retribution—that it was, in fact, caused by syphilis, the punishment for an old moral lapse being the deprivation of his most prized faculty. There is a considerable body of evidence to support this hypothesis, but it is by no means conclusive.

The radiant, joyous Second Symphony—Hector Berlioz called it "a ravishing picture of innocent pleasure"—was forming in his mind, and already ringing in his ears, as he tramped over the green meadows of Heiligenstadt, and pondered his dark fate. Only thus was he able to pass from crisis, tragedy, and the shadow of death itself to "the greater knowledge beyond."

"... a hot terror seizes upon me ..."

FOR MY BROTHERS KARL AND [JOHANN] BEETHOVEN

O ye men, who think or say that I am malevolent, stubborn, or misanthropic, how greatly do ye wrong me, you do not know the secret causes of my seeming, from childhood my heart and mind were disposed to the gentle feeling of good will, I was even ever eager to accomplish great deeds, but reflect now that for 6 years I have been in a hopeless case, aggravated by senseless physicians, cheated year after year in the hope of improvement, finally compelled to face the prospect of a *lasting malady* (whose cure will take years, or, perhaps, be impossible), born with an ardent and

217

lively temperament, even susceptible to the diversions of society, I was compelled early to isolate myself, to live in loneliness, when I at times tried to forget all this, O how harshly was I repulsed by the doubly sad experience of my bad hearing, and yet it was impossible for me to say to men speak louder, shout, for I am deaf.

Ah how could I possibly admit an infirmity in the *one sense* which should have been more perfect in me than in others, a sense which I once possessed in highest perfection, a perfection such as few surely in my profession enjoy or ever have enjoyed.—O I cannot do it, therefore forgive me when you see me draw back when I would gladly mingle with you, my misfortune is doubly painful because it must lead to my being misunderstood, for me there can be no recreation in society of my fellows, refined intercourse, mutual exchange of thought, only just as little as the greatest needs command may I mix with society.

I must live like an exile, if I approach near to people a hot terror seizes upon me, a fear that I may be subjected to the danger of letting my condition be observed—thus it has been during the last half year which I spent in the country, commanded by my intelligent physician to spare my hearing as much as possible, in this almost meeting my present natural disposition, although I sometimes ran counter to it, yielding to my inclination for society, but what a humiliation when one stood beside me and heard a flute in the distance and *I heard nothing,* or someone heard *the shepherd singing* and again I heard nothing, such incidents brought me to the verge of despair, but little more and I would have put an end to my life—only art it was that withheld me, ah it seemed impossible to leave the world until I had produced all that I felt called upon to produce, and so I endured this wretched existence—truly wretched, an excitable body which a sudden change can throw from the best into the worst state—Patience—it is said I must now choose for my guide, I have done so, I hope my determination will remain firm to endure until it pleases the inexorable Parcae to break the thread, perhaps I shall get better, perhaps not, I am prepared.

Forced already in my 28th year to become a philosopher, O it is not easy, less easy for the artist than for anyone else—Divine One thou lookest into my inmost soul, thou knowest it, thou knowest that love of man and desire to do good live therein. O men, when some day you read these words, reflect that ye did me wrong and let the unfortunate one comfort himself and find one of his kind who despite all the obstacles of nature yet did all that was in his power to be accepted among worthy artists and men. You my brothers Carl and [Johann] as soon as I am dead if Dr. Schmid is still alive ask him in my name to describe my malady and attach this document to the history of my illness so that so far as is possible at least the world may become reconciled with me after my death. At the same time I declare you two to be the heirs to my small fortune (if so it can be called), divide it fairly, bear with and help each other, what injury you have done me you know was long ago forgiven.

To you brother Carl I give special thanks for the attachment you have displayed toward me of late. It is my wish that your lives may be better and freer from care than I have had, recommend *virtue* to your children, it alone can give happiness, not money, I speak from experience, it was virtue that upheld me in misery, to it next to my art I owe the fact that I did not end my life by suicide.

Farewell and love each other—I thank all my friends, particularly *Prince Lichnowsky* and *Professor Schmid*—I desire that the instruments from Prince L. be preserved by one of you but let no quarrel result from this, so soon as they can serve you a better purpose sell them, how glad will I be if I can still be helpful to you in my grave—with joy I hasten toward death—if it comes before I shall have had an opportunity to show all my artistic capacities it will still come too early for me despite my hard fate and I shall probably wish that it had come later—but even then I am satisfied, will it not free me from a state of endless suffering? Come when thou wilt I shall meet thee bravely. Farewell and do not wholly forget me when I am dead. I deserve this of you in having often in life thought of you, how to make you happy, be so—

Ludwig van Beethoven
[Seal]

Heiglnstadt [*sic*],
   October 6th, 1802

For my brothers Carl and [Johann] to be read and executed after my death.

Heiglnstadt, October 10th, 1802, thus do I take my farewell of thee—and indeed sadly—yes that beloved hope—which I brought with me when I came here to be cured at least in a degree—I must wholly abandon, as the leaves of autumn fall and are withered so hope has been blighted, almost as I came—I go away—even the high courage—which often inspired me in the beautiful days of summer—has disappeared—O Providence—grant me at last but one day of pure joy—it is so long since real joy echoed in my heart —O when—O when, O Divine One—shall I find it again in the temple of nature and man—Never? no—O that would be too hard.

THE *Epilogue to this tragic testament consists of an incomparable series of masterpieces that reconstructed the universe of music. . . . Twenty-five years of supreme achievement, his greatest symphonies and songs, creations in every form and mood, were still ahead of him. At the* turning point marked by this letter, Beethoven, by a stupendous effort of will and by sheer elemental fortitude, determined not to be content with either passive resignation or vain and idle protests to an unlistening Providence. He decided quite simply to lift himself by his music beyond physicians, beyond patrons, friends, loved ones, beyond fate itself.

AARON BURR CHALLENGES ALEXANDER HAMILTON TO MEET HIM ON THE FIELD OF HONOR

AMERICAN history was made by this letter. It marks a turning point in the affairs of the new and struggling republic, early in the first decade of the nineteenth century.

Years of mounting antagonism, political and personal, between Alexander Hamilton and Aaron Burr, lay back of this challenge, and the resulting duel had fatal, melodramatic, and far-reaching political results. Aaron Burr had been Vice-President of the United States, was a brilliant lobbyist, a daring adventurer, and politically as ambitious as he was unscrupulous. Hamilton was a man of great personal charm and integrity, the financial genius who as first Secretary of the Treasury had put the new country on its economic feet.

For years, both in private conversation and intimate correspondence with his friends, Hamilton had been assailing Burr. His main weapons were rumor, intrigue, and gossip.

But for Hamilton, Burr might have been President. Receiving equal electoral votes for the vice-presidency and presidency respectively, Burr and Jefferson found their candidacy thrown into the House of Representatives. When the issue hung in the balance, Hamilton's persistent opposition turned the scales in favor of Jefferson. Later in 1804, when Burr sought the governorship of the state of New York, he again found himself opposed by Hamilton. Again Burr was defeated. Once more Burr retaliated by crafty and persistent countermaneuvers.

In his correspondence at about this time, Hamilton referred to Burr as "unprincipled, both as a public and a private man. . . ." Hamilton went on to say of his enemy: "He is determined, as I conceive, to make

AARON BURR TO ALEXANDER HAMILTON

"... you have invited the course I am about to pursue..."

his way to be the head of the popular party, and to climb per fas aut nefas [by hook or crook] to the highest honors of the State, and as much higher as circumstances may permit." This was not all. Hamilton went on to denounce Burr to all and sundry. He said Burr was "without probity," "a voluptuary by system," "a man of extreme and irregular ambition," "selfish to a degree which excludes all social affections, and decidedly profligate."

Finally a letter by one Charles D. Cooper was published in the newspapers, in which he said: "General Hamilton has come out decidedly against Burr; indeed when he was here he spoke of him as a dangerous man and ought not to be trusted. . . . I could detail to you a still more despicable opinion which General Hamilton has expressed of Burr."

At this point, Burr's patience and his secret and indirect retaliation came to an end. The hostility flared out openly, and Burr challenged Hamilton to a duel, as stated in the letter here quoted. The chances are that it was delivered by messenger June 22, 1804, though some authorities believe that it was never sent.

As to Burr's background, it is only necessary to add that he had been a captain, major, and lieutenant colonel in the Revolutionary Army at various times between 1776 and 1779, United States Senator from New York between 1791 and 1797, and third Vice-President of the United States.

The first Secretary of the Treasury, Alexander Hamilton, was born in 1757 at Nevis, British West Indies, the illegitimate offspring of Scotch and French parents. He was educated in the United States, partly at King's College (now Columbia), entering there at the age of seventeen. His brilliant military achievements in the American Revolutionary War and his personal courage won him an appointment on the staff of General George Washington, as confidential aide. At the decisive battle of Yorktown, he led the contingent that overwhelmed the first British defenses. After the war he founded the National Bank and established the young republic's financial credit, an achievement that won him his fame.

He showed moral courage of the highest order by openly publishing the details of his great love affair with Mrs. Reynolds, and thus cleared himself of all charges of having misused government funds. In politics, Alexander Hamilton fought vigorously and brilliantly for a strong central government. He played a prominent part in framing the Constitution and contributed brilliant papers to The Federalist. Hamilton's controversies with the more democratic Jefferson are famous in American history.

"...you have invited the course I am about to pursue..."

N. York June 22ᵈ 1804

SIR

Mr. V. Ness has this evening reported to me verbally that you refuse to answer my last letter, that you consider the course I have taken as intemperate and unnecessary and some other conversation which it is improper that I should notice.

My request to you was in the first instance prepared in a form the most simple in order that you might give to the affair that course to which you might be induced by your temper and your knowledge of facts. I relied with unsuspecting faith that from the frankness of a soldier and the candor of a gentleman I might expect an ingenuous declaration; that if, as I had reason to believe, you had used expressions derogatory to my honor, you would have had the spirit to maintain or the magnanimity to retract them, and, that if from your language injurious inferences had been improperly drawn, sincerity and decency would have pointed out to you the propriety of correcting errors which might then have been widely diffused.

With these impressions, I was greatly disappointed in receiving from you a letter which I could only consider as evasive and which in manner, is not altogether decorous. In one expectation however, I was not wholly deceived, for at the close of your letter I find an intimation, that if I should dislike your refusal to acknowledge or deny the charge, you were ready to meet the consequences. This I deemed a sort of defiance, and I should have been justified if I had chosen to make it the basis of an immediate message: Yet, as you had also said something (though in any opinion unfounded) of the indefiniteness of my request; as I believed that your communication was the offspring, rather of false pride than of reflection, and, as I felt the utmost reluctance to proceed to extremities while any other hope remained, my request was repeated in terms more definite. To this you refuse all reply, reposing, as I am bound to presume on the tender of an alternative insinuated in your letter.

Thus, Sir, you have invited the course I am about to pursue, and now by your silence impose it upon me. If, therefore your determinations are final, of which I am not permitted to doubt, Mr. Van Ness is authorised to communicate my further expectations either to yourself or to such friend as you may be pleased to indicate.

I have the honor to be

Yours respt
A. Burr

THREE weeks after the dispatch of this (or a similar) challenge, on July 11, 1804, the duelists met at sunrise on the cliffs of Weehawken Heights, across the Hudson from New York City. On this exact spot three years before, Hamilton's son, a boy of twenty, had been killed in a duel. Burr and Hamilton faced each other at ten paces. The challenger was forty-eight, his opponent forty-seven.

At the word "Present," which was the signal to fire, Burr fired first, his bullet entering Hamilton's side. Hamilton's shot was either discharged into the air or deliberately withheld, or perhaps even fired by accident. The eyewitness record is not clear. Burr's seconds later swore that Hamilton took deliberate aim, though a post-mortem testament stated that it had been his intention to withhold his fire. At any rate, a shot was fired from Hamilton's pistol, but it did not strike Burr.

The following day Hamilton died of his wound. Burr was indicted for murder but acquitted. About this time, Burr wrote to his son-in-law: "In New York I am to be disenfranchised and in New Jersey hanged. Having substantial objections to both, I shall not, for the present, hazard either, but shall seek another country." He undertook a filibustering expedition from New Orleans to Mexico, and engaged in treasonable conspiracies against the government. He died, an outcast and in disgrace, in 1836, thirty-two years after the fatal duel.

MICHAEL FARADAY APOLOGIZES FOR HIS INABIL-
ITY TO COMPOSE A LOVE LETTER

[A LETTER TO SARAH BARNARD]

THIS undated note from the brilliant physicist, who by his epoch-making researches and experiments paved the way for the application of electricity to modern industry, proves that though one may be able to summon up at will the principles of electrodynamics and the influence of the magnetic field on polarized light, one cannot necessarily synthesize the elements whereof a love letter is made. Michael Faraday lived from 1791 to 1867.

"... fancies swim before me ..."

Royal Institution: Thursday evening.
[December, 1820]

MY DEAR SARAH—It is astonishing how much the state of the body influences the powers of the mind. I have been thinking all the morning of the very delightful and interesting letter I would send you this evening, and now I am so tired, and yet have so much to do, that my thoughts are quite giddy, and run round your image without any power of themselves to stop and admire it. I want to say a thousand kind and, believe me, heartfelt things to you, but am not master of words fit for the purpose; and still, as I ponder and think on you, chlorides, trials, oil, Davy, steel, miscellanea, mercury, and fifty other professional fancies swim before and drive me further and further into the quandary of stupidness.

From your affectionate

Michael

NEVERTHELESS, *shortly after this letter was written, Sarah Barnard became Michael Faraday's devoted wife for many years. Theirs was a notably long and happy marriage.*

THE LOVES AND LETTERS
OF PERCY BYSSHE SHELLEY

[A SERIES COVERING FOUR YEARS]

IN HIS celebrated essay on Shelley, Francis Thompson spoke of "the unteachable folly of a love that made its goal its starting-point and firmly expected spiritual rest from each new divinity, though it had found none from the divinity's antecedent. . . . He left a woman not because he was tired of her arms, but because he was tired of her soul. . . ."

The three letters that follow confirm and illustrate this tendency and shed a wealth of light on the romantic ecstasies and marital adventures of the poet.

MARY GODWIN'S FATHER CONFIDES TO A FRIEND THE SECRET OF "THE SHELLEY SCANDAL"

[A LETTER TO JOHN TAYLOR]

HARRIET WESTBROOK was a schoolgirl of sixteen when she was first attracted to Shelley, then living in penury in London after having been cut off by his father at the age of nineteen. Despite parental objection based on Shelley's reputation as an atheist and radical, they eloped to Edinburgh in 1811. Three years later, Shelley tired of Harriet, when he was attracted to Mary Wollstonecraft Godwin, the beautiful and talented daughter of the noted political writer and freethinker, William Godwin. Harriet spread the slander that Godwin had sold his daughter to Shelley, and unfolded the details of the intrigue in a letter to Catherine Nugent:

"Mary was determined to secure him. She is to blame. She heated his imagination by talking of her mother, and going to her grave with him every day, till at last she told him she was dying in love for him, accompanied with the most violent gestures and vehement expostulations. He thought of me and my sufferings, and begged her to get the better of a passion as degrading to him as to herself. She then told him she would die—he had rejected her, and what appeared to her as the sublimest virtue was to him a crime. Why could we not all live together? I as his sister. She as his wife? He had the folly to believe this possible and sent for me, then residing in Bath. You may suppose how I felt at the disclosure. I was laid up for a fortnight after. I could do nothing for myself. He begged me

230

to live. The doctors gave me over. They said, ' 'twas impos-
possible.' I saw his despair. The agony of my beloved sister; and,
owing to the great strength of my constitution, I lived."

Mary offered to give up Shelley; Shelley tried to commit suicide, but
all three lived, and on July 18, 1814, Mary and Shelley eloped to the
Continent. Two years later Harriet drowned herself in the Serpentine.
The climax of the elopement is described most dramatically in the
following letter from Mary Godwin's father to John Taylor:

". . . a married man . . . has run away with my daughter."

Skinner Street,
Aug. 27, 1814

DEAR SIR
I have a story to tell you of the deepest melancholy. I should
not intrude this story at all upon you, if I could help it: first, because
it is my temper, as far as with convenience I can, to shut up my sorrows in my own bosom, & not disturb all my friends indiscriminately
with matters in which they can afford me no aid; & secondly, because
I am anxious to confine this story to the deepest secrecy, & not by
any indiscretion of mine to allow a breath of it to escape to the
world. . . . You are already acquainted with the name of Shelley,
the gentleman who more than twelve months ago undertook by his
assistance to rescue me from my pecuniary difficulties. Not to keep
you longer in suspense, he, a married man, has run away with my
daughter. I cannot conceive of an event of more accumulated
horror.

231

. . . He lodged at an inn in Fleet Street, & took his meals with me. I had the utmost confidence in him; I knew him susceptible of the noblest sentiments; he was a married man, who had lived happily with his wife for three years. Accordingly the first week of his visit passed in perfect innocence; . . .

On Sunday, June 26, he accompanied Mary, & her sister, Jane Clairmont, to the tomb of Mary's mother, one mile distant from London; & there, it seems, the impious idea first occurred to him of seducing her, playing the traitor to me, & deserting his wife. On Wednesday, the 6th of July, the transaction of the loan was completed; & on the evening of that very day he had the madness to disclose his plans to me, & to ask my consent. I expostulated with him with all the energy of which I was master, & with so much effect that for the moment he promised to give up his licentious love, & return to virtue. I applied all my diligence to waken up a sense of honour & natural affection in the mind of Mary, & I seemed to have succeeded. They both deceived me. In the night of the 27th Mary & her sister Jane escaped from my house; and the next morning when I rose, I found a letter on my dressing-table, informing me what they done. . . .

I had been of opinion from the first that Mary could only be withheld from ruin by her mind; & in that, by a series of the most consummate dissimulation, she made me believe I had succeeded. I formed the plan of sending her from home, knowing the violence of Shelley's temper, & far from certain what scenes he might be capable of acting: but I was well aware that in sending her from home I should be doing good, if she concurred with me, & concealed her retreat from her betrayer, but that if she were capable of an opposite conduct, I should be rather throwing her into his power.

You will imagine our distress. If anything could have added to it, it was this circumstance of Jane's having gone with her sister. Jane we were, & still are, most anxious to recover immediately; & there-

232

fore . . . it was agreed that Mrs. G should set off after them by the evening mail. She overtook them at Calais. I had made it a condition in suffering her to depart, that she should avoid seeing Shelley, who had conceived a particular adversion to her as a dangerous foe to his views, & might be capable of any act of desperation. Mrs. Godwin wrote to Jane . . . who . . . promised to return with her to England the next morning. But when morning arrived . . . all her resolutions were subverted. . . . Mrs. Godwin returned once more, alone. . . .

At Mrs. Godwin's request . . . I forward to you a small parcel by this day's mail, containing the copies of two letters I wrote to Shelley, between the time of his disclosing his licentious passion to me & the catastrophe. From them you will perceive fully, what were my feelings, & how I conducted myself on the subject. You, I believe, are acquainted with my character on these points, & would, I doubt not, without such an explanation do me justice. But I have many enemies; & Mrs. Godwin thinks I may stand in need of vindication. We are divided in this particular, between justification, & (what we infinitely prefer) the entire suppression of all knowledge of the affair. This, for the present at least, we owe to the poor girls, who may be brought back to the path of duty, time enough to prevent a stigma from being fastened on their characters. I had a thousand times rather remain unvindicated, than publish the tale to a single human creature to whom it might remain unknown. . . . These papers . . . are the only copies I possess, & I request you therefore to return them with speed.

When I use the word stigma, I am sure it is wholly unnecessary to say that I apply it in a very different sense to the two girls. Jane has been guilty of indiscretion only, & has shown a want of these filial sentiments, which it would have been most desirable to us to have discovered in her: Mary has been guilty of a crime.

Yours

William Godwin

233

MARY WOLLSTONECRAFT GODWIN WRITES A NOTE TO PERCY BYSSHE SHELLEY A FEW HOURS BEFORE ELOPING WITH HIM

ACCORDING to that indefatigable virtuoso of letter collecting, Dr. A. S. W. Rosenbach, this is one of the most prized love letters in English history. In fact, the doctor found it necessary to buy an entire library in England to capture this brief communication.

"Heaven bless my love . . ."

MY OWN LOVE:
I do not know by what compulsion I am to answer you, but your porter says I must, so I do. By a miracle I saved your five pounds & I will bring it. I hope, indeed, oh my loved Shelley, we shall indeed be happy. I meet you at three and bring heaps of Skinner street news. Heaven bless my love and take care of him!

His Own Mary

PERCY BYSSHE SHELLEY IMPLORES MARY GODWIN SHELLEY TO BRING THE BLUE-EYED DARLINGS TO ITALY

I<small>N</small> *1818, Shelley escorted Mary's sister Claire (Jane Clairmont) to Italy in pursuit of her heart's desire, Lord Byron. Byron loaned Shelley his villa in Este, whereupon Shelley, overjoyed at such good fortune, sent for Mary and the children. As a result of the long and trying trip across Italy in the heat, the baby Clara died before reaching Este.*

". . . scold me, if I have done wrong, and kiss me,
if I have done right . . ."

Bagni di Lucca,
Sunday morning, 23rd Aug., 1818.

M<small>Y</small> DEAREST MARY,
We arrived here last night at twelve o'clock, and it is now before breakfast the next morning. I can of course tell you nothing of the future, and though I shall not close this letter till post-time, yet I do not know exactly when that is. Yet, if you are still very impatient, look along the letter, and you will see another date, when I may have something to relate. . . . Well, but the time presses. I am now going to the banker's to send you money for the journey, which I shall address to you at Florence, Post Office. Pray come instantly to Este, where I shall be waiting in the utmost anxiety for

your arrival. You can pack up directly you get this letter, and employ the next day on that. . . . I have been obliged to decide on all these questions without you.

I have done for the best—and, my own beloved Mary, you must soon come and scold me, if I have done wrong, and kiss me, if I have done right, for I am sure I don't know which—and it is only the event that can show. We shall at least be saved the trouble of introductions, and have formed acquaintances with a lady who is so good, so beautiful, so angelically mild, that were she as wise too she would be quite a ——. Her eyes are like a reflection of yours. Her manners are like yours when you know and like a person.

Do you know, dearest, how this letter was written? By scrap and patches and interrupted every minute. The gondola is now coming to take me to the banker's. Este is a little place and the house found without difficulty. I shall count four days for this letter, one day for packing, four for coming here—and the ninth or tenth day we shall meet.

I am too late for the post, but I send an express to overtake it. Enclosed is an order for fifty pounds. If you knew all that I have to do! Dearest love, be well, be happy, come to me. Confide in your own constant and affectionate

P. B. S.

Kiss the blue-eyed darlings for me, and do not let William forget me. Clara cannot recollect me.

A N ironic epilogue to the Shelley-Godwin affair is, as Francis Thompson says in his essay on Shelley: "When he found Mary Shelley wanting, he seemed to have fallen into the mistake of Wordsworth, who complained in a charming piece of unreasonableness that his wife's love, which had been a fountain, was now only a well."

PERCY BYSSHE SHELLEY INVITES JOHN KEATS TO JOIN HIM IN ITALY

Before Shelley left England for Italy in 1818, he knew Keats only slightly. When The Revolt of Islam was published, Blackwood's went out of its way to say that "unlike Keats, Shelley was at least a gentleman."

Once established at Pisa, Shelley found himself at the peak of his poetic power. Here he wrote "Ode to the West Wind," "To a Skylark," and other great poems. The universe, in the phrase of Francis Thompson, became "a box of toys for this enchanted child," and "he danced in and out of the gates of Heaven: its floor was littered with his broken fancies. . . ."

About this time Shelley received word that a new volume of poems by Keats had just appeared in London, and for the first time was enjoying a good critical reception. But with this came reports of the desperate decline in the poet's physical condition. Thereupon Shelley promptly dispatched the following invitation*:

* The exact chronological order in the Keats letters that follow on page 240 has been slightly disregarded here so that the Keats-Shelley correspondence might be integrated. See also the cycle of Shelley letters beginning on page 229.

"... you are capable of the greatest things ..."

Pisa, 27 July, 1820.

MY DEAR KEATS,
I hear with great pain the dangerous accident you have undergone, and Mr. Gisborne, who gives me the account of it, adds that you continue to wear a consumptive appearance. This consumption is particularly fond of people who write such good verses as you have done, and with the assistance of an English winter it can often indulge its selection. I do not think that young and amiable poets are bound to gratify its taste; they have entered into no bond with the Muses to that effect.

But seriously (for I am joking on what I am very anxious about) I think you would do well to pass the winter after so tremendous an accident, in Italy, and if you think it as necessary as I do, so long as you continue to find Pisa or its neighbourhood agreeable to you, Mrs. Shelley unites with myself in urging the request, that you would take up your residence with us. You might come by sea to Leghorn (France is not worth seeing, and the sea is particularly good for weak lungs), which is within a few miles of us. You ought, at all events, to see Italy, and your health, which I suggest as a motive, might be an excuse to you.

I spare declamation about the statues, and the paintings, and the ruins, and what is a greater piece of forbearance, about the mountains streams and fields, the colours of the sky, and the sky itself.

I have lately read your "Endymion" again and even with a new sense of the treasures of poetry it contains, though treasures poured forth with indistinct profusion. This, people in general will not endure, and that is the cause of the comparatively few copies which have been sold. I feel persuaded that you are capable of the greatest things, so you but will.

I always tell Ollier to send you copies of my books.—"Prometheus Unbound" I imagine you will receive nearly at the same time with this letter. "The Cenci" I hope you have already received—it was studiously composed in a different style.

"Below the good how far! but far above the great."

In poetry I have sought to avoid system and mannerism; I wish those who excel me in genius would pursue the same plan.

Whether you remain in England, or journey to Italy, believe that you carry with you my anxious wishes for your health, happiness and success, wherever you are, or whatever you undertake, and that I am,

Yours sincerely,

P. B. Shelley

To THIS invitation, Keats replied, somewhat sardonically, somewhat humorously, and yet appreciatively, in the letter quoted on the next page:

JOHN KEATS ACKNOWLEDGES THE INVITATION
TO VISIT PERCY BYSSHE SHELLEY AT PISA

". . . an English winter would put an end to me . . ."

Hampstead, August, 1820.

MY DEAR SHELLEY,
I am very much gratified that you, in a foreign country, and with a mind almost over-occupied, should write to me in the strain of the letter beside me. If I do not take advantage of your invitation, it will be prevented by a circumstance I have very much to heart to prophesy. There is no doubt that an English winter would put an end to me, and do so in a lingering, hateful manner. Therefore, I must either voyage or journey to Italy, as a soldier marches up to a battery.

My nerves at present are the worst part of me, yet they feel soothed that, come what extreme may, I shall not be destined to remain in one spot long enough to take a hatred of any four particular bedposts. I am glad you take any pleasure in my poor poem, which I would willingly take the trouble to unwrite, if possible, did I care so much as I have done about reputation. I received a copy of "The Cenci," as from yourself, from Hunt. There is only one part of it I am judge of—the poetry and dramatic effect, which by many spirits nowadays is considered the Mammon.

A modern work, it is said, must have a purpose, which may be the God. An artist must serve Mammon; he must have "self-concentration"—selfishness, perhaps. You, I am sure, will forgive me for sincerely remarking that you might curb your magnanimity, and be more of an artist, and load every rift of your subject with ore. The thought of such discipline must fall like cold chains upon you, who perhaps never sat with your wings furled for six months together.

And is not this extraordinary talk for the writer of "Endymion," whose mind was like a pack of scattered cards? I am picked up and sorted to a pip.

My imagination is a monastery, and I am its monk. I am in expectation of "Prometheus" every day. Could I have my own wish effected, you would have it still in manuscript, or be now putting an end to the second act. I remember you advising me not to publish my first blights, on Hampstead Heath. I am returning advice upon your hands. Most of the poems in the volume I send you, have been written above two years, and would never have been published but for hope of gain; so you see I am inclined enough to take your advice now. I must express once more my deep sense of your kindness, adding my sincere thanks and respects for Mrs. Shelley.

In the hope of soon seeing you,

I remain most sincerely yours,

John Keats

THE following month Keats made his way to Italy with Severn, a friend planning to study art in Rome. But he never saw Shelley. Shortly after he took lodgings in the Piazza di Spagna, Keats grew progressively worse, and the rest of the trip to Pisa was out of the question. He died on February 23, 1821, at the age of twenty-six.* Grief over the death of Keats, as well as intense indignation at the cruelty of the critics

* See the farewell of Keats to Fanny Brawne, on page 248.

toward the poetry of his friend, inspired Shelley to write Adonais the following month in Pisa. The elegy was patterned on Bion's lament for Adonis, and after showing the muses, the seasons, the dreams, the desires, the pleasures, and the sorrows all weeping at the bier, rises "to a triumphant declaration of the poet's immortality." When Shelley himself was drowned on July 8 of the following year, on his way from Leghorn to Lerici, he carried in his pocket the manuscript of his "The Indian Serenade" and the poems of Keats and Sophocles. Shelley's last poem, The Triumph of Life, remained unfinished.

JOHN KEATS HESITATES ON THE THRESHOLD OF A CAREER IN BUSINESS

[A LETTER TO HIS SISTER FANNY]

FOR one brief moment in this letter the soul of Adonais hovered, like a star, about the possibility of quitting poetry for the business of tea brokerage.

The year 1819 was in many ways the most critical one of the twenty-four John Keats had lived up to that time. Born in 1795 in Moorfields, London, the son of a stable keeper, and orphaned at an early age, he had studied medicine and worked in a hospital before publishing his first poems in 1817. They were received indifferently. The following year, when he published Endymion, he was subjected to the full fury of the mighty critics on Blackwood's and to the savage and condescending abuse of the Quarterly Review.

Referring to the "scandalous critiques" of Endymion, Byron wrote in the topical Don Juan, ". . . 'Tis strange the soul, that fiery particle, should let itself be snuffed out by an article. . . ." To worsen matters, Keats' health took a critical turn, his slender funds began to run out, family troubles accumulated, his brother George departed for America, and his own love affair with Fanny Brawne* went through its most desperate anguish of jealousy and uncertainty. The second great volume of his poetry was to come a year later. Through all these crises the luxuriant images of The Eve of St. Agnes and the soaring melodies and wild flights of his deathless lyrics were doubtless beginning to take shape in his mind.

At this time, his sister Fanny and Leigh Hunt, through whom he met

* See his letter to her, on page 248, and the interchange of letters between Shelley and Keats beginning on page 237.

243

Shelley, were the two confidants toward whom Keats turned, and the devotion and solace he received from them are reflected in the letters they exchanged.

Many students rank the letters of Keats with his poems. In the mass they form what Christopher Morley called "one of the few inexhaustible books in English literature . . . the most thrilling and honorable reporting in our tongue, reporting the kind of things that people actually feel. . . ." Together with his sonnets and odes, these letters form the true autobiography of John Keats.

This is, therefore, an appropriate place to quote some representative excerpts from some other letters of Keats—all pertaining to the practice of his art:

"Poetry should strike the reader as a wording of his own highest thoughts, and appear almost a remembrance." [LETTER TO JOHN TAYLOR]

"The simple imaginative mind may have its rewards in the repetition of its own silent working, coming continually on the spirit with a fine suddenness." [LETTER TO BENJAMIN BAILEY]

"Some think me meddling, others silly, others foolish . . . I am content to be thought all this because I have in my own heart so great a resource." [LETTER TO GEORGE AND GEORGIANA KEATS]

"Poetry must work out its own salvation in a man; it cannot be matured by laws and precept, but by sensations and watchfulness. . . . Praise or blame has but a momentary effect on the man whose love of beauty in the abstract makes him a severe critic on his own words. J. S. is perfectly right in regard to the slip-shod Endymion. That it is so is no fault of mine. . . . It is as good as I had the power to make it—by myself. Had I been nervous about its being a perfect piece, and with that view asked advice, and trembled over every page, it would not have been written; for it is not in my nature to fumble—I will write independently.—I have written independently without Judgment. I may write

Wednesday Morn?

My dearest Girl,

I have been a walk this morning with a book in my hand, but as usual I have been occupied with nothing but you: I wish I could say in an agreeable manner. I am tormented day and night. They talk of my going to Italy 'tis certain I shall never recover if I am to be so long separate from you: yet with all this devotion to you I cannot persuade myself into any confidence of you. Past experience connected with the fact of my long separation from you gives me agonies which are scarcely to be talked of. When your mother comes I shall be very sudden and expert in asking her whether you have been to Mrs Dilkes, for she might say no to make me easy. I am literally worn to death, which seems my only recourse. I cannot forget what has pass'd. What? nothing with a man of the world, but to me deathful. I will get rid of this as much as possible. When you were in the habit of flirting with Brown you would have left off, could your own

JOHN KEATS TO FANNY BRAWNE
"Love is not a plaything..."

independently, and with Judgment hereafter. . . . In Endymion, I leaped headlong into the Sea, and thereby have become better acquainted with the Soundings, the quicksands, and the rocks, than if I had stayed upon the green shore, and piped a silly pipe, and took tea and comfortable advice." [LETTER TO JAMES AUGUSTUS HESSEY]

"We have read fine things, but never feel them to the full until we have gone the same steps as the author. . . . I find I cannot exist without poetry—without eternal poetry—half the day will not do—the whole of it—I began with a little, but habit has made me a Leviathan—I had become all in a Tremble from not having written any thing of late. The Sonnet over leaf did me some good. . . . I shall forthwith begin my Endymion, which I hope I shall have got some way into by the time you come, when we will read our verses in a delightful place I have set my heart upon near the Castle. . . ." [LETTER TO JOHN HAMILTON REYNOLDS]

In the letter that follows,* Keats explains to his sister that his guardian Mr. Abbey, who was in the tea business, had just given him an opportunity to enter upon a career of commerce. He discusses his "literary hopes" and refers to "some poems" he is "preparing":

". . . Tea Brokerage . . . will not suit me."

Wentworth Place, Monday Morn
[December 20, 1819]

MY DEAR FANNY,
When I saw you last, you ask'd me whether you should see me again before Christmas. You would have seen me if I had

* Taken out of its exact chronological place, so that the series of Keats letters might be integrated.

been quite well. I have not, though not unwell enough to have prevented me—not indeed at all—but fearful le[s]t the weather should affect my throat which on exertion or cold continually threatens me. By the advice of my Doctor I have had a wa[r]m great Coat made and have ordered some thick shoes—so furnish'd I shall be with you if it holds a little fine before Christmas day.

I have been very busy since I saw you especially the last Week and shall be for some time, in preparing some Poems to come out in the Spring. . . . My hopes of success in the literary world are now better than ever. Mr. Abbey, on my calling on him lately, appeared anxious that I should apply myself to something else— He mentioned Tea Brokerage. I supposed he might perhaps mean to give me the Brokerage of his concern, which might be executed with little trouble and good profit; and therefore said I should have no objection to it especially as at the same time it occur[r]ed to me that I might make over the business to George—I questioned him about it a few days after. His mind takes odd turns. When I became a Suitor, he became coy. He did not seem so much inclined to serve me. He described what I should have to do in the progress of business. It will not suit me. I have given it up. . . .

Mr. Brown and I go on in our old dog trot of Breakfast, dinner (not tea for we have left that off) supper Sleep, Confab, stirring the fire and reading. . . . On Tuesday I am going to hear some schoolboys Speechify on breaking up day—I'll lay you a pocket pi[e]ce we shall have "My name is norval." . . . This moment Bentley brought a Letter from George for me to deliver to Mrs Wylie—I shall see her and it before I see you. The direction was in his best hand, written with a good Pen and sealed with Tassi[e]'s Shakspeare such as I gave you—We judge of people's hearts by their Countenances; may we not judge of Letters in the same way? if so, the Letter does not contain unpleasant news—Good or bad

246

spirits have an effect on the handwriting. This direction is at least unnervous and healthy. Our Sister is also well, or George would have made strange work with Ks and Ws. The little Baby is well or he would have formed precious vowels and Consonants—He sent off the Letter in a hurry, or the mail bag was rather a wa[r]m birth, or he has worn out his Seal, for the Shakespeare's head is flattened a little. This is close muggy weather as they say at the Ale houses—

I am, ever, my dear Sister

Yours affectionately

John Keats

SHORTLY *after he wrote this letter, Keats was to learn, in his own words, that "circumstances are like Clouds, continually gathering and bursting." In a letter he later wrote, he went on to say, "While we are laughing, the seed of some trouble is put into the wide, arable land of events. . . . While we are laughing, it sprouts, it grows and suddenly bears a poison fruit which we must pluck." Four years were little room into which to crowd all the things John Keats had to say. He published his first poem at the age of twenty-two, and was dead at the age of twenty-six.*

JOHN KEATS TELLS FANNY BRAWNE HE CANNOT LIVE WITHOUT HER

ON THE SALE BY AUCTION OF KEATS' LOVE-LETTERS

These are the letters which Endymion wrote
   To one he loved in secret, and apart,
And now the brawlers of the auction mart
Bargain and bid for each poor blotted note,
Ay, for each separate pulse of passion quote
   The latest price—I think they love not Art
   Who break the crystal of a poet's heart
That small and sickly eyes may glare or gloat.

Is it not said, that many years ago
   In a far Eastern Town some soldiers ran
   With torches through the midnight, and began
To wrangle for mean raiment, and to throw
   Dice for the garments of a wretched man,
Not knowing the God's wonder or his woe?

OSCAR WILDE

THE crucial and tragic letter which follows is one of the many that Keats later cursed himself for writing. It shows the depths of torture and anguish of his ill-starred devotion to Fanny Brawne. His acute consumption had just taken a desperate turn; only the sunshine of Italy, he felt, could save his life; he was about to leave for Rome, "torn with jealousy and forebodings" when he wrote these burning lines.*

Fanny Brawne and John Keats first met in December, 1818. He was

---

* See the Shelley letter inviting Keats to Italy, on page 237 and his reply, on page 240.

twenty-three and she sixteen, the girl living in the house next door. He called her "beautiful, graceful, silly, fashionable and strange. . . ." At the time he was writing Hyperion. What began as a casual flirtation became within a week an intense romance and finally a secret and tragic passion, for Keats was already stricken, and marriage was clearly impossible. Even when he was too sick to write poetry, he poured out his heart in letters to Fanny Brawne. His "Bright Star" Sonnet is a paraphrase of one of his letters to her, written in the first days of their engagement.

In one of his love letters he wrote: "I wish I were in your arms, full of faith, or that a thunderbolt would strike me. . . ."

Again, on July 8, 1819, he wrote to Fanny: "I never knew before, what such love as you have made me feel, was; I did not believe in it; my Fanny was afraid of it, lest it should burn me up. But if you will fully love me, though there may be some fire 'twill not be more than we can bear when moistened and bedewed with Pleasures. . . . I love you the more in that I believe you have liked me for my own sake and for nothing else. I have met with women whom I really think would like to be married to a Poem and to be given away by a Novel." He signed this letter "Ever yours, my love!"

Another letter to Fanny Brawne contained this revealing and characteristic passage:

"I have no limit now to my love. I have been astonished that men could die martyrs of religion. I have shuddered at it. I shudder no more. I could be martyrd for my religion—love is my religion—I could die for you. My creed is love and you are its only tenet. You have ravish'd me away by a power I cannot resist. . . . My love is selfish. I cannot breathe without you. . . . Yours for ever."

The exact date of this farewell letter is not known. Some students say it was written July 5, 1820; others say it was somewhat later in the year. We know that, about this time, Keats had gone to Kentish Town in a vain attempt to check the ravages of tuberculosis. The disease intensified both *his love and jealousy. In vain he had tried the seashores of England. In vain, Fanny Brawne and her mother had nursed him. And in bitterness he wrote these words:*

"Love is not a plaything . . ."

Wednesday Morng. [Kentish Town, 1820]

MY DEAREST GIRL,
I have been a walk this morning with a book in my hand, but as usual I have been occupied with nothing but you: I wish I could say in an agreeable manner. I am tormented day and night. They talk of my going to Italy. 'Tis certain I shall never recover if I am to be so long separate from you: yet with all this devotion to you I cannot persuade myself into any confidence of you.

Past experience connected with the fact of my long separation from you gives me agonies which are scarcely to be talked of. When your mother comes I shall be very sudden and expert in asking her whether you have been to Mrs. Dilke's, for she might say no to make me easy. I am literally worn to death, which seems my only recourse. I cannot forget what has pass'd. What? nothing with a man of the world, but to me dreadful.

I will get rid of this as much as possible. When you were in the habit of flirting with Brown you would have left off, could your own heart have felt one half of one pang mine did. Brown is a good sort of Man—he did not know he was doing me to death by inches. I feel the effect of every one of those hours in my side now; and for that cause, though he has done me many services,

250

though I know his love and friendship for me, though at this moment I should be without pence were it not for his assistance, I will never see or speak to him until we are both old men, if we are to be. I *will* resent my heart having been made a football. You will call this madness. I have heard you say that it was not unpleasant to wait a few years—you have amusements—your mind is away—you have not brooded over one idea as I have, and how should you?

You are to me an object intensely desireable—the air I breathe in a room empty of you is unhealthy. I am not the same to you —no—you can wait—you have a thousand activities—you can be happy without me. Any party, any thing to fill up the day has been enough.

How have you pass'd this month? Who have you smil'd with? All this may seem savage in me. You do not feel as I do—you do not know what it is to love—one day you may—your time is not come.

Ask yourself how many unhappy hours Keats has caused you in Loneliness. For myself I have been a Martyr the whole time, and for this reason I speak; the confession is forc'd from me by the torture.

I appeal to you by the blood of that Christ you believe in: Do not write to me if you have done anything this month which it would have pained me to have seen. You may have altered—if you have not—if you still behave in dancing rooms and others societies as I have seen you—I do not want to live—if you have done so I wish this coming night may be my last.

I cannot live without you, and not only you but *chaste* you; *virtuous* you. The Sun rises and sets, the day passes, and you follow the bent of your inclination to a certain extent—you have no conception of the quantity of miserable feeling that passes through me in a day.—Be serious! Love is not a plaything—and

251

again do not write unless you can do it with a crystal conscience.
I would sooner die for want of you than ——

Yours for ever

J. Keats

FOR more than a century the recipient of this letter, "the girl who shared the fate of John Keats," was regarded as a "lightheaded, coquettish minx" unworthy of the great poet. Today, in the light of the recently disclosed letters of Fanny Brawne to the poet's sister, the verdict has been radically changed. She emerges now as a person who not only tried valiantly to save his life, but hoped and intended to marry him, and to some extent even appreciated his poetry.

Shortly after writing this letter, Keats paid his last farewell to Fanny Brawne, knowing it was forever, and hastened to Rome. As Francis Thompson put it, "He was first half chewed in London and finally spit dying into Italy." On shipboard, he wrote his last sonnet; on November 30, 1820, he wrote his last letter from Rome. On February 23, 1821, at the age of 26, he was dead. "Here lies one whose name was writ in water. . . ." Several of Fanny Brawne's unread letters were buried with him. Their contents were undisclosed to the world.

After the death of Keats, Fanny Brawne lived with the poet's sister in the house at Hampstead. The posthumous poems were still unpublished, the genius of John Keats unrecognized. Twelve years later she married a banker.

IN AN AUCTION ROOM

(LETTER OF JOHN KEATS TO FANNY BRAWNE)
ANDERSON GALLERIES, MARCH 15, 1920

How about this lot? said the auctioneer;
One hundred, may I say, just for a start?

Between the plum-red curtains, drawn apart,
A written sheet was held . . . And strange to hear
(Dealer, would I were steadfast as thou art)
The cold quick bids. (Against you in the rear!)
The crimson salon, in a glow more clear
Burned bloodlike purple as the poet's heart.

Song that outgrew the singer! Bitter Love
That broke the proud hot heart it held in thrall—
Poor script, where still those tragic passions move—
Eight hundred bid, fair warning; the last call;
The soul of Adonais, like a star. . . .
Sold for eight hundred dollars—Doctor R!

CHRISTOPHER MORLEY

LORD BYRON TELLS THE COUNTESS GUICCIOLI
THAT HE CANNOT CEASE TO LOVE HER

THE letters and journals of George Gordon, Lord Byron, fill six volumes. After the scandal caused in England by his divorce from a completely respectable and completely incompatible wife, Byron, at the age of twenty-eight, already world famous for more than four years, handsome, extravagant, reckless, brilliant, and crippled, wandered aimlessly about Europe, apostrophizing freedom and taking his loves where he found them.

In the words of Matthew Arnold, he was the "romantic hero at odds with the world and calling on all sympathetic readers to view the pageant of his bleeding heart." His intense awareness of his lameness, and his equally intense admiration of his own fascination for women, drove him to produce legends about himself. His letters have been described as "wildly exclamatory, heavily underlined, with pages blotted and blistered with tears. . . ."

Teresa, Countess Guiccioli, at sixteen had married an old and wealthy Italian nobleman. She was golden-haired, poised, well read, and gentle. In 1819, when she was eighteen and he thirty-one, Byron met her and fell passionately in love. Here is one of his letters* to her:

* The exact chronological sequence has been disregarded, so that the earlier cycles of Keats and Shelley letters could be integrated.

254

"... my destiny rests with you ..."

Bologna, August 25, 1819.

MY DEAREST TERESA,—I have read this book in your garden;—my love, you were absent, or else I could not have read it. It is a favourite book of yours, and the writer was a friend of mine. You will not understand these English words, and *others* will not understand them,—which is the reason I have not scrawled them in Italian. But you will recognize the handwriting of him who passionately loved you, and you will divine that, over a book which was yours, he could only think of love.

In that word, beautiful in all languages, but most so in yours— *Amor mio*—is comprised my existence here and hereafter. I feel I exist here, and I feel that I shall exist hereafter,—to *what* purpose you will decide; my destiny rests with you, and you are a woman, eighteen years of age, and two out of a convent, I wish that you had staid there, with all my heart,—or, at least, that I had never met you in your married state.

But all this is too late. I love you, and you love me,—at least, you *say so*, and *act* as if you *did* so, which last is a great consolation in all events. But *I* more than love you, and cannot cease to love you.

Think of me, sometimes, when the Alps and ocean divide us,— but they never will, unless you *wish* it.

Byron

255

THERE was no need for the "Alps and ocean" to divide them. The Countess, no less susceptible than her predecessors to Don Juan's charms, entered upon an affair which at first was tolerated, according to an old Italian custom, by her senile husband; then given a quasi-legal status by papal dissolution of her marriage. For two years she was a stabilizing influence in the life of her chaotic lover. When they parted, it was not in bitterness but with the nostalgic affection of a love that had run its course.

In 1823, Byron went abroad to Greece in his fight for freedom. He died there of a fever on April 19, 1824.

WILLIAM CULLEN BRYANT BREAKS THE NEWS
TO MOTHER

I N THIS kindly and witty letter the early American poet, chiefly famous
for Thanatopsis, and later a celebrated editor of the New York
Evening Post, describes the emotions of a man of twenty-six on his
wedding day. His bride was Frances Fairchild, and his home was in
Roslyn, Long Island.

". . . I was given to understand that I was married . . ."

[June, 1821]

D EAR MOTHER: I hasten to send you the melancholy intelligence of what has lately happened to me.

Early on the evening of the eleventh day of the present month
I was at a neighboring house in this village. Several people of both
sexes were assembled in one of the apartments, and three or four
others, with myself, were in another. At last came in a little elderly
gentleman, pale, thin, with a solemn countenance, hooked nose,
and hollow eyes. It was not long before we were summoned to
attend in the apartment where he and the rest of the company
were gathered. We went in and took our seats; the little elderly
gentleman with the hooked nose prayed, and we all stood up.
When he had finished, most of us sat down. The gentleman with
the hooked nose then muttered certain cabalistical expressions
which I was too much frightened to remember, but I recollect

that at the conclusion I was given to understand that I was married to a young lady of the name of Frances Fairchild, whom I perceived standing by my side, and I hope in the course of a few months to have the pleasure of introducing to you as your daughter-in-law, which is a matter of some interest to the poor girl, who has neither father nor mother in the world. . . .

I looked only for goodness of heart, an ingenuous and affectionate disposition, a good understanding, etc., and the character of my wife is too frank and single-hearted to suffer me to fear that I may be disappointed. I do myself wrong; I did not look for these nor any other qualities, but they trapped me before I was aware, and now I am married in spite of myself.

Thus the current of destiny carries us along. None but a madman would swim against the stream, and none but a fool would exert himself to swim with it. The best way is to float quietly with the tide. . . .

Your affectionate son,

William

THEY lived happily ever after, and were only separated by death fifty years later.

VICTOR HUGO CASTS HIMSELF HUMBLY AT THE FEET OF ADÈLE FOUCHER

As CHILDREN Victor and Eugène Hugo had played with their little neighbor and cousin, Adèle Foucher, in the garden of Les Feuillantines. As young men, both fell under the spell of her beauty and charm. At seventeen, Victor was a golden-haired young Apollo who had already published his first poetry. He and Adèle became engaged secretly, determined to marry despite the opposition of the Hugo family to a match unworthy of their exalted rank. For three years, Victor and Adèle exchanged secret messages. His were written with all the headlong passion and exaggeration of his romantic, energetic temperament. The letter printed below was written after he had heard that, as a reward for supporting the royalist traditions in his recently published poems, he was to receive a pension from Louis XVIII and could marry Adèle:

"... why is there no word for this but joy?"

Friday evening, March 15th, 1822.

After the two delightful evenings spent yesterday and the day before, I shall certainly not go out tonight, but will sit here at home and write to you. Besides, my Adèle, my adorable and adored Adèle, what have I not to tell you? O, God! for two days, I have been asking myself every moment if such happiness is not a dream. It seems to me that what I feel is not of earth. I cannot yet comprehend this cloudless heaven.

259

You do not yet know, Adèle, to what I had resigned myself. Alas! do I know it myself? Because I was weak, I fancied I was calm; because I was preparing myself for all the mad follies of despair, I thought I was courageous and resigned. Ah! let me cast myself humbly at your feet, you who are so grand, so tender and so strong! I had been thinking that the utmost limit of my devotion could only be the sacrifice of my life; but you, my generous love, were ready to sacrifice for me the repose of yours.

Adèle, to what follies, what delirium, did not your Victor give way during these everlasting eight days! Sometimes I was ready to accept the offer of your admirable love; I thought that if pushed to the last extremity by the letter from my father, I might realize a little money, and then carry you away—you, my betrothed, my companion, my wife—away from all those who might want to disunite us; I thought we would cross France, I being nominally your husband, and go into some other country which would give us our rights. By day we would travel in the same carriage, by night sleep under the same roof.

But do not think, my noble Adèle, that I would have taken advantage of so much happiness. Is it not true that you would never have done me the dishonor of thinking so? You would have been the object most worthy of respect, the being most respected, by your Victor; you might on the journey have even slept in the same chamber without fearing that he would have alarmed you by a touch, or even have looked at you. Only I should have slept, or watched wakefully in a chair, or lying on the floor beside your bed, the guardian of your repose, the protector of your slumbers. The right to defend and to watch over you would have been the only one of a husband's rights that your slave would have aspired to, until a priest had given him all the others. . . .

Adèle, oh! do not hate me, do not despise me for having been so weak and abject when you were so strong and so sublime.

Think of my bereavement, of my loneliness, of what I expected from my father; think that for a week I had looked forward to losing you, and do not be astonished at the extravagance of my despair. You—a young girl—were admirable. And indeed, I feel as if it would be flattering an angel to compare such a being to you. You have been privileged to receive every gift from nature, you have both fortitude and tears. Oh, Adèle, do not mistake these words for blind enthusiasm—enthusiasm for you has lasted all my life, and increases day by day. My whole soul is yours. If my entire existence had not been yours, the harmony of my being would have been lost, and I must have died—died inevitably.

These were my meditations, Adèle, when the letter that was to bring me hope or else despair arrived. If you love me, you know what must have been my joy. What I know you may have felt, I will not describe.

My Adèle, why is there no word for this but joy? Is it because there is no power in human speech to express such happiness?

The sudden bound from mournful resignation to infinite felicity seemed to upset me. Even now I am still beside myself and sometimes I tremble lest I should suddenly awaken from this dream divine.

Oh, now you are mine! At last you are mine! Soon—in a few months, perhaps, my angel will sleep in my arms, will awaken in my arms, will live there. All your thoughts at all moments, all your looks will be for me; all my thoughts, all my moments, all my looks, will be for you! My Adèle! . . .

And now you will belong to me! Now I am called on earth to enjoy celestial felicity. I see you as my young wife, then a young mother, but always the same, always my Adèle, as tender, as adored in the chastity of married life as in the virgin days of your first love— Dear love, answer me—tell me if you can conceive the happiness of love immortal in an eternal union! And that will be ours some day. . . .

My Adèle, no obstacle will now discourage me, either in my writing or in my attempt to gain a pension, for every step I take to attain success in both will bring me nearer to you. How could anything now seem painful to me? Do not think so ill of me as to believe that, I implore you. What is a little toil, if it conquers so much happiness? Have I not a thousand times implored heaven to let me purchase it at the price of my blood? Oh! how happy I am! how happy I am going to be!

Adieu, my angel, my beloved Adèle! Adieu! I will kiss your hair and go to bed. Still I am far from you, but I can dream of you. Soon perhaps you will be at my side. Adieu; pardon the delirium of your husband who embraces you, and who adores you, both for this life and another.

Your picture?

Six months later Victor and Adèle were married in the presence of both families. But Victor's brother Eugène, overcome at witnessing the marriage, lost his mind completely and had to be sent to an asylum. It was not a good omen. That the marriage lasted until Adèle's death in 1868 was proof of her "angelic" nature. Through the births and deaths of many children, through Victor's flagrant unfaithfulness, exile, disgrace, and triumph,* Adèle remained always a dignified wife, respected and loved by her husband, despite his deviations from marital fidelity.

When Léon Daudet, Victor Hugo's grandson, wrote his biography more than a hundred years later, he revealed the full story of "a great writer and a great lover who had Paris at his feet in his twenties . . .

* See Elizabeth Barrett Browning's letter to Napoleon III, pleading for Victor Hugo, on page 326.

an incorrigible Don Juan whom no woman could resist. . . ." This book, based on the correspondence of Victor Hugo, told how Hugo finally discovered "the double betrayal of his life, that of his wife Adèle with his friend Sainte-Beuve, that drove him to the great affair of his life, his liaison with the popular actress, Juliette Drouet. . . ."

FRANZ SCHUBERT HUMBLY PETITIONS HIS ROYAL HIGHNESS FOR THE POST OF ASSISTANT CONDUCTOR AT THE IMPERIAL COURT OF VIENNA

WITHOUT any time for anything but music, without any apparent awareness of his own poverty and suffering, without any help from the great or recognition from the humble, Franz Schubert lived his brief span of thirty-one years in a tumult of unpremeditated song.

Franz Schubert was born in Vienna in 1797 and died there in 1828. His father was a penurious schoolmaster who tried desperately to raise a family of fourteen children.

At the age of eleven, Franz Schubert was a singer in the court-chapel choir directed by Antonio Salieri. In his early youth he wrote a pitiful letter to an elder brother, asking for a few kreuzers a month, and adding: "You know by experience how sometimes one wants to eat a roll and a few apples and all the more when after a modest dinner one can only look forward to a wretched supper eight and a half hours later." At sixteen Schubert wrote his first symphony, at eighteen a Mass and The Erlking. Before his nineteenth year, he had written numerous string quartets, sonatas, Masses, five symphonies, and two hundred and fifty songs. In his eighteenth year alone he poured out, on music paper that he could scarcely afford to buy, five operas, two symphonies, two Masses, and one hundred and forty-six songs. He wrote fifteen songs in two days. Hark, Hark, the Lark! was literally dashed off on the back of a tavern bill-of-fare, and that same day he also composed Who Is Sylvia?

About this time Schubert also began to write his long series of petitions and applications for imperial employment—an art in which he was forced to be prolific. In 1816, for example, he wrote the Most Honorable Imperial and Royal Civic Guard headquarters in Vienna, humbly begging to be considered favorably for appointment to the vacant post of music director in Laibach, a provincial capital almost three hundred miles from Vienna. He set forth that "he has acquired such knowledge and skill in all branches of composition, in the practice of the organ and the violin as well as in singing that, as the enclosed certificates will show, of all candidates for this post he will be found to be the best qualified." Schubert referred to the "friendly recommendation" of his teacher in composition, Herr von Salieri, Chief Kapellmeister, and ended his letter by declaring that "in the event of a favorable answer he solemnly promises to make the best possible use of his power so as to give complete satisfaction." Salieri did not keep his word to Schubert. He recommended another pupil, and Franz Schubert, the young assistant teacher at his father's school at No. 10 Himmelpfortgrunde, Vienna, did not get the post for which he petitioned so humbly.

This was the darkest period of Schubert's life. He knew hunger, frustration, the routine agonies of elementary teaching, the dank atmosphere of a shabby schoolhouse and a poverty-stricken, multitudinous family. Inwardly he may have been seething with revolt and wrath; outwardly he was serene, and always he was composing music. When his application for the post at Laibach was refused, he plunged headlong into the carefree life of the musical set in Vienna. Befriended by Franz von Schober, he became the center of a Bohemian group that called themselves the Schubertians.

In his twenty-first year, Schubert was appointed music teacher of the family of Count Janós Esterházy at his country seat in Hungary. He was treated like a servant, and housed with the gardeners and scullions. Some of his loveliest and most enduring music, including the incredibly lyrical "Forellen" Quintet, was composed in this period. In 1822, he began work on the "Unfinished" Symphony. His health was beginning to weaken. Balked in his operatic ambitions by harsh impresarios, he also was blackballed from the Society of the Friends of Music. But symphonies, oratorios, chamber music, and songs in endless profusion were pouring from his pen. He composed almost as rapidly as a copyist could set down the notes on paper. In a letter to a friend about this time, Schubert called himself "the most unfortunate and miserable man in the world."

In 1826, shortly after he completed the "Death and the Maiden" quartet, Schubert resumed his pitiful letter-writing campaign in a desperate effort to find some degree of economic security. The following application he addressed to the Emperor Francis II:

"... at the present time without employment ..."

YOUR MAJESTY!
Most gracious Emperor!

With the deepest submission the undersigned humbly begs Your Majesty graciously to bestow upon him the vacant position of Vice-*Kapellmeister* to the Court, and supports his application with the following qualifications:

(1) The undersigned was born in Vienna, is the son of a school-teacher, and is 29 years of age.

(2) He enjoyed the privilege of being for five years a Court Chorister at the Imperial and Royal College School.

(3) He received a complete course of instruction in composition from the late Chief *Kapellmeister* to the Court, Herr Anton Salieri, and is fully qualified, therefore, to fill any post as *Kapellmeister*.

(4) His name is well known, not only in Vienna but throughout Germany, as a composer of songs and instrumental music.

266

(5) He has also written and arranged five Masses for both smaller and larger orchestras, and these have already been performed in various churches in Vienna.

(6) Finally, he is at the present time without employment, and hopes in the security of a permanent position to be able to realize at last those high musical aspirations which he has ever kept before him.

Should Your Majesty be graciously pleased to grant this request, the undersigned would strive to the utmost to give full satisfaction.

Your Majesty's most obedient humble servant,

Franz Schubert

H IS Most Gracious Majesty did not even acknowledge, let alone grant, Schubert's humble petition. The young composer had no friends near the seats of the mighty, and after a year's delay, the appointment was given to someone else. Schubert, who had only two years more for writing either masterpieces of music or letters of application, quietly went back to his symphonies, sonatas, songs, and quartets. In 1827, he was a torchbearer at Beethoven's funeral.

During the year 1828, just before the end, Schubert composed with a supreme outburst of creative energy. As Ralph Bates has expressed it in his notable biographical study, "Schubert must have been drunk with musical excitement . . . and it must have seemed to him that the only thing left to do with a life that had failed so of normal achievement was to surrender it entirely to music. . . ." In this last and tragic year Schubert composed the great C Major Symphony, generally called "the Seventh," actually the tenth, or last. Referring to "the splendor . . . the white magnificence . . ." of this symphony, Bates adds: "I suppose no man hearing this music can escape that sense of witnessing the universe of unseen law and shining constellation. . . ."

On November 19, 1828, a few months after completing this symphony, without even having an opportunity to hear it, Franz Schubert died of typhus. He was buried near Beethoven, under an epitaph composed by his friend, the poet Grillparzer: "Music has here entombed a rich Treasure but still fairer Hopes."

HENRY D. THOREAU EXPLAINS TO RALPH WALDO EMERSON THAT DIVINE COMMODITIES ARE NEAR AND CHEAP

M Y PROFESSION," wrote Henry David Thoreau, "is always to be alert, to find God in nature, to know his lurking places, to attend to all the oratorios, the operas in nature. . . ."

Above all, Thoreau sought to reduce life to the simplest terms, to "live deep and suck out all the marrow of existence," to get, like a thrifty, prudent Yankee, a full measure in the market place of man. Steeped though he was in mysticism, transcendentalist in his visions, he was fundamentally a man of practical common sense. The favorite question he asked of his fellow Americans was: "Are you getting your money's worth?" That was the core of his philosophy, the heart of his "oaken unknowability," the true secret that raised this "homely, cantankerous, schrewd, and witty Yankee" to the level of genius.

Henry Seidel Canby's definitive and masterly biography of Thoreau, published in 1939, deflates many legends about the man of Concord. He was not a misanthropic, women-hating hermit of the long wintry silences. He loved life. But he wanted to live it in his own way, without extravagance, without the spurious distractions of nonessentials. In fact, he believed his time was "too valuable to waste in making money." The pleasures Thoreau sought were the durable ones; those he rejected were, for him, meretricious and evanescent. Far from being ascetic, he said he "sometimes felt like a hound or a panther."

Born in Concord, Massachusetts, on July 12, 1817, Thoreau was a schoolteacher, lecturer, pencil manufacturer, surveyor, and intimate friend of Emerson. In his twenty-eighth year, he borrowed his neighbor Alcott's ax, and with his own hands began the construction of a forest

269

cabin for a two-year sojourn by the shores of Walden Pond. Incidentally, Van Wyck Brooks reminds us that Thoreau took pains to return the ax with a sharper edge.

But Thoreau's life was not one of "quiet desperation." It was only a twenty-minute walk to Emerson's home. The retreat in the woods had its true inviolability in the inner sense—in his contemplations of nature, in his honesty with himself, in his "nuggety, sparing, undecorated prose," compared by Clifton Fadiman with "the inevitability of and effectiveness of a well-aimed bullet . . . and the lasting quality of a great Madeira." This was the sort of writing he poured out in a series of journals, letters, essays, and nature studies that made him world famous.

Thoreau's weekly budget was twenty-seven cents. He raised his own beans and potatoes and lived on fourteen dollars a year. His idea during this experiment was to work only six weeks a year, repairing fences, building boats, surveying the land. When he needed a little more cash for a microscope, he took on a few extra jobs. He knew the countryside "like a bird or a fox."

Thus Thoreau escaped the bitter complexities of so-called civiliza-tion—chiefly by reducing his wants, simplifying his life, and freeing himself from all the "pother about possessions." Taking Emerson's dic-tum to heart, he did not want his cow to milk him. Instead, he admired the ancient Mexicans, who made a ritual of burning all their goods every fifty years. He wanted freedom, mobility, "a chance to measure his own capacities."

"Who could say," he wrote, "that if a man advance boldly, in the direc-tion of his dreams, endeavoring to live the life he had imagined, he could not meet with a success he had never expected on common hours?"

Emerson said that with health and a day he could make the pomp of emperors seem ridiculous. Thoreau did it even without health, for he inherited a susceptibility to tuberculosis.

When Thoreau was fresh from Harvard, in his twentieth year, he met Emerson,* then thirty-four, "at the height of his powers." It was Emer-

* See Emerson's letter to Walt Whitman, on page 323.

270

son who gave him inspiration, through the pages of his essay on "Nature," who gave him a home, a philosophy, and "the courage to break through dead doctrines." He called Thoreau "the boy" and regarded him as his "eyes and ears" in the countryside. Thoreau in turn called Emerson his "friend and brother." Dr. Canby points out that "Thoreau was made by two books, 'Nature' and the Bhagavad-Gita." Like Emerson he found "reason and faith . . . perpetual youth . . . a decorum and sanctity . . . a perennial festival . . ." in the woods.

According to Thoreau, "As the inner life fails, people run desperately to the post office." He remarked that he hadn't in all his life received more than two or three letters that were worth the postage. These were strange sentiments from a man who himself wrote such frank and honest letters of self-disclosure. Two years before his retirement to Walden Pond, Thoreau, at the age of twenty-six, penned these Emersonian thoughts to "the one man who knew him best and loved him," Ralph Waldo Emerson:

"We communicate like the burrows of foxes, in silence and darkness, under ground."

February 12, 1843.

DEAR FRIEND,—As the packet still tarries, I will send you some thoughts, which I have lately relearned, as the latest public and private news.

How mean are our relations to one another! Let us pause till they are nobler. A little silence, a little rest, is good. It would be sufficient employment only to cultivate true ones.

The richest gifts we can bestow are the least marketable. We hate the kindness which we understand. A noble person confers

271

no such gift as his whole confidence: none so exalts the giver and the receiver; it produces the truest gratitude. Perhaps it is only essential to friendship that some vital trust should have been reposed by the one in the other. I feel addressed and probed even to the remote parts of my being when one nobly shows, even in trivial things, an implicit faith in me. When such divine commodities are so near and cheap, how strange that it should have to be each day's discovery! A threat or a curse may be forgotten, but this mild trust translates me. I am no more of this earth; it acts dynamically; it changes my very substance. I cannot do what before I did. I cannot be what before I was. Other chains may be broken, but in the darkest night, in the remotest place, I trail this thread. Then things cannot *happen*. What if God were to confide in us for a moment! Should we not then be gods?

How subtle a thing is this confidence! Nothing sensible passes between; never any consequences are to be apprehended should it be misplaced. Yet something has transpired. A new behavior springs; the ship carries new ballast in her hold. A sufficiently great and generous trust could never be abused. It should be cause to lay down one's life,—which would not be to lose it. Can there be any mistake up there? Don't the gods know where to invest their wealth? Such confidence, too, would be reciprocal. When one confides greatly in you, he will feel the roots of an equal trust fastening themselves in him. When such trust has been received or reposed, we dare not speak, hardly to see each other; our voices sound harsh and untrustworthy. We are as instruments which the Powers have dealt with. Through what straits would we not carry this little burden of a magnanimous trust! Yet no harm could possibly come, but simply faithlessness. Not a feather, not a straw, is intrusted; that packet is empty. It is only *committed* to us, and, as it were, all things are committed to us.

The kindness I have longest remembered has been of this sort,

—the sort unsaid; so far behind the speaker's lips that almost it already lay in my heart. It did not have far to go to be communicated. The gods cannot misunderstand, man cannot explain. We communicate like the burrows of foxes, in silence and darkness, under ground. We are undermined by faith and love. How much more full is Nature where we think the empty space is than where we place the solids!—full of fluid influences. Should we ever communicate but by these? The spirit abhors a vacuum more than Nature. There is a tide which pierces the pores of the air. These aerial rivers, let us not pollute their currents. What meadows do they course through? How many fine mails there are which traverse their routes! He is privileged who gets his letter franked by them.

I believe these things.

Henry D. Thoreau

Two years after this letter, Thoreau began his two-year retirement. Most of the rest of his life he spent on a village street—talking, writing, philosophizing, earning his living and his immortality. His diary filled thirty volumes. According to Canby, there were four women in his life, in addition to his "chattering mother and sisters." One of these was Lidian Emerson, the second wife of the man to whom he addressed this letter. He called her his "mother-sister." Thoreau lived for a long time in the Emerson household.

In 1849, two years after he had completed his stay at Walden Pond, he published A Week on the Concord and Merrimac Rivers, and five years after that, Walden. He died in 1862 at the age of forty-five. His essay on "Civil Disobedience," written after he spent the night in jail for non-payment of taxes, is said to have inspired Gandhi's doctrine of non-resistance.

In later years Thoreau and Emerson differed and disagreed, as disciple and teacher frequently do, when both are geniuses, both ever-growing. But at Thoreau's funeral Emerson spoke these words about "this erect and spotless person":

"The country knows not yet, or in the least part, how great a son it has lost. It seems an injury that he should leave in the midst his broken task, which none else can finish. . . . But he, at least, is content. His soul was made for the noblest society, he had in a short life exhausted the capabilities of this world; wherever there is knowledge, wherever there is virtue, wherever there is beauty, he will find a home."

THE LOVE LETTERS
OF ROBERT BROWNING
AND ELIZABETH BARRETT

[A SERIES]

ERE is the correspondence that chronicles the tranquil beginning and the dramatic climax of what was doubtless the perfect Victorian idyl—complete with midnight elopements, swooning maidens, outraged parents, and the other appurtenances of "plush-and-rose-water romance." In these letters, we can trace the history of the courtship and marriage of two great nineteenth-century poets. They give us in their own words, "at midnight and in the silence of the sleep-time," the inmost music of "two hearts beating each to each." They record the devotion and the passion which inspired the best known of Elizabeth Barrett Browning's Sonnets From the Portuguese:

How do I love thee? Let me count the ways.
I love thee to the depth and breadth and height
My soul can reach, when feeling out of sight
For the ends of Being and ideal Grace.
I love thee to the level of everyday's
Most quiet need, by sun and candlelight.
I love thee freely, as men strive for right;
I love thee purely, as they turn from praise.
I love thee with the passion put to use
In my old griefs, and with my childhood's faith.
I love thee with a love I seemed to lose
With my lost saints—I love thee with the breath,
Smiles, tears, of all my life!—and, if God choose,
I shall but love thee better after death.

ROBERT BROWNING TELLS ELIZABETH BARRETT THAT HE LOVES HER VERSES WITH ALL HIS HEART

ELIZABETH BROWNING was the eldest daughter of Edward Moulton-Barrett, who had inherited a large fortune in Jamaica. Her autocratic father ruthlessly opposed the idea of marriage for any of his children. After an earlier residence in Herefordshire and Devon, the family moved to London, settling at 50 Wimpole Street.

At the age of thirty, Elizabeth was practically an invalid. When her first poems appeared in Bulwer-Lytton's New Monthly Magazine, she met William Wordsworth. In 1844 she published a volume of poems that elicited the following letter of praise from Robert Browning. Of this, she wrote to a friend: "I had a letter from Browning, the poet, last night, which threw me into ecstasies—Browning, the author of Paracelsus, the king of the mystics."

"... this great living poetry of yours ..."

New Cross, Hatcham, Surrey.
[January 10th, 1845]

I LOVE your verses with all my heart, dear Miss Barrett,—and this is no off-hand complimentary letter that I shall write,—whatever else, no prompt matter-of-course recognition of your genius, and there a graceful and natural end of the thing.

Since the day last week when I first read your poems, I quite laugh to remember how I have been turning and turning again in my mind what I should be able to tell you of their effect upon me, for in the first flush of delight I thought I would this once get out of my habit of purely passive enjoyment, when I do really enjoy, and thoroughly justify my admiration—perhaps even, as a loyal fellow-craftsman should, try and find fault and do you some little good to be proud of hereafter!—but nothing comes of it all—so into me has it gone, and part of me has it become, this great living poetry of yours, not a flower of which but took root and grew—Oh, how different that is from lying to be dried and pressed flat, and prized highly, and put in a book with a proper account at top and bottom, and shut up and put away . . . and the book called a 'Flora,' besides!

After all, I need not give up the thought of doing that, too, in time; because even now, talking with whoever is worthy, I can give a reason for my faith in one and another excellence, the fresh strange music, the affluent language, the exquisite pathos and true new brave thought; but in this addressing myself to you—your own self, and for the first time, my feeling rises altogether.

I do, as I say, love these books with all my heart—and I love you too. Do you know I was once not very far from seeing—really seeing you? Mr. Kenyon said to me one morning 'Would you like to see Miss Barrett?' then he went to announce me,—then he returned . . you were too unwell, and now it is years ago, and I feel as at some untoward passage in my travels, as if I had been close, so close, to some world's-wonder in chapel or crypt, only a screen to push and I might have entered, but there was some slight, so it now seems, slight and just sufficient bar to admission, and the half-opened door shut, and I went home my thousands of miles, and the sight was never to be?

278

Well, these Poems were to be, and this true thankful joy and pride with which I feel myself,

Yours ever faithfully,
Robert Browning

ELIZABETH BARRETT, impressed and delighted, pounced upon the opportunity of corresponding with the poet, and lost no time in answering:

ELIZABETH BARRETT ACKNOWLEDGES HER DEBT TO ROBERT BROWNING

". . . from the bottom of my heart."

50 Wimpole Street: Jan. 11, 1845.

I THANK you, dear Mr. Browning, from the bottom of my heart. You meant to give me pleasure by your letter—and even if the object had not been answered, I ought still to thank you. But it is thoroughly answered. Such a letter from such a hand! Sympathy is dear—very dear to me: but the sympathy of a poet, and of such a poet, is the quintessence of sympathy of me! Will you take back my gratitude for it?—agreeing, too, that of all the commerce done in the world, from Tyre to Carthage, the exchange of sympathy for gratitude is the most princely thing!

For the rest you draw me on with your kindness. It is difficult to get rid of people when you once have given them too much pleasure—*that* is a fact, and we will not stop for the moral of it. What I was going to say—after a little natural hesitation—is, that if ever you emerge without inconvenient effort from your 'passive state,' and will *tell* me of such faults as rise to the surface and strike you as important in my poems, (for of course, I do not think of troubling you with criticism in detail) you will confer a lasting obligation on me, and one which I shall value so much, that I covet it at a distance.

280

I do not pretend to any extraordinary meekness under criticism and it is possible enough that I might not be altogether obedient to yours. But with my high respect for your power in your Art and for your experience as an artist, it would be quite impossible for me to hear a general observation of yours on what appear to you my master-faults, without being the better for it hereafter in some way. I ask for only a sentence or two of general observation—and I do not ask even for *that*, so as to tease you— but in the humble, low voice, which is so excellent a thing in women—particularly when they go a-begging!

The most frequent general criticism I receive, is, I think, upon the style,—'if I *would* but change my style'! But *that* is an objection (isn't it?) to the writer bodily? Buffon says, and every sincere writer must feel, that '*Le style c'est l'homme;*' a fact, however, scarcely calculated to lessen the objection with certain critics.

Is it indeed true that I was so near to the pleasure and honour of making your acquaintance? and can it be true that you look back upon the lost opportunity with any regret? *But*—you know —if you had entered the 'crypt,' you might have caught cold, or been tired to death, and *wished* yourself 'a thousand miles off;' which would have been worse than travelling them. It is not my interest, however, to put such thoughts in your head about its being 'all for the best;' and I would rather hope (as I do) that what I lost by one chance I may recover by some future one. Winters shut me up as they do dormouse's eyes; in the spring, *we shall see*: and I am so much better that I seem turning round to the outward world again. And in the meantime I have learnt to know your voice, not merely from the poetry but from the kindness in it. Mr. Kenyon often speaks of you—dear Mr. Kenyon!—who most unspeakably, or only speakably with tears in my eyes,—has been my friend and helper, and my book's friend and helper! critic and sympathiser, true friend of all hours! You know him well enough, I think, to understand that I must be grateful to him.

I am writing too much,—and notwithstanding that I am writing too much, I will write of one thing more. I will say that I am your debtor, not only for this cordial letter and for all the pleasure which came with it, but in other ways, and those the highest: and I will say that while I live to follow this divine art of poetry, in proportion to my love for it and my devotion to it, I must be a devout admirer and student of your works. This is in my heart to say to you—and I say it.

And for the rest, I am proud to remain,

Your obliged and faithful

Elizabeth B. Barrett

How this friendship developed into a romantic attachment and marriage is developed in the next letter, quoted on the following page.

ELIZABETH BARRETT BROWNING TELLS HER SISTERS HOW SHE AND ROBERT BROWNING TOOK THEIR DESTINIES IN THEIR OWN HANDS

[A LETTER TO HENRIETTA AND ARABEL BARRETT]

THE letters just quoted have long been available in the standard volumes of the Browning correspondence, but in 1935 the more intimate letters, never revealed before, were first made public. From this collection, bought at auction for $40,000 by the United Features Syndicate, and brilliantly edited by William Rose Benét, is now printed the crucial letter recording the turning point of this poetic idyl.

The correspondence which started when Robert Browning first praised Elizabeth Barrett's poems soon flowered into visits and courtship. Gradually he persuaded her to marry him, despite her father's violent objections. Browning's own family also disapproved of the marriage, because Elizabeth was six years older than he and an invalid. The whole affair was kept a secret from Mr. Barrett. During the summer Elizabeth's health improved and on September 12, 1846, she and Browning were married at the parish church of St. Pancras. They went to Italy for the winter and the following spring finally settled at the Palazzo Guidi (the "Casa Guidi" of Mrs. Browning's poems) in Florence. All this is recorded with a wealth of intimate detail in this long, rambling sisterly letter:

283

"Papa thinks that I have sold my soul—
for genius . . . mere genius."

[Roanne] October 2, 1846.

I THANK and bless you my dearest Henrietta and Arabel . .
my own dearest kindest sisters!—what I suffered in reaching
Orleans,—at last holding all these letters in my hands, can only
be measured by my deep gratitude to you, and by the tears and
kisses I spent upon every line of what you wrote to me . . dearest
kindest that you are. The delay of the week in Paris brought me
to the hour of my death warrant at Orleans—my 'death warrant'
I called it at the time, I was so anxious and terrified. Robert
brought in a great packet of letters . . . and I held them in my
hands, not able to open one, and growing paler and colder every
moment. He wanted to sit by me while I read them, but I would
not let him. I had resolved never to let him do *that*, before the
moment came—so, after some beseeching, I got him to go away
for ten minutes, to meet the agony alone, and with more courage
so, according to my old habit you know—And besides, it was right
not to let him read . . .

They were very hard letters, those from dearest Papa and dearest George—To the first I had to bow my head—I do not seem
to myself to have deserved that full cup, in the intentions of this
act—but he is my father and he takes his own view, of course, of
what is before him to judge of. But for George, I thought it hard,
I confess, that he should have written to me so with a sword. To
write to me as if I did not love you all,—*I* who would have laid

284

down my life at a sign, if it could have benefitted one of you *really* and essentially:—with the proof, you should have had life and happiness at a sign.

It was hard that he should use his love for me to half break my heart with such a letter—Only he wrote in excitement and in ignorance. I ask of God to show to him and the most unbelieving of you, that never, never did I love you better, all my beloved ones, than when I left you—than in that day, and that moment. . . .

Now I will tell you—Robert who had been waiting at the door, I believe, in great anxiety about me, came in and found me just able to cry from the balm of your tender words—I put your two letters into his hands, and *he*, when he had read them, said with tears in his eyes, and kissing them between the words—"I love your sisters with a deep affection—I am inexpressibly grateful to them,—It shall be the object of my life to justify this trust, as they express it here." . . .

Dearest Henrietta and Arabel,—how I suffered that day—that miserable Saturday . . when I had to *act a part to you*—how I suffered! and how I had to think to myself that if I betrayed one pang of all, I should involve you deeply in the grief which otherwise remained my own. And Arabel to see through it, notwithstanding! I was afraid of her—she looked at me so intently, and was so grave . . my dearest, dearest Arabel! Understand both of you, that if, from the apparent necessities of the instant, I consented to let the ceremony precede the departure by some few days, it was upon the condition of not seeing him again in that house and till we went away.

We parted, as we met, at the door of Marylebone Church—he helped me at the communion table, and not a word passed after. I looked like death, he has said since. You see we were afraid of a sudden removal preventing everything . . or at least, laying

285

the unpleasantness on me of a journey to London *previous* to the ceremony, which particularly I should have hated, for very obvious reasons. There was no elopement in the case, but simply a private marriage; and to have given the least occasion to a certain class of observations, was repugnant to both of us. . . . Wilson knew nothing till the night before. What I suffered under your eyes, you may guess—it was in proportion to every effort successfully made to disguise the suffering. Painful it is to look back upon now—Forgive me for whatever was expiated in the deepest of my heart.

With your letters at Orleans, I had one from dearest Mr. Kenyon in reply to those which we had written to him at the last. Nothing could be more generously and trustingly kind—and to poor Robert it was a great relief, as the verdict of a friend whom he loved and looked up to on many grounds. I will transcribe to you what Mr. Kenyon says; *for you*—you will understand how it is of great price to us. "My dearest E. B. B. I received part of your husband's letters yesterday. To speak briefly as I must, I sympathise in all you have both been thinking and feeling, and in all you have done. Nothing but what is generous in thought and action could come from you and Browning. And the very peculiar circumstances of your case have transmuted what might have been otherwise called 'Imprudence' into 'Prudence,' and apparent wilfulness into real necessity.—To speak personally of you both, I know no two persons so worthy of each other; and to speak personally *to* you both, be assured that out of your own households, you can have no warmer and more affectionate well wisher than I am. It is a pleasant vision to me to think that, if I live, I may hereafter enjoy your joint society and affection, as hitherto I have derived happiness from each of you singly". . . .

The one or two sentences omitted, (for I have not room) are in harmony with all the rest. Dearest, kindest Mr. Kenyon, how

I love him better than all!—Also I had kind notes from Miss Mitford, Nelly Bordman and Mr. Jago, who sent me a prescription for the draughts with ever so many good wishes. . . . I wrote to Jane when I was in Paris . . or rather about to leave it—but to Minny I have not written yet—when the fatigue gives me half an hour I will do it, be sure. I thank you for those letters you speak of having written for me.

Did you get my long letter from Paris? and Trippy, my short note from Havre. Ah, dear Trippy! let her not think hardly of me. No one can judge of this act, except some one who knows thoroughly the man I have married. He rises on me hour by hour. If ever a being of a higher order lived among us with a glory round his head, in these latter days, he is such a being.

Papa thinks that I have sold my soul—for *genius* . . . mere genius. Which I might have done when I was younger, if I had had the opportunity . . but am in no danger of doing now. For my sake, for the love of me, from an infatuation which from first to last has astonished me, he has consented to occupy for a moment a questionable position.

But those who question most, will do him justice fullest—and we must wait a little with resignation. In the meanwhile, what he is, and what he is to *me*, I would fain teach you.—Have faith in me to believe it. He puts out all his great faculties to give me pleasure and comfort . . charms me into thinking of *him* when he sees my thoughts wandering . . . forces me to smile in spite of all of them—if you had seen him that day at Orleans.

He laid me down on the bed and sate by me for hours, pouring out floods of tenderness and goodness, and promising to win back for me, with God's help, the affection of such of you as were angry. And he loves me more and more. Today we have been together a fortnight, and he said to me with a deep, serious tenderness . . "I kissed your feet, my Ba, before I married you—but

287

now I would kiss the ground under your feet, I love you with a so much greater love." And this is true, I see and feel. I feel to have the power of making him happy . . I feel to have it in my hands. It is strange that anyone so brilliant should love me,—but true and strange it is . . and it is impossible for me to doubt it any more. Perfectly happy therefore we should be, if I could look back on you all without this pang. His family have been very kind. His father considered him of age to judge, and never thought of interfering otherwise than of saying at the last moment, "Give your wife a kiss for me" this, when they parted. His sister sent me a little travelling writing desk, with a word written, "E. B. B. from her sister Sarianna." Nobody was displeased at the reserve used towards them, understanding that there were reasons for it which did not detract from his affection for them and my respect.

I told you that Mrs. Jameson was travelling with us, and that we had seen a great deal of her in Paris. She repeats of Robert that she never knew anyone of so affluent a mind and imagination combined with a nature and manners so sunshiny and captivating. Which she well may say . . for he encases us from morning till night—thinks of everybody's feelings . . is witty and wise . . (and foolish too in the right place) charms cross old women who cry out in the diligence "mais, madame, mes jambes!" talks Latin to the priests who enquire at three in the morning whether Newman and Pusey are likely "lapsare in erroribus" (you will make out that) and forgets nothing and nobody . . . except himself . . it is the only omission. He has won Wilson's heart I do assure you—and by the way, Wilson is excellent and active beyond what I could have expected of her. Most affectionate and devoted she has been to me throughout, and now she is not scared by the French, but has learnt already to get warm water and coffee and bread and butter. . . . By the way, what does George mean by speaking of "Arabel or Minny my accomplices"? Does he not

288

believe me when I have spoken the very contrary of such a thing? —or is it that dear Minny has spoken too gently of me to be unblamed? For my Arabel, I know her as I love her . . and do not ask how she spoke.

But I think . . think . . of the suffering I caused you, my own, own Arabel, that evening! I tremble thinking of you that evening—my own dearest dearest Arabel! Oh, do not fancy that new affections can undo the old. I love you now even more, I think. Robert is going to write to you from Pisa, and to Henrietta also. He loves you as his sisters, he says, and wishes that you were with us, and hopes that one day you will be with us . . staying and travelling with us . . exactly as I do myself. And I must not forget to tell you what Mrs. Jameson said the other day to me . . "Well, it is the most charming thing to see you and Mr. Browning together. If two persons were to be chosen from the ends of the earth for perfect union and fitness, there could not be a greater congruity than between you two—" which I tell you, because I think it will please you to hear what is an honest impression of hers, though far too great a compliment to me. . . . And for the rest, if he is brilliant and I am dull, (socially speaking) *Love makes a level*, which is my comfort.

Two separate (not following, of course) nights we have passed in the diligence—and I have had otherwise a good deal of fatigue which has done me no essential harm. I am taken such care of; so pillowed by arms and knees . . so carried up and down stairs against my will . . so spoilt and considered in every possible way. Also the change of air does me good. I am able to do more—and when we get to our rest at Pisa, the fatigue will leave no trace, I think, except of good. You would stare however to see me thrown abroad out of all my habits!—I seem to be in a feverish dream. Tomorrow we take the railroad to Lyons, and the next day embark on the Rhone. At Avignon, we pause a day and go to Vaucluse to hunt Petrarch's footsteps. Today I have not been allowed to stir from this bed where I write, because last night we were travelling—and there has been a table brought close to it (foreign fashion, Arabel!) for Robert to dine on and to make me dine. . . .

I am so glad that you are in the country—Do write—and write . . and tell me everything, and tell me if you like Little Bookham. Half of my soul is with you. May God help you my own beloved ones. Give my best love to dear Mr. Boyd, to whom I shall write in time. And let Mrs. Martin understand the same. And do you feel and know, that as for me . . for my position as a wife . . it is awfully happy for this world. He is too good and tender, and beyond me in all things, and we love each other with a love that grows instead of diminishing. I speak to you of such things rather than of the cathedral at Bourges, because, it is of these, I feel sure, that you desire knowledge rather.

I am going to write to Papa—and to George—very soon, I shall. Ah—dear George would not have written so, if he had known my whole heart, yet he loved me while he wrote, as I felt with every pain the writing caused me. Dear George,—I love him to his worth. And my poor Papa! My thoughts cling to you all, and will not leave their hold. Dearest Henrietta and Arabel let me be as ever and for ever

Your fondly attached

Ba

. . . I meant you to have the letters an hour after I left Wimpole Street. It was very unhappy—I grieve for it. As to going to Bookham, I had thought of that once—but the wrong to you would have been greater, to have spoilt and clouded the new scene, instead of allowing it to be a resource to you. Be happy, my dearest ones—I will write, be sure.

MR. BARRETT did not forgive his daughter, and there was never any reconciliation.

Except for occasional visits to Rome, Paris, and London, the Brownings lived happily in Florence from 1847 until Elizabeth's death in 1861. The Sonnets From the Portuguese were written during the courtship and were never seen by anyone until after the marriage. Elizabeth presented them to her husband at Pisa. A child—the famous "Pen"—was born in 1849.

In "Epilogue to Asolando," the last work to come from Robert Browning's pen, a work deemed by many students to be his authentic self-portrait, appears this stanza:

> Oh, to love so, to be so loved, yet so mistaken!
> What had I on earth to do
> With the slothful, with the mawkish, the unmanly?
> Like the aimless, helpless, hopeless, did I drivel!
> —Being—who?

EDGAR ALLAN POE REVEALS THE SECRET OF "THE TERRIBLE EVIL WHICH CAUSED THE IRREGULARITIES SO PROFOUNDLY LAMENTED"

[A LETTER TO GEORGE EVELETH]

INTO forty bitter, delirious, and lyric years Edgar Allan Poe crowded a wealth of melody, a rare and disciplined genius for creative criticism, and a vivid pageant of tales grotesque and arabesque.

Born in Boston in 1809, orphaned at the age of two, Poe was raised by a guardian who had little understanding of, and less sympathy for, the unruly talents of his ward. Despite his brilliant record at college, Poe's youth was marred by gambling, drinking, poverty, and constant difficulties with his guardian. He was expelled from the University of Virginia and court-martialed at West Point. His early manhood was darkened by that unholy trinity of genius, the hostility of critics, the indifference of the public, and the harsh terms of publishers. Through them all he said poetry was for him "not a purpose but a passion."

Poe secretly married his beautiful cousin, Virginia Clemm, when she was only thirteen, and he twenty-four. It was her mother, Maria, whose energy and devotion tided the young couple through fourteen years of poverty-stricken marriage. The child-wife had "bright liquid eyes and an unearthly pallor." To Poe, her beauty was doubtless

> ". . . Like those Nicæan barks of yore,
> That gently, o'er a perfumed sea,
> The weary, wayworn wanderer bore
> To his own native shore."

ing an author you must imitate him, ape him, out-Herod Herod. She is grossly dishonest.
abuses Lowell, for example, (the best of our poets, perhaps) on account of a personal quarrel
him. She has omitted all mention of me for the same reason — although a short time
the issue of her book, she praised me highly in the Tribune. I enclose you her criticism
you may judge for yourself. She praised "Witchcraft" because Mathews (who toadies her)
it. In a word, she is an ill-tempered and very inconsistent old maid:— avoid her.
Nothing was omitted in "Marie Roget" but what I omitted myself:— all that is mystifi-
on. The story was originally published in Snowden's "Lady's Companion". The "naval officer"
committed the murder (or rather the accidental death arising from an attempt at abor-
composed it; and the whole matter is now well understood — but, for the sake of relatives
is a topic on which I must not speak further. 8 — "The Gold Bug" was originally sent to
am, but he not liking it, I got him to take some critical papers instead, and sent
The Dollar Newspaper which had offered $100 for the best story. It obtained the premi-
and made a great noise. 9 — The "necessities" were pecuniary ones. I referred to a
r at my poverty on the part of the Mirror. 10 — You say — "Can you hint to me what
the terrible evil" which caused the irregularities so profoundly lamented?" Yes; I
do more than hint. This "evil" was the greatest which can befall a man. Six years
a wife, whom I loved as no man ever loved before, ruptured a blood-vessel in singing. Her
was despaired of. I took leave of her forever & underwent all the agonies of her death. She re-
ed partially and I again hoped. At the end of a year the vessel broke again — I went through
isely the same scene. Again in about a year afterward. Then again — again — again &
once again at varying intervals. Each time I felt all the agonies of her death — and
each accession of the disorder I loved her more dearly & clung to her life with more des-
te pertinacity. But I am constitutionally sensitive — nervous in a very unusual degree.
came insane, with long intervals of horrible sanity. During these fits of absolute uncon-
rness I drank, God only knows how often or how much. As a matter of course,
enemies referred the insanity to the drink rather than the drink to the insanity.
d indeed, nearly abandoned all hope of a permanent cure when I found one in the
h of my wife. This I can & do endure as becomes a man — it was the horrible
ever-ending oscillation between hope & despair which I could not longer have
ured without total loss of reason. In the death of what was my life, then, I
ne a new but — oh God! how melancholy an existence!

And now, having replied to all your queries let me refer to The Stylus. I am resolved
my own publisher. To be controlled is to be ruined. My ambition is great. If I succeed, I put
of (within 2 years) in possession of a fortune & infinitely more. My plan is to go through the
& west & endeavor to interest my friends so as to commence with a list of at least
subscribers. With this list I can take the matter into my own hands. There are some few
y friends who have sufficient confidence in me to advance their subscriptions — but
all events succeed I will. Can you or will you help me? I have room to say no more.
Truly, yours — E. A. Poe.

EDGAR ALLAN POE TO GEORGE EVELETH
"...the horrible never-ending oscillation between hope and despair..."

Certainly it was a strange household, shifting about from place to place, but always sustained by the tender regard that all three felt for one another.

Even Poe's wild fits of despondency, usually ending in excessive drinking and the use of drugs, could not shatter the devotion of his girl-wife and her mother. In this letter to George Eveleth, who was a young medical student from Phillips, Maine, and an early admirer of Poe's work, probably the first to hail him as a genius, Poe describes vividly the slow agony of Virginia's death; and with his usual fecundity, outlines some literary plans. Strangely enough, Poe and Eveleth never met. It is the most intimate sort of letter, revealing as it does the deepest secret of Poe's life, and the reason for his untimely and tragic death. Dr. A. S. W. Rosenbach, who acquired the original, truly called it "a confession wrenched from the soul of a man who has reached the heights and depths. . . ."

". . . the horrible never-ending oscillation
between hope & despair . . ."

New-York—Jan. 4, 1848.

MY DEAR SIR—Your last, dated July 26, ends with—"Write will you not?" I have been living ever since in a constant state of intention to write, and finally concluded not to write at all until I could say something definite about The Stylus and other matters.

You perceive that I now send you a Prospectus—but before I speak further on this topic, let me succinctly reply to various points in your letter.

293

1—"Hawthorne" is out—how do you like it?

2—"The Rationale of Verse" was found to come down too heavily (as I forewarned you it did) upon some of poor Colton's personal friends in Frogpondium—the "pundits," you know; so I gave him "a song" for it & took it back. The song was "Ulalume a Ballad" published in the December number of the Am. Rev. I enclose it as copied by the Home Journal (Willis's paper) with the editor's remarks—please let me know how you like "Ulalume".

As for the "Rat. of Verse" I sold it to Graham at a round advance on Colton's price, and in Graham's hands it is still—but not to remain even there; for I mean to get it back, revise or rewrite it (since "Evangeline" has been published) and deliver it as a lecture when I go South & West on my Magazine expedition.

3—I have been "so still" on account of preparation for the magazine campaign—also have been working at my book—nevertheless I have written some trifles not yet published—some which have been.

4—My health is better—best. I have never been so well.

5—I do not well see how I could have otherwise replied to English. You must know him, (English) before you can well estimate my reply. He is so thorough a "blatherskite" that to have replied to him with *dignity* would have been the extreme of the ludicrous. The only true plan—not to have replied to him at all —was precluded on account of the nature of some of his accusations—forgery for instance. To such charges, even from the Autocrat of all Asses—a man is *compelled* to answer. There he had me. Answer him I must. But how?

Believe me there exists no such dilemma as that in which a gentleman is placed when he is forced to reply to a blackguard. If he have any genius then is the time for its display. I confess to you that I rather *like* that reply of mine in a literary sense—

and so do a great many of my friends. It fully answered its purpose beyond a doubt—would to Heaven every work of art did as much!

You err in supposing me to have been "peevish" when I wrote the reply:—the peevishness was all "put on" as a part of my argument—of my plan:—so was the "indignation" with which I wound up. How could I be either peevish or indignant about a matter so well adapted to further my purposes? Were I able to afford so expensive a luxury as personal and especially as *refutable* abuse, I would willingly pay any man $2000 per annum, to hammer away at me all the year round. I suppose you know that I sued the Mirror & got a verdict. English eloped.

5—The "common friend" referred to is Mrs. Frances S. Osgood, the poetess.

6—I agree with you only in part as regards Miss Fuller. She has some general, but no particular, critical powers. She belongs to a *school* of criticism—the Göthean, æsthetic, eulogistic. The creed of this school is that, in criticising an author you must imitate him, ape him, out-Herod Herod. She is grossly dishonest. She abuses Lowell, for example, (the best of our poets, perhaps) on account of a personal quarrel with him. She has omitted all mention of me for the same reason—although, a short time before the issue of her book, she praised me highly in the Tribune. I enclose you her criticism that you may judge for yourself. She praised "Witchcraft" because Mathews (who toadies her) wrote it. In a word, she is an ill-tempered and very inconsistent old maid—avoid her.

7—Nothing was omitted in "Marie Roget" but what I omitted myself:—all *that* is mystification. The story was originally published in Snowden's "Lady's Companion". The "naval officer" who committed the murder (or rather the accidental death arising from an attempt at abortion) *confessed* it; and the whole matter is now well understood—but, for the sake of relatives, this is a topic on which I must not speak further.

8—"The Gold Bug" was originally sent to Graham; but he not liking it, I got him to take some critical papers instead, and sent it to The Dollar Newspaper which had offered $100 for the best story. It obtained the premium, and made a great noise.

9—The "necessities" were pecuniary ones. I referred to a sneer at my poverty on the part of the Mirror.

10—You say—"Can you *hint* to me what was the terrible evil "which caused the irregularities so profoundly lamented?" Yes; I can do more than hint. This "evil" was the greatest which can befall a man. Six years ago, a wife, whom I loved as no man ever loved before, ruptured a blood-vessel in singing. Her life was despaired of. I took leave of her forever & underwent all the agonies of her death. She recovered partially and I again hoped.

At the end of a year the vessel broke again—I went through precisely the same scene. Again in about a year afterward. Then again—again—again & even once again at varying intervals.

Each time I felt all the agonies of her death—and at each accession of the disorder I loved her more dearly & clung to her life with more desperate pertinacity. But I am constitutionally sensitive—nervous in a very unusual degree. I became insane, with long intervals of horrible sanity. During these fits of absolute unconsciousness I drank, God only knows how often or how much.

As a matter of course, my enemies referred the insanity to the drink rather than the drink to the insanity. I had indeed, nearly abandoned all hope of a permanent cure when I found one in the *death* of my wife. This I can & do endure as becomes a man—it was the horrible never-ending oscillation between hope & despair which I could *not* longer have endured, without total loss of reason. In the death of what was my life, then, I receive a new, but—oh God! how melancholy an existence!

And now, having replied to all your queries let me refer to The

Stylus. I am resolved to be my own publisher. To be controlled is to be ruined. My ambition is great. If I succeed, I put myself (within 2 years) in possession of a fortune & infinitely more. My plan is to go through the South & West & endeavor to interest my friends so as to commence with a list of at least 500 subscribers. With this list I can take the matter into my own hands. There are some few of my friends who have sufficient confidence in me to advance their subscriptions—but at all events succeed I will. Can you or will you help me? I have room to say no more.

Truly Yours—

E. A. Poe

A YEAR before this letter was written, Edgar Allan Poe's wife died. A year after it was written, he himself followed. In the light of this dark confession, many of Poe's lyrics and a few of his deathly tales and eerie romances assume a clearer, if more tragic, significance—the second and final stanzas of "Annabel Lee," for example:

> I was a child and she was a child,
>   In this Kingdom by the sea;
> But we loved with a love that was more than love
>   I and my Annabel Lee;
> With a love that the winged seraphs of heaven
>   Coveted her and me.

> . . . For the moon never beams, without bringing me dreams
>   Of the beautiful Annabel Lee;
> And the stars never rise, but I feel the bright eyes
>   Of the beautiful Annabel Lee;
> And so, all the night-tide, I lie down by the side
>   Of my darling—my darling—my life and my bride,
>   In the sepulchre there by the sea
>   In her tomb by the sounding sea.

DOSTOEVSKY DESCRIBES HIS SENSATIONS WHEN
HE HAD BUT ONE MINUTE TO LIVE

[A LETTER TO HIS BROTHER MIHAIL]

Nᴏᴛ until many years after the melodramatic events immediately preceding this letter did Dostoevsky write his greatest novels. In his earlier years, he had frequently foregathered with other young Russian radicals to study the French socialist writers and the problems of political reform in his own land. When he was twenty-five he published his first book, Poor People. In 1849, when he was twenty-eight, he and a group of his comrades were arrested, tried as "conspirators," and sentenced to death. Only a few moments before the hour set for the execution they learned that they were to be deported, imprisoned, but not killed. These few seconds in which Dostoevsky hung between life and death left their profound mark. In this extraordinary letter to his brother, written a day later, he writes at once like one in prison about to die, and one resurrected from the dead:

"... the sentence of death was read ..."

The Peter and Paul Fortress,
December 22, 1849

MIHAIL MIHAILOVICH DOSTOEVSKY,
Nevsky Prospect, opposite Gryazny Street,
in the house of Neslind

Brother, my precious friend! all is settled! I am sentenced to four years' hard labor in the fortress (I believe, of Orenburg), and after that to serve as a private. Today, the 22nd of December, we were taken to the Semionov Drill Ground. There the sentence of death was read to all of us, we were told to kiss the Cross, our swords were broken over our heads, and our last toilet was made (white shirts). Then three were tied to the pillar for execution. I was the sixth. Three at a time were called out; consequently, I was in the second batch and no more than a minute was left me to live.

I remembered you, brother, and all yours; during the last minute you, you alone, were in my mind, only then I realized how I love you, dear brother mine! I also managed to embrace Plescheyev and Durov who stood close to me, and to say good-by to them. Finally the retreat was sounded, and those tied to the pillar were led back, and it was announced to us that His Imperial Majesty granted us our lives. Then followed the present sentences. Palm alone has been pardoned, and returns with his old rank to the army.

I was just told, dear brother, that today or tomorrow we are to

299

be sent off. I asked to see you. But I was told that this was impossible; I may only write you this letter: make haste and give me a reply as soon as you can.

I am afraid that you may somehow have got to know of our death sentence. From the windows of the prison van, when we were taken to the Semionov Drill Ground, I saw a multitude of people; perhaps the news reached you, and you suffered for me. Now you will be easier on my account.

Brother! I have not become downhearted or low-spirited. Life is everywhere life, life in ourselves, not in what is outside us. There will be people near me, and to be a *man* among people and remain a man for ever, not to be downhearted nor to fall in whatever misfortunes may befall me—this is life; this is the task of life. I have realized this. This idea has entered into my flesh and into my blood.

Yes, it's true! The head which was creating, living with the highest life of art, which had realized and grown used to the highest needs of the spirit, that head has already been cut off from my shoulders. There remain the memory and the images created but not yet incarnated by me. They will lacerate me, it is true! But there remains in me my heart and the same flesh and blood which can also love, and suffer, and desire, and remember, and this, after all, is life. *On voit le soleil!* Now, good-by, brother! Don't grieve for me!

Now about material things: my books (I have the Bible still) and several sheets of my manuscript, the rough plan of the play and the novel (and the finished story *A Child's Tale*) have been taken away from me, and in all probability will be got by you. I also leave my overcoat and old clothes, if you send to fetch them. Now, brother, I may perhaps have to march a long distance. Money is needed. My dear brother, when you receive this letter, and if there is any possibility of getting some money, send it to

300

me at once. Money I need now more than air (for one particular purpose). Send me also a few lines. Then if the money from Moscow comes—remember me and do not desert me. Well, that is all! I have debts,[1] but what can I do? . . .

Kiss your wife and children. Remind them of me continually; see that they do no forget me. Perhaps, we shall yet meet some time! Brother, take care of yourself and of your family, live quietly and carefully. Think of the future of your children. . . .

Live positively. There has never yet been working in me such a healthy abundance of spiritual life as now. But will my body endure? I do not know. I am going away sick, I suffer from scrofula. But never mind! Brother, I have already gone through so much in life that now hardly anything can frighten me. Let come what may!

At the first opportunity I shall let you know about myself. Give the Maikovs my farewell and last greetings. Tell them that I thank them all for their constant interest in my fate. Say a few words for me, as warm as possible, as your heart will prompt you, to Eugenia Petrovna.[2] I wish her much happiness and shall ever remember her with grateful respect. Press the hands of Nikolay Apollonovich,[3] and Apollon Maikov, and also of all the others. Find Yanovsky. Press his hand, thank him. Finally, press the hands of all who have not forgotten me. And those who have forgotten me—remember me to them also. Kiss our brother Kolya. Write a letter to our brother Andrey and let him know about me. Write also to Uncle and Aunt. This I ask you in my own name, and greet them for me. Write to our sisters: I wish them happiness.

And maybe, we shall meet again some time, brother! Take care of yourself, go on living, for the love of God, until we meet.

[1] Money owed by Dostoevsky to Krayevsky was paid by A Child's Tale.
[2] Eugenia Petrovna was the mother of the poet Apollon Maikov, Dostoevsky's friend.
[3] N. A. Maikov, the father of A. N. Maikov.

Perhaps some time we shall embrace each other and recall our youth, our golden time that was, our youth and our hopes, which at this very instant I am tearing out from my heart with my blood, to bury them.

Can it indeed be that I shall never take a pen into my hands? I think that after the four years there may be a possibility. I shall send you everything that I may write, if I write anything, my God! How many imaginations, lived through by me, created by me anew, will perish, will be extinguished in my brain or will be spilt as poison in my blood! Yes, if I am not allowed to write, I shall perish. Better fifteen years of prison with a pen in my hands!

Write to me more often, write more details, more, more facts. In every letter write about all kinds of family details, of trifles, don't forget. This will give me hope and life. If you knew how your letters revived me here in the fortress! These last two months and a half, when it was forbidden to write or receive a letter, have been very hard on me. I was ill. The fact that you did not send me money now and then worried me on your account; it meant you yourself were in great need! Kiss the children once again; their lovely little faces do not leave my mind. Ah, that they may be happy! Be happy yourself too, brother, be happy!

But do not grieve, for the love of God, do not grieve for me! Do believe that I am not downhearted, do remember that hope has not deserted me. In four years there will be a mitigation of my fate. I shall be a private soldier—no longer a prisoner, and remember that some time I shall embrace you. I was today in the grip of death for three quarters of an hour; I have lived it through with that idea; I was at the last instant and now I live again!

If anyone has bad memories of me, if I have quarreled with anyone, if I have created in anyone an unpleasant impression—tell them they should forget it, if you manage to meet them. There is no gall or spite in my soul; I should dearly love to embrace any one of my former friends at this moment. It is a comfort, I experienced it today when saying good-by to my dear ones before death. I thought at that moment that the news of the execution would kill you. But now be easy, I am still alive and shall live in the future with the thought that some time I shall embrace you. Only this is now in my mind.

What are you doing? What have you been thinking today? Do you know about us? How cold it was today!

Ah, if only my letter reaches you soon! Otherwise I shall be for four months without news of you. I saw the envelopes in which you sent money during the last two months; the address was written in your hand, and I was glad that you were well.

When I look back at the past and think how much time has been wasted in vain, how much time was lost in delusions, in errors, in idleness, in ignorance of how to live, how I did not value time, how often I sinned against my heart and spirit—my heart bleeds. Life is a gift, life is happiness, each minute might have been an age of happiness. *Si jeunesse savait!* Now, changing my life, I am being reborn into a new form. Brother! I swear to you that I shall not lose hope and shall preserve my spirit and heart in purity. I shall be reborn to a better thing. That is my whole hope, my whole comfort!

The life in prison has already sufficiently killed in me the demands of the flesh which were not wholly pure; I took little heed of myself before. Now privations are nothing to me, and, therefore, do not fear that any material hardship will kill me. This cannot be! Ah! To have health!

Good-by, good-by, my brother! When shall I write you again? You will receive from me as detailed an account as possible of my journey. If I can only preserve my health, then everything will be right!

Well, good-by, good-by, brother! I embrace you closely, I kiss

303

you closely. Remember me without pain in your heart. Do not grieve, I pray you, do not grieve for me! In the next letter I shall tell you of how I go on. Remember then what I have told you: plan out your life, do not waste it, arrange your destiny, think of your children. Oh, to see you, to see you! Good-by! Now I tear myself away from everything that was dear; it is painful to leave it! It is painful to break oneself in two, to cut the heart in two. Good-by! Good-by! But I shall see you, I am convinced—I hope; do not change, love me, do not let your memory grow cold, and the thought of your love will be the best part of my life. Good-by, good-by, once more! Good-by to all! Your brother

Fiodor Dostoevsky

Dec. 22, 1849

At my arrest several books were taken away from me. Only two of them were prohibited books. Won't you get the rest for yourself? But there is this request: one of the books was *The Work of Valerian Maikov*: his critical essays—Eugenia Petrovna's copy. It was her treasure, and she lent it to me. At my arrest I asked the police officer to return that book to her, and gave him the address. I do not know if he returned it to her. Make inquiries! I do not want to take this memory away from her. Good-by, good-by, once more!—Your

F. Dostoevsky

[*On the margins:*]

I do not know if I shall have to march or go on horses. I believe I shall go on horses. Perhaps!

Once again press Emily Fiodorovna's hand, kiss the little ones. Remember me to Krayevsky: perhaps . . .

Write me more particularly about your arrest, confinement, and liberation.

AFTER four years in prison, Dostoevsky's sentence was commuted. But throughout his greatest work he alludes again and again to the shattering experiences of 1849—as indicated by the actual phrasing of the titles of three of his famous novels: The House of Death (1861), Memoirs from Underground (1864), and Crime and Punishment (1866).

CHARLES DICKENS TELLS HIS WIFE THAT THEIR INFANT DAUGHTER HAS DIED

As RECENTLY as 1939 the three-volume Nonesuch Edition of Ten Thousand Letters of Charles Dickens was first published, containing "the tears, the laughter, the daemonic drive of the man." The letter that follows is one of the most poignant in the whole collection.

The completion of David Copperfield marked the happiest period in the life of Charles Dickens. He was thirty-seven years old, a prolific author, confident of success, happily married, and the father of a large family. Then his fortunes changed. His father died; both his wife and his ninth child, the infant Dora, were taken ill.

This letter has a double pathos. As little Dora lay ill at home, Dickens, having left his sick wife at Great Malvern, was presiding at a dinner in honor of the Actors' Theatrical Fund. His friend, John Forster, was called from the meeting to take the message of the child's death. He returned to hear Dickens saying: "Many . . . have come from the scenes of sickness, of suffering, aye, even of death itself, to play their parts before us. Yet how often it is with all of us that in our several spheres we have to do violence to our own feelings and to hide our hearts in carrying on this fight for life, if we would bravely discharge in it our duties and responsibilities."

The next day, Dickens broke the news to his frail wife in this tragic, tender letter.

". . . read this letter very slowly . . ."

Devonshire-terrace
Tuesday morning, 15th April, 1851

M Y DEAREST KATE,—Now observe, you must read this letter very slowly and carefully. If you have hurried on thus far without quite understanding (apprehending some bad news) I rely on your turning back and reading again.

Little Dora, without being in the least pain, is suddenly stricken ill. There is nothing in her appearance but perfect rest—you would suppose her quietly asleep, but I am sure she is very ill, and I cannot encourage myself with much hope of her recovery. I do not (and why should I say I do to you, my dear?) I do not think her recovery at all likely.

I do not like to leave home, I can do no good here, but I think it right to stay. You will not like to be away, I know, and I cannot reconcile it to myself to keep you away. Forster, with his usual affection for us, comes down to bring you this letter and to bring you home, but I cannot close it without putting the strongest entreaty and injunction upon you to come with perfect composure—

> to remember what I have often told you, that we never can expect to be exempt, as to our many children, from the afflictions of other parents, and that if—if when you come I should even have to say to you, "Our little baby is dead," you are to do your duty to the rest, and to show yourself worthy of the great trust you hold in them.

307

If you will only read this steadily I have a perfect confidence in your doing what is right.

Ever affectionately,

Charles Dickens

MANY years later the world was to discover that the marriage of Charles and Catherine Hogarth Dickens was by no means a happy one. They separated in 1858, after twenty-two years of married life. The year before he had fallen in love with a blonde actress named Ellen Ternan.

On May 9, 1929, at the age of eighty-nine, Mrs. Kate Perugini, third child of Catherine and Charles Dickens, died and left to her biographer this candid declaration: "I loved my father better than any man in the world. I loved him for his faults. . . . My father was a wicked man—a very wicked man. . . ."

THREE TYPICAL LETTERS OF
ABRAHAM LINCOLN

[TO HIS STEPBROTHER, AN OLD COMRADE, AND
MRS. BIXBY]

THESE three letters, written respectively in 1848, 1855, and 1864, reveal three phases of Lincoln's hard-won wisdom—his homely common sense in practical affairs, his political vision and integrity, and his brooding compassion. They range from simple shrewdness to inspired foresight, from heroic leadership to a sublime tenderness. Together they show the depths and spiritual development of one whom, in the words of his friend Herndon, "God rolled through his fiery furnace."

In these letters we find a firsthand and intimate disclosure of the legendary qualities which inspired the apostrophe of Edwin Markham at the dedication of the Lincoln Memorial in Washington in 1922:

The color of the ground was in him, the red earth,
The smack and tang of elemental things.
                    Sprung from the West,
He drank the valorous youth of a new world,
The strength of virgin forests braced his mind,
The hush of spacious prairies still his soul.
His words were oaks in acorns;
                    And his thoughts
Were roots that firmly gripped the granite truth.

ABRAHAM LINCOLN REFUSES TO LEND HIS STEP-BROTHER EIGHTY DOLLARS

[A LETTER TO JOHN D. JOHNSTON]

THIS is a letter which reveals the more intimate, the more homely phase of Lincoln's life, and provides a vivid contrast to the moral grandeur of some of his more famous utterances. Here "the man of sorrows" writes as Poor Richard might have written when faced with a problem in family relationships. He reads a sermon on thrift and diligence to a wayward kinsman. It is a model of clear thinking and straightforward writing.

At the time of this letter, Lincoln's stepmother, Sally Bush Lincoln, was living on a farm in Coles County, Illinois. Her son, who had husked corn in Indiana with Lincoln, wrote him asking for a loan. This was his reply:

"... go to work 'tooth and nail' ..."

[Dec. 24, 1848]

DEAR JOHNSTON:
Your request for eighty dollars, I do not think it best to comply with now. At the various times when I have helped you a little, you have said to me, "We can get along very well now," but in a very short time I find you in the same difficulty again.

311

Now this can only happen by some defect in your conduct. What that defect is, I think I know. You are not *lazy*, and still you *are* an *idler*. I doubt whether since I saw you, you have done a good whole day's work, in any one day. You do not very much dislike to work, and still you do not work much, merely because it does not seem to you that you could get much for it.

This habit of uselessly wasting time, is the whole difficulty; it is vastly important to you, and still more so to your children, that you should break this habit. It is more important to them, because they have longer to live, and can keep out of an idle habit before they are in it, easier than they can get out after they are in.

You are now in need of some ready money; and what I propose is, that you shall go to work, "tooth and nail," for somebody who will give you money for it.

Let father and your boys take charge of your things at home—prepare for a crop, and make the crop, and you go to work for the best money wages, or in discharge of any debt you owe, that you can get. And to secure you a fair reward for your labor, I now promise you that for every dollar you will, between this and the first of May, get for your own labor either in money or in your own indebtedness, I will then give you one other dollar.

By this, if you hire yourself at ten dollars a month, from me you will get ten more, making twenty dollars a month for your work. In this, I do not mean you shall go off to St. Louis, or the lead mines, or the gold mines, in California, but I mean for you to go at it for the best wages you can get close to home—in Coles County.

Now if you will do this, you will soon be out of debt, and what is better, you will have a habit that will keep you from getting in debt again. But if I should now clear you out, next year you will be just as deep in as ever. You say you would almost give your place in Heaven for $70 or $80. Then you value your place in Heaven very cheaply, for I am sure you can with the offer I make you get the seventy or eighty dollars for four or five months' work. You say if I furnish you the money you will deed me the land, and if you don't pay the money back, you will deliver possession—

Nonsense! If you can't now live with the land, how will you then live without it? You have always been kind to me, and I do not now mean to be unkind to you. On the contrary, if you will but follow my advice, you will find it worth more than eight times eighty dollars to you.

Affectionately

Your brother

A. Lincoln

EVEN in the massive documentation of The Prairie Years, by Carl Sandburg, there is no recorded evidence as to whether or not Lincoln's stepbrother took this letter to heart, but it is reasonable to assume that the advice of "Honest Abe" proved effective.

ABRAHAM LINCOLN OPENS HIS HEART TO AN OLD COMRADE

[A LETTER TO JOSHUA F. SPEED]

JOSHUA SPEED was an "enlightened Southerner" who favored slavery but opposed the bitter agitation that was taking place over it in the 1840's and 1850's. He was, moreover, an old friend of Abraham Lincoln, in many ways his most intimate correspondent, with the exception of William Herndon. Years before young Herndon had clerked in Josh Speed's store. According to Carl Sandburg, "Speed and Lincoln slept in the same big room over the store and some nights talked each other to sleep."

During Lincoln's wavering courtship of Mary Todd, he and Speed exchanged long and friendly letters. Following Lincoln's marriage in 1842, and after Speed had moved to Louisville, Kentucky, the correspondence dwindled until it almost ceased, chiefly because Mrs. Lincoln did not like Speed and did all she could to keep the old friends apart.

At the time of this letter, Lincoln's interest in politics was becoming active again, following the lull which took place with his unsuccessful term in Congress, ending in 1849. He became greatly interested in opposing the Kansas-Nebraska Act, which was steered through the Senate under the sponsorship of Stephen A. Douglas early in 1854. The following year he was disappointed in his own senatorial aspirations, but continued to campaign against the Kansas-Nebraska Act, a crucial piece of legislation in the whole issue of slavery. It was at this time he wrote to his old friend on the subject.

The 1841 trip to which Lincoln refers in this letter was one that he had taken with Speed himself from Louisville to Springfield. This was just after Lincoln's breakdown, following his difficulties with Mary Todd on

314

the fatal first of January of that year—difficulties which made his life "a domestic hell."

Many authorities on Lincoln's life feel that this is one of the most revealing, and politically and historically one of the most significant, letters from the pen of Abraham Lincoln.

". . . differ we must."

Springfield, August 24, 1855

DEAR SPEED:
You know what a poor correspondent I am. Ever since I received your very agreeable letter of the 22d of May I have been intending to write you an answer to it. You suggest that in political action, now, you and I would differ. I suppose we would; not quite as much, however, as you may think. You know I dislike slavery, and you fully admit the abstract wrong of it. So far there is no cause of difference. But you say that sooner than yield your legal right to the slave, especially at the bidding of those who are not themselves interested, you would see the Union dissolved. I am not aware that any one is bidding you yield that right; very certainly I am not. I leave that matter entirely to yourself. I also acknowledge your rights and my obligations under the Constitution in regard to your slaves. I confess I hate to see the poor creatures hunted down and caught and carried back to their stripes and unrequited toil; but I bite my lips and keep quiet.

In 1841 you and I had together a tedious low-water trip on a steamboat from Louisville to St. Louis. You may remember, as I well do, that from Louisville to the mouth of the Ohio there

315

were on board ten or a dozen slaves shackled together with irons. That sight was a continued torment to me, and I see something like it every time I touch the Ohio or any other slave border. It is not fair for you to assume that I have no interest in a thing which has, and continually exercises, the power of making me miserable. You ought rather to appreciate how much the great body of the Northern people do crucify their feelings, in order to maintain their loyalty to the Constitution and the Union. I do oppose the extension of slavery because my judgment and feeling so prompt me, and I am under no obligations to the contrary. If for this you and I must differ, differ we must.

You say, if you were President, you would send an army and hang the leaders of the Missouri outrages upon the Kansas elections; still, if Kansas fairly votes herself a slave State she must be admitted, or the Union must be dissolved. But how if she votes herself a slave State unfairly, that is, by the very means for which you say you would hang men? Must she still be admitted, or the Union dissolved? That will be the phase of the question when it first becomes a practical one.

In your assumption that there may be a fair decision of the slavery question in Kansas, I plainly see you and I would differ about the Nebraska law. I look upon that enactment not as a law, but as a violence from the beginning. It was conceived in violence, is maintained in violence, and is being executed in violence. I say it was conceived in violence, because the destruction of the Missouri Compromise, under the circumstances, was nothing less than violence. It was passed in violence, because it could not have passed at all but for the votes of many members in violence of the known will of their constituents. It is maintained in violence, because the elections since clearly demand its repeal; and the demand is openly disregarded.

316

You say men ought to be hung for the way they are executing the law; I say the way it is being executed is quite as good as any of its antecedents. It is being executed in the precise way which was intended from the first, else why does no Nebraska man express astonishment or condemnation? Poor Reeder is the only public man who has been silly enough to believe that anything like fairness was ever intended, and he has been bravely undeceived. . . .

You inquire where I now stand. That is a disputed point. I think I am a Whig; but others say there are no Whigs, and that I am an Abolitionist. When I was at Washington, I voted for the Wilmot proviso as good as forty times; and I never heard of any one attempting to unwhig me for that. I now do no more than oppose the extension of slavery. I am not a Know-Nothing; that is certain. How could I be? How can any one who abhors the oppression of negroes be in favor of degrading classes of white people? Our progress in degeneracy appears to me to be pretty rapid. As a nation we began by declaring that "all men are created equal." We now practically read it "all men are created equal, except negroes." When the Know-Nothings get control, it will read "all men are created equal, except negroes and foreigners and Catholics." When it comes to this, I shall prefer emigrating to some country where they make no pretense of loving liberty,—to Russia, for instance, where despotism can be taken pure, and without the base alloy of hypocrisy.

Mary will probably pass a day or two in Louisville in October. My kindest regards to Mrs. Speed. On the leading subject of this letter, I have more of her sympathy than I have of yours; and yet let me say I am

Your friend forever,

A. Lincoln

317

THE following year, 1856, "saw bonfires for the new Republican party of Illinois." Then came the debates with Stephen A. Douglas, the election to the presidency, the Civil War, the Emancipation Proclamation—all following inevitably from the sentiments expressed and the conflicts and events recorded in this letter.

ABRAHAM LINCOLN CONSOLES MRS. LYDIA BIXBY ON THE LOSS OF FIVE SONS IN THE CIVIL WAR

THIS is one of the most quoted letters in American history. Viscount Bryce said of it: "I do not know where the nobility of self-sacrifice for a great cause, and of the consolation which the thought of a sacrifice so made should bring, is set forth with such simple and pathetic beauty. Deep must be the fountains from which there issues so pure a stream."

Carl Sandburg has said of it: "More darkly than the Gettysburg speech the letter wove its awful implication that human freedom so often was paid for with agony. . . ." In these words Lincoln "performed a rite, managing language as though he might be a ship captain at midnight by lantern light, dropping black roses into the immemorial sea for mystic remembrance and consecration. . . . Here was a piece of the American Bible. . . ."

It is interesting to compare this Lincoln letter with one that Kaiser Wilhelm is reputed to have sent on a somewhat similar occasion to a mother whose nine sons had fallen on the field of battle. The Emperor wrote: "His Majesty the Kaiser hears that you have sacrificed nine sons in defense of the Fatherland in the present war. His Majesty is immensely gratified at the fact, and in recognition is pleased to send you his photograph with frame and autograph signature."

Mrs. Bixby first came to the attention of President Lincoln as "the bitter year of 1864" was drawing to a close. Governor Andrew of Massachusetts wrote him about the case of a widow living at 15 Dover Street, Boston. According to information he had received from his State Adjutant General, William Schouler, she had sent five sons into the Union armies, and all had been killed in action. Two years before, the Governor had given her forty dollars to defray her traveling expenses for a hospital visit with one of these wounded sons. The Adjutant General's report stated: "About ten days ago, Mrs. Bixby came to my office and showed me five letters from five company commanders, and each letter informed the poor women of the death of one of her sons. Her last remaining son was recently killed in the fight on the Weldon Railroad."

Carl Sandburg has pointed out that though this document came to Lincoln in mid-October of a crucial year in the nation's major political crisis, he characteristically refrained from writing an immediate letter to Mrs. Bixby that might have been made public for campaign purposes. Instead, he waited until November 21 and then wrote the following letter, which he had forwarded to her through the War Department and Adjutant General Schouler:

"*. . . how weak and fruitless must be any word of mine . . .*"

Executive Mansion
Washington, Nov. 21, 1864

TO MRS. BIXBY, Boston, Mass.
   Dear Madam,
   I have been shown in the files of the War Department a statement of the Adjutant General of Massachusetts that you are the mother of five sons who have died gloriously on the field of battle. I feel how weak and fruitless must be any word of mine which should attempt to beguile you from the grief of a loss so overwhelming. But I cannot refrain from tendering you the consolation that may be found in the thanks of the republic they died to

Executive Mansion
Washington, Nov 21. 1864

To Mrs Bixby, Boston, Mass,

Dear Madam,

I have been shown in the files of the War Department a statement of the Adjutant General of Massachusetts that you are the mother of five sons who have died gloriously on the field of battle. I feel how weak and fruitless must be any word of mine which should attempt to beguile you from the grief of a loss so overwhelming. But I cannot refrain from tendering you the consolation that may be found in the thanks of the republic they died to save. I pray that our Heavenly Father may assuage the anguish of your bereavement, and leave you only the cherished memory of the loved and lost, and the solemn pride that must be yours to have laid so costly a sacrifice upon the altar of freedom.

Yours very sincerely and respectfully,

A. Lincoln.

ABRAHAM LINCOLN TO MRS. LYDIA BIXBY

"…how weak and fruitless must be any word of mine…"

save. I pray that our Heavenly Father may assuage the anguish of your bereavement, and leave you only the cherished memory of the loved and lost, and the solemn pride that must be yours to have laid so costly a sacrifice upon the altar of freedom.

Yours very sincerely and respectfully,
A. Lincoln

IT MAY come as a shock to some readers to learn that this masterpiece of compassion was not completely based on fact. Someone had blundered, and Lincoln was misinformed. In the first place, it appears from later military researches that Mrs. Bixby originally protested against the enlistment of her sons in the Civil War. Furthermore, all five did not die gloriously on the field of battle. Sergeant Charles Bixby was killed in action at Fredericksburg; Private Oliver Bixby was killed in action at Petersburg; Henry was taken prisoner, exchanged, and returned to his mother in good health; George deserted to the enemy, and Edward not only deserted but fled the country. His mother swore that he had enlisted (against her will) at the age of sixteen and that he had periods of insanity. His discharge papers were therefore authorized, but he deserted and went to sea before they were issued.

The subsequent history of this letter, as recorded in Carl Sandburg's monumental biography of Abraham Lincoln, is extremely interesting:

"The President of the United States took Mrs. Bixby as a symbol, as a transfigured American mother who deserved enshrinement for loyalty and heroic service. It was just as well perhaps that no one recorded what Mrs. Bixby may have exclaimed as her eyes fluttered over the written words of the President of the United States. The letter was literary. She was literate, not literary. Her cue was silence."

Adjutant General Schouler gave out a copy of the letter to the Boston newspapers. Before many weeks it was reprinted all over the world.

Although later research had found errors in the first War Department records, and thus changed the facts upon which Lincoln's consolatory letter to Mrs. Lydia Bixby was based, the substance, as Sandburg has pointed out, remains unchanged: "Whether all five had died on the field of battle, or only two, four of her sons had been poured away into the river of war. The two who had deserted were as lost to her as though dead. The one who had returned alive had fought at Gettysburg. If sacrifice could be transmitted into cold figures, she deserved some kind of a token, some award approaching the language Lincoln had employed. Lincoln was not deceived."

The letter is now an incontestable part of America's heritage, but at the Civil War's dark end, it was a subject of raging controversy. Lincoln's enemies denounced it as "cheap and ostentatious." One newspaper even asked why the President was shedding these tears for Mrs. Bixby's sons while his own two sons were "kept at home in luxury, far from the dangers of the field." At the time Tad Lincoln was eleven years old and Robert was twenty-one, and, as Sandburg says, "His father was letting a mother of unsound mind have her way that the boy should not go where he might be killed."

RALPH WALDO EMERSON GREETS WALT WHITMAN AT THE BEGINNING OF A GREAT CAREER

It has been estimated that Ralph Waldo Emerson left to his literary executor more than four thousand letters. Until 1938 more than two thousand of these had never been published.

The great transcendentalist was born in Boston in 1803. After his education at Harvard and training for the Unitarian ministry, Emerson made his first success as a lecturer. His stirring discourses on self-reliance won him immediate fame. "It was a doctrine of supreme value to a comparatively youthful country which had hitherto felt very keenly a sense of dependence upon Europe," says F. H. Pritchard.

This point of view naturally enhanced the appeal of Whitman's Leaves of Grass to Emerson.

"I was simmering, simmering," wrote Walt Whitman. "Emerson brought me to a boil."

The poet referred, no doubt, to the fact that when Leaves of Grass first appeared in a volume of ninety-four pages in 1855, and was completely neglected by both the critics and the public, a letter from Emerson to Whitman, published in the New York Tribune, created widespread discussion and stimulated the first demand for the book. This is what Emerson wrote:

"... the wonderful gift of 'Leaves of Grass.'"

Concord 21 July
Mass^{tts} 1855

DEAR SIR,
I am not blind to the worth of the wonderful gift of "Leaves of Grass." I find it the most extraordinary piece of wit & wisdom that America has yet contributed. I am very happy in reading it, as great power makes us happy. It meets the demand I am always making of what seems the sterile and stingy Nature, as if too much handiwork or too much lymph in the temperament were making our Western wits fat and mean. I give you joy of your free & brave thought. I have great joy in it. I find incomparable things said incomparably well, as they must be. I find the courage of *treatment*, which so delights us, & which large perception only can inspire.

I greet you at the beginning of a great career, which must yet have had a long foreground somewhere, for such a start. I rubbed my eyes a little to see if this sunbeam were no illusion; but the solid sense of the book is a sober certainty. It has the best merits, namely, of fortifying & encouraging.

I did not know until I, last night, saw the book advertised in a newspaper, that I could trust the name as real & available for a post-office.

I wish to see my benefactor, & have felt much like striking my tasks, & visiting New York to pay you my respects.

R. W. Emerson
[To] Mr Walter Whitman

At the advice of Charles A. Dana, editor of the New York Sun, Whitman appended Emerson's letter to the second and enlarged edition of Leaves of Grass, which appeared the following year, in 1856. The endorsement of so famous and respected a philosopher helped to sell the book but did not too greatly impress a public, outraged and rather vitriolic in its abuse of both the poems and the poet. Soon after writing this letter, Emerson met Whitman. Although the two men were separated by a world of culture and tradition, and were as different as the cultivated lawns of Emerson's Cambridge from the wild dunes of Whitman's Long Island, nevertheless their mutual admiration lasted all their lives.

At one point, however, Emerson's enthusiasm for Leaves of Grass cooled considerably. This was the occasion when Whitman refused to expunge some of the "strong words" to which the philosopher objected.

ELIZABETH BARRETT BROWNING IMPLORES NA-
POLEON III TO PARDON VICTOR HUGO

NAPOLEON III (Louis Napoleon), first President, then Emperor of the French, naturally had little sympathy for a powerful and gracious man of letters like Victor Hugo, who not only had the audacity to speak his mind but the genius to speak it magnificently.* Shortly after Hugo wrote his violent satire, Les Châtiments, he was banished because of his anti-Bonapartist sentiments. This banishment inspired Elizabeth Barrett Browning (who herself was living in exile for reasons of health) to write this impassioned and disinterested plea for a fellow artist—one whom she knew only through his work.* It is a ringing manifesto in defense of a poet's sensitive temperament and integrity.

"It is a woman's voice, Sire, which dares to utter what many yearn for in silence."

SIRE,
  I am only a woman and have no claim on your Majesty's attention except that of the weakest on the strongest. Probably my very name as the wife of an English poet and as named itself a little among English poets, is unknown to your Majesty. I never approached my own sovereign with a petition, nor am skilled in the way of addressing kings. Yet having, through a studious and

* See the earlier letters of Elizabeth Barrett, on page 275, and an earlier letter of Victor Hugo, on page 259.

326

make an exception of him as God made an exception
of him when He gave him genius, and call him
back without condition to his country and
his daughters' grace.

I have written these words without the knowledge
of any. Naturally I should have preferred as
a woman to have addressed them through the mediation
of the tender-hearted Empress Eugénie; but, a
wife myself, I felt it would be harder for her
majesty to pardon an offence against the
Emperor Napoleon, than it could be for the
Emperor.

And I am driven by an irresistible impulse
to your Majesty's feet to ask this grace. It
is a woman's voice, Sire, which dares to utter
what many yearn for in silence. I have believed
in Napoleon the Third. Passionately loving the
democracy, I have understood from the beginning
that it was to be served throughout Europe in you
and by you. I have trusted you for doing greatly.
I will trust you besides for pardoning nobly.
You will be Napoleon in this also.

    Elizabeth Barrett Browning.

ELIZABETH BARRETT BROWNING TO NAPOLEON III
"It is a woman's voice, Sire, which dares to utter what many yearn for in silence."

thoughtful life, grown used to great men (among the Dead at least) I cannot feel entirely at a loss in speaking to the Emperor Napoleon.

And I beseech you to have patience with me while I supplicate you. It is not for myself nor for mine.

I have been reading with wet eyes and a swelling heart (as many who love and some who hate your Majesty have lately done) a book called the 'Contemplations' of a man who has sinned deeply against you in certain of his political writings, and who expiates rash phrases and unjustifiable statements in exile in Jersey. I have no personal knowledge of this man; I never saw his face; and certainly I do not come now to make his apology. It is indeed precisely because he cannot be excused, that, I think, he might worthily be forgiven. For this man, whatever else he is not, is a great poet of France, and the Emperor who is the guardian of her other glories should remember him and not leave him out.

Ah sire, what was written on "Napoleon le petit" does not touch your Majesty; but what touches you is, that no historian of the age should have to write hereafter, "While Napoleon the Third reigned Victor Hugo lived in exile." What touches you is, that when your people count gratefully the men of commerce, arms and science secured by you to France, no voice shall murmur, "But where is our poet?" What touches you is, that, however statesmen & politicians may justify his exclusion, it may draw no sigh from men of sentiment and impulse, yes, and from women like myself. What touches you is, that when your own beloved young prince shall come to read these poems (and when you wish him a princely nature, you wish, sire, that such things should move him) he may exult to recall that his imperial father was great enough to overcome this great poet with magnanimity.

Ah Sire, you are great enough! You can allow for the peculiarity of the poetical temperament, for the temptations of high gifts, for the fever in which poets are apt to rage and suffer beyond the measure of other men. You can consider that when they hate most causelessly, there is a divine love in them somewhere,—and that when they see most falsely they are loyal to some ideal light. Forgive this enemy, this accuser, this traducer. Disprove him by your generosity. Let no tear of an admirer of his poetry drop upon your purple. Make an exception of him as God made an exception of him when He gave him genius, and call him back *without condition* to his country and his daughter's grave.

I have written those words without the knowledge of any. Naturally I should have preferred as a woman to have addressed them through the mediation of the tender-hearted Empress Eugénie,— but, a wife myself, I felt it would be harder for her majesty to pardon an offence against the Emperor Napoleon, than it could be for the Emperor.

And I am driven by an irresistible impulse to your Majesty's feet to ask this grace. It is a woman's voice, Sire, which dares to utter what many yearn for in silence. I have believed in Napoleon the Third. Passionately loving the democracy, I have understood from the beginning that it was to be served throughout Europe in you and by you. I have trusted you for doing greatly. I will trust you besides for pardoning nobly. You will be Napoleon in this also.

Elizabeth Barrett Browning

LIKE *many other letters written in white heat, this one was actually never mailed. Victor Hugo remained in exile until after Napoleon III suffered military disaster and was himself banished from France. Thus was poetic justice vindicated by the turn of historic events.*

328

THOMAS BABINGTON MACAULAY PEERS INTO THE FUTURE AND PREDICTS THAT THE AMERICAN REPUBLIC WILL BE LAID WASTE BY BARBARIANS IN THE TWENTIETH CENTURY

[A LETTER TO HENRY S. RANDALL]

ON AUGUST 18, 1937, President Franklin D. Roosevelt, in an address celebrating the three hundred and fiftieth anniversary of the birth of Virginia Dare in Fort Raleigh, North Carolina, brought to light an amazing prophecy made by Thomas Babington Macaulay in 1857, regarding the future of democracy in America. This almost forgotten letter, written by the famous historian eighty years before, instantly became front-page news and floodlighted the major policies and objectives of the New Deal.

Macaulay was Britain's outstanding historical scholar of the nineteenth century. At the age of eight, this precocious child, son of a noted philanthropist and pioneer of abolition, had written a history of the world. He was particularly active in Britain's antislavery reform movement during the first part of the nineteenth century; he campaigned for the Reform Act of 1832. At the age of thirty he entered Parliament and added to his reputation as essayist and critic new honors as an orator and statesman. Following his active political career, he devoted his life to historical labors and, with the possible exception of Gibbon, became the most popular historian in England.

The background of the letter quoted by President Roosevelt is particularly interesting. Henry S. Randall, American biographer of Jefferson, received four significant letters from his British correspondent, Lord

Macaulay. The correspondence began after Randall sent Macaulay an autograph of George Washington and copies of his own four-volume history of Colonial New York State. Randall was Secretary of State in New York from 1851 to 1853 and noted for his treatises on sheep husbandry. He had been the youngest delegate to the Democratic National Convention of 1835.

Macaulay's letters, which Randall made public after his death, were first published in The Southern Literary Messenger in Richmond, Virginia, in 1860. They were reprinted in London papers and caused wide controversial discussion because of their searching criticism of the American system of government.

President Roosevelt was not the first chief magistrate of the United States to quote from this correspondence. President Garfield used Macaulay as a target in a Congressional campaign speech at Cornell University in 1878.

In referring to this letter, President Roosevelt drew a parallel between the New Deal and the campaign of Andrew Jackson against the small group of directors of the Bank of the United States and their supporters in the United States Senate who believed in the conduct of government "by a self-perpetuating group at the top of the ladder." He then went on to say ". . . that this was the clear line of demarcation—the fundamental difference of opinion in regard to American institutions—is proved by an amazingly interesting letter which Lord Macaulay wrote in 1857 to an American friend":

"Your Constitution is all sail and no anchor . . ."

[May 23, 1857]
Holly Lodge, Kensington, London

DEAR SIR,
You are surprised to learn that I have not a high opinion of Mr. Jefferson, and I am surprised at your surprise. I am certain that I never wrote a line, and that I never . . . uttered a word indicating an opinion that the supreme authority in a state ought to be intrusted to the majority of citizens told by the head, in other words, to the poorest and most ignorant part of society.

I have long been convinced that institutions purely democratic must, sooner or later, destroy liberty, or civilisation, or both. . . .

I have not the smallest doubt that, if we had a purely democratic government here, the effect would be the same. . . . You may think that your country enjoys an exemption from these evils. . . . I am of a very different opinion. Your fate I believe to be certain, though it is deferred by a physical cause. As long as you have a boundless extent of fertile and unoccupied land, your labouring population will be far more at ease than the labouring population of the old world; and, while that is the case, the Jeffersonian polity may continue to exist without causing any fatal calamity.

But the time will come when New England will be as thickly peopled as old England. Wages will be as low, and will fluctuate as much with you as with us. You will have your Manchesters and Birminghams, and in those Manchesters and Birminghams, hundreds of thousands of artisans will assuredly be sometimes out of

331

work. Then, your institutions will be fairly brought to the test. Distress everywhere makes the labourer mutinous and discontented, and inclines him to listen with eagerness to agitators who tell him that it is a monstrous iniquity that one man should have a million while another cannot get a full meal.

In bad years there is plenty of grumbling here, and sometimes a little rioting. But it matters little. For here the sufferers are not the rulers. The supreme power is in the hands of a class, numerous indeed, but select; of an educated class, of a class which is, and knows itself to be, deeply interested in the security of property and the maintenance of order. Accordingly, the malcontents are firmly, yet gently, restrained. The bad time is got over without robbing the wealthy to relieve the indigent. The springs of national prosperity soon begin to flow again: work is plentiful: wages rise; and all is tranquillity and cheerfulness. . . .

. . . I cannot help foreboding the worst. It is quite plain that your government will never be able to restrain a distressed and discontented majority. . . . The day will come when . . . a multitude of people, none of whom has had more than half a breakfast, or expects to have more than half a dinner, will choose a Legislature. . . . On one side is a statesman preaching patience, respect for vested rights. . . . On the other is a demagogue ranting about the tyranny of capitalists . . . and asking why anybody should be permitted to drink Champagne and to ride in a carriage, while thousands of honest folks are in want of necessaries. . . . I seriously apprehend that you will, in some such season of adversity . . . do things which will prevent prosperity from returning; that you will act like people who should in a year of scarcity devour all the seed corn, and thus make the next year a year, not of scarcity, but of absolute famine. . . . There is nothing to stop you. Your Constitution is all sail and no anchor. . . . Either some Cæsar or Napoleon will seize the reins of government with a strong hand; or your republic will be . . . laid waste by barbarians in the twentieth Century as the Roman Empire was in the fifth. . . .

Thomas Babington Macaulay

COMMENTING on the quoted letter, President Roosevelt said, "Macaulay was, in other words, opposed to what we call 'popular government.' That, my friends, with all due respect to Lord Macaulay, is an excellent representation of the cries of alarm which rise today from the throats of American Lord Macaulays. They tell you that America drifts toward the Scylla of dictatorship on the one hand, or the Charybdis of anarchy on the other. Their anchor for the salvation of the ship of state is Macaulay's anchor: . . . 'supreme power . . . in the hands of a class, numerous indeed, but select; of an educated class, of a class which is, and knows itself to be, deeply interested in the security of property and the maintenance of order.' "

One commentator, discussing President Roosevelt's citation of this letter, pointed out that the past, rather than the future, had obviously been Macaulay's specialty, and added that America's record as a republic and a democracy from 1857 to 1937 was the most effective and most ironic commentary on Lord Macaulay's prophecy. Another commentator added that "like Christianity, democracy had not failed . . . it just hadn't been tried. . . ." and that "the cure for the ills of democracy was still more democracy. . . ."

JOHN BROWN BIDS FAREWELL TO HIS FAMILY
THE NIGHT BEFORE HE IS EXECUTED

JOHN BROWN's fanatical devotion to the Abolitionist cause before the Civil War is an epic chapter in American history. Ever since he had gone to Kansas in 1855 to live with five of his twenty sons, he had led a series of messianic raids on the pro-slavery forces, had clashed with state officials and soldiers in a series of bloody massacres, and had become the object of a relentless man hunt. Finally the Virginia authorities captured him at Harpers Ferry and in 1859 sentenced him to death.

"I submit to arrest," he said, "knowing full well that I shall be hanged for this attempt to end the evils of slavery. But after I am dead, the evil will remain and you and all other patriots will come to learn that it can be purged from this guilty world only with blood."

Brown asked the commanding general for permission to spend his last night on earth with his wife. The request was not granted. According to Brown's biographer, Oswald Garrison Villard, it was "the only time in all his imprisonment that he gave way to anger or passion." But when the parting came, both husband and wife "exhibited a composure, either feigned or real, that was truly surprising."

With his wife gone, John Brown devoted himself to his last letter and to "a brief but calm sleep." Here is the farewell letter to his family:

334

JOHN BROWN TO HIS FAMILY

"*I am waiting the hour of my public* murder
with great composure of mind . . ."

Charlestown, Prison, Jefferson Co., Va.
30th Nov 1859

MY DEARLY Beloved Wife, Sons: & Daughters, Everyone
As I now begin what is probably the last letter I shall
ever write to any of you; I conclude to write you all at the same
time. . . . I am waiting the hour of my public *murder* with great
composure of mind, & cheerfulness: feeling the strongest assurance
that in no other possible way could I be used to so much advance
the cause of God; & of humanity: & that nothing that either I or
all my family have sacrificed or suffered: *will be lost.*

The reflection that a *wise & merciful, as well as just & holy God:*
rules not only the affairs of *this world*; but of all worlds; is a rock
to set our feet upon; under all circumstances: *even* those more
severely *trying ones*: into which our own follies; & rongs have
placed us. I have now no doubt but that our seeming *disaster*: will
ultimately result in the most *glorious success*. So my dear *shattered
& broken* family be of good cheer; & believe & trust in God; "*with
all your heart & with all your soul*;" for "*he doeth All things well.*"
Do not feel ashamed on my account; nor *for one moment* despair
of the cause; or grow *weary of well doing*. I bless God; I never felt
stronger confidence in the certain and near approach of a *bright
Morning*; & a *glorious day*; than I have felt; & do now feel; since
my confinement here.

I am endeavouring to "return" like a "poor Prodigal" as *I am*,

335

to my Father: against whom I have *always* sined: *in the hope*; that he may kindly, & forgivingly "meet me: though *a verry great way off*." Oh my dear Wife & Children would "to God" you could know how I have been "travelling in birth for you" *all*: that no one of you "may fail of the grace of God, through Jesus Christ:" that no one of you may be blind to the truth: & glorious "light of *his* word," in which Life; & Immortality; are brought to light.

I beseech you *every one* to make the bible your *dayly* & *Nightly study*; with a *childlike honest, candid, teachable spirit*: out of love and respect for your husband; & Father: & I beseech *the God* of *my Fathers*; to open all your eyes to a discovery of *the truth*. You *cannot imagine* how much you may *soon need* the consolations of the Christian religion.

Circumstances like my own; for more than a month past; convince me beyond *all doubt*: of our great *need*: of something more to rest our hopes on; than merely our own vague theories framed up, while our *prejudices* are excited; or our *vanity* worked up to its highest pitch.

Oh do not trust your eternal all uppon the boisterous Ocean, without *even a Helm*; or *Compass* to *aid* you in steering. I do *not ask any* of you; to throw *away your reason*: I only ask you, to make a candid & sober *use of your reason*: My dear younger children will you listen to the last poor admonition of one who can only love you? Oh be determined at once to give your whole hearts to God; & let *nothing* shake; or alter; that resolution. You need have no fear of *regreting it*.

Do not be vain; and thoughtless: but *sober minded*. And let me entreat you all to love *the whole remnant* of our once great family: "with a pure *heart fervently*." Try to *build again*: your broken walls: & to make *the utmost* of every *stone* that is left. Nothing can so tend to make life a blessing as the consciousness that you *love: & are beloved*: & "love ye the stranger" *still*. It is ground of

336

the utmost comfort to my mind: to know that so many of you as have had the opportunity; have given full proof of your fidelity to the great family of man.

Be faithful until death. From the exercise of habitual love to man: it cannot be very hard: to learn to love his maker. I must yet insert a reason for my firm belief in the Divine inspiration of the Bible: notwithstanding I am (perhaps naturally) skeptical: (certainly not, credulous.) I wish you all to consider it most thoroughly; when you read the blessed book; & see whether you can not discover such evidence yourselves. It is the purity of heart, feeling, or motive: as well as word, & action which is everywhere insisted on; that distinguish it from all other teachings; that commends it to my conscience; whether my heart be "willing, & obedient" or not. The inducements that it holds out; are another reason of my conviction of its truth: & genuineness: that I cannot here omit; in this my last argument for the Bible.

Eternal life; is that my soul is "panting after" this moment. I mention this; as reason for endeavouring to leave a valuable copy of the Bible to be carefully preserved in remembrance of me: to so many of my posterity; instead of some other things of equal cost.

I beseech you all to live in habitual contentment with verry moderate circumstances: & gains, of worldly store: & most earnestly to teach this: to your children; & Childrens Children; after you: by example: as well; as precept. Be determined to know by experience as soon as may be: whether bible instruction is of Divine origin or not; which says; "Owe no man anything but to love one another." John Rogers wrote to his children, "Abhor the arrant whore of Rome." John Brown writes to his children to abhor with undiing hatred, also: that "sum of all vilainies;" Slavery.

Remember that "he that is slow to anger is better than the mighty: and he that ruleth his spirit; than he that taketh a city." Remember also: that "they that be wise shall shine; and they that

337

turn many to *righteousness: as the stars forever; & ever."* And now dearly beloved Farewell, To God & the word of his grace I comme[n]d you all.

Your Affectionate Husband & Father

John Brown

To THE bitter end, John Brown fought the good fight. He was "faithful unto death." Within a year and a half after his execution, the Civil War began, and a nation was torn asunder before the Abolitionist cause was finally vindicated.

THOMAS HUXLEY STRIPS HIMSELF OF THE HOPES AND CONSOLATIONS OF THE MASS OF MANKIND

[A LETTER TO CHARLES KINGSLEY]

STANDING beside the open grave of his little son, his heart "full of submission and without bitterness," Thomas Huxley here examines the "mischievous and delusive" arguments for immortality. In this soul-searching communication to a distinguished clergyman, written when he was close to a complete nervous breakdown, Huxley explores, as only one of the world's great champions of pure science can explore them, matters of life and death. In his own words he speaks "more openly and distinctly" than he has ever spoken before to any human being, except his wife. Refusing to lie, refusing to grovel, refusing to compromise, refusing to be crushed by his own cruel bereavement or by his wife's "inconsolable grief," the man who coined the term "agnostic" here defends a free man's first principles.

Leonard Huxley, son and biographer of Thomas Huxley, has said of his father's famous letter: "It sets forth the grounds of his own philosophy as to the ends of life and the hope of immortality, and affords insight into the very depths of his nature. It is a rare outburst at a moment of intense feeling, in which, more completely than in almost any other writing of his, intellectual clearness and moral fire are to be seen uniting in a veritable passion for truth."

Thomas Huxley lived from 1825 to 1895, made notable and original discoveries in the field of natural science, and won fame for his magnificent prose style and his inspired and incorruptible leadership of the forces of scientific truth in the controversy that raged about the doctrine of evolution. This letter was written only one year after the publication of The Origin of Species, by Huxley's contemporary and hero, Charles Darwin.* Both these great leaders of the nineteenth century were then being savagely denounced by the churchmen as infidels, atheists, and heretics.

When Huxley's friend, the Reverend Charles Kingsley, noted alike as churchman and novelist, author of Westward Ho!, Hereward the Wake, and Water Babies, wrote Thomas Huxley a long letter of sympathy and condolence on the death of his son, the scientist replied as follows:

"Sit down before fact as a little child . . ."

14 Waverley Place, Sept. 23, 1860.

MY DEAR KINGSLEY—I cannot sufficiently thank you, both on my wife's account and my own, for your long and frank letter, and for all the hearty sympathy which it exhibits—and Mrs. Kingsley will, I hope, believe that we are no less sensible of her kind thought of us. To myself your letter was especially valuable, as it touched upon what I thought even more than upon what I said in my letter to you.

My convictions, positive and negative, on all the matters of which you speak, are of long and slow growth and are firmly rooted. But the great blow which fell upon me seemed to stir them to their foundation, and had I lived a couple of centuries earlier I could have fancied a devil scoffing at me and them—and asking me what profit it was to have stripped myself of the hopes and

* See Darwin's letter on page 361, and John Stuart Mill's letter on page 358.

consolations of the mass of mankind? To which my only reply was and is—Oh devil! truth is better than much profit. I have searched over the grounds of my belief, and if wife and child and name and fame were all to be lost to me one after the other as the penalty, still I will not lie.

And now I feel that it is due to you to speak as frankly as you have done to me. An old and worthy friend of mine tried some three or four years ago to bring us together—because, as he said, you were the only man who would do me any good. Your letter leads me to think he was right, though not perhaps in the sense he attached to his own words.

To begin with the great doctrine you discuss. I neither deny nor affirm the immortality of man. I see no reason for believing in it, but, on the other hand, I have no means of disproving it.

Pray understand that I have no a priori objections to the doctrine. No man who has to deal daily and hourly with nature can trouble himself about a priori difficulties. Give me such evidence as would justify me in believing anything else, and I will believe that. Why should I not? It is not half so wonderful as the conservation of force, or the indestructibility of matter. Whoso clearly appreciates all that is implied in the falling of a stone can have no difficulty about any doctrine simply on account of its marvellousness.

But the longer I live, the more obvious it is to me that the most sacred act of a man's life is to say and to feel, "I believe such and such to be true." All the greatest rewards and all the heaviest penalties of existence cling about that act.

The universe is one and the same throughout; and if the condition of my success in unravelling some little difficulty of anatomy or physiology is that I shall rigorously refuse to put faith in that which does not rest on sufficient evidence, I cannot believe that the great mysteries of existence will be laid open to me on other terms.

It is no use to talk to me of analogies and probabilities. I know what I mean when I say I believe in the law of the inverse squares, and I will not rest my life and my hopes upon weaker convictions. I dare not if I would.

Measured by this standard, what becomes of the doctrine of immortality?

You rest in your strong conviction of your personal existence, and in the instinct of the persistence of that existence which is so strong in you as in most men.

To me this is as nothing. That my personality is the surest thing I know—may be true. But the attempt to conceive what it is leads me into mere verbal subtleties. I have champed up all that chaff about the ego and the non-ego, about noumena and phenomena, and all the rest of it, too often not to know that in attempting even to think of these questions, the human intellect flounders at once out of its depth.

It must be twenty years since, a boy, I read Hamilton's essay on the unconditioned, and from that time to this, ontological speculation has been a folly to me. When Mansel took up Hamilton's argument on the side of orthodoxy (!) I said he reminded me of nothing so much as the man who is sawing off the sign on which he is sitting, in Hogarth's picture. But this by the way.

I cannot conceive of my personality as a thing apart from the phenomena of my life. When I try to form such a conception I discover that, as Coleridge would have said, I only hypostatise a word, and it alters nothing if, with Fichte, I suppose the universe to be nothing but a manifestation of my personality. I am neither more nor less eternal than I was before.

Nor does the infinite difference between myself and the animals alter the case. I do not know whether the animals persist after they disappear or not. I do not even know whether the infinite difference between us and them may not be compensated by *their*

342

persistence and my cessation after apparent death, just as the humble bulb of an annual lives, while the glorious flowers it has put forth die away.

Surely it must be plain that an ingenious man could speculate without end on both sides, and find analogies for all his dreams. Nor does it help me to tell me that the aspirations of mankind—that my own highest aspirations even—lead me towards the doctrine of immortality. I doubt the fact, to begin with, but if it be so even, what is this but in grand words asking me to believe a thing because I like it.

Science has taught to me the opposite lesson. She warns me to be careful how I adopt a view which jumps with my preconceptions, and to require stronger evidence for such belief than for one to which I was previously hostile.

My business is to teach my aspirations to conform themselves to fact, not to try and make facts harmonise with my aspirations.

Science seems to me to teach in the highest and strongest manner the great truth which is embodied in the Christian conception of entire surrender to the will of God. Sit down before fact as a little child, be prepared to give up every preconceived notion, follow humbly wherever and to whatever abysses nature leads, or you shall learn nothing. I have only begun to learn content and peace of mind since I have resolved at all risks to do this.

There are, however, other arguments commonly brought forward in favour of the immortality of man, which are to my mind not only delusive but mischievous. The one is the notion that the moral government of the world is imperfect without a system of future rewards and punishments. The other is: that such a system is indispensable to practical morality. I believe that both these dogmas are very mischievous lies.

With respect to the first, I am no optimist, but I have the firmest belief that the Divine Government (if we may use such a phrase to express the sum of the "customs of matter") is wholly just. The more I know intimately of the lives of other men (to say nothing of my own), the more obvious it is to me that the wicked does *not* flourish nor is the righteous punished. But for this to be clear we must bear in mind what almost all forget, that the rewards of life are contingent upon obedience to the *whole* law —physical as well as moral—and that moral obedience will not atone for physical sin, or *vice versa.*

The ledger of the Almighty is strictly kept, and every one of us has the balance of his operations paid over to him at the end of every minute of his existence.

Life cannot exist without a certain conformity to the surrounding universe—that conformity involves a certain amount of happiness in excess of pain. In short, as we live we are paid for living.

And it is to be recollected in view of the apparent discrepancy between men's acts and their rewards that Nature is juster than we. She takes into account what a man brings with him into the world, which human justice cannot do. If I, born a bloodthirsty and savage brute, inheriting these qualities from others, kill you, my fellow-men will very justly hang me, but I shall not be visited with the horrible remorse which would be my real punishment if, my nature being higher, I had done the same thing.

The absolute justice of the system of things is as clear to me as any scientific fact. The gravitation of sin to sorrow is as certain as that of the earth to the sun, and more so—for experimental proof of the fact is within reach of us all—nay, is before us all in our own lives, if we had but the eyes to see it.

Not only, then, do I disbelieve in the need for compensation, but I believe that the seeking for rewards and punishments out of this life leads men to a ruinous ignorance of the fact that their inevitable rewards and punishments are here.

If the expectation of hell hereafter can keep me from evil-doing, surely a *fortiori* the certainty of hell now will do so? If a man could be firmly impressed with the belief that stealing damaged him as much as swallowing arsenic would do (and it does), would not the dissuasive force of that belief be greater than that of any based on mere future expectations?

And this leads me to my other point.

As I stood behind the coffin of my little son the other day, with my mind bent on anything but disputation, the officiating minister read, as a part of his duty, the words, "If the dead rise not again, let us eat and drink, for to-morrow we die." I cannot tell you how inexpressibly they shocked me. Paul had neither wife nor child, or he must have known that his alternative involved a blasphemy against all that was best and noblest in human nature. I could have laughed with scorn. What! because I am face to face with irreparable loss, because I have given back to the source from whence it came, the cause of a great happiness, still retaining through all my life the blessings which have sprung and will spring from that cause, I am to renounce my manhood, and, howling, grovel in bestiality? Why, the very apes know better, and if you shoot their young, the poor brutes grieve their grief out and do not immediately seek distraction in a gorge.

Kicked into the world a boy without guide or training, or with worse than none, I confess to my shame that few men have drunk deeper of all kinds of sin than I. Happily, my course was arrested in time—before I had earned absolute destruction—and for long years I have been slowly and painfully climbing, with many a fall, towards better things. And when I look back, what do I find to have been the agents of my redemption? The hope of immortality or of future reward? I can honestly say that for these fourteen years such a consideration has not entered my head. No, I can tell you exactly what has been at work. *Sartor Resartus* led me to know that a deep sense of religion was compatible with the entire absence of theology.

Secondly, science and her methods gave me a resting-place independent of authority and tradition. Thirdly, love opened up to me a view of the sanctity of human nature, and impressed me with a deep sense of responsibility.

If at this moment I am not a worn-out, debauched, useless carcass of a man, if it has been or will be my fate to advance the cause of science, if I feel that I have a shadow of a claim on the love of those about me, if in the supreme moment when I looked down into my boy's grave my sorrow was full of submission and without bitterness, it is because these agencies have worked upon me, and not because I have ever cared whether my poor personality shall remain distinct for ever from the All from whence it came and whither it goes.

And thus, my dear Kingsley, you will understand what my position is. I may be quite wrong, and in that case I know I shall have to pay the penalty for being wrong. But I can only say with Luther, "Gott helfe mir, Ich kann nichts anders."

I know right well that 99 out of 100 of my fellows would call me atheist, infidel, and all the other usual hard names. As our laws stand, if the lowest thief steals my coat, my evidence (my opinions being known) would not be received against him.

But I cannot help it. One thing people shall not call me with justice, and that is—a liar. As you say of yourself, I too feel that I lack courage; but if ever the occasion arises when I am bound to speak, I will not shame my boy.

I have spoken more openly and distinctly to you than I ever have to any human being except my wife.

If you can show me that I err in premises or conclusion, I am ready to give up these as I would any other theories. But at any rate you will do me the justice to believe that I have not reached my conclusions without the care befitting the momentous nature of the problems involved.

346

And I write this the more readily to you, because it is clear to me that if that great and powerful instrument for good or evil, the Church of England, is to be saved from being shivered into fragments by the advancing tide of science—an event I should be very sorry to witness, but which will infallibly occur if men like Samuel of Oxford are to have the guidance of her destinies—it must be by the efforts of men who, like yourself, see your way to the combination of the practice of the Church with the spirit of science. Understand that all the younger men of science whom I know intimately are *essentially* of my way of thinking. (I know not a scoffer or an irreligious or an immoral man among them, but they all regard orthodoxy as you do Brahmanism.) Understand that this new school of the prophets is the only one that can work miracles, the only one that can constantly appeal to nature for evidence that it is right, and you will comprehend that it is of no use to try to barricade us with shovel hats and aprons, or to talk about our doctrines being "shocking."

I don't profess to understand the logic of yourself, Maurice, and the rest of your school, but I have always said I would swear by your truthfulness and sincerity, and that good must come of your efforts. The more plain this was to me, however, the more obvious the necessity to let you see where the men of science are driving, and it has often been in my mind to write to you before.

If I have spoken too plainly anywhere, or too abruptly, pardon me, and do the like to me.

My wife thanks you very much for your volume of sermons.— Ever yours very faithfully,

T. H. Huxley

347

Thomas huxley's clear and courageous utterance has become a classic statement of the scientist's attitude toward free inquiry and an unshackled search for truth.

A few months after this letter was written another son was born in the Huxley family, giving the bereaved mother some measure of comfort.

RICHARD WAGNER DEMANDS AN IMMEDIATE LOAN OF TEN THOUSAND FRANCS FROM ONE OF HIS ADMIRERS

[AN EXCHANGE OF LETTERS WITH BARON ROBERT VON HORNSTEIN]

AT THE time of these letters, in 1861, Richard Wagner was in a low, almost desperate, spiritual state. But the arrogant demands he made on his disciples and admirers were still insistent, clamorous, and arbitrary. Discouraged by the fact that after fifty-seven rehearsals Tristan and Isolde had been abandoned as "a hopeless production," and plagued by debts, family scandals, and critical ridicule, Wagner was at this stage of his career virtually a wanderer and a failure. But his genius-intoxicated vanity never wavered, and his ego was "inexhaustibly predatory."

When Baron Robert von Hornstein's son Ferdinand first published the memoirs of his father in 1908, he tactfully withheld the following correspondence from the book "out of consideration for Wagner and his family." Subsequently, however, after the publication of Wagner's auto-biography, which contained a bitter reference to Baron von Hornstein, Ferdinand changed his mind and made public the correspondence as further evidence of the "pettiness of Wagner's rancor against this young man from whom, notwithstanding his disparagement of him, he was willing to borrow money." The letters tell their own story:

"... do not shrink from a sacrifice."

19, Quai Voltaire, Paris,
12th December 1861

DEAR HORNSTEIN,
I hear that you have become rich. In what a wretched state I myself am you can easily guess from my failures. I am trying to retrieve myself by seclusion and a new work. In order to make possible this way to my preservation—that is to say, to lift me above the most distressing obligations, cares, and needs that rob me of all freedom of mind—I require an immediate loan of ten thousand francs. With this I can again put my life in order, and again do productive work.

It will be rather hard for you to provide me with this sum; but it will be possible if you WISH it, and do not shrink from a sacrifice. This, however, I desire, and I ask it of you against my promise to endeavor to repay you in three years out of my receipts.

Now let me see whether you are the right sort of man!

If you prove to be such for me,—and why should not this be expected of someone someday?—the assistance you give me will bring you into very close touch with me, and next summer you must be pleased to let me come to you for three months at one of your estates, preferably in the Rhine district.

I will say no more just now. Only as regards the proposed loan I may say that it would be a great relief to me if you could place even six thousand francs at my disposal immediately; I hope then to be able to arrange to do without the other four thousand francs until

March. But nothing but the immediate provision of the whole sum can give me the help which I so need in my present state of mind.

Let us see, then, and hope that the sun will for once shine a little on me. What I need now is a success; otherwise—I can probably do nothing more!

Yours,

Richard Wagner

IN *My Life, Richard Wagner later explained that he thought he was "conferring an honor" upon Baron von Hornstein when he made this request, and was "greatly surprised" when he received the following reply "expressing terror" at the suggestion:*

"I regret that I cannot be of service to you."

DEAR HERR WAGNER,

You seem to have a false idea of my riches. I have a modest (*hübsch*) fortune on which I can live in plain and decent style with my wife and child. You must therefore turn to really rich people, of whom you have plenty among your patrons and patronesses all over Europe. I regret that I cannot be of service to you.

As for your long visit to "one of my estates," at present I cannot contrive a long visit; if it should become possible later I will let you know.

I have read in the papers with great regret that the production of "Tristan and Isolde" will not take place this winter. I hope that

351

it is only a question of time, and that we shall yet hear the work. Greetings to you and your wife.

From yours,

Robert von Hornstein

BUT Wagner still insisted on the last word, and in a letter dated December 27, 1861, from Paris, he sharply rebuked his prospective benefactor for his "impropriety," adding: "You should not have presumed to advise me in any way, even as to who is really rich; and you should have left it to myself to decide why I do not apply to the patrons and patronesses to whom you refer. If you are not prepared to have me at one of your estates, you could have seized the signal opportunity I offered you of making the necessary arrangements for receiving me in some place of my choice. It is consequently offensive of you to say that you will let me know when you will be prepared to have me. You should have omitted the wish you express with regard to my Tristan; your answer could only pass muster on the assumption that you are totally ignorant of my works. Let this end the matter. I reckon on your discretion, as you can on mine."

The following year, Wagner's difficulties were temporarily and rather luxuriously solved when he accepted the hospitality of Ludwig II, King of Bavaria, at Munich. Here he lived in splendor. The King even paid many of his debts for him. At Munich Wagner directed the first performance of Tristan and Isolde, and here he finally completed Die Meistersinger and the last opera of the Ring—Götterdämmerung.

Deems Taylor has touched on the heart of the whole matter in these words:

"When you consider what Wagner wrote—thirteen operas and music dramas, eleven of them still holding the stage, eight of them unquestionably worth ranking among the world's great musicodramatic masterpieces—when you listen to what he wrote, the debts and heartaches that people had to endure from him don't seem much of a price . . . a few thousand dollars' worth of debts are not too heavy a price to pay for the Ring trilogy. What if he was faithless to his friends and to his wives? He had one mistress to whom he was faithful to the day of his death: Music."

FRIEDRICH NIETZSCHE CONFIDES A SECRET TO RICHARD WAGNER

WHEN Friedrich Nietzsche was still a young man, he made the acquaintance of Richard Wagner, then thirty years his senior, who at the time was the storm center of German culture. Wagner's excessive vanity was touched by the headlong worship of this brilliant young philosopher, who was then composing sonatas for the piano. "Without music," said Nietzsche, "life would be a mistake."

Richard Wagner became a crucial influence in Nietzsche's life. When they first met, the great composer was living near Basel, where Nietzsche was teaching classical philology at the university. They spent Christmas together in 1869, the superman of music acting as host and teacher, the young philosopher of the superman serving as pupil and disciple.

Inspired by Wagner, Nietzsche set to work on his first book, The Birth of Tragedy Out of the Spirit of Music. Brooding from an Alpine solitude, he then set down this nuclear declaration from which was eventually to develop the main themes of his entire philosophy: "I felt for the first time that the strongest and highest will to life does not find expression in a miserable struggle for existence, but in a Will to War, a Will to Power, a Will to Overpower."

Nietzsche hailed Wagner as "another Aeschylus, restoring myths and symbols, and uniting music and drums again in Dionysian ecstasy . . . a Siegfried who has never learned the meaning of fear. . . ." The forthcoming operatic festival at Bayreuth he saluted reverently as signifying "the morning sacrament on the day of battle."

But soon the young hero-worshiper became critical, searching, and gradually disillusioned. When Wagner exulted in his "supreme triumph" of The Ring of the Nibelungs, and the world of princes and the princes

354

of the world were at his feet in homage, Nietzsche's apocalyptic vision pierced through the curtain of theatrical splendor: he was shocked and terrorized by what he found. Realizing that the shining knight-errant of Siegfried had become the high priest of Parsifal, Nietzsche, unwilling to serve any longer as an acolyte, and now full-grown to philosophic stature, refused to burn incense. But Wagner openly and arrogantly demanded it. Thus began the famous Nietzsche-Wagner controversy, which developed into a deep-rooted quarrel and finally led to a complete break between the old friends.

At last Nietzsche silently abandoned his god and hero, declaring himself "tired with disgust of all that is feminism and undisciplined rhapsody in that romanticism, that idealistic lying, that softening of the human conscience, which had conquered here one of the bravest souls."

The cultural feud was now irreconcilable. When Nietzsche found himself again a neighbor of Wagner at Sorrento, where the composer was at work on Parsifal, they did not even speak. The former satellite, now an uncompromising philosopher, had no sympathy for the reigning titan of music. He deemed Wagner a mountebank, exalting "pity, flesh-less love, and the fool in Christ." That, in substance, was the cause of Nietzsche's celebrated clash with the supreme egomaniac of the new music drama—a controversy which, in the words of H. L. Mencken, was "for so long the subject of vague rumors and dark whispers."

Shortly before Nietzsche wrote the following letter to Wagner, the composer, as a conciliatory gesture, had sent an inscribed copy of the newly published score of Parsifal to Nietzsche, who at the time was working on Human, All-Too Human, expounding his latest theory of art, in direct opposition to Wagner's. When the gift arrived, Nietzsche, greatly moved, and realizing, as his sister put it, "what a great shock the Wag-nerian party would receive upon reading this book," decided to publish it anonymously, and wrote this letter imparting to Wagner privately the secret of its authorship, "without surrendering one iota of his own independence of thought." *The letter is undated but was probably written sometime between 1878 and 1880.*

"I have the most curious feeling of solitude and multitude . . ."

IN SENDING you this book, I place my secret in the hands of you and your noble wife with the greatest confidence and assume that is now your secret. I wrote this book; in it I have revealed my innermost views upon men and things and for the first time, have traveled around the entire periphery of my thoughts. This book was a great consolation to me at a period full of paroxysms and misery and it never disappointed me when all else failed to console me. I think it not improbable that I am still living just because I was able to write such a book.

I was obliged to resort to a pseudonym for several reasons; in the first place, because I did not wish to counteract the effect of my earlier works, and secondly, because this was my only means of preventing a public and private befouling of my personal dignity (something I am *no longer* able to endure on account of the state of my health) and finally and chiefly, because I wish to make possible a *scientific* discussion in which all of my intelligent friends could take part, unrestrained by any feelings of delicacy, as has hitherto been the case whenever I have published anything. No one will speak or write *against my name!*

I know of no one of them who entertains the ideas expressed in *this* book and must confess to a great curiosity as to the counter arguments which such a book will provoke.

356

I feel very much like an officer who has stormed a breastwork despite his severe wounds; he has reached the *top* and unfurled his flag, and notwithstanding the terrifying spectacle by which he is surrounded, experiences much more joy than sorrow.

Although I know of no one who shares my views, as I have already said, I am conceited enough to think that I have not thought individually but collectively. I have the most curious feeling of *solitude and multitude*; of being a herald who has hastened on in advance without knowing whether the band of knights is following or not—in fact, whether they are still living.

*T*HE *letter was never actually sent to Wagner. As for the book, Nietzsche refused to sanction the anonymous publication of a work that, according to his publishers, could sell only with the author's name on the cover. Therefore Nietzsche scrupulously went over the manuscript to eliminate all allusions that might wound Wagner. Instead of the original letter he sent Wagner a copy of Human, All-Too Human, with this inscription: "Friend—Nothing binds us now. But we have taken pleasure in one another up to the point where one advanced the ideas of the other, even though these were diametrically opposed to his own." But Wagner could not be objective about his ideas. He demanded worship, adulation, unquestioning loyalty. As Nietzsche's sister expressed it, Wagner saw in Human, All-Too Human nothing but "the apostacy of his former pupil—more than that, of the favorite disciple and a genius to boot . . . and therefore this occasion had the effect of a blow and an insult. The break was final. . . ." In his last delirium, just before his death in 1900, Nietzsche saw a picture of his old hero, and remarked tenderly: "Him I loved much."*

JOHN STUART MILL RESCUES HIS GREATEST RIVAL IN PHILOSOPHY, HERBERT SPENCER, FROM IMPENDING RUIN

In 1858, Herbert Spencer conceived his master plan of "a series of works in which he would show the evolution of matter and mind from nebula to man, and from savage to Shakespeare." He was then nearly forty years old and already an invalid, and poor. This grand scheme for his crowning lifework developed while he was revising his essays for collective publication and was struck by the unity and sequence of the ideas he had expressed. In the words of Will Durant, "The notion came to him, like a burst of sunlight through opened doors, that the theory of evolution might be applied in every science as well as in biology; that it could explain not only species and genera but planets and strata, social and political history, moral and esthetic conceptions. That was the first concept of Spencer's Synthetic Philosophy."

Spencer's immediate problem was to finance his staggering undertaking and at the same time to make a living. When he received a bequest of $2500 from an uncle, he resigned the editorship of The Economist. He sought advance subscriptions for his intended volumes, hoping meantime "to live from hand to mouth." On the basis of an outline, he secured pledges from an imposing list of noted scientists and men of letters, including Kingsley, Lyell, Sir Joseph Hooker, Tyndall, Buckle, Froude, Alexander Bain, Herschel, and others. Altogether, about six hundred sponsors made possible a fund of $1500 a year, and Spencer set to work.

In 1862, after the publication of Part One of First Principles, a storm of controversy arose. Huxley defended the evolutionists and scholars

358

against the onslaughts of the outraged bishops.* As a result of the Battle of the Books (over First Principles and The Origin of Species), Spencer's subscribers fell away, and many promised payments were defaulted. Soon his funds and his courage were both exhausted, and he was reluctantly forced to announce the abandonment of the whole project. At this dramatic moment, Spencer received the following letter from his great rival in philosophy, John Stuart Mill:

"... it is a simple proposal of cooperation for an important public purpose ..."

February 4, 1866

DEAR SIR:
　　On arriving here last week, I found the December *livraison* of your *Biology*, and I need hardly say how much I regretted the announcement in the paper annexed to it. . . . I propose that you should write the next of your treatises, and that I should guarantee the publisher against loss. . . . I beg that you will not consider this proposal in the light of a personal favour, though even if it were I should still hope to be permitted to offer it. But it is nothing of the kind—it is a simple proposal of cooperation for an important public purpose, for which you give your labour and have given your health. I am, Dear Sir,
　　　　　　　　Very truly yours,
　　　　　　　　　　　　J. S. Mill

* See the letter of Huxley to Kingsley, on page 339, and the letter of Charles Darwin, on page 361.

AT FIRST, Spencer rejected Mill's offer, firmly but courteously. But Mill insisted and actually persuaded many of his friends to subscribe. Again Spencer objected. At this point, a group of American admirers of Spencer joined forces with Mill and made available a $7000 fund, of which the interest or dividends were to go to Spencer. This Spencer accepted. The colossal task of research and study was resumed and faithfully prosecuted for forty years until all the Synthetic Philosophy was finally published. . . .

In 1896 Spencer wrote to Andrew Carnegie, one of his admirers: "You will readily understand why after having continued to fritter away my small resources until I was nearly stopped by impending ruin . . . in my seventy-seventh year these long-postponed marks of honor have no attraction for me. . . ." Carnegie replied: "You had a message so far in advance that recognition was not to be expected. . . . Why, my dear friend, what do you mean by complaining of neglect, abuse, scorn? These are the precious rewards of teachers of mankind."

In The Importance of Living, Lin Yutang reminds us that a few days before his death Herbert Spencer had the eighteen volumes of the Synthetic Philosophy piled on his lap, and . . . "as he felt their cold weight wondered if he would not have done better could he have a grandchild in their stead. . . ."

CHARLES DARWIN IS OVERJOYED TO SEE A THE-
ORY ALMOST PROVED TRUE

[A LETTER TO ALFRED RUSSEL WALLACE]

THE author of The Origin of Species has set forth in this letter a few friendly observations about scientific collaboration, about the butterflies, the dragonflies, and sexual selection among the Malayans. Here we are permitted to peer over Darwin's shoulder and see the scientific mind in its supreme genius actually at work on a specific problem.

Darwin said that his own success was due chiefly to "the love of science, unbounded patience in long reflecting over any subject, industry in observing and collecting facts, and a fair share of invention as well as of common sense. . . . I have steadily endeavoured to keep my mind free so as to give up any hypothesis, however much beloved (and I cannot resist forming one on every subject), as soon as facts are shown to be opposed to it."

The foundation for Darwin's scientific achievements was the famous journey he took as naturalist on the Beagle from 1831 to 1836 to Tahiti, New Zealand, St. Helena, Brazil, and the Azores. In 1837, on his return, we find his first notebooks' entries on the transmutation of the species. The previous March he had been greatly struck, while still on the voyage (and just twenty years old), by the character of South American foliage in the Galápagos Archipelago.

In 1838 Darwin first noted "specific evidence for the struggle for existence" and was impressed by the fact that "favourable variations would tend to be preserved and unfavorable ones destroyed." The result of this, he sensed, was the formation of new species. Thus he learned the idea of "progressive divergence."

361

On January 11, 1844, Darwin wrote: "At last gleams of light have come and I am almost convinced (quite contrary to the opinion I started out with) that species are not (it is like confessing a murder) immutable."

In 1856, when he was almost ready to publish his basic study on evolution, Darwin received a manuscript essay from A. R. Wallace, another great naturalist, an authority on life in the Malaysia. Wallace asked for Darwin's opinion, and Darwin was startled to find in the essay a complete abstract of his own theory. On the advice of his brother scientists, this led in July, 1858, to a joint essay for the Linnaean Society "On the Tendency of Species to Form Varieties and Species by Natural Means of Selection."

On October 15, 1859, Charles Darwin wrote to Thomas Huxley* from Yorkshire: "I am here hydropathising and coming to life again after having finished my accursed book [The Origin of Species] which could have been easy work to anyone else but half-killed me. . . . I am far from expecting to convert you to many of my heresies."

Finally Darwin's epochal masterpiece appeared in 1859, under the title On the Origin of Species by Means of Natural Selection, or the Preservation of Favoured Races in the Struggle for Life. The first edition of 1250 copies was exhausted on publication day.

In the letter that follows we can catch a glimpse of the type of investigation, verification, and creative thinking that went into all of Darwin's work:

* See the famous Thomas Huxley letter to Rev. Charles Kingsley on page 339.

"... resolved to publish a little essay on the origin of Mankind ..."

Down, February 26 [1867]

MY DEAR WALLACE,—Bates was quite right; you are the man to apply to in a difficulty. I never heard anything more ingenious than your suggestion,* and I hope you may be able to prove it true. That is a splendid fact about the white moths; it warms one's very blood to see a theory thus almost proved to be true. With respect to the beauty of male butterflies, I must as yet think that it is due to sexual selection. There is some evidence that dragon-flies are attracted by bright colours; but what leads me to the above belief, is so many male Orthoptera and Cicadas having musical instruments. This being the case, the analogy of birds makes me believe in sexual selection with respect to colour in insects. I wish I had strength and time to make some of the experiments suggested by you, but I thought butterflies would not pair in confinement. I am sure I have heard of some such difficulty. Many years ago I had a dragon-fly painted with gorgeous colours, but I never had an opportunity of fairly trying it.

The reason of my being so much interested just at present about sexual selection is, that I have almost resolved to publish a little essay on the origin of Mankind, and I still strongly think (though I failed to convince you, and this, to me, is the heaviest blow

* That conspicuous caterpillars or butterflies, which are distasteful to birds, are protected by being easily recognized and avoided.

363

possible) that sexual selection has been the main agent in forming the races of man.

By the way, there is another subject which I shall introduce in my essay, namely, expression of countenance. Now, do you happen to know by any odd chance a very good-natured and acute observer in the Malay Archipelago, who you think would make a few easy observations for me on the expression of the Malays when excited by various emotions? For in this case I would send to such person a list of queries. I thank you for your most interesting letter, and remain,

Yours very sincerely,
Ch. Darwin

A YEAR after this letter was written, in 1868, the subject it discussed was developed in greater detail by Darwin in a work entitled Variations of Animals and Plants Under Domestication. Finally, The Descent of Man and Selection in Relation to Sex was published by Darwin in 1871—a topic also touched on in this letter of 1867.

With respect to religion, Darwin said: "Disbelief crept over me at a very slow rate but was at last complete. The rate was so slow that I felt no distress."

EMILY DICKINSON FINDS ECSTASY IN THE MERE
SENSE OF LIVING

[A LETTER TO COLONEL THOMAS WENTWORTH HIGGINSON]

EMILY DICKINSON, the recluse of Amherst, and Colonel Higginson, man of letters, met only rarely, perhaps on only one occasion. But for twenty-four years they carried on an extraordinary friendship through their letters. The note printed here is typical of the "stark intensity" that characterized her side of their "literary philandering." Here we have one of the few prose revelations from the poet described by Lewis Gannett as the "sherry-eyed, chestnut-haired girl who shut herself away in her father's Amherst house and for close to thirty years never stepped out of it."

In 1862, in her thirty-second year, she began her correspondence with Colonel Thomas Wentworth Higginson through a "stray note of admiration" she sent him for an article in The Atlantic Monthly. Addressing him as "Dear Master" in the letter that followed, she invited his critical suggestions on her poetry.

Various scholars have guessed at the identity of the one great romance in Emily's life. Some have hinted that it was the Reverend George Gould, others Lieutenant Edward Hunt, husband of her friend, Helen Fiske, author of Ramona. It was for the last-named friend that Emily Dickinson is alleged to have made "the supreme renunciation." Another possibility is the Unitarian law student, B. F. Newton, who married soon after leaving Amherst. In any case, there is every reason to believe that the chief subject of her correspondence with Colonel Higginson was not love, but poetry.

According to George Frisbie Whicher, Emily Dickinson's love poems were nothing "more than the reverberations in an uncommonly sensitive nature of a devotion whispered in the heart's chambers, but never outwardly expressed, save in poetry."

The genius of Emily Dickinson has been superbly characterized by Louis Untermeyer: "Her personal magic is in everything she touched; in the agony of separation, a railway train, the wind tapping 'like a tired man,' a dog's 'belated feet, like intermittent plush'—all are invested with intimations of eternity. Startling in its details, tremendous in its casual implications, this poetry, built on epigram and paradox, has a range unsurpassed even by Walt Whitman. . . . Emily Dickinson, within her four walls, beheld more than is ever seen with the physical eye. She did not need the world who contained a universe. . . ."

". . . no fire can ever warm me . . ."

August 1870

TRUTH is such a rare thing, it is delightful to tell it.

I find ecstasy in living; the mere sense of living is joy enough.

How do most people live without any thoughts? There are many people in the world,—you must have noticed them in the street,— how do they live? How do they get strength to put on their clothes in the morning?

If I read a book and it makes my whole body so cold no fire can ever warm me, I know that is poetry. If I feel physically as if the top of my head were taken off, I know that is poetry. These are the only ways I know it. Is there any other way?

366

A T EMILY DICKINSON's *funeral in 1886 (she lived to the age of fifty-six),* Colonel Higginson *read a poem by Emily Brontë on immortality,* which he said "was a favorite of Emily Dickinson's, who has just put it on—if she could ever have been said to put it off."

Mme Martha Dickinson Bianchi, Emily Dickinson's niece and biographer, by whose permission this letter is reprinted, wrote to the editor concerning its inclusion in this anthology of letters: "I think it would amuse my Aunt Emily to be yoked with the Apostle Paul. I hope I am not too late to assure her of this particular fact."

BENJAMIN DISRAELI OFFERS TO FREE THOMAS CARLYLE FROM COMMON CARES IN THE SUNSET OF HIS LIFE

HERE is a characteristic letter from the crafty Prime Minister who was noted for his flowery speech and his courtly deference to Queen Victoria.

When Disraeli delivered his first address in the House of Commons, he was laughed down, but bravely answered that some day his fellow members would have to listen to him. They did. Disraeli won his first renown as a novelist, his greater fame as a statesman and empire-builder.

Prompted, perhaps, by the conferring of the Prussian Order of Merit upon Carlyle for his Frederick the Great, the Prime Minister offered Carlyle the Grand Cross of the Bath and a pension in the elegant communication that follows:

"A Government should recognise intellect."

(Confidential)

Bournemouth, Dec. 27, 1874.

SIR, A Government should recognise intellect. It elevates and sustains the tone of a nation. But it is an office which, adequately to fulfil, requires both courage and discrimination, as there is a chance of falling into favouritism and patronising mediocrity, which, instead of elevating the national feeling, would eventually degrade or debase it.

368

In recommending Her Majesty to fit out an Arctic expedition, and in suggesting other measures of that class, her Government have shown their sympathy with science. I wish that the position of high letters should be equally acknowledged; but this is not so easy, because it is in the necessity of things that the test of merit cannot be so precise in literature as in science.

When I consider the literary world, I can see only two living names which, I would fain believe, will be remembered; and they stand out in uncontested superiority. One is that of a poet; if not a great poet, a real one; and the other is your own.

I have advised the Queen to offer to confer a baronetcy on Mr. Tennyson, and the same distinction should be at your command, if you liked it. But I have remembered that, like myself, you are childless, and may not care for hereditary honours. I have therefore made up my mind, if agreeable to yourself, to recommend to Her Majesty to confer on you the highest distinction for merit at her command, and which, I believe, has never yet been conferred by her except for direct services to the State. And that is the Grand Cross of the Bath.

I will speak with frankness on another point. It is not well that, in the sunset of your life, you should be disturbed by common cares. I see no reason why a great author should not receive from the nation a pension as well as a lawyer and a statesman. Unfortunately the personal power of Her Majesty in this respect is limited; but still it is in the Queen's capacity to settle on an individual an amount equal to a good fellowship, and which was cheerfully accepted and enjoyed by the great spirit of Johnson, and the pure integrity of Southey.

Have the goodness to let me know your feelings on these subjects.

I have the honour to remain, Sir,

Your faithful Servant,

B. Disraeli

369

BENJAMIN DISRAELI TO THOMAS CARLYLE

CARLYLE, who had frequently objected to Disraeli's imperial policies, courteously but firmly declined the proferred honors. He deliberately rejected the distinction of burial in Westminster Abbey and chose to lie beside his parents in his native village of Ecclefechan, in Scotland.

SARAH BERNHARDT TELLS VICTORIEN SARDOU WHY PARIS IS A VAST DESERT OF DESOLATION WITHOUT HIM

THE "divine Sarah" was a prodigious correspondent. She wrote letters with the same tempestuous animation that marked her entire life. To this talent she added a weakness for incurring debts and a genius for dominating the theater of her time.

Born in Paris in 1844, Sarah Bernhardt was raised in a convent. She overcame her youthful stage fright by an incomparable memory and a golden voice, and thus started a stage career that soon dazzled three continents. Her romantic attachment to Sardou, the poet-playwright, author of Fedora, written expressly for Bernhardt, lasted for many years. She was openly the aggressor and the pursuer. It was her definite policy in love. Seeing him by chance in a café-dansant in Paris, she determined to win him—and did. Here is a typical letter she sent to him:

"Your words are my food, your breath my wine."

[undated]

WONDERFUL BOY,

Where are you tonight? Your letter came only an hour ago—cruel hour—I had hoped you would spend it with me here.

Paris is a morgue without you: before I knew you, it was Paris, and I thought it heaven; but now it is a vast desert of desolation and loneliness. It is like the face of a clock, bereft of its hands.

371

All the pictures that hung in my memory before I knew you have faded and given place to our radiant moments together.

Now I cannot live apart from you—your words, even though bitter—dispel all the cares of the world and make me happy; my art has been suckled by them and softly rocked in their tender cradle; they are as necessary to me now as sunlight and air.

I am as hungry for them as for food. I am thirsty for them, and my thirst is overwhelming. Your words are my food, your breath my wine. You are everything to me.

Your Sarah

A<small>T THE</small> age of seventy, Sarah Bernhardt lost one of her legs but continued her triumphant tour of Europe and America. On the eve of her death, when seventy-eight years of age, she acted for the screen. She died in London in 1923, and after her death and Sardou's, their love letters were published.

PIOTR ILYICH TCHAIKOVSKY RECEIVES AN INVOLUNTARY CONFESSION FROM HIS BENEFACTRESS, NADEJDA PHILARETOVNA VON MECK

[AN EXCHANGE OF LETTERS]

WHEN Catherine Drinker Bowen and Barbara von Meck issued their volume of Tchaikovsky's selected correspondence under the title Beloved Friend in February, 1937, the world learned for the first time the full details of "one of the strangest and most pathetic love stories in history." The thirteen-year intimacy between the Russian composer and his benefactress "who fell in love with him and his music, and who supported, consoled, and mothered him, wrote him almost daily letters, arranged his daily life, but never talked with him face to face," is chronicled in these moving and pathetic letters. In their wild emotional outbursts we can decipher the secret—implicit perhaps also in his music—which turned the young dilettante into a tragic figure.

As a young man, Tchaikovsky was "a stock figure out of Turgeniev— elegant, superficial, foppish, and diffuse." He came of a completely unmusical family and was, in fact, raised for the law.

When they began corresponding in 1876, Tchaikovsky was thirty-six and Nadejda von Meck forty-five, a proud aristocrat just widowed and a recluse. She fell in love with both him and his music when she heard Nikolai Rubinstein play Tchaikovsky's Tempest. The composer was then already excessively shy, largely because he feared the world might learn his deepest secret—his lack of normal capacity to love women. His

373

distant and adoring admirer, Mme von Meck, was the mother of twelve children.

When Rubinstein arranged to introduce Tchaikovsky and Mme von Meck by letter, she made it clear that she had no wish to meet him, just as he had no wish to meet her. They said they felt closer because of this stipulation. Thus began the extraordinary friendship.

Tchaikovsky was soon afterward virtually trapped into an unwilling marriage with a pupil at the Conservatory, Antonina Ivanovna Miliukova. Antonina, it appears, had sent Tchaikovsky an effusive "fan letter," which he foolishly answered. He soon tried to discourage her attentions, but she threatened suicide. Even after he confessed his homosexuality, Antonina was not dismayed. He gave in to her pleas, and they were married on July 18, 1877.

At the time, Tchaikovsky was composing the score of Eugen Oniegin, and identified Antonina with Tatiana in the opera. After two terror-stricken weeks with his bride, he tried in vain to commit suicide by drowning, and finally, with money advanced by Mme von Meck, fled from her in hysteria and panic. Rubinstein and Tchaikovsky's brother, Modest, broke to Antonina the news of the impossibility of Tchaikovsky's ever returning to her. Already half-mad, she survived the separation forty years, dying in an insane asylum in 1917.

Mme von Meck then settled an annuity of six thousand rubles on Tchaikovsky. This "overwhelming good fortune, this unquestioning and undemanding kindness," inspired a burst of creative energy, climaxed by the completion of the Fourth Symphony, dedicated to Mme von Meck. The music referred to in this letter is the piano arrangement of that symphony. Two years later, she wrote her protégé as follows:

". . . do you know what a wicked person I am?"

Brailov
Sept. 26, 1879
Friday at 8 A.M.

HOW sorry I am, my dearest, that you feel so badly in Petersburg, but—forgive me—I am glad you are homesick for Brailov. I doubt if you could ever understand how jealous I am of you, in spite of the absence of personal contact between us. Do you know that I am jealous in the most unpardonable way, as a woman is jealous of the man she loves? Do you know that when you married it was terribly hard for me, as though something had broken in my heart? The thought that you were near that woman was bitter and unbearable.

And do you know what a wicked person I am? I rejoiced when you were unhappy with her! I reproached myself for that feeling. I don't think I betrayed myself in any way, and yet I could not destroy my feelings. They are something a person does not order.

I hated that woman because she did not make you happy, but I would have hated her a hundred times more if you had been happy with her. I thought she had robbed me of what should be mine only, what is my right, because I love you more than anyone and value you above everything in the world.

If this knowledge bothers you, forgive my involuntary confession. I have spoken out. The reason is, the symphony. But I believe it is better for you to know that I am not such an idealistic person as you think. And then, it cannot change anything in our relationship. I don't want any change. I should like to be sure that nothing will be changed as my life draws to its close, that nobody . . . But that I have no right to say. Forgive me and forget all I have said— my mind is upset.

Forgive me, please, and realize that I feel well and that I am in need of nothing. Good-by, dear friend; forget this letter, but do not forget your heartily loving,

N. von Meck

P.S. Would you mind, please, acknowledging the receipt of this letter?

To THIS letter, Tchaikovsky, in the sincere and heartfelt strain that marked most of his music, sent the following answer:

". . . the deepest and most secret gropings of my soul."

Grankino

Oct. 10, 1879

IT IS impossible to say how glad I was to see your handwriting and to know we were again in communication. Jurgenson forgot to tell me that the piano arrangement of our symphony had at last been published, so your letter was the first news I had of it. I am tremendously elated that you are satisfied with the arrangement, which in truth is well and skillfully done.

As for the music itself, I knew beforehand that you would like it; how could it have been otherwise? I wrote it with you constantly in mind. At that time, I was not nearly so intimate with you as now, but already I sensed vaguely that no one in the world could respond more keenly to the deepest and most secret gropings of my soul. No musical dedication has ever been more seriously meant. It was spoken not only on my part but on yours; the symphony was not, in truth, mine but ours. Forever it will remain my favorite work, as the monument of a time when upon a deep, insidiously growing mental disease, upon a whole series of unbearable sufferings, grief and despair, suddenly, hope dawned and the sun of happiness began to shine—and that sun was embodied in the person to whom the symphony was dedicated.

I tremble to think what might have happened if fate had not sent you to me. I owe you everything: Life, the chance to pursue freedom—that hitherto unattainable ambition, and such abundance of good fortune as had never occurred to me even in dreams.

I read your letter with gratitude and love too strong for expression in any medium but music. May I be able some time to express it thus!

Dear friend, may you keep well. I wish it for you more than for myself. Reading how our symphony caused you sleepless nights, I felt my heart constricted. I want my music henceforth to be a source of joy and consolation, and with all my strength I desire for you a spirit well and calm.

Yours,
P. Tchaikovsky

THIRTEEN years after it was started, the strange epistolary intimacy was abruptly brought to an end. Nadejda von Meck, either because she had finally heard of her protégé's "dark secret" or because she was depressed by her son's death and her own illness, abruptly discontinued the annuity in October, 1890, falsely blaming her step on financial reverses. The real truth reached Tchaikovsky, and he was sore at heart. The following year he went to New York for what was musically and outwardly a triumphal tour. But just before his first concert with the Philharmonic he was weeping bitterly and alone in his New York hotel room. . . . In his last year he composed his "Pathétique," or Sixth, Symphony, described by Havelock Ellis as a "homosexual tragedy." When Tchaikovsky died in 1893 at the age of fifty-three (a few months before the death of his patroness), he was reproachfully murmuring the name of Nadejda.

GUY DE MAUPASSANT AND MARIE BASHKIRTSEFF
INTRIGUE EACH OTHER'S CURIOSITY

[AN EXCHANGE OF LETTERS]

THESE are the headlong letters of a "would-be George Sand." Marie Bashkirtseff died of tuberculosis at twenty-four. This gifted Russian girl—naïve, witty, morbid, fearless, and passionately introspective—has captivated many readers by her published letters and journals. They provide a key not only to her own complex nature but to the literary, artistic, and social world of upper-class Europe in the late nineteenth century.

From the age of twelve, when she began her celebrated diary, Marie had indulged in many tempestuous (if merely epistolary) love affairs with unwitting heroes of her choice, including the ex-King Francis II and the Duke of Hamilton. She attained only modest success as a painter and musician, but won fame from her journals and letters. What measure of posthumous and frustrated glory she won came from her own desperate efforts to be a romantic correspondent of her celebrated contemporaries.

Shortly before her death, Marie Bashkirtseff was prompted by one of these romantic impulses to write to Guy de Maupassant, a rising literary star, whose widely heralded conquests of the heart had endowed him for her with the attributes of an Apollo. In a mood characteristically compounded of audacity, sentiment, and irony, she wrote her first letter to him, hiding behind the name "Miss Hastings," which had first served as the title for his story, recently published in Le Gaulois, and later entitled "Miss Harriet."

"... with romantic dreams of becoming the confidante of your beautiful soul ..."

MONSIEUR:

I read your works, I might almost say, with delight. In truth to nature, which you copy with religious fidelity, you find an inspiration that is truly sublime, while you move your readers by touches of feeling so profoundly human, that we fancy we see ourselves depicted in your pages, and love you with an egotistical love. Is this an unmeaning compliment? Be indulgent, it is sincere in the main.

You will understand that I should like to say many fine and striking things to you, but it is rather difficult, all at once, in this way. I regret this all the more as you are sufficiently great to inspire one with romantic dreams of becoming the confidante of your beautiful soul, always supposing your soul to be beautiful.

If your soul is not beautiful, and if "those things are not in your line," I shall regret it for your sake, in the first place; and in the next I shall set you down in my mind as a maker of literature, and dismiss the matter from my thoughts.

For a year past I have had the wish to write to you and was many times on the point of doing so, but—sometimes I thought I exaggerated your merits and that it was not worth while. Two days ago, however, I saw suddenly, in the *Gaulois*, that someone had honored you with a flattering epistle and that you had inquired the address of this amiable person in order to answer him. I at once became jealous, your literary merits dazzled me anew and—here is my letter.

And now let me say that I shall always preserve my incognito for you. I do not even desire to see you from a distance—your countenance might not please me—who can tell? All I know of you now is that you are young and that you are not married, two essential points, even for a distant adoration.

But I must tell you that I am charming; this sweet reflection will stimulate you to answer my letter. It seems to me that if I were a man I should wish to hold no communication, not even an epistolary one, with an old fright of an Englishwoman, whatever might be thought by

Miss Hastings
P.O. Station of the Madeleine

DE MAUPASSANT'S *curiosity was clearly piqued, for, unlike Zola and Goncourt, who received letters of this type from Marie, he acknowledged this letter from an "unknown" by replying as follows:*

"What charm can mysterious correspondence add to relationships?"

MADAME:
My letter surely will not be what you expected. At the outset I want to thank you for your kindness to me and for your compliments. Now let us talk like sensible people.

You ask to become my confidante. By what right? I do not

know you. Why should I tell you—a person unknown, whose mind, temperament, and so on, may not be in tune with the quality of my intellect—what perhaps I would tell, aloud and intimately, to the women who are my friends? Wouldn't that be the conduct of an idiot, of an unfaithful friend?

What charm can mysterious correspondence add to relationships? Does not all the sweetness of affection—chaste affection—between man and woman come for the most part, from the joy of meeting, of speaking to one another, and of visualizing, in letters to one's friend, her face depicted between one's eyes and the paper?

How could one transcribe the intimacies of one's innermost being and address them to one whose figure, the color of whose hair, whose smile and aspect, one is unacquainted with?

You allude to one letter which I received recently. It was from a man who asked my advice. Now look. To return to letters from unknown women. In the last two years, I have received in the neighborhood of fifty or sixty. How am I to choose from these women the confidante of my soul, as you put it?

When they are willing to reveal themselves and become acquainted as in the world of respectable society, then a relationship of friendliness and confidence can be established; otherwise, why should I neglect the charming friends I know for a friend who may be charming, but is unknown; that is to say, who may be disagreeable, both visually and intellectually? All this is not very gallant, is it? But if I throw myself at your feet, could you believe me faithful in my moral affections?

Pardon, Madame, the reasoning of a man more practical than poetical, and believe me to be your grateful and devoted

Guy de Maupassant

P.S. Pardon the erasures in my letter. I cannot write without making them and have no time to recopy.

THE correspondence flourished for a time. In her answer to Maupassant's letter, Marie Bashkirtseff poked fun at her hero. "Only sixty fan letters?" she said in effect. "You're not as popular as I supposed. And I refuse to be merely number sixty-one. I am more amusing than that."

The letters soon reflected other moods; Maupassant, confessing that he wrote from boredom, bid in vain for "Miss Hastings'" sympathy. She, however, refused to take him seriously. He then pretended to think Miss Hastings a man, and she promptly fell in with his fancy.

Finally Marie was bored with the whole affair and wanted to stop writing, but Maupassant, now thoroughly interested, renewed his efforts to discover her identity. She never revealed it.

In her last letter of all, Marie wrote with characteristic candor: "Your terrestrial envelope does not interest me, but does mine you? Suppose you had the bad taste not to find me wonderful, do you think I should like it, however pure my intentions?" So the strange correspondence closed. There is a legend that shortly before her death, she and Maupassant met. In a churchyard at Passy a chapel is dedicated to her, and in Nice a street bears her name.

BILL NYE BECOMES POSTMASTER OF LARAMIE, WYOMING, AND HELPS THE AMERICAN REPUBLIC MARCH ONWARD AND UPWARD WITH THE ARTS

[A LETTER TO GENERAL FRANK HATTON]

THIS *brief note helped Bill Nye (Edgar Wilson Nye) leap to nation-wide fame overnight. Before he undertook the local postmastership with this hilarious letter of acceptance, addressed to his chief in Washington, he was an unknown newspaperman laboring modestly on The Daily Boomerang of Laramie City, Wyoming. The letter was widely reprinted, and soon the new postmaster became one of America's favorite humorists. He wrote Bill Nye's History of the United States. Born in 1850, he died in 1896.*

". . . I may at times appear haughty and indifferent . . ."

Office of *Daily Boomerang*, Laramie City, Wy.,
August 9, 1882.

MY DEAR GENERAL:
I have received by telegraph the news of my nomination by the President and my confirmation by the Senate, as postmaster at Laramie, and wish to extend my thanks for the same.

I have ordered an entirely new set of boxes and post office outfit, including new corrugated cuspidors for the lady clerks.

384

I look upon the appointment, myself, as a great triumph of eternal truth over error and wrong. It is one of the epochs, I may say, in the Nation's onward march toward political purity and perfection. I do not know when I have noticed any stride in the affairs of state which so thoroughly impressed me with its wisdom.

Now that we are co-workers in the same department, I trust that you will not feel shy or backward in consulting me at any time relative to matters concerning post office affairs. Be perfectly frank with me, and feel perfectly free to just bring anything of that kind right to me. Do not feel reluctant because I may at times appear haughty and indifferent, cold or reserved. Perhaps you do not think I know the difference between a general delivery window and a three-m quad, but that is a mistake. My general information is far beyond my years.

With profoundest regard, and a hearty endorsement of the policy of the President and the Senate, whatever it may be,

I remain, sincerely yours,

Bill Nye, P.M.

Gen. Frank Hatton, Washington, D. C.

A YEAR later, on October 1, 1883, writing from the "Postoffice Divan" of Laramie City, Wyoming, once more, Bill Nye solemnly bid farewell to all his greatness and renounced his high post of duty in an equally florid letter to President Chester A. Arthur. With due ceremony he turned over the great seal and the key to the front door. This great and unselfish gesture came at a time when Nye's term of office still had three years to go. "I must, therefore, beg pardon for my eccentricity in resigning. It will be best, perhaps, to keep the heart-breaking news from the ears of European powers until the dangers of a financial panic are fully past. Then hurl it broadcast with a sickening thud."

385

P. T. BARNUM OFFERS GENERAL ULYSSES S. GRANT
A JOB

I N 1884, at the age of sixty-two, seven years after his second term as President had ended, Ulysses S. Grant was in distressing financial straits. As a result of a bank failure, he owed W. H. Vanderbilt $250,000, which he had no means of repaying. Instead, he made over to his creditor all his own personal property as well as that of his wife. Hearing of this, "The Greatest Showman on Earth," the self-styled "Prince of Humbugs," called on Grant, whom he had met before, and corroborated in person the astonishing offer printed below:

"I will give you one hundred thousand dollars cash . . ."

New York, January 12, 1885

TO GENERAL U. S. GRANT, twice President of the United States, etc.:

Honored Sir: The whole world honors and respects you. All are anxious that you should live happy and free from care. While they admire your manliness in declining the large sum recently tendered you by friends, they still desire to see you achieve financial independence in an honorable manner. Of the unique and valuable trophies with which you have been honored, we all have read, and all have a laudable desire to see these evidences of love and respect bestowed upon you by monarchs, princes and people throughout the globe.

While you would confer a great and enduring favor on your

386

fellow-men and women by permitting them to see these trophies you could also remove existing embarrassments in a most satisfactory and honorable manner. I will give you one hundred thousand dollars cash, besides a proportion of the profits, if I may be permitted to exhibit these relics to a grateful and appreciative public, and I will give satisfactory bonds of half a million dollars for their safe-keeping and return.

These precious trophies of which all your friends are so proud, would be placed before the eyes of your millions of admirers in a manner and style at once pleasing to yourself and satisfactory to the best elements of the entire community. Remembering that the mementoes of Washington, Napoleon, Frederick the Great and many other distinguished men have given immense pleasure to millions who have been permitted to see them, I trust you will in the honorable manner proposed, gratify the public and thus inculcate the lesson of honesty, perseverence and true patriotism so admirably illustrated in your career.

I have the honor to be truly your friend and admirer,

P. T. Barnum

MOST politely, General Grant declined the offer, on the grounds that Mr. Vanderbilt had promised to give the Grant relics to a museum in Washington, where everyone could see them. "Yes, General," Barnum replied, "but millions of persons who will never visit Washington will regret I had never brought these historic relics where they would see them."

General Grant recouped his fortunes to a large extent by completing his Personal Memoirs, under heroic circumstances, while he was dying of cancer of the throat. He finished the last page four days before his death, in July, 1885, six months after his interchange of letters with P. T. Barnum.

387

WILLIAM RANDOLPH HEARST, FRESH FROM HARVARD, SEEKS FUN, FAME, AND FORTUNE WITH A NEWSPAPER OF HIS OWN

[A LETTER TO HIS FATHER]

JUST dismissed from Harvard, because of "overindulgence in a passion for pranks," William Randolph Hearst, at the age of twenty-two, felt an overmastering desire to have a newspaper of his own—to try out his own unorthodox theories of journalism. Five years before, his multimillionaire father had taken over for debt a "limp rag of a newspaper" called The San Francisco Examiner. The bearded pioneer of the California gold rush of '49 rated the property "far beneath a single foal of his famous racing horses or the least lucrative of his ranches and mines ranging from Alaska to Mexico." But the son saw it as the golden opportunity for a career of his own. He outlined these ideas in the following letter to his father, which was never made public until more than fifty years later, when Hearst declared: "At that time my father was the only person in the world who, in my modest opinion, knew more than I did, although I have learned since, to my consternation, that quite a number of other people in this surprising world are gifted with thought reservoirs of a more spectacular order than my own."

"... I am convinced that I could run a newspaper successfully."

1885 [Washington]

DEAR FATHER:
I have just finished and dispatched a letter to the Editor of the *Examiner* in which I recommended Eugene Lent to his favorable notice, and commented on the illustrations, if you may call them such, which have lately disfigured the paper. I really believe that the *Examiner* has furnished what is thus far the crowning absurdity of illustrated Journalism, in illustrating an article on the chicken show by means of the identical Democratic roosters used during the late campaign. In my letter to the editor, however, I did not refer to this for fear of offending him, but I did tell him that in my opinion the cuts that have recently appeared in the paper bore an unquestionable resemblance to the Cuticura Soap advertisements; and I am really inclined to believe that our editor has illustrated many of his articles from his stock on hand of cuts representing gentlemen before and after using that efficacious remedy.

In case my remarks should have no effect and he should continue in his career of desolation, let me beg of you to remonstrate with him and thus prevent him from giving the finishing stroke to our miserable little sheet.

I have begun to have a strange fondness for our little paper— a tenderness like unto that which a mother feels for a puny or deformed offspring, and I should hate to see it die now after it

389

had battled so long and so nobly for existence; in fact, to tell the truth, I am possessed of the weakness, which at some time or other of their lives, pervades most men; I am convinced that I could run a newspaper successfully.

Now if you should make over to me the *Examiner*—with enough money to carry out my schemes—I'll tell you what I would do!

In the first place I would change the general appearance of the paper and make seven wide columns where we now have nine narrow ones, then I would have the type spaced more, and these two changes would give the pages a much cleaner and neater appearance.

Secondly, it would be well to make the paper as far as possible original, to clip only when absolutely necessary and to imitate only some such leading journal as the New York *World* which is undoubtedly the best paper of that class to which the *Examiner* belongs—that class which appeals to the people and which depends for its success upon enterprise, energy and a certain startling originality and not upon the wisdom of its political opinions or the lofty style of its editorials: And to accomplish this we must have—as the *World* has—active, intelligent and energetic young men; we must have men who come out West in the hopeful buoyancy of youth for the purpose of making their fortunes and not a worthless scum that has been carried there by the eddies of repeated failures.

Thirdly, we must advertise the paper from Oregon to New Mexico and must also increase our number of advertisements if we have to lower our rates to do it, thus we can put on the first page that our circulation is such and our advertisements so and so and constantly increasing.

And now having spoken of the three great essential points let us turn to details. The illustrations are a detail, though a very important one. Illustrations embellish a page; illustrations attract the eye and stimulate the imagination of the masses and materially aid the comprehension of an unaccustomed reader and thus are of particular importance to that class of people which the *Examiner* claims to address. Such illustrations, however, as have heretofore appeared in the paper, nauseate rather than stimulate the imagination and certainly do anything but embellish a page.

Another detail of questionable importance is that we actually or apparently establish some connection between ourselves and the New York *World*, and obtain a certain prestige in bearing some relation to that paper. We might contract to have important private telegrams forwarded or something of that sort, but understand that the principal advantage we are to derive is from the attention such a connection would excite and from the advertisement we could make of it. Whether the *World* would consent to such an arrangement for any reasonable sum is very doubtful, for its net profit is over one thousand dollars a day and no doubt it would consider the *Examiner* as beneath its notice. Just think, over one thousand dollars a day and four years ago it belonged to Jay Gould and was losing money rapidly.

And now to close with a suggestion of great consequence, namely, that all these changes be made not by degrees but at once so that the improvement will be very marked and noticeable and will attract universal attention and comment.

There is little to be said about my studies. I am getting on in all of them well enough to be able to spend considerable time in outside reading and in Journalistic investigation. There is, moreover, very little to be said about Washington, for Congress is as stupid as it is possible to conceive of and has been enlivened only once during our stay and that the other day when Wise of Virginia sat on Boutelle of Maine for attempting to revive the dissensions of the war. So heavily, indeed, did Mr. Wise sit on

Boutelle that I fear the latter gentlemen has not even yet recovered his characteristic rotundity of form.

Well, good-by. I have given up all hope of having you write to me, so I suppose I must just scratch along and trust to hearing of you through the newspapers. By the way, I heard you had bought 2000 acres of land the other day and I hope some of it was the land adjoining our ranch that I begged you to buy in my last letter.

Your affectionate son,

W. R. Hearst

THE letter either persuaded or convinced Senator Hearst, and in March, 1887, his young son took possession of The San Francisco Examiner. Thus began a spectacular career in journalism which has left its mark on the American scene for more than fifty years. Hearst's biographer, John K. Winkler, has thus summed him up as "an American phenomenon":

"Courted by kings, premiers, presidents; watched by Wall Street and the financial great of the earth; feared or fawned upon by politicians in every city and state in the nation, this astonishing master of the art of attracting attention and swaying the multitude holds himself personally as aloof as the Dalai Lama. Hence the general belief that Hearst is a man of mystery. Hearst is not a mysterious man; he is a mystifying man.

"His frontiers are perhaps as irregular as those of any human being that ever puzzled a biographer. Those who know him best unhesitatingly set him down as a genius. Their memories teem with incidents that show him incomparably brave, unbelievably timorous, generous, mean, altruistic, selfish! To some he is a Gladstone, a Pitt, a Parnell; to others a Nero, a Caligula, an Iago. No man knows him completely; some know him partially; all men who have come into contact with him agree *that he is about the most interesting individual that ever crossed their path."*

On February 5, 1937, the "Lord of San Simeon" continued the dynastic cycle by writing a note to his own son on the twenty-fifth anniversary of one of his many newspapers, The Atlanta Georgian. In this he passed on the heritage to the next generation and set down his newspaper philosophy in terms of his own actual achievements rather than of mere hopes and promises. Most of the features and promises young Hearst outlined in his youthful letter of 1885 were actually carried out in the following decades. In the process of doing so, he built a fabulous network of newspapers, magazine syndicates, motion-picture companies, gold mines, real-estate holding companies, and related industries and enterprises.

Now in his seventy-seventh year, Hearst lives in magnificent splendor and solitude, still directing, somewhat less actively, his far-flung newspaper and magazine empire, writing with craftsmanlike regularity and telegraphic speed and energy a daily column called "In the News." Many, but by no means all, of the art treasures he assembled with princely extravagance during the last half century have recently been sold at auction. Colleagues of Mr. Hearst still believe that "the Chief" is by far the most brilliant writer, the most forceful commentator, and the best all-around newspaperman on the Hearst staff of many thousands.

MARK TWAIN REFUSES TO SANCTION A DRAMATIZATION OF *TOM SAWYER*

[A LETTER TO NUMBER 1365]

Mark Twain's letters range from the depths of misanthropic despair to the inspired heights of Gargantuan humor. After a boyhood in Missouri, a youth in Mississippi, and an apprenticeship as printer and steamboat pilot, he first attained renown with his travel letters from Europe. Winning world fame with Tom Sawyer, Life on the Mississippi, and Huckleberry Finn, he extended it by his eloquence on the lecture platform and deepened it by profound and pessimistic philosophical studies.

Just before his own death at the age of seventy-five, Mark Twain suffered a "double disaster" within the span of thirteen days, when his wife died and his invalid daughter "was set free from the swindle of this life." A grief-stricken letter of desolation he wrote at that time has been read by the editor of this anthology. It is a classic of despair. Unfortunately it cannot yet be made public.

Another famous Mark Twain letter revealing his characteristic attitude toward his own masterpieces is the one in which he acknowledged a librarian's suggestion (in 1905) that Tom Sawyer and Huckleberry Finn be removed from the children's room, because "their mischievous and deceitful practices" made them "poor examples for youth." To this Mark Twain replied by stating: "I am greatly troubled by what you say. I wrote Tom Sawyer & Huck Finn for adults exclusively, & it always distresses me when I find that boys & girls have been allowed access to them. The mind that becomes soiled in youth can never again be washed clean. I know this by my own experience, & to this day I cherish an unappeasable bitterness against the unfaithful guardians of my young life, who not only permitted but compelled me to read an unexpurgated Bible through before I was 15 years old. None can do that and ever draw a clean sweet breath again this side of the grave. Ask that young lady— she will tell you so.

"Most honestly do I wish that I could say a softening word or two in defense of Huck's character, since you wish it, but really in my opinion it is no better than God's (in the Ahab chapter and 97 others) & those of Solomon, David, Satan & the rest of the sacred brotherhood.

"If there is an Unexpurgated in the Children's Department won't you please help that young woman remove Huck from that questionable companionship?"

The letter that follows was written at the height of Mark Twain's reputation, when he was fifty-two years of age. It seems that the manager of a traveling theatrical company had dramatized Tom Sawyer and asked the author's permission to use his name in announcing the production. Flinging prudence to the winds, the manager "took the liberty" of offering Mark Twain a free ticket to the performance. Here is Mark Twain's reply:

"Tom Sawyer is . . . a hymn . . ."

Hartford, Sept. 8, '87.

DEAR SIR,—And so it has got around to you, at last; and you also have "taken the liberty." You are No. 1365. When 1364 sweeter and better people, including the author, have tried to dramatize Tom Sawyer and did not arrive, what sort of show do you suppose you stand? That is a book, dear sir, which cannot be dramatized. One might as well try to dramatize any other hymn.

Tom Sawyer is simply a hymn, put into prose form to give it a worldly air.

Why the pale doubt that flitteth dim and nebulous athwart the forecastle of your third sentence? Have no fears. Your piece will be a Go. It will go out the back door on the first night. They've all done it—the 1364. So will—1365. Not one of us ever thought of the simple device of half-soling himself with a stove-lid. Ah, what suffering a little hindsight would have saved us. Treasure this hint.

How kind of you to invite me to the funeral. Go to; I have attended a thousand of them. I have seen Tom Sawyer's remains in all the different kinds of dramatic shrouds there are. You cannot start anything fresh. Are you serious when you propose to pay my expence—if that is the Susquehannian way of spelling it? And can you be aware that I charge a hundred dollars a mile when I travel for pleasure? Do you realize that it is 432 miles to Susquehanna? Would it be handy for you to send me the $43,-200 first, so I could be counting it as I come along; because railroading is pretty dreary to a sensitive nature when there's nothing sordid to buck at for Zeitvertreib.

Now as I understand it, dear and magnanimous 1365, you are going to re-create Tom Sawyer dramatically, and then do me the compliment to put me in the bills as father of this shady offspring. Sir, do you know that this kind of compliment has destroyed people before now? Listen.

Twenty-four years ago, I was strangely handsome. The remains of it are still visible through the rifts of time. I was so handsome that human activities ceased as if spellbound when I came in view, and even inanimate things stopped to look—like locomotives, and district messenger boys and so-on. In San Francisco, in rainy season I was often mistaken for fair weather. Upon one occasion I was traveling in the Sonora region, and stopped for an hour's nooning, to rest my horse and myself. All the town came out to look. A Piute squaw named her baby for me,—a voluntary compliment which pleased me greatly.

Other attentions were paid me. Last of all arrived the president and faculty of Sonora University and offered me the post of Professor of Moral Culture and Dogmatic Humanities; which I accepted gratefully, and entered at once upon my duties. But my name had pleased the Indians, and in the deadly kindness of their hearts they went on naming their babies after me. I tried to stop it, but the Indians could not understand why I should object to so manifest a compliment. The thing grew and grew and spread and spread and became exceedingly embarrassing. The University stood it a couple of years; but then for the sake of the college they felt obliged to call a halt, although I had the sympathy of the whole faculty.

The president himself said to me, "I am as sorry as I can be for you, and would still hold out if there were any hope ahead; but you see how it is: there are a hundred and thirty-two of them already, and fourteen precincts to hear from. The circumstance has brought your name into most wide and unfortunate renown. It causes much comment—I believe that that is not an over-statement. Some of this comment is palliative, but some of it— by patrons at a distance, who only know the statistics without the explanation,—is offensive, and in some cases even violent. Nine students have been called home. The trustees of the college have been growing more and more uneasy all these last months —steadily along with the implacable increase in your census— and I will not conceal from you that more than once they have touched upon the expediency of a change in the Professorship of Moral Culture. The coarsely sarcastic editorial in yesterday's Alta, —headed Give the Moral Acrobat a Rest—has brought things to a crisis, and I am charged with the unpleasant duty of receiving your resignation."

I know you only mean me a kindness, dear 1365, but it is a most deadly mistake. Please do not name your Injun for me. Truly yours.

THIS letter was never mailed by Mark Twain. Instead, he wrote to the manager as follows from New York on September 8, 1887:

Dear Sir,—Necessarily I cannot assent to so strange a proposition. And I think it but fair to warn you that if you put the piece on the stage, you must take the legal consequences.

Yours respectfully,
S. L. Clemens.

Thirteen years later, a Mr. Kester asked permission to make a play out of Tom Sawyer and received this reply from the author:

I should like to see Tom Sawyer staged. You need not submit the play to my approval. . . . Turn the book upside down and inside out if you want to. If you wish to add people, incidents, morals, immorals, or anything else, do so with a free hand. My literary vanities are dead and nothing I have written is sacred to me.

Sincerely yours,
S. L. Clemens.

Years later, the editors of The New Yorker framed this letter in their reception room, "where once an editor died like a dog for taking a comma out of a couplet."

ROBERT LOUIS STEVENSON DEFENDS A SAINT AND HERO WHO TASTED OF OUR COMMON FRAILTY

[AN OPEN LETTER TO THE REVEREND DR. C. M. HYDE OF HONOLULU]

ON THE night of February 25, 1890, in Sydney, Australia, Robert Louis Stevenson summoned his wife, his daughter, and his son, and announced that he had something serious to lay before them. The story of this dramatic family conclave has been reconstructed for us in Graham Balfour's celebrated biography of R.L.S.

"His demeanor," says Balfour, "showed a ferocity of indignation and his eyes literally blazed with a burning light."

What Stevenson had to relate forms the background of this impassioned philippic flung by him through the Far Eastern mails at the Reverend Dr. Hyde—a missive in which the words seem literally pressed from the grapes of wrath.

On his trip to the South Seas, seeking sunlight and health, Stevenson had visited the leper colony at Molokai, one of the Hawaiian group. There were some nuns on the boat with him, who had dedicated the remainder of their lives to caring for the lepers.

"My horror of the horrible is about my weakest point," he wrote to his wife, "but the moral loveliness at my elbow blotted out all else; and when I found out that one of them was crying, poor soul, quietly under her veil, I cried a little myself; then I felt as right as a trivet, only a little crushed to be there so uselessly."

Stevenson remained over a week on the island, and saw everything at the leper colony. Afterwards he wrote to his friend, Sidney Colvin: "The sight of so much courage, cheerfulness and devotion strung me too high to mind the infinite pity and horror of the sights. . . . I have seen sights that cannot be told. . . . Of old Damien, whose weakness and worse perhaps I heard fully, I think only the more. He was a European peasant, dirty, bigoted . . . but superb with generosity, residual candor and fundamental good-humor. . . . A man, with all the grime and paltriness of mankind, but a saint and a hero all the more for that."

The Damien to whom Stevenson referred was a priest of the leper colony, who had died two years before. One day, in a Sydney newspaper, Stevenson read with mounting anger a denunciation of Father Damien for being "coarse, dirty, headstrong, bigoted . . . disobedient . . . and not a pure man in his relation with women. . . ."

The author of these charges was the Reverend Dr. C. M. Hyde, a missionary of Stevenson's acquaintance, and Hyde's open letter to the press, it seems, had halted a plan to erect a tablet in honor of Father Damien. Instantly there was formed in Stevenson's mind a plan to defend Damien against this attack.

Stevenson wrote his reply to Dr. Hyde in white heat, then read it aloud to his assembled family. He pointed out to them that it was clearly libelous and gravely dangerous, since its publication might lead to a law suit and an award which could easily cause "the loss of his entire substance."

Without a dissenting voice, the family voted for the publication of the letter. In Balfour's Life of Robert Louis Stevenson, R.L.S. is quoted as saying, "I knew I was writing a libel. I thought he would bring action; I made sure I should be ruined. I asked leave of my gallant family, and the sense that I was signing away all I possessed kept me up to highwater mark, and made me feel every heroic insult."

Father Damien, the hero of this interchange of letters, was born in Belgium of devout Flemish stock and was marked for a business career by his family. "But his priestly vocation grew within and could not be denied . . ." and he was ordained and sent to the South Seas at the age of twenty-three.

Nine years later he volunteered for duty at the leper colony at Molokai. Freely, instinctively, he made this his life work. The next turning point of his life came in his forty-fifth year, on a Sunday in June, 1885, when he began his sermon not with the usual words "my brethren," but with the grim and compassionate salutation "we lepers." He died three years later, in 1888.

Inflamed with "holy anger" at Dr. Hyde's defamation of Damien, the concrete results of whose heroism he had but recently seen, Stevenson wrote this reply, which was privately printed and distributed first in Sydney, and then throughout the world.

"The least tender should be moved to tears; the most incredulous to prayer."

Sydney, February 25, 1890

SIR,—It may probably occur to you that we have met, and visited, and conversed; on my side, with interest. You may remember that you have done me several courtesies, for which I was prepared to be grateful. But there are duties which come before gratitude, and offences which justly divide friends, far more acquaintances. Your letter to the Reverend H. B. Gage is a document which, in my sight, if you had filled me with bread when I was starving, if you had sat up to nurse my father when he lay a-dying, would yet absolve me from the bonds of gratitude.

You know enough, doubtless, of the process of canonisation to be aware that, a hundred years after the death of Damien, there

401

will appear a man charged with the painful office of the *devil's advocate*. After that noble brother of mine, and of all frail clay, shall have lain a century at rest, one shall accuse, one defend him. The circumstance is unusual that the devil's advocate should be a volunteer, should be a member of a sect immediately rival, and should make haste to take upon himself his ugly office ere the bones are cold; unusual, and of a taste which I shall leave my readers free to qualify; unusual, and to me inspiring.

If I have at all learned the trade of using words to convey truth and to arouse emotion, you have at last furnished me with a subject.

For it is in the interest of all mankind and the cause of public decency in every quarter of the world, not only that Damien should be righted, but that you and your letter should be displayed at length, in their true colours, to the public eye.

To do this properly, I must begin by quoting you at large: I shall then proceed to criticise your utterance from several points of view, divine and human, in the course of which I shall attempt to draw again and with more specification the character of the dead saint whom it has pleased you to villify: so much being done, I shall say farewell to you for ever.

Honolulu, Aug. 2, 1889

Rev. H. B. Gage:

Dear Brother,—In answer to your inquiries about Father Damien, I can only reply that we who know the man are surprised at the extravagant newspaper laudations, as if he was a most saintly philanthropist. The simple truth is, he was a coarse, dirty man, headstrong and bigoted. He was not sent to Molokai, but went there without orders; did not stay at the leper settlement (before he became one himself), but circulated freely over the whole island (less than half the island is devoted to the lepers), and he came often to Honolulu. He had no hand in the reforms and improvements inaugurated, which were the work of our Board of Health, as occasion required and means were provided. He was not a pure man in his relations with women, and the leprosy of which he died should be attributed to his vices and carelessness. Others have done much for the lepers, our own ministers, the government physicians, and so forth, but never with the Catholic idea of meriting eternal life.—

Yours, etc.,

C. M. Hyde

To deal fitly with a letter so extraordinary, I must draw at the outset on my private knowledge of the signatory and his sect. It may offend others; scarcely you, who have been so busy to collect, so bold to publish, gossip on your rivals. And this is perhaps the moment when I may best explain to you the character of what you are to read: I conceive you as a man quite beyond and below the reticences of civility: with what measure you mete, with that shall it be measured you again; with you, at last, I rejoice to feel the button off the foil and to plunge home. And if in aught that I shall say I should offend others, your colleagues, whom I respect and remember with affection, I can but offer them my regret; I am not free, I am inspired by the consideration of interests far more large; and such pain as can be inflicted by anything from me must be indeed trifling when compared with the pain with which they read your letter. It is not the hangman, but the criminal, that brings dishonour on the house.

You belong, sir, to a sect—I believe my sect, and that in which my ancestors laboured—which has enjoyed, and partly failed to utilise, an exceptional advantage in the islands of Hawaii. The first missionaries came; they found the land already self-purged of its old and bloody faith; they were embraced, almost on their arrival, with enthusiasm; what troubles they supported came far more from whites than from Hawaiians; and to these last they stood (in a rough figure) in the shoes of God.

This is not the place to enter into the degree or causes of their failure, such as it is. One element alone is pertinent, and must here be plainly dealt with. In the course of their evangelical calling, they—or too many of them—grew rich. It may be news to you that the houses of missionaries are a cause of mocking on the streets of Honolulu. It will at least be news to you, that when I returned your civil visit, the driver of my cab commented on the size, the taste, and the comfort of your home. It would have been news certainly to myself, had any one told me that afternoon that I should live to drag such matter into print.

But you see, sir, how you degrade better men to your own level; and it is needful that those who are to judge betwixt you and me, betwixt Damien and the devil's advocate, should understand your letter to have been penned in a house which could raise, and that very justly, the envy and the comments of the passers-by. I think (to employ a phrase of yours which I admire) it "should be attributed" to you that you have never visited the scene of Damien's life and death. If you had, and had recalled it, and looked about your pleasant rooms, even your pen perhaps would have been stayed.

Your sect (and remember, as far as any sect avows me, it is mine) has not done ill in a worldly sense in the Hawaiian Kingdom. When calamity befell their innocent parishioners, when leprosy descended and took root in the Eight Islands, a *quid pro quo* was to be looked for. To that prosperous mission, and to you, as one of its adornments, God had sent at last an opportunity.

I know I am touching here upon a nerve acutely sensitive. I know that others of your colleagues look back on the inertia of your Church, and the intrusive and decisive heroism of Damien, with something almost to be called remorse. I am sure it is so with yourself; I am persuaded your letter was inspired by a certain

404

envy, not essentially ignoble, and the one human trait to be espied in that performance.

You were thinking of the lost chance, the past day; of that which should have been conceived and was not; of the service due and not rendered. *Time was*, said the voice in your ear, in your pleasant room, as you sat raging and writing; and if the words written were base beyond parallel, the rage, I am happy to repeat —it is the only compliment I shall pay you—the rage was almost virtuous.

But, sir, when we have failed, and another has succeeded; when we have stood by, and another has stepped in; when we sit and grow bulky in our charming mansions, and a plain, uncouth peasant steps into the battle, under the eyes of God, and succours the afflicted, and consoles the dying, and is himself afflicted in his turn, and dies upon the field of honour—the battle cannot be retrieved as your unhappy irritation has suggested. It is a lost battle, and lost for ever. One thing remained to you in your defeat—some rags of common honour; and these you have made haste to cast away.

Common honour; not the honour of having done anything right, but the honour of not having done aught conspicuously foul; the honour of the inert: that was what remained to you.

We are not all expected to be Damiens; a man may conceive his duty more narrowly, he may love his comforts better; and none will cast a stone at him for that. But will a gentleman of your reverend profession allow me an example from the fields of gallantry? When two gentlemen compete for the favour of a lady, and the one succeeds and the other is rejected, and (as will sometimes happen) matter damaging to the successful rival's credit reaches the ear of the defeated, it is held by plain men of no pretensions that his mouth is, in the circumstance, almost necessarily closed.

Your Church and Damien's were in Hawaii upon a rivalry to do well: to help, to edify, to set divine examples. You having (in one huge instance) failed, and Damien succeeded, I marvel it should not have occurred to you that you were doomed to silence; that when you had been outstripped in that high rivalry, and sat inglorious in the midst of your well-being, in your pleasant room —and Damien, crowned with glories and horrors, toiled and rotted in that pigstye of his under the cliffs of Kalawao—you, the elect, who would not, were the last man on earth to collect and propagate gossip on the volunteer who would and did.

I think I see you—for I try to see you in the flesh as I write these sentences—I think I see you leap at the word pigstye, a hyperbolical expression at the best. "He had no hand in the reforms," he was "a coarse, dirty man"; these were your own words; and you may think it possible that I am come to support you with fresh evidence.

In a sense, it is even so. Damien has been too much depicted with a conventional halo and conventional features; so drawn by men who perhaps had not the eye to remark or the pen to express the individual; or who perhaps were only blinded and silenced by generous admiration, such as I partly envy for myself—such as you, if your soul were enlightened, would envy on your bended knees.

It is the least defect of such a method of portraiture that it makes the path easy for the devil's advocate, and leaves for the misuse of the slanderer a considerable field of truth.

For the truth that is suppressed by friends is the readiest weapon of the enemy. The world, in your despite, may perhaps owe you something, if your letter be the means of substituting once for all a credible likeness for a wax abstraction. For, if that world at all remember you, on the day when Damien of Molokai shall be named Saint, it will be in virtue of one work: your letter to the Reverend H. B. Gage.

406

You may ask on what authority I speak. It was my inclement destiny to become acquainted, not with Damien, but with Dr. Hyde. When I visited the lazaretto Damien was already in his resting grave. But such information as I have, I gathered on the spot in conversation with those who knew him well and long: some indeed who revered his memory; but others who had sparred and wrangled with him, who beheld him with no halo, who perhaps regarded him with small respect, and through whose unprepared and scarcely partial communications the plain, human features of the man shone on me convincingly.

These gave me what knowledge I possess; and I learnt it in that scene where it could be most completely and sensitively understood—Kalawao, which you have never visited, about which you have never so much as endeavoured to inform yourself: for, brief as your letter is, you have found the means to stumble into that confession.

"Less than one-half of the island," you say, "is devoted to the lepers." Molokai—"*Molokai ahina*," the "grey," lofty, and most desolate island—along all its northern side plunges a front of precipice into a sea of unusual profundity. This range of cliff is, from east to west, the true end and frontier of the island.

Only in one spot there projects into the ocean a certain triangular and rugged down, grassy, stony, windy, and rising in the midst into a hill with a dead crater: the whole bearing to the cliff that overhangs it somewhat the same relation as a bracket to a wall. With this hint you will now be able to pick out the leper station on a map; you will be able to judge how much of Molokai is thus cut off between the surf and precipice, whether less than a half, or less than a quarter, or a fifth, or a tenth—or say, a twentieth; and the next time you burst into print you will be in a position to share with us the issue of your calculations.

I imagine you to be one of those persons who talk with cheerfulness of that place which oxen and wainropes could not drag you to behold. You, who do not even know its situation on the map, probably denounce sensational descriptions, stretching your limbs the while in your pleasant parlour on Beretania Street.

When I was pulled ashore there one early morning, there sat with me in the boat two sisters, bidding farewell (in humble imitation of Damien) to the lights and joys of human life. One of these wept silently; I could not withhold myself from joining her.

Had you been there, it is my belief that nature would have triumphed even in you; and as the boat drew but a little nearer, and you beheld the stairs crowded with abominable deformations of our common manhood, and saw yourself landing in the midst of such a population as only now and then surrounds us in the horror of a nightmare—what a haggard eye you would have rolled over your reluctant shoulder towards the house on Beretania Street!

Had you gone on; had you found every fourth face a blot upon the landscape; had you visited the hospital and seen the butt-ends of human beings lying there almost unrecognisable, but still breathing, still thinking, still remembering; you would have understood that life in the lazaretto is an ordeal from which the nerves of a man's spirit shrink, even as his eye quails under the brightness of the sun; you would have felt it was (even to-day) a pitiful place to visit and a hell to dwell in.

It is not the fear of possible infection. That seems a little thing when compared with the pain, the pity, and the disgust of the visitor's surroundings, and the atmosphere of affliction, disease, and physical disgrace in which he breathes.

I do not think I am a man more than usually timid; but I never recall the days and nights I spent upon that island promontory (eight days and seven nights), without heartfelt thankfulness that I am somewhere else. I find in my diary that I speak of my stay as a "grinding experience": I have once jotted in the margin,

408

"*Harrowing* is the word"; and when the *Mokolii* bore me at last towards the outer world, I kept repeating to myself, with a new conception of their pregnancy, those simple words of the song—

> *Tis the most distressful country that ever yet*
> *was seen.*

And observe: that which I saw and suffered from was a settlement purged, bettered, beautified; the new village built, the hospital and the Bishop-Home excellently arranged; the sisters, the doctor, and the missionaries, all indefatigable in their noble tasks.

It was a different place when Damien came there, and made his great renunciation, and slept that first night under a tree amidst his rotting brethren: alone with pestilence; and looking forward (with what courage, with what pitiful sinkings of dread, God only knows) to a lifetime of dressing sores and stumps.

You will say, perhaps, I am too sensitive, that sights as painful abound in cancer hospitals and are confronted daily by doctors and nurses. I have long learned to admire and envy the doctors and the nurses. But there is no cancer hospital so large and populous as Kalawao and Kalaupapa; and in such a matter every fresh case, like every inch of length in the pipe of an organ, deepens the note of the impression; for what daunts the onlooker is that monstrous sum of human suffering by which he stands surrounded. Lastly, no doctor or nurse is called upon to enter once for all the doors of that gehenna; they do not say farewell, they need not abandon hope, on its sad threshold; they but go for a time to their high calling, and can look forward as they go to relief, to recreation, and to rest. But Damien shut to with his own hand the doors of his own sepulchre.

I shall now extract three passages from my diary at Kalawao.

A. "Damien is dead and already somewhat ungratefully remembered in the field of his labours and sufferings. 'He was a good man, but very officious,' says one. Another tells me he had fallen (as other priests so easily do) into something of the ways and habits of thought of a Kanaka; but he had the wit to recognise the fact, and the good sense to laugh at" [over] "it. A plain man it seems he was; I cannot find he was a popular."

B. "After Ragsdale's death" [Ragsdale was a famous Luna, or overseer, of the unruly settlement] "there followed a brief term of office by Father Damien which served only to publish the weakness of that noble man. He was rough in his ways, and he had no control. Authority was relaxed; Damien's life was threatened, and he was soon eager to resign."

C. "Of Damien I begin to have an idea. He seems to have been a man of the peasant class, certainly of the peasant type: shrewd; ignorant and bigoted, yet with an open mind, and capable of receiving and digesting a reproof if it were bluntly administered; superbly generous in the least thing as well as in the greatest, and as ready to give his last shirt (although not without human grumbling) as he had been to sacrifice his life; essentially indiscreet and officious, which made him a troublesome colleague; domineering in all his ways, which made him incurably unpopular with the Kanakas, but yet destitute of real authority, so that his boys laughed at him and he must carry out his wishes by the means of bribes. He learned to have a mania for doctoring; and set up the Kanakas against the remedies of his regular rivals: perhaps (if anything matter at all in the treatment of such a disease) the worst thing that he did, and certainly the easiest.

"The best and worst of the man appear very plainly in his dealings with Mr. Chapman's money; he had originally laid it out" (intended to lay it out) "entirely for the benefit of Catholics, and even so not wisely; but after a long, plain talk, he admitted his error fully and revised the list. The sad state of the boys' home is in part the result of his lack of control; in part, of his own slovenly

410

ways and false ideas of hygiene. Brother officials used to call it 'Damien's Chinatown.' 'Well,' they would say, 'your Chinatown keeps growing.' And he would laugh with perfect good-nature, and adhere to his errors with perfect obstinacy.

"So much I have gathered of truth about this plain, noble human brother and father of ours; his imperfections are the traits of his face, by which we know him for our fellow; his martyrdom and his example nothing can lessen or annul; and only a person here on the spot can properly appreciate their greatness."

I have set down these private passages, as you perceive, without correction; thanks to you, the public has them in their bluntness. They are almost a list of the man's faults, for it is rather these that I was seeking: with his virtue, with the heroic profile of his life, I and the world were already sufficiently acquainted. I was besides a little suspicious of Catholic testimony; in no ill sense, but merely because Damien's admirers and disciples were the least likely to be critical. I know you will be more suspicious still; and the facts set down above were one and all collected from the lips of Protestants who had opposed the father in his life. Yet I am strangely deceived, or they build up the image of a man, with all his weaknesses, essentially heroic, and alive with rugged honesty, generosity, and mirth.

Take it for what it is, rough private jottings of the worst side of Damien's character, collected from the lips of those who had laboured with and (in your own phrase) "knew the man";—though I question whether Damien would have said that he knew you. Take it, and observe with wonder how well you were served by your gossips, how ill by your intelligence and sympathy; in how many points of fact we are at one, and how widely our appreciations vary. There is something wrong here; either with you or me. It is possible, for instance, that you, who seem to have so many ears in Kalawao, had heard of the affair of Mr. Chapman's money, and were singly struck by Damien's intended wrong-doing.

I was struck with that also, and set it fairly down; but I was struck much more by the fact that he had the honesty of mind to be convinced. I may here tell you that it was a long business; that one of his colleagues sat with him late into the night, multiplying arguments and accusations: that the father listened as usual with "perfect good-nature and perfect obstinacy"; but at the last, when he was persuaded—"Yes," said he, "I am very much obliged to you; you have done me a service; it would have been a theft." There are many (not Catholics merely) who require their heroes and saints to be infallible; to these the story will be painful; not to the true lovers, patrons, and servants of mankind.

And I take it, this is a type of our division; that you are one of those who have an eye for faults and failures; that you take a pleasure to find and publish them; and that, having found them, you make haste to forget the overvailing virtues and the real success which had alone introduced them to your knowledge. It is a dangerous frame of mind. That you may understand how dangerous, and into what a situation it has already brought you, we will (if you please) go hand-in-hand through the different phrases of your letter, and candidly examine each from the point of view of its truth, its appositeness, and its charity.

Damien was coarse.

It is very possible. You make us sorry for the lepers who had only a coarse old peasant for their friend and father. But you, who were so refined, why were you not there, to cheer them with the lights of culture? Or may I remind you that we have some reason to doubt if John the Baptist were genteel; and in the case of Peter, on whose career you doubtless dwell approvingly in the pulpit, no doubt at all he was a "coarse, headstrong" fisherman! Yet even in our Protestant Bibles Peter is called Saint.

Damien was *dirty*.

He was. Think of the poor lepers annoyed with this dirty comrade! But the clean Dr. Hyde was at his food in a fine house.

Damien was *headstrong*.

I believe you are right again; and I thank God for his strong head and heart.

Damien was *bigoted*.

I am not fond of bigots myself, because they are not fond of me. But what is meant by bigotry, that we should regard it as a blemish in a priest? Damien believed his own religion with the simplicity of a peasant or a child; as I would I could suppose that you do. For this I wonder at him some way off; and had that been his only character, should have avoided him in life. But the point of interest in Damien, which has caused him to be so much talked about and made him at last the subject of your pen and mine, was that, in him, his bigotry, his intense and narrow faith, wrought potently for good, and strengthened him to be one of the world's heroes and exemplars.

Damien *was not sent to Molokai, but went there without orders.*

Is this a misreading? or do you really mean the words for blame? I have heard Christ, in the pulpits of our Church, held up for imitation on the ground that His sacrifice was voluntary. Does Dr. Hyde think otherwise?

Damien *did not stay at the settlement, etc.*

It is true he was allowed many indulgences. Am I to understand that you blame the father for profiting by these, or the officers for granting them? In either case, it is a mighty Spartan standard to issue from the house on Beretania Street; and I am convinced you will find yourself with few supporters.

413

Damien *had no hand in the reforms, etc.*

I think even you will admit that I have already been frank in my description of the man I am defending; but before I take you up upon this head, I will be franker still, and tell you that perhaps nowhere in the world can a man taste a more pleasurable sense of contrast than when he passes from Damien's "Chinatown" at Kalawao to the beautiful Bishop-Home at Kalaupapa. At this point, in my desire to make all fair for you, I will break my rule and adduce Catholic testimony.

Here is a passage from my diary about my visit to the Chinatown, from which you will see how it is (even now) regarded by its own officials: "We went round all the dormitories, refectories, etc.—dark and dingy enough, with a superficial cleanliness, which he" [Mr. Dutton, the lay brother] "did not seek to defend. 'It is almost decent,' said he; 'the sisters will make that all right when we get them here.' " And yet I gathered it was already better since Damien was dead, and far better than when he was there alone and had his own (not always excellent) way. I have now come far enough to meet you on a common ground of fact; and I tell you that, to a mind not prejudiced by jealousy, all the reforms of the lazaretto, and even those which he most vigorously opposed, are properly the work of Damien. They are the evidence of his success; they are what his heroism provoked from the reluctant and the careless.

Many were before him in the field; Mr. Meyer, for instance, of whose faithful work we hear too little: there have been many since; and some had more worldly wisdom, though none had more devotion, than our saint. Before his day, even you will confess, they had effected little. It was his part, by one striking act of martyrdom, to direct all men's eyes on that distressful country. At a blow, and with the price of his life, he made the place illustrious and public. And that, if you will consider largely, was the one

414

reform needful; pregnant of all that should succeed. It brought money; it brought (best individual addition of them all) the sisters; it brought supervision, for public opinion and public interest landed with the man of Kalawao. If ever any man brought reforms, and died to bring them, it was he. There is not a clean cup or towel in the Bishop-Home, but dirty Damien washed it.

Damien was not a pure man in his relations with women, etc.

How do you know that? Is this the nature of the conversation in that house on Beretania Street which the cabman envied, driving past?—racy details of the misconduct of the poor peasant priest, toiling under the cliffs of Molokai?

Many have visited the station before me; they seem not to have heard the rumour. When I was there I heard many shocking tales, for my informants were men speaking with the plainness of the laity; and I heard plenty of complaints of Damien. Why was this never mentioned? and how came it to you in the retirement of your clerical parlour?

But I must not even seem to deceive you. This scandal, when I read it in your letter, was not new to me. I had heard it once before; and I must tell you how. There came to Samoa a man from Honolulu; he, in a public-house on the beach, volunteered the statement that Damien had "contracted the disease from having connection with the female lepers"; and I find a joy in telling you how the report was welcome in a public-house.

A man sprang to his feet; I am not at liberty to give his name, but from what I heard I doubt if you would care to have him to dinner in Beretania Street. "You miserable little ——" (here is a word I dare not print, it would so shock your ears). "You miserable little ——," he cried, "if the story were a thousand times true, can't you see you are a million times a lower —— for daring to repeat it?"

I wish it could be told of you that when the report reached you in your house, perhaps after family worship, you had found in your soul enough holy anger to receive it with the same expressions: ay, even with that one which I dare not print; it would not need to have been blotted away, like Uncle Toby's oath, by the tears of the recording angel; it would have been counted to you for your brightest righteousness. But you have deliberately chosen the part of the man from Honolulu, and you have played it with improvements of your own.

The man from Honolulu—miserable, leering creature—communicated the tale to a rude knot of beach-combing drinkers in a public-house, where (I will so far agree with your temperance opinions) man is not always at his noblest; and the man from Honolulu had himself been drinking—drinking, we may charitably fancy, to excess.

It was to your "Dear Brother, the Reverend H. B. Gage," that you chose to communicate the sickening story; and the blue ribbon which adorns your portly bosom forbids me to allow you the extenuating plea that you were drunk when it was done. Your "dear brother"—a brother indeed—made haste to deliver up your letter (as a means of grace, perhaps) to the religious papers; where, after many months, I found and read and wondered at it; and whence I have now reproduced it for the wonder of others.

And you and your dear brother have, by this cycle of operations, built up a contrast very edifying to examine in detail. The man whom you would not care to have to dinner, on the one side; on the other, the Reverend Dr. Hyde and the Reverend H. B. Gage: the Apia bar-room, the Honolulu manse.

But I fear you scarce appreciate how you appear to your fellow-men; and to bring it home to you, I will suppose your story to be true. I will suppose—and God forgive me for supposing it—that Damien faltered and stumbled in his narrow path of duty; I will suppose that, in the horror of his isolation, perhaps in the fever of incipient disease, he, who was doing so much more than he had sworn, failed in the letter of his priestly oath—he, who was so much a better man than either you or me, who did what we have never dreamed of daring—he too tasted of our common frailty. "O, Iago, the pity of it!" The least tender should be moved to tears; the most incredulous to prayer. And all that you could do was to pen your letter to the Reverend H. B. Gage!

Is it growing at all clear to you what a picture you have drawn of your own heart? I will try yet once again to make it clearer. You had a father: suppose this tale were about him, and some informant brought it to you, proof in hand: I am not making too high an estimate of your emotional nature when I suppose you would regret the circumstance? that you would feel the tale of frailty the more keenly since it shamed the author of your days? and that the last thing you would do would be to publish it in the religious press? Well, the man who tried to do what Damien did, is my father, and the father of the man in the Apia bar, and the father of all who love goodness; and he was your father too, if God had given you grace to see it.

Robert Louis Stevenson

THE following September, on sober second thought (we learn from Balfour), Stevenson considered it a mistake to have sent the letter in this form. He thought he "should have waited for his anger to cool and should have made the letter more impersonal and less egotistic."

In a letter to Mrs. Charles Fairchild, Stevenson characterized the letter as "barbarously rash" and went on to say, "If I did it now, it would defend Damien no less and would give less pain to those who are alive. . . . On the whole it was virtuous to defend Damien but it was harsh to strike so hard at Dr. Hyde. When I wrote the letter I believed he would bring an action, in which case I knew I could be beggared. And as yet there has come no action. The injured doctor has contented himself up to now with the truly innocuous vengeance of calling me a 'Bohemian crank' and I have deeply wounded one of his colleagues whom I esteemed and liked. . . . Well, such is life. . . ."

Almost fifty years later (we learn from The Second Woollcott Reader), Charles MacArthur and Alexander Woollcott speculated on the effect this historic correspondence had on the "astounded recipient":

"Did it crush the Cleric utterly? Did it hurry him to a mortified grave? Or was he armoured against such shafts? Did he bridle and say that he 'considered the source'? Did he, as MacArthur guessed, audibly derive comfort from the fact that his critic was a wretched Bohemian who had taken another man's wife away from him and carried her off to the wanton South Seas? Really, what could he expect?"

Actually, the Reverend Dr. Hyde was not crushed at all. He returned to the attack with an epistolary counterblast. On August 7, 1890, he wrote a letter to The Congregationalist, in which he said he had been "exposed to all the malodorous and scarifying missiles any blackguard may use who has access to the public press." But he went on to concede that Stevenson's letter was "brilliantly written."

Stevenson's letter was reprinted throughout the English-speaking world. He persistently declined to be paid for its use. To his publisher he wrote: "This letter is yours or any man's. . . . I draw the line at cannibalism. I could not eat a penny roll that this piece of bludgeoning had gained for me. . . ." Finally the Reverend Dr. Hyde was "bludgeoned into silence," unbroken even by the libel action that Stevenson feared. He died, as Stevenson prophesied in his letter, "remembered only by the virtue of one work: (his) letter to the Reverend H. B. Gage."

In 1936, the body of Father Damien was returned with full honors to his home in Belgium for burial in his homeland. It had been Damien's wish to be buried among the lepers whom he succored. For forty-six years his body had rested in Hawaiian soil. He remains in memory "one of the great martyrs in history"—his immortality guaranteed by a single burning letter written by Robert Louis Stevenson, who died in Samoa and was buried in a mountain grave overlooking the Pacific.

PIERRE CURIE ASKS MARIE SKLODOVSKA, A FORMER GOVERNESS AND A STUDENT OF PHYSICS, TO BE HIS WIFE

In 1893, Pierre Curie, although still virtually unknown in France, was enjoying considerable renown throughout the rest of Europe for his basic researches in magnetism and other branches of physics. He had developed an ultrasensitive method of measurement known as the "Curie Scale." Lord Kelvin himself publicly declared him a master. For this creative scientific work of the first magnitude, plus the instruction of thirty students, the French government was then paying him, at the age of thirty-five, a salary of three hundred francs a month—the wages of a competent factory worker. His title was Chief of the Laboratory at the School of Physics and Chemistry of the City of Paris.

Among his small group of friends it was said that Pierre Curie "was devoting body and soul to scientific research . . . and that "he loved nobody." In his diary, he had once written: "Women of genius are rare."

Then Pierre Curie met Marie Sklodovska. . . . She had come from Warsaw to study at the Sorbonne, had passed first in the physics examination the year before, and was just preparing for her examination in mathematics. Their first conversation, at the home of a common friend, as described by Eve Curie, "was soon reduced to scientific dialogue. . . . Marie, with a shade of timidity and deference, asked questions and listened to Pierre's suggestions. He in turn explained his plans, and described the phenomena of crystallography, which fascinated him, and upon which he was now engaged in research. How strange it was, the physicist thought, to talk to a woman of the work one loves, using technical terms, complicated formulae, and to see that woman, charming and young, become animated, understand, even discuss certain

420

details with an *infallible clear-sightedness. . . . How sweet it was!"*

The friendship thus started was pursued by Pierre Curie "with gentle tenacity." After Pierre had seen her in the laboratory in her "big linen smock, bent silently over her apparatus," he sent her a reprint of his latest publication, On Symmetry in Physical Phenomena: Symmetry of an Electric Field and of a Magnetic Field.

Before coming to Paris, Marie had been a governess. She was now living in a garret. "Disappointed and humiliated at the failure of her first idyl," according to her daughter and biographer, Eve, "Marie swore to love no one. She had ruled marriage out of her life's program and had built for herself a secret universe of implacable rigor, dominated by the passion for science."*

When Pierre first asked Marie to be his wife, she refused, but when she returned to Poland for the summer he continued his courtship by correspondence. This is one of the letters he wrote her at that time:

"*. . . any discovery that we may make, however small,*
will remain acquired knowledge."

August 10, 1894

NOTHING could have given me greater pleasure than to get news of you. The prospect of remaining two months without hearing about you had been extremely disagreeable to me: that is to say, your little note was more than welcome.

I hope you are laying up a stock of good air and that you will

* See a letter written in 1911 by Marie Curie and Henri Poincaré, recommending Albert Einstein for a professorship, on page 453.

come back to us in October. As for me, I think I shall not go anywhere; I shall stay in the country, where I spend the whole day in front of my open window or in the garden.

We have promised each other—haven't we?—to be at least great friends. If you will only not change your mind! For there are no promises that are binding; such things cannot be ordered at will. It would be a fine thing, just the same, in which I hardly dare believe, to pass our lives near each other, hypnotized by our dreams: your patriotic dream, our humanitarian dream, and our scientific dream.

Of all those dreams the last is, I believe, the only legitimate one. I mean by that that we are powerless to change the social order and, even if we were not, we should not know what to do; in taking action, no matter in what direction, we should never be sure of not doing more harm than good, by retarding some inevitable evolution. From the scientific point of view, on the contrary, we may hope to do something; the ground is solider here, and any discovery that we may make, however small, will remain acquired knowledge.

See how it works out: it is agreed that we shall be great friends, but if you leave France in a year it would be an altogether too Platonic friendship, that of two creatures who would never see each other again. Wouldn't it be better for you to stay with me? I know that this question angers you, and that you don't want to speak of it again—and then, too, I feel so thoroughly unworthy of you from every point of view.

I thought of asking your permission to meet you *by chance* in Fribourg. But you are staying there, unless I am mistaken, only one day, and on that day you will of course belong to our friends the Kovalskis.

Believe me your very devoted

Pierre Curie

I should be happy if you would write to me and give me the assurance that you intend to come back in October. If you write direct to Sceaux the letters would get to me quicker: Pierre Curie, 13 rue des Sablons, Sceaux (Seine).

WOULD it not," asks *Eve Curie, "in itself be a splendid title to fame to have inspired such letters?"*

When Marie returned to her Paris laboratory in October, Pierre resumed his courtship. *"He bore within him,"* writes *Eve Curie, "the same faith as his future wife, a faith which was even more wholehearted, purer by its lack of alloy. . . . He was even ready to sacrifice what people call happiness to another happiness known to him alone. He suggested, in other words, a purely friendly arrangement and even offered to go to Poland with Marie. He became a humble supplicant. . . ."* Thus for ten months the courtship continued.

Finally, in July, 1895, Marie wrote to a girlhood friend:

> When you receive this letter your Manya will have changed her name. I am about to marry the man I told you about last year in Warsaw. It is a sorrow to me to have to stay in Paris, but what am I to do? Fate has made us deeply attached to each other and we cannot endure the idea of separating.
>
> I haven't written, because all this was decided only a short time ago, quite suddenly. I hesitated for a whole year and could not resolve upon an answer. Finally I became reconciled to the idea of settling here. When you receive this letter, write to me: Mme Curie, School of Physics and Chemistry, 42 Rue Lhomond.
>
> That is my name from now on. My husband is a teacher in that school. Next year I shall bring him to Poland so that he will know my country,.and I shall not fail to introduce him to my dear little chosen sister, and I shall ask her to love him. . . .

On her wedding day, Marie Sklodovska asked a friend who offered her a wedding dress that she be kind enough to give her one that would be "practical and dark so that it could be worn in the laboratory." For their honeymoon they toured the countryside on bicycles and explored the woods on foot. They called it a "wedding tramp."

Thus was culminated the romance of Marie and Pierre Curie. Their life story has been beautifully summarized by Eve Curie:

> She was a woman; she belonged to an oppressed nation; she was poor; she was beautiful. A powerful vocation summoned her from her motherland, Poland, to study in Paris, where she lived through years of poverty and solitude. There she met a man whose genius was akin to hers. She married him; their happiness was unique. By the most desperate and avid effort they discovered a magic element, radium. This discovery not only gave birth to a new science and a new philosophy; it provided mankind with the means of treating a dreadful disease.

Perhaps this is a fitting place to repeat Einstein's famous tribute: "Marie Curie is, of all celebrated beings, the only one whom fame has not corrupted."

When Pierre Curie was killed by a wagon in a street accident in 1906, Mme Curie succeeded him as professor at the Sorbonne, resuming his lecture sequence at the precise point where he had left off. In 1921 she visited the United States and received from the hands of President Warren Gamaliel Harding, on behalf of the women of America, a gram of radium worth about $120,000. She died in 1934 as a result of an ailment aggravated by her radium experiments.

PAUL GAUGUIN AND AUGUST STRINDBERG COMPARE NOTES ON ART, BARBARISM, AND CIVILIZATION

[AN EXCHANGE OF LETTERS]

Paul Gauguin lived from 1848 to 1903.

An exhibitionistic misanthrope who was in turn sailor, stoker, successful stockbroker for thirty years, painter, and roué on several continents, Paul Gauguin, crippled in a fight with Breton sailors over his Javanese mistress, decided for the third and last time to leave civilization forever and return to his home in Tahiti, which only a few months before he had abandoned in boredom and disgust.

Gauguin was at heart half Parisian, half savage. Having instructed his Paris agent to sell all his pictures at auction for what they would bring, he wrote to August Strindberg, the Swedish poet and dramatist, who had formerly lived with him, asking for a preface for the catalogue. Strindberg's reply follows:

"I cannot grasp your art . . ."

You insist absolutely upon having the preface for your catalog which I wrote in remembrance of the winter 1894-5, when we were living here, behind the Institute, not far from the Pantheon, more important still, close to the cemetery of Montparnasse! I would have willingly given you this souvenir to take away with you to that isle of Oceania, where you wish to seek a decoration in harmony with your powerful stature and a breathing space, but I feel myself in an equivocal position from the outset, and I respond immediately to your request by an "I cannot," or, more brutally, by an "I will not." . . .

I cannot grasp your art, and I cannot love it. I know that this avowal will neither astonish nor wound you, because you seem to be only strengthened by the hatred of others; your personality, careful to remain intact, is pleased by the antipathy that it arouses. Perhaps with reason, for, from the instant when approved and admired, you obtain partisans, either they will rank you or classify you or give to your art a name which the younger men shall have used for five years to designate a superannuated style of painting. . . .

It was of Puvis de Chavannes that I thought last night, when to the southern sounds of mandolin and guitar, I saw on the walls of your studio an uproar of sunlit pictures, which pursued me in my sleep. I saw trees which no botanist will discover, animals unsuspected by Cuvier and men which only you can create.

A sea which pours forth from a volcano, a sky in which no God can live—Sir, said I in my dream, you have created a new heaven and earth, but I am not delighted in the midst of your creation. It is too sunny for me. I prefer more chiaroscuro. And in your paradise there lives an Eve who is not my ideal because truly I, too, have a feminine ideal or two!

Gauguin is not formed from the work of Chavannes, nor from that of Manet, nor from that of Bastien-Lepage.

Who is he then? He is Gauguin, the savage who hates a wearisome civilization; something of a Titan, who, jealous of his creator, in his idle moments makes his own little creation; a child who breaks up his toys to make others; he who denies and defies

426

the rabble, preferring to see the sky red, rather than blue, as they do.

Bon Voyage, Master: but come back here to me. I shall by that time perhaps have learned to understand your art better, which will permit me to make a true preface for a new catalog of a new sale, since I am beginning also to feel an immense need for becoming savage and creating a new world.

To THIS *letter from August Strindberg, Paul Gauguin replied in a manner that demonstrated, as many of his pictures did, what Thomas Craven has called "a splenetic grudge which ripened into an active contempt for civilization. . . ."*

"... she alone ... can remain naked before one's eyes."

I HAVE received today your letter; your letter, which is a preface for my catalog. I had the idea of asking you for a preface, when I saw you the other day in my studio playing the guitar and singing, your blue northern eyes gazing attentively at the pictures on the walls. I had then the presentiment of a revolt, of a shock between your civilization and my barbarism.

You suffer from your civilization. My barbarism is to me a renewal of youth.

Before the Eve of my choice, which I have painted in forms and harmonies of another world, your remembrances have perhaps evoked a sorrow of the past. The Eve of your civilized conception makes you and the rest of us almost always misogynists; the

427

old Eve, which in my studio frightens you, will perhaps smile at you less bitterly some day. This world of mine, which neither a Cuvier nor a botanist can find, will be a Paradise which I shall have only sketched out. And from this sketch to the realization of the dream is very far. What matter? To envisage happiness, is that not a foretaste of Nirvana?

The Eve that I have painted, she alone, logically, can remain naked before one's eyes. Yours in that simple state could not walk without shame and too beautiful (perhaps) would be the evocation of an evil and a sorrow.

GAUGUIN, showman par excellence, printed both letter and answer in the catalogue, raising it thus to the status of a milestone in the history of art criticism. With the 12,000 francs from the sale, he returned to Tahiti, where he died eight years later, dissolute, drugged, and diseased, still flinging his angry grievance against the world, but possessing to the last that uncompromising and vigorous sense of life that lives in his paintings.

WILLIAM JAMES DISCOVERS THAT HE HAS OMITTED THE DEEPEST PRINCIPLE OF HUMAN NATURE FROM HIS TEXTBOOK ON PSYCHOLOGY

[A LETTER TO HIS STUDENTS AT RADCLIFFE COLLEGE]

THE founder of "pragmatism" and brother of Henry James was born in New York in 1842 and died in 1910. He was educated abroad and at Harvard. Joining the faculty in 1872, he soon became head of a famous group of psychologists and philosophers that included Charles Peirce, George Santayana, Josiah Royce, and Hugo Munsterberg. His basic textbook, Principles of Psychology, described by Professor Irwin Edman as "the towering classic of modern times in its empirical interpretation of human nature," made him famous.

William James worshiped at the shrine of experience and is noted in the annals of philosophy for the "fresh communication of the incontrovertibleness, the primacy of firsthand experience." Half mystical, half practical, he said that "the ultimate test for us of what a truth means is indeed the conduct it dictates or inspires." But he did not merely contemplate life from an ivory tower. Those who knew him at close range and those who have read his voluminous correspondence realize he had a zest for life—"an almost agonized concern for deciphering the secret ultimates of nature and destiny."

At a university ceremony, the young ladies of his class at Radcliffe College presented William James with a lovely azalea plant. In acknowledgment of this gift, he wrote the following charming letter—a classic of graciousness and appreciation:

"... *the pride of my life and delight of my existence.*"

Cambridge, Apr. 6, 1896.

DEAR YOUNG LADIES,—I am deeply touched by your remembrance. It is the first time anyone ever treated me so kindly, so you may well believe that the impression on the heart of the lonely sufferer will be even more durable than the impression on your minds of all the teachings of Philosophy 2A. I now perceive one immense omission in my Psychology,—the deepest principle of Human Nature is the *craving to be appreciated*, and I left it out altogether from the book, because I had never had it gratified till now. I fear you have let loose a demon in me, and that all my actions will now be for the sake of such rewards. However, I will try to be faithful to this one unique and beautiful azalea tree, the pride of my life and delight of my existence. Winter and summer will I tend and water it—even with my tears. Mrs. James shall never go near it or touch it. If it dies, I will die too; and if I die, it shall be planted on my grave.

Don't take all this too jocosely, but believe in the extreme pleasure you have caused me, and in the affectionate feelings with which I am and shall always be faithfully your friend,

Wm. James

WILLIAM JAMES lived fourteen years following this gift and this letter—years described as "busy, exploring, variegated." In addition to his classic work on Principles of Psychology, he also wrote The Will to Believe, The Meaning of Truth, Pragmatism, Varieties of Religious Experience, and Human Immortality.

431

Part Three

LETTERS OF YESTERDAY AND TODAY

[FROM 1898 TO 1937]

ÉMILE ZOLA CHALLENGES THE PRESIDENT OF THE FRENCH REPUBLIC TO RESTORE FAITH IN HUMAN JUSTICE

ANATOLE FRANCE called Zola a moment of the conscience of man, and in this historic letter, which marked the climax of the Dreyfus case, we see how he earned that glorious tribute.

In 1894, Captain Alfred Dreyfus, a brilliant young French artillery officer of unimpeachable integrity, the son of a Jewish manufacturer, was charged, on the evidence of an intercepted letter to a German official, with selling documents of military value. He was tried, convicted on trumped-up evidence, stripped of his military honors and rank, and sentenced to life imprisonment on Devil's Island, off the coast of French Guiana. At a formal ceremony, Dreyfus was publicly degraded, his shoulder straps and buttons being cut away and his sword snapped in two. While a frenzied mob clamored for the "traitor's death," Dreyfus stood firm and flung back these clear words to the officers and the crowd: "I am innocent. Some day you shall know the truth. Vive la France."

In the ghastly isolation of Devil's Island, Dreyfus suffered unspeakable hardships. Six jailers watched him day and night, and he was subjected to both physical and mental tortures. Even after the authorship of the incriminating note was definitely attributed three years later to the notorious blackguard Esterhazy, justice was impeded by the obdurate refusal of the high command of the French Army to reverse the record and thus lose face with the nation. By this time, liberals all over France and throughout Europe were aroused to an impassioned interest in the case. The nation was torn asunder; a principle was at stake.

Émile Zola, at the zenith of his fame as a novelist, known the world over for his great naturalistic novels like Nana and Germinal, feared and

435

respected as "the shark" of letters, worshiped as the forsworn enemy of sham and injustice, had been interested from the start. Now, in January, 1898, he volunteered to wield his pen in the cause of right. When the obviously guilty Esterhazy was acquitted after a fantastic trial, Zola was consumed by a wrath truly titanic.

Deliberately laying himself open to charges of libel, Zola made use of the impressive array of facts marshaled by the liberals, and drafted, in his forty-eighth year, this famous open letter to President Félix Faure of France, printed in L'Aurore, a struggling liberal newspaper. It is undoubtedly one of the most terrible denunciations in all history. He spent a day writing it—"panting not only out of indignation, but out of fear that he might not be the first to write such a manifesto." This letter created tumultuous interest throughout the land. Georges Clemenceau, then a radical young journalist, supplied the celebrated title:

"J'accuse . . ."

[January, 1898]

MR. PRESIDENT,
Permit me, I beg you, in return for the gracious favors you once accorded me, to be concerned with regard to your just glory and to tell you that your record, so fair and fortunate thus far, is now threatened with the most shameful, the most effaceable blot.

You escaped safe and sane from the basest calumnies; you conquered all hearts. You seem radiant in the glory of a patriotic celebration . . . and are preparing to preside over the solemn triumph of our Universal Exposition, which is to crown our great century of work, truth and liberty. But what a clod of mud is

436

flung upon your name—I was about to say your reign—through this abominable Dreyfus affair. A court-martial has but recently, by order, dared to acquit one, Esterhazy—a supreme slap at all truth, all justice! And it is done; France has this brand upon her visage; history will relate that it was during your administration that such a social crime could be committed.

Since they have dared, I too shall dare. I shall tell the truth because I pledged myself to tell it if justice, regularly empowered did not do so, fully, unmitigatedly. My duty is to speak; I have no wish to be an accomplice. My nights would be haunted by the spectre of the innocent being, expiating under the most frightful torture, a crime he never committed.

And it is to you, Mr. President, that I shall out this truth, with all the force of my revolt as an honest man. To your honor, I am convinced that you are ignorant of the crime. And to whom, then, shall I denounce the malignant rabble of true culprits, if not to you, the highest magistrate in the country? . . .

I accuse Colonel du Paty de Clam of having been the diabolical agent of the judicial error, unconsciously, I prefer to believe, and of having continued to defend his deadly work during the past three years through the most absurd and revolting machinations.

I accuse General Mercier of having made himself an accomplice in one of the greatest crimes of history, probably through weak-mindedness.

I accuse General Billot of having had in his hands the decisive proofs of the innocence of Dreyfus and of having concealed them, and of having rendered himself guilty of the crime of lèse humanity and lèse justice, out of political motives and to save the face of the General Staff.

I accuse General Boisdeffre and General Gonse of being accomplices in the same crime, the former no doubt through religious prejudice, the latter out of esprit de corps.

437

I accuse General de Pellieux and Major Ravary of having made a scoundrelly inquest, I mean an inquest of the most monstrous partiality, the complete report of which composes for us an imperishable monument of naïve effrontery.

I accuse the three handwriting experts, MM. Belhomme, Varinard and Couard of having made lying and fraudulent reports, unless a medical examination will certify them to be deficient of sight and judgment.

I accuse the War Office of having led a vile campaign in the press, particularly in *l'Eclair* and *l'Echo de Paris* in order to misdirect public opinion and cover up its sins.

I accuse, lastly, the first court-martial of having violated all human right in condemning a prisoner on testimony kept secret from him, and I accuse the second court-martial of having covered up this illegality by order, committing in turn the judicial crime of acquitting a guilty man with full knowledge of his guilt.

In making these accusations I am aware that I render myself liable to articles 30 and 31 of Libel Laws of July 29, 1881, which punish acts of defamation. I expose myself voluntarily.

As to the men I accuse, I do not know them, I have never seen them, I feel neither resentment nor hatred against them. For me they are only entities, emblems of social malfeasance. The action I take here is simply a revolutionary step designed to hasten the explosion of truth and justice.

I have one passion only, for light, in the name of humanity which has borne so much and has a right to happiness. My burning protest is only the cry of my soul. Let them dare then to carry me to the court of appeals, and let there be an inquest in the full light of the day!

I am waiting.

Mr. President, I beg you to accept the assurances of my deepest respect.

Émile Zola

FOR this letter, Zola was promptly brought to trial, charged with criminal libel. The country was in a state of turmoil. Riots and disorders broke out all over France. During the trial, Zola and his colleagues on the defense, the outstanding intellectual liberals of the time, were in constant danger of mob violence.

In the farcical and feverish court proceedings, Zola and his lawyers were not permitted to bring into the record any pertinent facts regarding the Dreyfus case itself. Zola was thus naturally found guilty, sentenced to one year's imprisonment, and fined three thousand francs. Aided by liberal friends, he managed to escape from jail and fled to England.

During Zola's exile, Lieutenant Colonel Henry, one of the chief figures in the charges against Dreyfus, confessed to having forged the crucial documents implicating Dreyfus, and committed suicide. Esterhazy also admitted his share in the plot.

In 1899, almost six years after his conviction, Dreyfus was brought back from Devil's Island—his health broken—and finally "pardoned" for "treason under extenuating circumstances." But not until years later, on July 21, 1906, was he fully pardoned, reinstated in the army, legally cleared, and formally decorated on the very spot where he had been degraded twelve years before.

Zola returned triumphantly to France.

Dreyfus volunteered for active military service in the First World War, was made a lieutenant colonel in command of an artillery battery, and served brilliantly and bravely, first in the defense of Paris, later on the Western Front. He was finally made an officer of the Legion of Honor, and died in July, 1935, at the age of seventy-five.

Walter Littlefield, an authority on the case, has said that Dreyfus "to the end of his days believed that he was solely the victim of a judicial error, monstrous but comprehensible, and that most of the witnesses arrayed against him, all the judges who convicted him, were honest but mistaken men. . . On the contrary, they were neither honest nor mistaken. All knew Dreyfus to be innocent, or could easily have ascertained that fact. He was the selected instrument of an insidious conspiracy for

439

the destruction of the French republic. . . . At his second trial Dreyfus forbade his junior counsel, maître Labori, to deliver an address which would have exposed the conspirators in all their hideous guilt. This attitude was inspired not so much through fear of antagonizing his judges, as by a pitiful reluctance to have their faith in their army chief shattered, the moral and material decrepitude of the military hierarchy exposed to the Germans. His was a strange, enigmatical, almost unfathomable personality. . . ."

Zola never met, never even saw, the man for whose freedom he fought so valiantly, risking everything for an abstract principle. The author of "J'accuse" died in 1902 at the age of sixty-two.

JOSEPH CONRAD FINDS THAT PAGES ACCUMU-
LATE AND THE STORY STANDS STILL

IN AN earlier letter to Arthur Symons, Joseph Conrad had set forth his creed as a writer:

"One thing that I am certain of is that I have approached the object of my task, things human, in a spirit of piety. The earth is a temple where there is going on a mystery play, childish and poignant, ridiculous and awful enough, in all conscience. Once in, I've tried to behave decently. I have not degraded any quasi-religious sentiment by tears and groans; and if I have been amused or indignant, I've neither grinned nor gnashed my teeth. In other words, I've tried to write with dignity, not out of regard for myself, but for the sake of the spectacle, the play with an obscure beginning and an unfathomable dénouement.

"I don't think that this has been noticed. It is your penitent beating the floor with his forehead and the ecstatic worshipper at the rails that are obvious to the public eye. The man standing quietly in the shadow of the pillar, if noticed at all, runs the risk of being suspected of sinister designs. Thus I've been called a heartless wretch, a man without ideals and a poseur of brutality. But I will confess to you under seal of secrecy that I don't believe I am such as I appear to mediocre minds."

The writing of Joseph Conrad (born Korzenjowski) is as mystifying as his personality. The tributes of his many friends reveal him as a man infinitely picturesque and arresting. "One of the most original and sinister and sombre personalities of our time," Arthur Symons called him. "A gentleman adventurer who had sailed with Drake," he seemed to his friend and collaborator, Ford Madox Ford.

441

The very qualities that enabled Conrad to write with so heightened a sense of reality made his an agonizing life. His sensitivity, his intensity, his sardonic pity for the human race; these, combined with the acute physical torture of gout, would send him into black depths of depression, whence at last, buoyed up by a marvelous resilience, he would emerge triumphant. He lived from 1857 to 1924.

In 1894, twenty years after he had gone to sea, he submitted the manuscript of Almayer's Folly to Fisher Unwin, a London publisher. He was summoned to the publisher's office and there received by Edward Garnett, then a young assistant reader, by whose recommendation the book was accepted. It was Garnett who encouraged the young expatriate Pole to go on writing. They became friends and remained so for thirty years, until Conrad's death. In his letters to Garnett, as in all his letters, we are aware of a complex being, subtle, tender, exuberant, violent, tragic, buoyant, and, above all, loyal to his art and to his friends.

The following letter was written during one of his depressed periods while he was at work on The Rescue:

"All is darkness."

3rd Aug. 98

MY DEAR GARNETT

I am not dead tho' only half alive. Very soon I shall send you some Ms. I am writing hopelessly—but still I am writing. How I feel I cannot express. Pages accumulate and the story stands still.

I feel suicidal.

Drop me a line and tell me when and how you are. If you could come down it would be an act of real friendship and also of charity.

442

My kind regards and Jessie's love to your wife. Jess is knocked up with the boy's teething performances. He has (and she has also) a rough time of it.

I am afraid there's something wrong with my thinking apparatus. I am utterly out of touch with my work—and I can't get in touch. All is darkness.

Ever yours

Joseph Conrad

THE extent to which Conrad recovered from this dark and suicidal mood is evidenced by the procession of sixty works, including twenty famous novels, which subsequently came from his pen. Among his greatest works are Lord Jim, Chance, Nostromo, Victory, Typhoon, and The Arrow of Gold.

GEORGE BERNARD SHAW
AND ELLEN TERRY CARRY ON
A ROMANTIC CORRESPONDENCE
FOR TWENTY-FIVE YEARS

[A SERIES OF LETTERS]

SEVERAL times during the last few years Mrs. Patrick Campbell was on the verge of publishing her early romantic letters from George Bernard Shaw. To her formal request for permission to do so, G.B.S. wrote: "No, Stella, I will not play horse to your Lady Godiva. . . ."

But the publication of his "romantic correspondence" with Ellen Terry, Shaw not only sanctioned, but encouraged and graced with his own characteristic commentary.

Obviously the letters were never intended for publication. In them we see revealed, perhaps for the first time, a tender and compassionate Shaw not generally known to the world. From the collection of about two hundred letters of Miss Terry and a slightly smaller number written by Mr. Shaw a few representative examples and excerpts are quoted here.

In the first group of letters, we are made aware of Ellen Terry's fear

444

that if she and her famous correspondent met, he would be disappointed in her appearance off the stage. Hence her "determination to avoid the meeting at any cost."

G. B. S. to E. T. You will find me a disagreeably cruel-looking, middle-aged Irishman with a red beard; but that cannot be helped. . . .

E.T. to G.B.S. You are in the blues! You are only a boy. Forty is nothing when it's Irish. Be strong. Don't waste your time on any woman. Shake the world, you stupid (darling). . . .

G.B.S. to E.T. Up to the time I was 29, actually twenty-nine, I was too shabby for any woman to tolerate me. I stalked about in a decaying green coat, cuffs trimmed with the scissors, terrible boots, and so on. Then I got a job to do and bought a suit of clothes with the proceeds. A lady immediately invited me to tea, threw her arms round me, and said she adored me. I permitted her to adore, being intensely curious on the subject. Never having regarded myself as an attractive man, I was surprised; but I kept up appearances successfully. Since that time, whenever I have been left alone in a room with a female, she has invariably thrown her arms round me and declared she adored me. It is fate. Therefore beware. If you allow yourself to be left alone with me for a single moment, you will certainly throw your arms round me and declare you adore me. . . .

In a characteristic Shavian preface, Shaw himself warns the reader not to judge the correspondence "according to the code of manners which regulate polite letter writing in cathedral country towns," and adds: "As a correspondence between a churchwarden and a deaconess its implications would make its publication impossible. But the theatre, behind the scenes, has an emotional freemasonry of its own, certainly franker and arguably wholesomer than the stiffnesses of surburban society outside. . . . Actors, like Jews, were a race apart when Ellen Terry was

445

born into the theatre in 1848, and, like all segregated races, they preserved manners and customs peculiar to themselves."

Ellen Terry, in her autobiography, The Story of My Life, says her correspondence with Shaw began with a letter from her asking him what he thought of the chances of a composer-singer friend of hers. Their first exchange of letters was extremely formal. At the time Ellen Terry was forty-four and still acting with Henry Irving at the Lyceum Theatre. Shaw was eight years younger and had already established his renown in the field of music and revolutionary pamphleteering. Most of Ellen Terry's letters were written from her London home in Barkston Gardens, Earl's Court. In the early phases of the correspondence, Shaw was still unmarried and lived with his mother in lodgings in Fitzroy Square. Ellen Terry wrote many more letters than he did, but we have reason to believe that she destroyed many of his letters. Some were doubtless lost.

To those who complained that this twenty-five-year romance existed "only on paper," Shaw retorted: "Let them . . . remember that only on paper has humanity yet achieved glory, beauty, truth, knowledge, virtue, and abiding love. . . ."

George Jean Nathan once referred to the "Garbo-like fan letters" that made up this correspondence, characterizing it as "vegetarian amour—a game of epistolary post office. . . ."

ELLEN TERRY WARNS GEORGE BERNARD SHAW NOT TO WASTE HIMSELF UPON UNCONSIDERED TRIFLES

"You have become a habit with me . . ."

18 September 1896.
Savoy Hotel.

THE timeing plays (or rather the *not* timeing them!) is where one goes on the rocks for the first few nights, and it comes of not rehearsing, *for at least a week*, each act without a stop. One does that for the first time on the first night, and of course it's *wrong* at first.

I'm not good at knives and curses, but better at flying to lovers and enduring a good deal in the way of rocks and shocks.

What are you best at?

You seem to do everything.

But I remember you made me laugh, and amused me more than I was ever amused, when I saw Arms and the Man. But then Music (the which I fear I understand nothing of, but love the best of all). Are you best at that? Oh how frightful it must be to know a lot! No possible companionship, for most people know nothing at all! I'm nearly dead. Pray for me, "wish" for me. My head, and heart, and body all ache. I think I'm just *frightened*.

And, after all, as if anything mattered!

Why here's a letter from G. B. S. And he is a vegetarian, is he? I knew of his Jaegerish woolerish ways, but not of the carrots and beans.

447

Missfire! That's the word. That's what I am doing as I get older. And I shall have to give it up. You must advise me to, in public or private, I care not a ha'penny which, and strengthen me in my own opinion. You honour me by anything you say to me. I should like one thing, that you never mentioned me in print. It's different, it seems to me, now that we have met (?) But again, what does it matter? *How small.* Only it would be fun to me if you found all fault with me in the eyes of other people, and really, all the time, *liked* me, although with but as small a drop of liking as a wren's eye!

Ellen is a very small person even to consider for a moment such matters.

You have become a habit with me, Sir, and each morning before breakfast *I take you,* like a dear pill!

The only thing that distresses me (though it joys me too) is that you write back again quick—like thought—you kind Dear, when you ought not to waste yourself upon unconsidered trifles. Well, somehow you will be rewarded, I doubt not, and when Tuesday is past and gone, I'll only trouble you once in a long while, for my grandchildren shall have my time, and I'll take my comfort from them (Selfish!) At present need, they are too much in the milky way for their drooping grandmother, and your desperately tired and grateful

Ellen Terry

P. S. I won't send this off until to-morrow, and so let you escape for a day.

THE LETTER *from G.B.S. to Ellen Terry on the following pages shows how the romantic correspondence developed in the intervening* sixteen years.

GEORGE BERNARD SHAW IMPLORES ELLEN TERRY
TO THROW HIM A SCRAP OF HER BELOVED
WRITING

"Be my good angel . . ."

13 August 1912.
Hotel Excelsior, Nancy,
Meurthe-et-Moselle, France

DEAREST ELLEN,
What is a Philomathic Society? It sounds like stamp collecting. When you said you had no personal influence with me you told a wicked lie; but it served the man right for bothering you.

I am languishing here alone, with a broken automobile. I left Charlotte at Kissingen doing a cure (mud baths and such like) with her sister, and made a dash for the Alps. Unluckily the dash broke something vital in the auto; and I had to drag it here by rail through custom houses and over frontiers and all sorts of bothers to get it to the factory of its makers.

I now have a grotesque confession to make to you. I wrote a play* for Alexander which was really a play for Mrs Patrick Campbell. It is almost as wonderful a fit as Brassbound; for I am a good ladies' tailor, whatever my shortcomings may be. And the part is SO different, not a bit in the world like Lady Cicely. ("I should think not" you will say.) Then came the question, would *she* stand it? For, I repeat, this heroine wasnt a Lady Cicely Wayn-

* Refers to *Pygmalion.*

449

flete: she was Liza Doolittle, a flower girl, using awful language and wearing an apron and three ostrich feathers, and having her hat put in the oven to slay the creepy-crawlies, and being taken off the stage and washed, like Drinkwater. I simply didnt dare offer it to her. Well, I read it to a good friend of mine [Dame Edith Lyttelton], and contrived that she should be there. And she was there, reeking from Bella Donna. She saw through it like a shot. "You beast, you wrote this for me, every line of it: I can hear you mimicking my voice in it, etc. etc." And she rose to the occasion, quite fine and dignified for a necessary moment, and said unaffectedly she was flattered. And then—and then—oh Ellen; and then? Why, then I went calmly to her house to discuss business with her, as hard as nails, and, as I am a living man, fell head over ears in love with her in thirty seconds. And it lasted more than thirty hours. I made no struggle: I went in head over ears, and dreamed and dreamed and walked on air for all that afternoon and the next day as if my next birthday were my twentieth. And I said, among other things (to myself) "Now I shall amuse and interest Ellen again for at least one letter or two." Which I am accordingly trying to do.

One thing she said pleased me better than she knew. She said that Duse has leaden feet, and that the perfect people walked on air, "like Ellen Terry." I was tempted to reply that Ellen's feet were heavy enough when she was trampling on a man's heart; but I didnt.

Storms soon arose. She was clever enough to see that her business was not to accept the offers of Frohman and the others, but to get the profits of the play herself by going into management. Then came a terrible conflict over the question of the leading man. She wanted—whom do you think? Your Jim! I wouldnt have him at any price, because the part is essentially an English part of a certain type; and he would have been at a disadvantage in it. She proposed all sorts of impossible people. I proposed Loraine. She would not hear of him. I pressed my choice. She said awful things about him. I repeated them to him. He said unpardonable things about her. I repeated them to her. This sort of Shavian horseplay startled her: she said I was a mischief-maker. I made some more; and finally they had to assure one another of their undying esteem and admiration, which was what I wanted. But Loraine had to go to America to Supermanage himself into a solvent condition before coming back to play with her. And she said that she would never never play Liza. And so she went off to Aix-les-Bains, where she is at present. And I am plying her with the most wonderful love letters. To write love letters to you was like giving tracts to a missionary (not that I could help doing it for all that) for you could hold me at letter writing and play with me at love making; but there cannot be two women alive at the same time who could do that: she is a wonderful person in her way; but there is only one Ellen.

And now Gertrude Kingston is going to do Brassbound, having got an hour's start of Marie Tempest, who was that much too late. I suppose it must be let go now that you have exhausted it; but what will it be to me without you?

I shall be here for a few days still. Be my good angel to the extent of throwing me a scrap of your beloved writing.

G. B. S.

As a postscript to the entire cycle of letters, Shaw wrote in 1929: "Ellen Terry became a legend in her old age; but of that I have nothing to say; for we did not meet, and, except for a few broken letters, did not write; and she never was old to me."

A few days before Ellen Terry died in 1928, her daughter found a scrap of paper labeled "My Friends." On that roll of honor, the name of Charles Reade was written first. Directly beneath it was the name of Bernard Shaw.

HENRI POINCARÉ AND MARIE CURIE RECOMMEND ALBERT EINSTEIN FOR A PROFESSORSHIP AT ZURICH INSTITUTE

O CCASIONALLY, a great mark of genius is the ability to recognize genius in others. When Albert Einstein first published The Special Theory of Relativity in 1905, at the age of twenty-six, he "invited others to build on his work." At the time Einstein was doing routine work in the Swiss patent office. After hours he concentrated on the study of light—reconstructing the universe with a fountain pen and a pad of paper as his sole laboratory equipment. He had been married in 1903, and in the following two years he produced five scientific papers; the last of these was the epochal Special Theory.

Only a few thinkers and scientists paid attention to this publication in 1905, but in this small group was none other than Max Planck, the discoverer of the original quantum theory, who wrote Einstein a most encouraging letter of appreciation, hailing the special theory of relativity as "a revolution in human thought."

Six years later, Einstein, despite his growing international reputation, was still seeking a permanent university post. It was then (in 1911) that two great fellow workers in his own field of mathematics and physics— Henri Poincaré and Marie Curie—rallied to his support with a letter of recommendation "marked by the highest type of prophetic insight." The testimonial was drafted by Henri Poincaré but was signed by him and Madame Curie. It is in the form of a letter to the Federal Institute of Technology at Zurich:

"The future will give more and more proofs of the merits of Herr Einstein . . ."

[1911]

HERR EINSTEIN is one of the most original minds that we have ever met. In spite of his youth he already occupies a very honorable position among the foremost savants of his time. What we marvel at him, above all, is the ease with which he adjusts himself to new conceptions and draws all possible deductions from them. He does not cling to classical principles, but sees all conceivable possibilities when he is confronted with a physical problem. In his mind this becomes transformed into an anticipation of new phenomena that may some day be verified in actual experience. . . . The future will give more and more proofs of the merits of Herr Einstein, and the University that succeeds in attaching him to itself may be certain that it will derive honor from its connection with the young master.

Henri Poincaré
Marie Curie

SO DISTINGUISHED and so eloquent a recommendation naturally carried great weight with the Institute, and Einstein received the appointment, joining the faculty in 1912.

He held this post until 1914, when he was appointed director of the physics department of the Kaiser Wilhelm Institute in Berlin. The following year, at the age of thirty-six, he published his general relativity theory. Although it aroused great interest in the world of science, it remained almost totally unknown to the public until 1919, when its verification by photographs of the eclipse of that year made him world famous overnight, thanks largely to the enterprise and insight of Carr Van Anda, then managing editor of The New York Times, who happened to be passionately interested in mathematics and astronomy. The tribute Einstein accorded to Marie Curie*—that fame could not corrupt her— applies with equal validity to Einstein himself. In 1921, he received the Nobel prize in physics. In 1933, he left Nazi Germany, and for the last few years has been head of the mathematics department at the Institute for Advanced Study at Princeton, New Jersey.

* See the Curie correspondence starting on page 420.

CAPTAIN ROBERT FALCON SCOTT TELLS THE BRITISH PUBLIC THAT "THESE ROUGH NOTES AND OUR DEAD BODIES MUST TELL THE TALE"

O N THE honor roll of heroic adventure the name of the noted Polar explorer, Captain Robert Falcon Scott, of the British Navy, will always rank high. He was born in 1868 and was a midshipman at the age of fourteen. When he was thirty-one he organized the National Antarctic Expedition and in 1902 sailed in the Discovery on this first trip, which lasted three years. He failed to reach the South Pole, but acquired scientific data and experience of great value.

In 1910 Scott began his second Antarctic Expedition, sailing in the Terra Nuova. His journey took him to the vast ice-covered stretches of the Antarctic—"eternally frozen and surrounded by wind-whipped mountains," where the ice, in places, is two thousand feet thick.

Two years later, on January 18, 1912, Scott and four companions from the main party—Wilson, Bowers, Oates, and Evans—reached the South Pole, only to find that Amundsen had preceded them by thirty-five days. The Norwegian, who had kept his real destination secret by announcing he was going to the North Pole, had reached the South Pole on December 14, 1911. When Scott reached the spot he found Amundsen's tent still uncovered by snow.

Naturally dispirited, Scott and his companions started their seven-hundred-mile homeward journey, buoyed up somewhat by the thought that so far they had gone farther than even the most optimistic had dared to expect. But death cut short their homeward trek—a death as slow, as tortured, as heroic, as men have ever died. Food ran low, the

456

suffering from frostbite was severe. For a month at a time the temperature was 40° below zero. It was "tragedy all along the line."

On March 3, Scott wrote in his diary: "God help us, we can't keep up this pulling, that is certain. Amongst ourselves we are unendingly cheerful, but what each man feels in his heart I can only guess." Evans was the first to die.

One week later: "With great care, we might have a dog's chance, but no more."

On March 16: ". . . assuredly the end is not far." The next day Oates deliberately walked out alone in the blizzard to die "rather than be a drag on his comrades." His last words were, "I am just going outside and may be some time." He had slept through the night before, hoping not to wake, but he woke in the morning.

But not until March 29—after two weeks of unequal battle with the icy elements—do we get the last entry: "It seems a pity, but I do not think I can write more. R. Scott." Then, last of all: "For God's sake, look after our people."

Eight months later, the bodies of Scott and two companions were found by a searching party, within fifteen miles of the nearest supply camp. The three bodies were in their sleeping bags, half buried in snow. Beside them were the complete scientific records of the polar trip, letters to various persons, and Scott's message to the public—a stirring last testament of elemental courage.

In the accompanying note to his friend, Sir James M. Barrie, Scott wrote: "We are pegging out in a very comfortless spot. . . . We are showing that Englishmen can still die with a bold spirit, fighting it out to the end. . . . I am not at all afraid of the end, but sad to miss many a humble pleasure which I had planned for the future on our long marches. I may not have proved a great explorer, but we have done the greatest march ever made and come very near to great success." Captain Scott's farewell letter to his countrymen follows:

457

"Englishmen can still die with a bold spirit . . ."

[A MESSAGE TO THE BRITISH PUBLIC]

THE causes of the disaster are due not to faulty organisation, but to the misfortune in all risks which had to be undertaken.

1. The loss of pony transport in March 1911 obliged me to start later than I had intended, and obliged the limits of stuff transported to be narrowed.

2. The weather throughout the outward journey, and especially the long gale in 83° S., stopped us.

3. The soft snow in lower reaches of glacier again reduced pace.

We fought these untoward events with a will and conquered, but it cut into our provision reserve.

Every detail of our food supplies, clothing and depôts made on the interior ice-sheet and over that long stretch of 700 miles to the Pole and back, worked out to perfection. The advance party would have returned to the glacier in fine form and with surplus of food, but for the astonishing failure of the man whom we had least expected to fail. Edgar Evans was thought the strongest man of the party.

The Beardmore Glacier is not difficult in fine weather, but on our return we did not get a single completely fine day; this with a sick companion enormously increased our anxieties.

As I have said elsewhere we got into frightfully rough ice and Edgar Evans received a concussion of the brain—he died a natural death, but left us a shaken party with the season unduly advanced.

But all the facts above enumerated were as nothing to the

458

surprise which awaited us on the Barrier. I maintain that our arrangements for returning were quite adequate, and that no one in the world would have expected the temperatures and surfaces which we encountered at this time of the year. On the summit in lat. 85° 86° we had —20°, —30°. On the Barrier in lat. 80°, 10,000 feet lower, we had —30° in the day, —47° at night pretty regularly, with continuous head wind during our day marches. It is clear that these circumstances come on very suddenly, and our wreck is certainly due to this sudden advent of severe weather, which does not seem to have any satisfactory cause. I do not think human beings ever came through such a month as we have come through, and we should have got through in spite of the weather but for the sickening of a second companion, Captain Oates, and a shortage of fuel in our depôts for which I cannot account, and finally, but for the storm which has fallen on us within 11 miles of the depôt at which we hoped to secure our final supplies.

Surely misfortune could scarcely have exceeded this last blow. We arrived within 11 miles of our old One Ton Camp with fuel for one last meal and food for two days.

For four days we have been unable to leave the tent—the gale howling about us. We are weak, writing is difficult, but for my own sake I do not regret this journey, which has shown that Englishmen can endure hardships, help one another, and meet death with as great a fortitude as ever in the past. We took risks, we knew we took them; things have come out against us, and therefore we have no cause for complaint, but bow to the will of Providence, determined still to do our best to the last. But if we have been willing to give our lives to this enterprise, which is for the honour of our country, I appeal to our countrymen to see that those who depend upon us are properly cared for.

Had we lived, I should have had a tale to tell of the hardihood, endurance, and courage of my companions which would have

459

stirred the heart of every Englishman. These rough notes and our dead bodies must tell the tale, but surely, surely, a great rich country like ours will see that those who are dependent on us are properly provided for.

R. Scott

CAPTAIN SCOTT and his companions were buried beneath the tent where they were found, on an icy plain, halfway back from the South Pole. A cross fashioned of skis and a cairn with an inscription mark their grave, and above was placed the last line of Tennyson's Ulysses:

"To strive, to seek, to find, and not to yield. . . ."

This heart-rending farewell plea to the British public did not go unheeded. When the Lord Mayor of London started a fund for the dead men's families, almost half a million dollars was raised in short order. A surplus was set aside for the advancement of arctic and antarctic expeditions through the Scott Polar Research Institute at Cambridge. Amidst the trophies and relics of many heroic and adventurous journeys by men like Scott, Amundsen, and Shackleton is a bust of Scott himself, carved by his widow. On the façade of the Institute is a Latin inscription in letters three feet high:

"He sought the secrets of the Pole, he found the secrets of God."

RUPERT BROOKE TELLS AN ENGLISH FRIEND ABOUT THE ROMANTIC SPLENDORS OF THE SOUTH SEAS

[A LETTER TO EDWARD MARSH]

RUPERT BROOKE's death at the age of twenty-eight during the English Mediterranean campaign in the First World War was almost prophetically foreshadowed in his war poems. This letter, written just before the war, during a trip around the world, illustrates his many-sided nature, notably its vitality, humor, and sensitive appreciation. From the South Seas it gives back "the thoughts by England given," and re-echoes

> . . . laughter, learnt of friends, and gentleness,
> In hearts at peace, under an English heaven.

". . . brown and wild in the fair chocolate arms
of a Tahitian beauty . . ."

Somewhere near Fiji
November 15 (?), 1913

DEAR EDDIE, I'm conscious I haven't written to you for a long time:—though, indeed, my last letter was *posted* only a short time ago. When it, or when this, will get to you, God knows. About Christmas, I suppose, though it seems incredible.

461

My *reason* tells me that you'll be slurring through London mud in a taxi, with a heavy drizzle falling, and a chilly dampness in the air, and the theatres glaring in the Strand, and crowds of white faces. But I can't help *thinking* of you trotting through crisp snow to a country church, holly-decorated, with little robins picking crumbs all around, and the church-bells playing our brother Tennyson's *In Memoriam* brightly through the clear air. It may not be: it never has been:—that picture-postcard Christmas. But I shall think of you so.

You think of me, in a loin-cloth, brown and wild in the fair chocolate arms of a Tahitian beauty, reclining beneath a bread-fruit tree, on white sand, with the breakers roaring against the reefs a mile out, and strange brilliant fish darting through the pellucid hyaline of the sun-saturated sea.

Oh, Eddie, it's all true about the South Seas! I get a little tired of it at moments, because I am just too old for Romance. But there it is: there it wonderfully is: heaven on earth, the ideal life, little work, dancing and singing and eating, naked people of incredible loveliness, perfect manners, and immense kindliness, a divine tropic climate, and intoxicating beauty of scenery.

I came aboard and left Samoa two days ago. Before that I had been wandering with an "interpreter"—entirely genial and quite incapable of English—through Samoan villages. The last few days I stopped in one, where a big marriage-feast was going on. I lived in a Samoan house (the coolest in the world) with a man and his wife, nine children, ranging from a proud beauty of 18 to a round object of 1 year, a dog, a cat, a proud hysterical hen, and a gaudy scarlet and green parrot, who roved the roof and beams with a wicked eye; choosing a place whence to——, twice a day, with humorous precision, on my hat and clothes.

The Samoan girls have extraordinarily beautiful bodies, and

462

walk like goddesses. They're a lovely brown colour, without any black Melanesian admixture; their necks and shoulders would be the wild envy of any European beauty; and in carriage and face they remind me continually and vividly of my incomparable heartless and ever-loved X. Fancy moving among a tribe of X's! Can't you imagine how shattered and fragmentary a heart I'm bearing away to Fiji and Tahiti? And, oh dear! I'm afraid they'll be just as bad.

And Eddie, it's all True about, for instance, Cocoanuts. You tramp through a strange vast dripping tropical forest for hours, listening to weird liquid hootings from birds and demons in the branches above. Then you feel thirsty, so you send your boy up a great perpendicular palm. He runs up with utter ease and grace, cuts off a couple of vast nuts and comes down and makes holes in them. And they are chock-full of the best drink in the world.

Romance! Romance! I walked 15 miles through mud and up and down mountains, and swam three rivers, to get this boat. But if ever you miss me, suddenly, one day, from lecture-room B. in King's, or from the Moulin d'Or at lunch, you'll know that I've got sick for the full moon on these little thatched roofs, and the palms against the morning, and the Samoan boys and girls diving thirty feet into a green sea or a deep mountain pool under a water-fall—and that I've gone back.

Romance? That's half my time. The rest is Life—Life, Eddie, is what you get in the bars of the hotels in 'Frisco, or Honolulu, or Suva, or Apia, and in the smoking-rooms in these steamers. It is incredibly like a Kipling story, and all the people are very self-consciously Kiplingesque. Yesterday, for instance, I sat in the Chief Engineer's cabin, with the first officer and a successful beach-comber lawyer from the white-man's town in Samoa, drinking Australian champagne from breakfast to lunch. "To-day I am not well." The beach-comber matriculated at Wadham, and was sent down. Also, he rode with the Pytchley, quotes you Virgil, and discusses the ins and outs of the Peninsular campaign. And his repertoire of smut is enormous. Mere Kipling, you see, but one gets some good stories. Verses, of a school-boy kind, too. . . . *Sehr primitiv.* The whole thing makes a funny world.

I may pick up some mail, and hear from you, when I get to New Zealand. I'm afraid your post as my honorary literary agent, or grass-executor, is something of a sinecure. I can't write on the trail.

There's one thing I wanted to consult you about, and I can't remember if I mentioned it. I want some club to take an occasional stranger into, for a drink, and to read the papers in, and, sometimes, to have a quiet meal in. Where do you think I should go? . . . I want somewhere I needn't always be spick and span in, and somewhere I don't have to pay a vast sum.

There's nothing else in the way of my European existence, I think. That part of it which is left, out here, reads Ben Jonson. Kindly turn up his "New Inn" (which is sheer Meredith) and read Lovel's Song in Act IV. The second verse will dispel the impression of the first, that it is by Robert Browning. The whole thing is pure beauty.

No more. My love to everyone, from Jackson down to —— if you've made her acquaintance yet—Helena Darwin Cornford.* And to such as Wilfred (Gibson) and Denis (Browne) and yourself and a few more poor, pale-skinned stay-at-homes, a double measure. I have a growing vision of next summer term spent between King's and Raymond Buildings: a lovely vision. May it be.

Manina! Tofa!

Thy

Rupert

* Professor Henry Jackson, O. M.—and a baby born since his departure.

Two years later Rupert Brooke wrote his famous sonnet, The Soldier, beginning

> If I should die, think only this of me:
> That there's some corner of a foreign field
> That is for ever England.

And shortly afterward he was dead at Gallipoli.

D. H. LAWRENCE ADVISES A FRIEND ON LOVE
AND MARRIAGE

[A LETTER TO JOHN MIDDLETON MURRY]

"DIFFERENT, superior, and kind" were the words that Aldous Huxley employed to describe his friend and hero, D. H. Lawrence: "He looked at things with the eyes, so it seemed, of a man who had been at the brink of death and to whom, as he emerges from the darkness, the world reveals itself as unfathomably beautiful and mysterious. For Lawrence, existence was one continuous convalescence; it was as though he were nearly reborn from a mortal illness every day of his life."

The early characterization of Lawrence as a feverish, tortured, erotic, self-styled Dionysian rebel has of late been tempered and modified, largely by a calmer critical estimate of his work and a careful analysis of his recently published correspondence. The Lawrence legend has come down to earth.

Critics are now inclined to realize that he was not only one of the great lyric geniuses of modern literature, in the words of Clifton Fadiman "an expert on lusts, hatreds, emotions that none before dared pursue," but basically a man of good will and a great lover of life. Henry Seidel Canby has called him the "John Bunyan of the dark furies of the spirit, who earned his understanding of passion from lofty experience."

In 1912, at the age of twenty-six, this half-cockney English schoolteacher was earning fifteen shillings a week and already suffering from a bronchial condition aggravated by his early poverty. That year he persuaded Freiherrin Frieda von Richthofen, sister of the noted German aviator, to leave her husband and children and elope with him. Later she became his wife. About this time—the Sons and Lovers period—

466

Lawrence met John Middleton Murry, the literary critic, who was then associated with The Westminster Gazette. Lawrence and Murry soon became intimate friends. When Murry fell in love with Katherine Mansfield, then a struggling young short-story writer and critic contributing to his magazine, Lawrence and Murry discussed the prospective marriage in the most searching manner, and one of Lawrence's most memorable letters is devoted to this subject. It follows:

". . . a woman who loves a man would sleep on a board."

Lerici, per Fiascherino,
Golfo della Spezia, Italy.
Thursday (1913).

DEAR MURRY,—
    I'm going to answer your letter immediately, and frankly.
When you say you won't take Katherine's money, it means you don't trust her love for you. When you say she needs little luxuries, and you couldn't bear to deprive her of them, it means you don't respect either yourself or her sufficiently to do it.

It looks to me as if you two, far from growing nearer, are snapping the bonds that hold you together, one after another. I suppose you must both of you consult your own hearts, honestly. She must see if she really *wants* you, wants to keep you and to have no other man all her life. It means forfeiting something. But the only principle I can see in this life, is that one *must* forfeit the less for the greater. Only one must be thoroughly honest about it.

She must say, "Could I live in a little place in Italy, with Jack, and be lonely, have rather a bare life, but be happy?" If she could, then take her money. If she doesn't want to, don't try.

467

But don't beat about the bush. In the way you go on, you are inevitably coming apart. She is perhaps beginning to be unsatisfied with you. And you can't make her more satisfied by being unselfish. You must say, "How can I make myself most healthy, strong, and satisfactory to myself and to her?" If by being lazy for six months, then be lazy, and take her money. It doesn't matter if she misses her luxuries: she won't die of it. What luxuries do you mean?

If she doesn't want to stake her whole life and being on you, then go to your University abroad for a while, alone. I warn you, it'll be hellish barren.

Or else you can gradually come apart in London, and then flounder till you get your feet again, severally, but be clear about it. It lies between you and Katherine, nowhere else.

Of course you can't dream of living long without work. Couldn't you get the *Westminster* to give you *two* columns a week, abroad? You must *try*. You must stick to criticism. You ought also to plan a book, either on some literary point, or some man. I should like to write a book on English heroines. You ought to do something of that sort, but not so cheap. Don't try a novel—try essays—like Walter Pater or somebody of that style. But you can do something *good* in that line; something concerning *literature* rather than life.

And you must rest, and you and Katherine must heal, and come together, before you do *any serious* work of any sort. It's the split in the love that drains you. You see, while she doesn't really love you, and is not satisfied, you show to frightful disadvantage. But it would be a pity not to let your mind flower—it might, under decent circumstances, produce beautiful delicate things, in perception and appreciation. And *she* has a right to provide the conditions. But not if you don't trust yourself nor her nor anybody, but go on slopping, and pandering to her smaller side.

If you work yourself sterile to get her chocolates, she will most

468

justly detest you—she is *perfectly* right. She doesn't want you to sacrifice yourself to her, you fool. Be more natural, and positive, and stick to your own guts. You spread them on a tray for her to throw to the cats.

If you want things to come right—if you are ill and exhausted, then take her money to the last penny, and let her do her own housework. Then she'll know you love her. You can't blame her if she's not satisfied with you. If I haven't had enough dinner, you can't blame me. But, you fool, you squander yourself, not for *her*, but to provide her with petty luxuries she doesn't really want. You insult her. A woman unsatisfied must have luxuries. But a woman who loves a man would sleep on a board.

It strikes me you've got off your lines, somewhere you've not been man enough: you've felt it rested with your honour to give her a place to be proud of. It rested with your honour to give her a man to be satisfied with—and satisfaction is never accomplished even physically unless the man is strongly and surely himself, and doesn't depend on anything but his own *being* to make a woman love him. You've tried to satisfy Katherine with what you could earn for her, give her: and she will only be satisfied with what you are.

And you don't know what you are. You've never come to it. You've always been dodging round, getting Rhythms and flats and doing criticism for money. You are a fool to work so hard for Katherine—she hates you for it—and quite right. You want to be strong in the possession of your own soul. Perhaps you will only come to that when this affair of you and her has gone crash. I should be sorry to think that—I don't believe it. You must save yourself, and your self-respect, by making it complete between Katherine and you—if you devour her money till she walks in rags, if you are both outcast. Make her certain—don't pander to her—stick to *yourself*—do what you *want* to do—don't consider

469

her—she hates and loathes being considered. You insult her in saying you wouldn't take her money.

The University idea is a bad one. It would further disintegrate you.

If you are disintegrated, then get integrated again. Don't be a coward. If you are disintegrated your first duty is to yourself, and you may use Katherine—her money and everything—to get right again. You're not well, man. Then have the courage to get well. If you are strong again, and a bit complete, she'll be satisfied with you. She'll love you hard enough. But don't you see, at this rate, you distrain on her day by day and month by month. I've done it myself.

Take your rest—do *nothing* if you like for a while—though I'd do a *bit*. Get better, first and foremost—use anybody's money, to do so. Get better—and do things you like. Get yourself into condition. It drains and wearies Katherine to have you like this. What a fool you are, what a fool. Don't bother about her—what she wants or feels. Say, "I am a man at the end of the tether, therefore I become a man blind to everything but my own need." But keep a heart for the long run.

Look. We pay 60 lire a month for this house: 25 lire for the servant; and food is very cheap. You could live on 185 lire a month in plenty—and be greeted as "Signoria" when you went out together —it is the same as "Guten Tag, Herrschaften;" that would be luxury enough for Katherine.

Get up, lad, and be a man for yourself. It's the man who dares to take, who is independent, not he who gives.

I think Oxford did you harm.

It is beautiful, wonderful, here.

A ten-pound note is 253 lire. We could get you, I believe, a jolly nice apartment in a big garden, in a house alone, for 80 lire a month. Don't waste yourself—don't be silly and floppy. You know what you *could* do—you *could* write—then prepare yourself: and

470

first make Katherine at rest in her love for you. Say "This I will certainly do"— it would be a relief for her to hear you. Don't be a child—don't keep that rather childish charm. Throw everything away, and say, "Now I act for my own good, at last."

We are getting gradually nearer again, Frieda and I. It is very beautiful here. . . .

D. H. Lawrence

KATHERINE MANSFIELD, the subject of this letter from Lawrence to Murry, was born Kathleen Beauchamp in Wellington, New Zealand, in 1888, daughter of a banker. After winning school prizes for youthful writing, she went to England at the age of thirteen and studied in London colleges—years she later regarded as wasted. In 1911 she published In a German Pension and subsequently met John Middleton Murry and with him edited a magazine called Rhythm, later The Blue Review.

Shortly after the letter quoted above, Murry and Miss Mansfield were married. The extent to which Murry took to his heart the advice of his friend may be only guessed at from his own writings, and from the overtones of the stories Katherine Mansfield wrote at the time in various cities of Europe, where she was desperately seeking to find sunlight and health.

One of her greatest triumphs in the short-story form, for which she has been compared to Chekhov, is The Garden Party. She herself described it as "a mordant little tale of the diversity of life and how we try to fit in everything, Death included."

In September, 1915, Katherine Mansfield wrote to her husband: "Is it just my fancy—the beauty of this house to-night? This round lamp on the round table, the rich flowers, the tick of the clock dropping into the quiet—and the dark outside and the apples swelling and a swimming sense of deep water. May brought me this evening some of this year's apples . . . 'Good to eat' . . . They are small and coloured like pale strawberries. I wish that you were with me. It is not because you are absent that I feel so free of distraction, so poised and so still. I feel that I am free even of sun and wind, like a tree whose every leaf has turned. . . ."

Katherine Mansfield died in 1923, at the age of thirty-five, and her epitaph was the phrase from Shakespeare: "Out of the nettle, danger, we pluck the flower, safety."

LEON TROTSKY WARNS AN OLD SOCIALIST COMRADE TO HEED THE MUTED RUMBLE OF APPROACHING EVENTS

I N THIS letter, written a year before the outbreak of the Russian Revolution, we see one of its two organizers and leaders not only predicting with amazing accuracy the course it was to take, but revealing in intimate detail the dynamic ideas and bold actions which made it possible.* It is a significant commentary on socialist theory in war and peace, on revolutionary ideology as both cause and effect of one of the great crises of history.

Leon Trotsky, born Lev Davidovich Bronstein, was born in 1877. He was first arrested by the Russian authorities for his revolutionary activities when he was twenty-one. "Revolution was his father and mother." Exiled to Siberia, he escaped to England, where he met Lenin.

In 1905, on his return to Russia, Trotsky became President of the St. Petersburg Soviet, and promulgated and developed his theory of "permanent revolution," holding that socialism could not succeed in one country alone. He was arrested again, and this time escaped to Vienna. Until his assassination he was an active revolutionary leader, carrying out his doctrines in the arena of world history, as military chieftain, statesman, and colleague of Lenin, and eventually, in exile once again, chronicling them as a historian.

As in many of Trotsky's manifestoes and orations, this letter is colored by a "passionate closeness to events." Like his monumental History of the Russian Revolution, it gives us an opportunity to "hear the past and the future exchanging shots."

* See the correspondence between Czar Nicholas II and the Czarina, on the eve of the Russian Revolution, on page 485.

473

In that spirit Leon Trotsky sent this open letter—perhaps one of the most brilliant examples of polemic scorn in the whole history of letter writing—to a Frenchman named Jules Guesde, a former socialist comrade. The occasion was Trotsky's expulsion from France, ordered by the wartime National Coalition Ministry, which Guesde, forsaking his earlier radical ideas to ally himself with "the Socialist patriots," had recently joined. The letter was written in Paris, just before Trotsky's projected departure for Switzerland. At the last minute, however, the Swiss visa was countermanded, and Trotsky went to Spain instead.

The "ten days that shook the world" were not far off, and the man who was shortly to help Lenin direct them here expounds his uncompromising doctrines in a corrosive communication to a former revolutionary colleague. Feeling that Guesde had betrayed not only an old coworker but also the first principles of socialism and his own integrity, Trotsky wrote:

"We expect them, we summon them, we prepare for them!"

Paris, October 11th, 1916.

TO M. the Minister of State, Jules Guesde:

Before quitting the soil of France, under the escort of a police officer, who personifies the liberties over whose defense you stand guard in the National Cabinet, I deem it my duty to express to you a few thoughts which, while they will most likely not be of any use to you, will at least be of use *against* you. In expelling me from France, your colleague, the Minister of War, did not think fit to indicate the causes for prohibiting the Russian newspaper, *Nashe Slovo* (Our Word), one of whose editors I was, and which had, for two years, suffered all the torments of a censorship, operating under the aegis of this same Minister of War.

Still, I shall not conceal from you the fact that for me there is no mystery about the reasons for my expulsion. You felt the need of adopting repressive measures against an international socialist, against one of those who refuse to accept the part of defender or ready slave of the imperialist war.

But while the reasons for this measure have not been communicated to me, who am the one concerned, and at whom it is directed, they have been stated by M. Briand to the deputies and to the journalists.

In Marseilles last August, a group of mutinying Russian soldiers killed their colonel. The investigation is alleged to have disclosed that a number of these soldiers were in possession of copies of *Nashe Slovo*. In any case, this is the explanation given by M. Briand in an interview with Deputy Longuet and with the president of the Chamber Committee of Foreign Affairs, M. Leygues, who, in turn, transmitted this version to the journalists of the Russian bourgeois press.

To be sure, M. Briand did not dare to assert that *Nashe Slovo*, which was subject to his own censorship, was directly responsible for the killing of the officer. His thoughts may be expressed as follows: In view of the presence of Russian soldiers in France, it is necessary to sweep *Nashe Slovo* and its editors off the soil of the Republic. For a Socialist newspaper that refuses to spread illusions and lies may—in the memorable phrase of M. Renaudel—"put a bee in the bonnet" of the Russian soldiers and lead them into the dangerous path of reflection.

Unfortunately, however, for M. Briand, his explanation is based upon a scandalous anachronism. A year ago, Gustave Hervé, at that time still a member of the permanent Administrative Commission of your party, wrote that if Malvy were to kick out of

475

France those Russian refugees guilty of revolutionary internation-alism, he, Hervé, guaranteed that the public opinion of his janitors would accept such a measure without any objection. Obviously, there can be no doubt that Hervé quaffed his inspiration in a ministerial closet. At the end of July the same Hervé whispered, semi-officially, that I was to be expelled from France.

At about the same time—i.e., still before the killing of the colonel in Marseilles—Professor Durkheim, the President of the Commission for Russian Refugees, appointed by the Government, informed a representative of the refugees of the impending sup-pression of *Nashe Slovo* and the expulsion of its editors (*vide, Nashe Slovo*, July 30, 1916.)

Thus everything had been arranged in advance, even the public opinion of M. Hervé's janitors. They waited only for a pretext to strike the final blow. And the pretext was found: at the oppor-tune moment, the unfortunate Russian soldiers—acting in some-body's interests—killed their colonel.

This providential coincidence invites an assumption which, I fear, may offend your still virginal ministerial modesty. The Rus-sian journalists who made a special investigation of the Marseilles incident have established the fact that in this affair, as almost always in such cases, an active rôle was played by an *agent provo-cateur*. It is easy to understand what was his aim, or rather the aim of the well-paid blackguards who directed him. They re-quired some excess or another on the part of the Russian soldiers in order, first, to justify that régime of the knout which is still somewhat offensive to the French authorities, and then to create a pretext for measures to be taken against Russian refugees who take advantage of French hospitality in order to demoralize Rus-sian soldiers in wartime.

It is not hard to acknowledge that the instigators of this scheme did not themselves believe that the affair would go so far, or that such was their intention. It is probable that they hoped to achieve ampler results by smaller sacrifices. But undertakings of this sort always involve an element of professional risk. In this case, however, the victim was not the *provocateur* himself, but Colonel Krause and those who killed him. Even the patriotic Russian journalists, who are hostile to *Nashe Slovo*, have advanced the theory that copies of our paper may have been given to the soldiers, at the right moment, by the same *agent provocateur*.

Try, Mr. Minister, just try to institute, through the services of M. Malvy, an investigation along this line! You do not see that anything could be gained by such an investigation? Neither do I. Because—let us speak openly—*agents provocateurs* are at least just as valuable for the alleged "national defense" as Socialist ministers. And you, Jules Guesde, after having assumed responsibility for the foreign policy of the Third Republic, for the Franco-Russian alliance and its consequences, for the territorial ambitions of the Tsar, and for all the aims and methods of this war—it remains for you to accept, along with the symbolic detachments of Russian soldiers, the in no way symbolic exploits of the *provocateurs* of His Majesty, the Tsar.

At the beginning of the war, when generous promises were spread with a lavish hand, your closest companion, Sembat, vouchsafed the Russian journalists a glimpse of the highly beneficial influence to be exerted by the allied democracies upon the internal régime of Russia. Moreover, this was the supreme argument used persistently but without success by the government socialists of France and Belgium to reconcile the Russian revolutionists with the Tsar.

Twenty-six months of constant military collaboration, of communion with generalissimi, diplomats, and parliamentarians, the visits of Viviani and Thomas to Tsarkoe Selo, in short, twenty-six months of incessant "influence" exerted by the Western democ-

477

racies upon Tsarism, have only served to strengthen in our land the most arrogant reaction, moderated only by chaos in the administration and have succeeded, at the same time, in transforming the internal régime of England and France until they have become very similar to that of Russia. As may be seen, the generous promises of M. Sembat are cheaper than his coal. The luckless fate of the right of asylum is thus but a striking symptom of police and military martinet rule prevalent on both sides of the Channel.

Lloyd George, the hangman of Dublin, the imperialist incarnate, with the manners of a drunken clergyman, and M. Aristide Briand, for whose characterization I beg to refer you, Jules Guesde, to your articles of earlier days—these two figures best express the spirit of the present war, its rectitude, its morality, with its appetites both of class and individual. Can there be a worthier partner for Messrs. Lloyd George and Briand than M. Sturmer, this truly Russian German, who has made a career by clinging to the cassocks of the Metropolitans and the skirts of the court bigots? What an incomparable trio! Decidedly, history could have found no better colleagues and chieftains for Guesde, the minister.

How is it possible for an honest socialist not to fight against you! You have transformed the socialist party into a docile choir which accompanies the chorus-masters of capitalist brigandage in an epoch when bourgeois society—whose deadly enemy you, Jules Guesde, used to be—has disclosed its true nature to the very core. From the events which were prepared by a whole period of worldwide depredation and whose consequences we so often predicted, from all the blood that has been shed, from all the suffering and misfortune, from all the crimes, from all the rapaciousness and felonies of the Governments, you, Jules Guesde, you draw but one single lesson for the French proletariat: that Wilhelm II and Franz Joseph are two criminals, who, contrary to Nicholas II and

478

M. Poincaré, fail to respect the rules and regulations of international law.

An entire new generation of French working youth, new millions of workers morally awakened for the first time by the thunderbolts of the war, learn about the causes of this catastrophe of the Old World only what the Yellow Book of MM. Delcassé, Poincaré, Briand wants to tell them. And you, old Chief of the proletariat, you sink to your knees before this Evangel of the peoples, and you renounce all that you learned and taught in the school of the class struggle.

French Socialism, with its inexhaustible past, with its magnificent phalanx of fighters and martyrs, has at last found—what a fall, what a disgrace!—a Renaudel to translate, during the most tragic period of the world's history, the lofty thoughts of the Yellow Book into the language of a press of the same color.

The Socialism of Babeuf, of Saint-Simon, of Fourier, of Blanqui, of the Commune, of Jaurès, and of Jules Guesde—yes, of Jules Guesde too!—has at last found its Albert Thomas to consult with Romanov concerning the surest ways of capturing Constantinople; has found its Marcel Sembat to promenade his dilettante nonchalance over the corpses and the ruins of French civilization; and it has found its Jules Guesde to follow—he too—the chariot of the triumpher Briand.

And you believed, you hoped that the French proletariat, which has been bled white in this senseless and hopeless war by the crime of the ruling classes, would continue to tolerate quietly, to the end, this shameful pact between official socialism and the worst enemies of the proletariat. You were mistaken. An opposition has come forward. In spite of martial law and the frenzy of nationalism which, whatever its form, be it royalist, radical, or socialist, always preserves its capitalistic substance—the revolutionary opposition is advancing step by step and gaining ground every day.

Nashe Slovo, the paper that you have strangled, lived and breathed in the atmosphere of awakening French socialism. Torn from the soil of Russia by a counter-revolution which triumphed thanks to the aid of the French Bourse,—which you, Jules Guesde, are now serving—the group of *Nashe Slovo* was privileged to echo, even if in the incomplete form imposed upon it by censorship— the voice of the French section of the new International, which is raising its head amidst the horrors of the fratricidal war.

In our capacity as "undesirable foreigners" who linked our fate with that of the French opposition, we are proud of having sustained the first blows of the French Government—your government, Jules Guesde!

We have the honor, together with Monatte, Merrheim, Soumoneau, Rosmer, Bourderon, Loriot, Guilbeaux, and so many others, to be accused, all of us, of being pro-German. The Paris weekly of your friend Plekhanov, who shared with you your glory as he now shares with you your fall, denounced us week after week to the police of M. Malvy, as agents of the German General Staff. Time was when you knew the value of such accusations, for you yourself had the great honor of being their target. Now you put your stamp of approval upon M. Malvy by summing up, for the Government of National Defense, the reports of the stool pigeons. Yet, my political files contain a very recent prison sentence pronounced upon me, *in contumacium*, during the war, by a German court, for my pamphlet, "The War and the International."

But even aside from this brutal fact, which ought to make an impression even upon the police-brain of M. Malvy, I believe I have the right to assert that we revolutionary internationalists are far more dangerous enemies of German reaction than all the Governments of the Allies taken together.

Their hostility to Germany is, at the bottom, nothing but the simple rivalry of the competitor; whereas our revolutionary hatred of its ruling class is indestructible.

Imperialist competition may again unite the enemy brethren of today. Were the plans for the total destruction of Germany to be realized, England and France, after a decade, would again approach the Empire of the Hohenzollerns, to defend themselves against the excessive power of Russia. A future Poincaré would exchange telegrams of congratulations with Wilhelm or with his heir; Lloyd George, in the peculiar language of the clergyman and the boxer, would curse Russia, as the bulwark of barbarism and militarism; Albert Thomas, as the French ambassador to the Kaiser, would receive lilies of the valley from the hands of the court ladies of Potsdam, as he did so recently from the Grand Duchesses of Tsarkoe Selo.

All the banalities of present-day speeches and articles would be warmed over, and M. Renaudel would have to change, in his articles, only the proper names, a job entirely within his capacities.

As for us—we shall remain what we have been and are, sworn enemies of Germany's rulers, for we hate German reaction with the same revolutionary hatred that we have vowed against Tsarism or against the French plutocracy. And when you dare, you and your newspaper lackeys, to applaud Liebknecht, Mehring, Luxemburg, Zetkin, as intrepid enemies of the Hohenzollerns, you cannot deny that they are of our own stripe, our comrades in arms. We are allied with them against you and your masters by the indissoluble unity of the revolutionary struggle.

Perhaps you console yourself with the thought that we are few in number? Yet we are greater in number than the police of every grade believe. In their professional myopia, they do not see the spirit of revolt that is arising from every hearth of suffering and spreading throughout France, throughout all of Europe, in the workmen's suburbs and in the countryside, in the shops and in the trenches.

You have incarcerated Louise Soumoneau* in one of your prisons; but have you thereby diminished the despair of the women of this land? You can arrest hundreds of Zimmerwaldists, after having ordered your press to besmirch them again with police calumnies. But can you return the husbands to their wives? Can you restore the sons to their mothers, the fathers to their children, strength and health to the sick? Can you return, to a duped and debilitated people, the trust in those who have deceived them?

Jules Guesde, get out of your military automobile, leave the cage in which the capitalist state has imprisoned you. Look about! Perhaps fate will have pity, for the last time, upon your wretched old age, and let you hear the muted rumble of approaching events. We expect them, we summon them, we prepare for them! The fate of France would be too frightful if the Calvary of its working masses did not lead to a great revenge, to our revenge, where there will be no room for you, Jules Guesde, and for yours.

Expelled by you, I leave France with a profound faith in our triumph. Over and above your head I send fraternal greetings to the French proletariat, which is awakening to its grand destiny. Without you and against you, long live Socialist France.

Leon Trotsky

B Y AN ironic twist of history, Leon Trotsky was to return to France almost twenty years later—this time as an exile from the Union of Socialist Soviet Republics that he helped to bring into being during the epochal events that followed almost immediately after the writing of this

* Leader of the woman's section of the French socialists; imprisoned for anti-war activities; joined the communist party when founded; and expelled from it in 1925 for supporting Trotsky.

letter. In 1917, after perilous and secret wanderings as an exile in many lands, Trotsky reached Russia just as the masses, in his own historic phrase, "were entering the sphere of rulership over their own destiny." He organized and led the insurrection of October, 1917, became People's Commissar for Foreign Affairs and, after the Treaty of Brest-Litovsk, Commissar for War. In this capacity he defended, consolidated, and extended the revolutionary victories, directing the Red Army in a war against the counterrevolutionary forces, with fighting on fourteen fronts, a battle line seven thousand miles long.

After Lenin's death in 1923 (see his Testament to the Communist Party in this anthology),* Trotsky was outvoted in the Soviet councils. In 1927, he was expelled from the Communist Party by Stalin and exiled to Turkestan.

Again the odyssey of the old exile was resumed. In 1929 Trotsky found himself in Constantinople, writing his History of the Russian Revolution. Finally, four years later, the police edict of M. Malvy, described in the 1916 letter to Jules Guesde, was reversed, his French visa was at last granted, and he found a brief and somewhat precarious sanctuary at Barbizon, near Paris.

By the cumulative irony of history, events now repeated themselves once more with a strange and melodramatic twist. The Soviet ambassador to France, Vladimir Potemkin, was under orders from Trotsky's implacable enemy, Stalin, to bring pressure on the French government, because of "the new and warm friendship between Paris and Moscow," to expel Trotsky once more. The Kremlin charged that Trotsky, then seeking to recover his health in France, was responsible for the Kirov assassination and a plot against the Stalin government. Trotsky in turn charged that Stalin was betraying the Russian Revolution. And so "the unreconstructed Bolshevik" took up his wanderings once more.

In 1936, Trotsky established a temporary home in Norway. The next

* On page 491.

year he found sanctuary in Mexico, where, on August 21, 1940, he was assassinated by a member of his barricaded household, Jacques Mornard van den Dreschd. Trotsky was convinced that his murderer was directed by the hand of Stalin, and his last words, whispered to his secretary, were: "Please say to our friends I am sure of the victory of the Fourth International. Go forward!"

NICHOLAS II, THE LAST CZAR OF IMPERIAL RUSSIA, IS ASSURED BY HIS WIFE, ON THE EVE OF THE REVOLUTION, THAT ALL IS WELL AT HOME

BETWEEN the lines of this letter we can hear the "roar of the underground tremors" that marked the impending collapse of the Russian monarchy.

"The empire did not fall," wrote Bernard Pares in a massive study of that subject, "because of the revolution, but the revolution came because the empire fell. The cause of the ruin came not at all from below, but from above, and what overthrew the Romanovs was the Romanovs themselves. . . ." Pares compared the whole story to something that "happened far back in the Middle Ages, when it was still thought possible to regard a sixth of the world as a personal estate, and to govern one hundred and seventy millions of humanity from a lady's drawing room."

At the time the letter quoted below was written by the Czarina to the Czar, in the midst of the First World War, His Imperial Majesty was at general headquarters, in conference with his grand dukes and field marshals. The idea of a palace revolution was already in the air, and the Czarina was inextricably enmeshed in "mystic debaucheries" with Rasputin, described as "our dear friend" in the letter that follows. She had no way of realizing that the "death agony of the monarchy" was to come within three months. The Imperial family still enjoyed an income of more than a million dollars a month, and owned privately fifty million dollars in land, and eighty million dollars in pearls and rubies and other precious jewels.

As Trotsky says in The History of the Russian Revolution, "The ruling classes were desperately trying to save themselves from a revolution by getting rid of the Czar and his circle. . . . They wanted to, but they did not dare. . . . The possessing classes were completely monarchist, by virtue of interests, habits, and cowardice. But they wanted a monarchy without Rasputin. The monarchy answered them: 'Take me as I am. . . .' "

In response to demands for "a decent ministry," the Czarina sent to the Czar at headquarters an apple from the hands of Rasputin, and urged that he eat it "in order to strengthen his will. . . ."

"Be Peter the Great, Ivan the Terrible, Emperor Paul," she commanded. "Crush them all under your feet!"

Trotsky points out that all this was taking place "against the purple background of war, with the privileged classes meantime devouring the joys of life."

According to Trotsky, the Czarina, to whom the Czar submitted in everything, was at the time probably betraying Russian military secrets and even the heads of the Allied chieftains to the enemy. It will be recalled that she was born Princess Alex of Hesse-Darmstadt, and was the granddaughter of Queen Victoria. The ruling classes, moreover, were "diffident about the palace revolution, because they felt that the cure might prove more ruinous than the disease."

Against this setting we can best appreciate the following intimate letter from the Czarina to the Czar, which was found in a black box in the last prison of the Imperial family, when the Bolsheviks excavated the Romanov archives after the Revolution. The document itself is taken from The Letters of the Czarina Alexandra Fiedorovna to the Czar Nicolai II.

"... you are the Master ..."

Tsarskoje Selo, Dec. 4th, 1916

MY VERY PRECIOUS ONE,
Goodbye, sweet Lovy!

Its great pain to let you go—worse than ever after the hard times we have been living & fighting through. But God who is all love & mercy has let the things take a change for the better, —just a little more patience & deepest faith in the prayers & help of our Friend—then all will go well. I am fully convinced that great & beautiful times are coming for yr. reign & Russia. Only keep up your spirits, let no talks or letters pull you down—let them pass by as something unclean & quickly to be forgotten.

Show to all, that you are the Master & your will shall be obeyed —the time of great indulgence & gentleness is over—now comes your reign of will & power, & they shall be made to bow down before you & listen your orders & to work how & with whom you wish—obedience they must be taught, they do not know the meaning of that word, you have spoilt them by yr. kindness & all forgivingness.

Why do people hate me? Because they know I have a strong will & when am convinced of a thing being right (when besides blessed by Gregory), do not change my mind & that they can't bear. But its the bad ones.

Remember Mr. Philipps words when he gave me the image with the bell. As you were so kind, trusting & gentle, I was to be yr. bell, those that came with wrong intentions wld. not be able to

487

approach me & I wld. warn you. Those who are afraid of me, don't look me in the eyes or are up to some wrong, never like me.—Look at the black ones—then Orlov & Drenteln—Witte—Kokovtzev—Trepov, I feel it too—Makarov—Kaufmann—Sofia Ivanovna—Mary—Sandra Obolensky etc., but those who are good & devoted to you honestly & purely—love me,—look at the simple people & military. The good & bad clergy its all so clear & therefore no more hurts me as when I was younger. Only when one allows oneself to write you or me nasty impertinent letters—you must punish.

Ania told me about *Balaschov* (the man I always disliked). I understood why you came so awfully late to bed & why I had such pain & anxiety waiting. Please, Lovy, tell Frederiks to write him a strong *reprimand* (he & *Nicolai Mikhailovitch* & *Vass* make one in the club)—he has such a high court-rank & dares to write, unasked. And its not the first time—in bygone days I remember he did so too. Tear up the letter, but have him firmly reprimanded —tell *Voyeikov* to remind the old man—such a smack to a conceited member of the Council of the Empire will be very useful.

We cannot now be trampled upon. Firmness above all!—Now you have made *Trepov's* son A.D.C. you can insist yet more on his working with *Protopopov*, he must prove his gratitude.—Remember to forbid *Gurko* speaking & mixing himself into politics —it ruined *Nikolasha* & Alexeiev,—the latter God sent this illness clearly to save you fr. a man who was lossing his way & doing harm by listening to bad letters & people, instead of listening to yr. orders about the war & being obstinate. And one has set him against me—proof—what he said to old *Ivanov*.—

But soon all this things will blow over, its getting clearer & the weather too, which is a good sign, remember.

And our dear Friend is praying so hard for you—a man of God's near one gives the strength, faith & hope one needs so sorely. And others cannot understand this great calm of yours &

therefore think you don't understand & try to ennervate, frighten & prick at you. But they will soon tire of it.

Should Mother dear write, remember the Michels are behind her.—Don't heed & take to heart—thank God, she is not here, but kind people find means of writing & doing harm.—All is turning to the good—our Friends dreams means so much. Sweety, go to the *Moghilev* Virgin & find peace & strength there—look in after tea, before you receive, take Baby with you, quietly—its so calm there —& you can place yr. candels. Let the people see you are a christian Sovereign & don't be shy—even such an example will help others.—

How will the lonely nights be? I cannot imagine it. The consolation to hold you tightly clasped in my arms—it lulled the pain of soul & heart & I tried to put all my endless love, prayers & faith & strength into my caresses. So inexpressibly dear you are to me, husband of my heart. God bless you & my Baby treasure—I cover you with kisses; when sad, go to Baby's room & sit a bit quietly there with his nice people. Kiss the beloved child & you will feel warmed & calm. All my love I pour out to you, Sun of my life.—

Sleep well, heart & soul with you, my prayers around you—God & the holy Virgin will never forsake you ——

Ever your very, very,

Own

NINE *days later, the Czarina wrote again to the Czar, addressing him as "My own dearest Angel" and thanking him for his card from headquarters. In this letter she assured him that things were calmer and better at home, adding: "Only one wants to feel your hand—how long years people have told me the same—'Russia loves to feel the whip' —it's their nature—tender love and then the iron hand to punish the* guide.—*How I wish I could pour my will into your veins! The Virgin is above you, for you, remember the miracle—our friend's vision. . . ."* (The friend referred to, as in the first letter, was Rasputin.) The Czarina ended with the statement that she was busy writing Christmas cards and a hurried P.S. urging the Czar to have Rodzianko's uniform taken off.

The Czar acknowledged these letters from the Czarina with "tender thanks for the severe written scolding," and signed himself "Your poor little weak-willed hubby."

Three days later, on the night of December 16-17, Rasputin was lured to a little party by Prince Yussupov and put to death, with cyanide of potassium in his wine and a bullet in his heart.

"Around the body of the 'Holy Friend,'" wrote Trotsky, "the former horse thief murdered by grand dukes, the Czar's family must have seemed outcast even to themselves. . . . The noose of hopelessness was drawing tighter." Within a few weeks, "The dynasty fell by shaking, like rotten fruit, before the Revolution even had time to approach its first problem."

When the Russian armies mutinied after three years of bloody warfare, and the masses not only clamored for bread and land, but began actually seizing them, the Czar abdicated, and he and his whole family were imprisoned on March 17, 1917. On July 16, 1918 they were executed by a self-appointed revolutionary firing squad in a dusty cellar at the foot of the Urals, and a dynasty that had begun in Byzantium and had given to history such names as the first Vladimir, Ivan the Terrible, Peter the Great, Catherine II, the first Alexander, and a whole series of Little White Fathers came to an end.

LENIN WARNS THE COMMUNIST PARTY THAT STALIN IS CONCENTRATING TOO MUCH POWER IN HIS OWN HANDS

[LENIN'S DEATHBED TESTAMENT]

For the authentic text of this historic letter the editor of this anthology is directly indebted to Max Eastman, author of Since Lenin Died and translator of Trotsky's History of the Russian Revolution. He has also supplied his own record and interpretation of the background.

"On Christmas, 1922,* lying on his deathbed and deprived of the power of speech, Lenin wrote a letter predicting the inevitable struggle between Trotsky and Stalin, analyzing the characters of the two men, and indicating the action which the party ought to take to avoid a split. The almost uncanny political sagacity of Lenin was never more clearly revealed than in that brief letter, which has been called his Testament to the party. The letter was locked up in the safe and declared nonexistent by Stalin and his associates in power, because it contained a vigorous criticism of Stalin himself and the advice that he be removed from his commanding position as General Secretary of the party. I have correct citations from the letter in 1925 in my book Since Lenin Died, but was compelled to give them on my own authority. My citations were denounced and denied all over the world by the official Communist press, including the Politburo in Moscow. On October 18, 1926—at the height of a militant effort of the Opposition to carry out the will of Lenin in regard to the General Secretary—I published the following translation of the full text of the Testament in The New York Times, using the money received in the

* The difference in the date line on the letter is due to the Russian calendar.

491

further propagation of Bolshevik ideas. This text is complete, accurate, and entirely to be relied on."

Nicolai Lenin (born Vladimir Ilich Ulyanov) was born in 1870, in a family of middle-class intellectuals; his wife, Krupskaya, was the daughter of an impoverished nobleman. After studying for the law, Lenin was exiled to Siberia for "demonstrations against the authorities." After the brief revolution of 1905, Lenin lived in England and Switzerland, where he carried on the propaganda and developed the Marxian doctrines that laid the foundation for the Russian Revolution, for which he returned to his homeland in 1917.

Joseph Stalin (born Joseph Vissarionovitch Dzugashvili) was born in 1879, in Tiflis, the son of a cobbler. At the age of seventeen he became a revolutionary agitator, and advanced to great power in the Bolshevik councils, becoming general Secretary of the Central Committee of the Russian Communist party in 1917, and succeeding Lenin as dictator of the USSR after his death in 1924.

"Stalin is too rude . . ."

BY THE stability of the Central Committee, of which I spoke before, I mean measures to prevent a split, so far as such measures can be taken. For, of course, the White Guard in Russkaya Mysl (I think it was S. E. Oldenburg) was right when, in the first place, in his play against Soviet Russia he banked on the hope of a split in our party, and when, in the second place, he banked for that split on serious disagreements in our party.

Our party rests upon two classes, and for that reason its instability is possible, and if there cannot exist an agreement between those classes its fall is inevitable. In such an event it would be useless to take any measures or in general to discuss the stability of our Central Committee. In such an event no measures would prove capable of preventing a split. But I trust that is too remote a future, and too improbable an event, to talk about.

I have in mind stability as a guarantee against a split in the near future, and I intend to examine here a series of considerations of a purely personal character.

I think that the fundamental in the matter of stability—from this point of view—is such members of the Central Committee as Stalin and Trotsky. The relation between them constitutes, in my opinion, a big half of the danger of that split, which might be avoided, and the avoidance of which might be promoted, in my opinion, by raising the number of members of the Central Committee to fifty or one hundred.

Comrade Stalin, having become General Secretary, has concentrated an enormous power in his hands; and I am not sure that he always knows how to use that power with sufficient caution. On the other hand Comrade Trotsky, as was proved by his struggle against the Central Committee in connection with the question of the People's Commissariat of Ways of Communication is distinguished not only by his exceptional abilities—personally he is, to be sure, the most able man in the present Central Committee; but also by his too far-reaching self-confidence and a disposition to be too much attracted by the purely administrative side of affairs.

These two qualities of the two most able leaders of the present Central Committee might, quite innocently, lead to a split; if our party does not take measures to prevent it, a split might arise unexpectedly.

I will not further characterize the other members of the Central Committee as to their personal qualities. I will only remind you that the October episode of Zinoviev and Kamenev was not, of course, accidental, but that it ought as little to be used against them personally as the non-Bolshevism of Trotsky.

Of the younger members of the Central Committee, I want to say a few words about Bukharin and Piatakov. They are, in my opinion, the most able forces (among the youngest), and in regard to them it is necessary to bear in mind the following: Bukharin is not only the most valuable and biggest theoretician of the party, but also may legitimately be considered the favorite of the whole party; but his theoretical views can only with the very greatest doubt be regarded as fully Marxist, for there is something scholastic in him (he never has learned, and I think never has fully understood, the dialectic).

And then Piatakov—a man undoubtedly distinguished in will and ability, but too much given over to administration and the administrative side of things to be relied on in a serious political question.

Of course, both these remarks are made by me merely with a view to the present time, or supposing that these two able and loyal workers may not find an occasion to supplement their knowledge and correct their one-sidedness.
December 25, 1922.

Postscript: Stalin is too rude, and this fault, entirely supportable in relations among us Communists, becomes insupportable in the office of General Secretary. Therefore, I propose to the comrades to find a way to remove Stalin from that position and appoint to it another man who in all respects differs from Stalin only in superiority—namely, more patient, more loyal, more polite and more attentive to comrades, less capricious, etc. This circumstance may seem an insignificant trifle, but I think that from the point of view of preventing a split and from the point of view of the relation between Stalin and Trotsky which I discussed above, it is not a trifle, or it is such a trifle as may acquire a decisive significance.

Lenin

Jan. 4, 1923.

M AX EASTMAN *has also supplied the following note, giving his own view of the consequences of this letter of Lenin:*

"There is increasing pathos in Lenin's last warning to his party, as time proves how far-seeing it was, and how futile. We see him attempting vainly with a dying hand to stay the stride towards power of the super-fascist who should supplant him and destroy his hopes. Stalin has banished Trotsky, 'the ablest man in the executive committee,' and killed all the others whom Lenin saw fit to mention in this letter. He has killed, jailed, or banished all the old leaders of the Bolsheviks, the colleagues upon whom Lenin relied intimately. There is not one left. And he has built upon the ruins of Lenin's so carefully pondered plan for a workers' and peasants' republic a totalitarian state. And that is but the modern name for tyranny."

In a selection of excerpts from the writings of Stalin just issued in America under the title Stalin's Kampf, there appears a statement the dictator made to Kamenev, as recorded in his own jottings:

"To choose one's victim, to prepare one's plans minutely, to stake an implacable vengeance, and then to go to bed . . . there is nothing sweeter in the world."

BARTOLOMEO VANZETTI BIDS FAREWELL TO DANTE SACCO ON THE EVE OF HIS EXECUTION

IN APRIL 15, 1920, two shoe-factory employees named Parmenter and Berardelli, carrying a large sum of money through the streets of South Braintree, Massachusetts, were attacked by two men, or perhaps three, and mortally injured. Their assailants, who had used revolvers, escaped in an automobile with the stolen money. Charged with the crime, Bartolomeo Vanzetti and Nicola Sacco, two obscure immigrants, one a fish peddler and the other a shoemaker, were arrested. Their names soon became symbols of sacrifice to blind or blundering justice.

For seven years they languished in jail while embattled lawyers fought through protracted and tantalizing trials. Liberals the world over, aghast at the prisoners' conviction on scant and perjured evidence, fought for their release. In 1920, America was in the throes of a violent "Red scare," and feeling against all radicals ran high, especially in the Massachusetts court where this case was tried.

Finally, on August 21, 1927, Vanzetti, the idealistic dreamer, whose anarchistic views had done much to impair his chances of freedom, wrote this moving letter to the son of his friend Sacco. As Lewis Gannett expressed it: "Two semi-illiterate Italian idealists put on paper stumbling and beautiful sentences which will be remembered along with Nathan Hale's regret that he had only one life to give for his country and William Lloyd Garrison's 'I am in earnest. I will not equivocate; I will not excuse; I will not retreat a single inch; and I will be heard.'"

496

*" . . . seven years, four months and seventeen days
of unspeakable tortures and wrong . . ."*

August 21, 1927. From the Death House
of Massachusetts State Prison

MY DEAR DANTE:
I still hope, and we will fight until the last moment, to revindicate our right to live and to be free, but all the forces of the State and of the money and reaction are deadly against us because we are libertarians or anarchists.

I write little of this because you are now and yet too young to understand these things and other things of which I would like to reason with you.

But, if you do well, you will grow and understand your father's and my case and your father's and my principles, for which we will soon be put to death.

I tell you now that all that I know of your father, he is not a criminal, but one of the bravest men I ever knew. Some day you will understand what I am about to tell you. That your father has sacrificed everything dear and sacred to the human heart and soul for his fate in liberty and justice for all. That day you will be proud of your father, and if you come brave enough, you will take his place in the struggle between tyranny and liberty and you will vindicate his (our) names and our blood.

If we have to die now, you shall know, when you will be able to understand this tragedy in its fullest, how good and brave your

497

father has been with you, your father and I, during these eight years of struggle, sorrow, passion, anguish and agony.

Even from now you shall be good, brave with your mother, with Ines, and with Susie—brave, good Susie*—and do all you can to console and help them.

I would like you to also remember me as a comrade and friend to your father, your mother and Ines, Susie and you, and I assure you that neither have I been a criminal, that I have committed no robbery and no murder, but only fought modestly to abolish crimes from among mankind and for the liberty of all.

Remember Dante, each one who will say otherwise of your father and I, is a liar, insulting innocent dead men who have been brave in their life. Remember and know also, Dante, that if your father and I would have been cowards and hypocrits and rinnegetors of our faith, we would not have been put to death. They would not even have convicted a lebbrous dog; not even executed a deadly poisoned scorpion on such evidence as that they framed against us. They would have given a new trial to a matricide and abitual felon on the evidence we presented for a new trial.

Remember, Dante, remember always these things; we are not criminals; they convicted us on a frame-up; they denied us a new trial; and if we will be executed after seven years, four months and seventeen days of unspeakable tortures and wrong, it is for what I have already told you; because we were for the poor and against the exploitation and oppression of the man by the man.

The documents of our case, which you and other ones will collect and preserve, will prove to you that your father, your mother, Ines, my family and I have sacrificed by and to a State Reason of the American Plutocratic reaction.

The day will come when you will understand the atrocious cause

* Faithful friend of Mrs. Sacco, with whom she and her children lived during the last years of the case.

of the above written words, in all its fullness. Then you will honor us.

Now Dante, be brave and good always. I embrace you.

P.S. I left the copy of *An American Bible* to your mother now, for she will like to read it, and she will give it to you when you will be bigger and able to understand it. Keep it for remembrance. It will also testify to you how good and generous Mrs. Gertrude Winslow has been with us all. Good-bye Dante.

Bartolomeo

T HE following day, just after midnight, Sacco and Vanzetti were put to death in the electric chair. As Sacco sat in the chair he shouted in Italian, "Long live anarchy!" and in English bid farewell to his wife, his child, his mother, and his friends. Vanzetti "protested innocence, denied crime, admitted some sin." His last words were, "I wish to forgive some people for what they are now doing to me."

The complete record of the case has been published in six large volumes and summarized by many impartial lawyers, judges, and historians, virtually all of them agreeing that the evidence against Sacco and Vanzetti was not sufficient to convict them, that Judge Webster Thayer was "guilty of gross and damaging prejudice," and that the Committee of Inquiry directed by President A. Lawrence Lowell of Harvard carried on its investigation "in an unsatisfactory manner." Most students of the case believe that the murders for which these two men were indicted, convicted, and executed were in reality committed by notorious and confessed gangsters.

CHRISTOPHER MORLEY INSPIRES THE TALE OF A WAYSIDE INN

[A LETTER TO T. A. DALY]

SIMEON STRUNSKY said of Christopher Morley that his love for the city of New York was one of the great love affairs of history. But apparently there was an earlier idyl in his life—a romantic attachment characteristically described in this nostalgic and iridescent letter to a boon companion, a letter running over with "large tabling and belly cheer."

No section of the Dewey Decimal System of Library Classification—not even the sprawling 800's devoted to Literature—is broad enough to take care of the teeming Morley items of the last twenty years, from The Eighth Sin, Kathleen, Parnassus on Wheels, and The Haunted Bookshop of his early Oxford and Doubleday period, down through Where the Blue Begins, Thunder on the Left, and John Mistletoe, to such recent novels as Human Being and Kitty Foyle. William Bolitho declared that "no other American writer is more sure of being in print a hundred years hence."

Morley has been, in his varied moods, poet, essayist, lecturer, sage, editor, columnist, anthologist, "Old Quercus" of The Saturday Review of Literature, founder of the Three Hours for Lunch Club and The Baker Street Irregulars, doctor of humane letters, minister plenipotentiary for the ancient convivialities, and bibliodisiac extraordinary for the American reading public. He claims, however, to have retired from all this and says he is working, secretly and persistently, on a long projected textbook of English Literature.

In this letter Kit Morley implores a devoted kinsprit and a noted bard to apostrophize a vanished Mermaid Tavern of Philadelphia. Readers

500

of Kitty Foyle will have noticed that Dooner's was the good Irish hostelry frequented by Old Man Foyle himself.

"... where the piddling and the picayune and the
petit larceny of life get brushed away ..."

Roslyn Heights, Long Island
April 15, 1928

TOM darling, I see in the paper tonight that Ed Dooner's dead. Won't you write a piece about him? I mean a real whale of a piece like you damn well ought to, a piece that wallows in the deep, rises to the top here and there to snoof an iridescent shower and then slabsides downward again into the lazy greenwards like that blessed young whale I saw from the *Caronia's* topsides just gently loitering himself in the warm Atlantic one day last August. . . .

So should you meander yourself in this piece, it must be something that'll get reprinted from here to Kingdom West, all full of the endless decencies of those hambone and whisky days, the lit'ry associations of the dear old hotel, how it was as masculine as firemen's suspenders and the sort of place where bishops and men with bubukle noses both felt equally at home, like the immortal Conniving House of Irish fame; a tavern where there was neither pimping nor skimping but where any of the genuine kidney, from Shakespeare to Lew Fields, would have known themselves somewhere near the third waistcoat button of life.

Ed was the one I knew, wasn't he? the quiet gentlemanly fellow with glimmering eyes, eyes just a little moistened always, so that

501

CHRISTOPHER MORLEY TO T. A. DALY

one rather wanted to take just the torn-off corner of a very soft piece of blotting paper and seep them a bit; and a sadness that slipped in and out of his face, and he was fond of music. I imagine a piece that would have in it the best of Ed and the best of You and the best of the Dooner's you introduced me to, the colored waiters and the old mosaic above the bar, and Lord do you remember that hottest of hell's hot days in early summer, 1917, when I first had lunch with you there? and we ate steaming hot ham in our shirt sleeves and drank shandygaff, I think, though maybe you insisted on whisky? . . .

My eye slips away from this typewriter to the little painting of a bull terrier's head that hung over the old cashier's desk in the dining-room (I think that's where it was) that you salvaged for me when the place broke up . . . together with those dear old Dooner spoons and cruets and Friday finnan-haddie-platters you got for me, bless your old skull. . . .

Such a piece might drag literature into the picture ever and anon: and gosh knows it's fair enough to regard Dooner's as a sort of symbolic provincial Mermaid Tavern, for surely there as much as any place in Philadelphia (if my guess is right) the essence that lies behind literature and all the arts was alive and frolic; and I can see Ed coming up so very quietly to our table to ask you if everything was jake. Why do I associate him with the violin? Did he have a son who was a violinist, or something of the sort? Or am I dreaming? The floor was squares of black and white tile, wasn't it? I was always pleased by the little photo in the lobby, of Morley's Hotel in Trafalgar Square, that famous old hostelry also abdicated from its destiny. I remember the tablet on the Ludlow Street corner. And who forgets the great party we had on the occasion of the Three Hrs for Lunch Club official visit to Philadelphia, which must have been one of the last of Dooner's great affairs?

It must have been a good life to be an innkeeper of that sort.

502

There was charity in it, there was honor in it, there was merriment, there was always enough annoyance and complication and care to keep one busy and alert and free from the morbid dubiousness of the poet and philosopher. By running it for gents only, one purged away many of the vexing problems that presumably harass the general roof-giver.

I want to see you sit down and let the old pen and the flagon of green ink just mosey about the general idea of Ed Dooner, the quiet artist in living, and Dooner's, the Institution, and the whole theory of the host and how it is that literature is likely to get itself born around and about such places where the piddling and the picayune and the petit larceny of life get brushed away and we feel that we are larger than we know.

There was something essentially Catholic, I mean Papist, about that place as I remember it: one surrendered to it as the troubled soul does (eventually, I dare say) to the Church Universal. It was a Steve O'Grady kind of place; a parish priest kind of place; I expect there was usually some dust under the beds, and the engravings on the walls were sure to be of the Landseer type; the ventilation was dense, and I expect some of the guests slept in their union suits; yet there was a kind of obese holiness about it too. (I mustn't go on like this, but I want somehow by hook or by crook—shepherd's crook—to get you steamed up with the idea of doing a piece about Dooner's that will bug out the eyes of the uninitiate.)

Because the gist of Dooner's, as I think about it this moment, was that the right kind of person knew as soon as he stepped into it that it was real. The steam that floated up from those plates of cabbage was a genuine exhalation: the perspiration on the coon waiters was actual sweat: the men who sat at the little tables in the barroom for their lunch were identifiable as comic and struggling human beings, destined for agony and disappointment and bawdy stories.

503

It was a Liam O'Flaherty and Shaemus Stephens sort of place, a John Drew and Otis Skinner sort of place, a place for mannerly old troupers and, I imagine, for cagy old ward leaders with hairy ears, well pickled in a thousand vats of compromise and graft; all the good-tempered, grizzling ruffians who live by their wits and by knowing how easy most of us are.

I suppose any man who sees that long procession of human life go past maybe gets that sad look in his eyes that Ed Dooner had. . . . But listen, you're writing this piece, not me. I want you to reach up and grab holt of something high and queer and shiny and lean on it and let loose a picture of what Dooner's meant. A Mark Twain kind of place. An Edgar Allan Poe kind of place. A fireman save my child kind of place. A sleep with the window closed kind of place and hang your scapular on the back of a chair. A terrapin soup and catch the late train for Villanova kind of place. (I hear you grunting.) A Comédie Humaine kind of place. A Joyce Kilmer kind of place.

And you, old shark, are the lad to sit down and do for the vanished Dooner's what Lamb did (let's say) for the Old Benchers of the Inner Temple . . . who were not baseball players as the youngest generation probably imagine.

Send me the copy and watch my smoke.

God bless you. David Bone is due in tonight, after being away three months on a Mediterranean cruise and a winter lay-up. I hope to see him tomorrow, and I shall tell everyone I meet that you are going to do the trick about Dooner's. Then I'll tell you (when it's done) my schemes for marketing it as a little book next fall. Your fortune is made.

Hey: my love to The Cravenbird, Jim the Quiz-editor; and where is Bart up to these days? Damme, I'm coming over some day to have lunch with youse guys: but I'm working trying to write a book. It's a fact, a Book.

I think affectionately of Ed Dooner, although I knew him so little.

Kit

O BVIOUSLY *Christopher Morley was himself writing the essay for which he was clamoring, but T. A. Daly took him at his word and wrote* The House of Dooner—The Last of the Friendly Inns. *He employed both prose and poetry, incorporated his friend's letter, and then improvised freely on the theme. The resulting book was published in 1928 by the David McKay Company, of Philadelphia. . . . Dooner's itself, alas! had already vanished when Morley's letter was written. It was torn down in 1924, and part of the huge new Federal Reserve Bank covers the ancient premises.*

H. L. MENCKEN ADMITS TO A PHILOSOPHER THAT GOD HAS TREATED HIM WITH VAST PO-LITENESS

[A LETTER TO WILL DURANT]

NOTED as a newspaperman, editor, author, and critic, the Sage of Baltimore is both a prompt and prodigious letter writer. His brief notes and his long letters are both marked by his torrential style, his militant manner, and his colorful images. Born in Baltimore in 1880, Henry L. Mencken has been associated almost all his adult life with the Baltimore Sun papers. From 1914 to 1923 he was coeditor of Smart Set; the following year, with George Jean Nathan, he founded The American Mercury and subsequently was sole editor until 1933. In addition to his long series of Prejudices and Prefaces, he has done important scholarly work in philology climaxed by The American Language. Music is one of his main interests.

The letter printed below (written in 1933) was prompted by a request from Will Durant, author of The Story of Philosophy, who was conducting a Socratic symposium of his own and asked Mencken (among others) to explain what meaning life held for him.

"... if He really exists, [He] deserves to be denounced instead of respected."

YOU ask me, in brief, what satisfaction I get out of life, and why I go on working. I go on working for the same reason that a hen goes on laying eggs. There is in every living creature an obscure but powerful impulse to active functioning. Life demands to be lived. Inaction, save as a measure of recuperation between bursts of activity, is painful and dangerous to the healthy organism —in fact, it is almost impossible. Only the dying can be really idle.

The precise form of an individual's activity is determined, of course, by the equipment with which he came into the world. In other words, it is determined by his heredity. I do not lay eggs, as a hen does, because I was born without any equipment for it. For the same reason I do not get myself elected to Congress, or play the violoncello, or teach metaphysics in a college, or work in a steel mill. What I do is simply what lies easiest to my hand. It happens that I was born with an intense and insatiable interest in ideas, and thus like to play with them. It happens also that I was born with rather more than the average facility for putting them into words. In consequence, I am a writer and editor, which is to say, a dealer in them and concoctor of them.

There is very little conscious volition in all this. What I do was ordained by the inscrutable fates, not chosen by me. In my boyhood, yielding to a powerful but still subordinate interest in exact facts, I wanted to be a chemist, and at the same time my poor father tried to make me a business man. At other times, like any

507

other relatively poor man, I have longed to make a lot of money by some easy swindle. But I became a writer all the same, and shall remain one until the end of the chapter, just as a cow goes on giving milk all her life, even though what appears to be her self-interest urges her to give gin.

I am far luckier than most men, for I have been able since boyhood to make a good living doing precisely what I have wanted to do—what I would have done for nothing, and very gladly, if there had been no reward for it. Not many men, I believe, are so fortunate. Millions of them have to make their livings at tasks which really do not interest them. As for me, I have had an extraordinarily pleasant life, despite the fact that I have had the usual share of woes. For in the midst of those woes I still enjoyed the immense satisfaction which goes with free activity. I have done, in the main, exactly what I wanted to do. Its possible effects upon other people have interested me very little. I have not written and published to please other people, but to satisfy myself, just as a cow gives milk, not to profit the dairyman, but to satisfy herself. I like to think that most of my ideas have been sound ones, but I really don't care. The world may take them or leave them. I have had my fun hatching them.

Next to agreeable work as a means of attaining happiness I put what Huxley called the domestic affections—the day to day intercourse with family and friends. My home has seen bitter sorrow, but it has never seen any serious disputes, and it has never seen poverty. I was completely happy with my mother and sister, and I am completely happy with my wife. Most of the men I commonly associate with are friends of very old standing. I have known some of them for more than thirty years. I seldom see anyone, intimately, whom I have known for less than ten years. These friends delight me. I turn to them when work is done with unfailing eagerness. We have the same general tastes, and see the world much alike. Most of them are interested in music, as I am. It has given me more pleasure in this life than any other external thing. I love it more every year.

As for religion, I am quite devoid of it. Never in my adult life have I experienced anything that could be plausibly called a religious impulse. My father and grandfather were agnostics before me, and though I was sent to Sunday-school as a boy and exposed to the Christian theology I was never taught to believe it. My father thought that I should learn what it was, but it apparently never occurred to him that I would accept it. He was a good psychologist. What I got in Sunday-school—beside a wide acquaintance with Christian hymnology—was simply a firm conviction that the Christian faith was full of palpable absurdities, and the Christian God preposterous. Since that time I have read a great deal in theology—perhaps much more than the average clergyman—but I have never discovered any reason to change my mind.

The act of worship, as carried on by Christians, seems to me to be debasing rather than ennobling. It involves grovelling before a Being who, if He really exists, deserves to be denounced instead of respected. I see little evidence in this world of the so-called goodness of God. On the contrary, it seems to me that, on the strength of His daily acts, He must be set down a most stupid, cruel and villainous fellow. I can say this with a clear conscience, for He has treated me very well—in fact, with vast politeness. But I can't help thinking of his barbaric torture of most of the rest of humanity. I simply can't imagine revering the God of war and politics, theology and cancer.

I do not believe in immortality, and have no desire for it. The belief in it issues from the puerile egos of inferior men. In its Christian form it is little more than a device for getting revenge upon those who are having a better time on this earth. What the meaning of human life may be I don't know: I incline to suspect

509

that it has none. All I know about it is that, to me at least, it is very amusing while it lasts. Even its troubles, indeed, can be amusing. Moreover, they tend to foster the human qualities that I admire most—courage and its analogues. The noblest man, I think, is that one who fights God, and triumphs over Him. I have had little of this to do. When I die I shall be content to vanish into nothingness. No show, however good, could conceivably be good forever.

H. L. Mencken

HAD space permitted, another characteristic Mencken letter would have been included here—the one in which he pays homage to his musical gods. In this letter he says of Franz Schubert: "The fellow was scarcely human. His merest belch was as lovely as the song of the sirens. He sweated beauty as naturally as a Christian sweats hate. . . ." Mencken once traveled eighty miles to hear a Schubert octet. The horn player failed to show up, and Mencken played his part on the piano.

Since writing the letter quoted above to Will Durant, Mencken has published A Treatise on the Gods: A Philosophic Study on Right and Wrong and a nostalgic record of his first twelve years, entitled, as is fitting for a man treated by God with vast politeness, Happy Days.

LION FEUCHTWANGER ADDRESSES AN INQUIRY TO THE NAZI OCCUPANT OF HIS CONFISCATED HOUSE

[AN OPEN LETTER TO MR. X]

THE celebrated author of Jew Süss, The Ugly Duchess, and The Oppermanns was born in 1884. In addition to his novels, he achieved fame as a poet-philosopher and as a man of letters generally.

At the beginning of March, 1933, while Feuchtwanger was visiting in America, the Nazis confiscated his home and destroyed his library and his writings. In September, they gave his house to an important member of the National Socialist Party. On receiving this news, Feuchtwanger addressed the following letter to the occupant of his house:

"Thou shalt dwell in houses thou hast not builded."

DEAR SIR:
      I do not know your name or how you came into possession of my house. I only know that two years ago the police of the Third Reich seized all my property, personal and real, and handed it over to the stock company formed by the Reich for the confiscation of the properties of political adversaries (chairman of the board: Minister Goering). I learned this through a letter from the mortgagees. They explained to me that under the laws of the Third Reich con-

fiscations of property belonging to political opponents concern themselves only with credit balances. Although my house and my bank deposits, which had also been confiscated, greatly exceeded in value the amount of the mortgage, I would be obliged to continue the payment of interest on the mortgage, as well as my German taxes, from whatever money I might earn abroad. Be that as it may, one thing is certain—you, Herr X are occupying my house and I, in the opinion of German judges, must pay the costs.

How do you like my house, Herr X? Do you find it pleasant to live in? Did the silver-gray carpets in the upper rooms come to grief while the S. A. men were looting? My houseman sought safety in these upper rooms, as, I being in America at the time, the gentlemen seemed to determine to take it out on him. Those carpets are very delicate, and red is a strong color, hard to eradicate. The rubber tiling in the hallways was also not primarily designed with the boots of the S. A. men in mind.

Have you any notion why I had the semi-inclosed terrace built on the roof? Frau Feuchtwanger and I used it for our morning setting-up exercises. Would you mind seeing to it that the pipes of the shower don't freeze? . . .

I wonder to what use you have put the two rooms which formerly contained my library? I have been told, Herr X, that books are not very popular in the Reich in which you live, and whoever shows interest in them is likely to get into difficulties. I, for instance, read your Führer's book and guilelessly remarked that his 140,000 words were 140,000 offenses against the spirit of the German language. The result of this remark is that you are now living in my house. Sometimes I wonder to what uses bookcases can be put in the Third Reich. In case you should decide to have them ripped out, be careful not to damage the wall. . . .

By the way, is our street still called Mahlerstrasse? Have the masters of your Reich overlooked that the composer, Gustav Mahler,

512

LION FEUCHTWANGER TO MR. X

for whom the street is named, was a Jew, or has Richard Strauss brought this fact to their attention?

And what have you done with my terrarium which stood at one of the windows of my study? Did you actually kill my turtles and my lizards because their owner was an "alien"? And were the flower beds and the rock garden much damaged when the S. A. men, shooting as they ran, pursued my sorely beaten servant across the garden into the woods beyond?

Doesn't it sometimes seem odd to you that you should be living in my house? Your Führer is not generally considered a friend of Jewish literature. Isn't it, therefore, astounding that he should have such a strong predilection for the Old Testament? I myself have heard him quote with much fervor, 'An eye for an eye, a tooth for a tooth' (by which he may have meant, 'A confiscation of property for literary criticism'). And now, through you, he has fulfilled a prophecy of the Old Testament—the saying, 'Thou shalt dwell in houses thou hast not builded.'

With many good wishes for our house,

Lion Feuchtwanger

P.S. On the other hand, perhaps you think my statement that your "Führer" writes bad German is justified by the fact that you are now living in my house?

THERE is no record of any reply by Mr. X. . . . Feuchtwanger's novel published in 1934, The Oppermanns, won international acclaim for its inspired and masterly indictment of the Hitler regime. The author then moved to France. His last novel, Paris Gazette, was written during his exile there. . . . He is currently (July, 1940) reported as being in a German concentration camp, although there is also an unconfirmed report that he succeeded in making his escape to Portugal.

THOMAS MANN INDICTS THE HITLER REGIME
FOR ITS SECRET AND OPEN CRIMES

[A LETTER TO THE DEAN OF THE PHILOSOPHICAL FACULTY
OF THE UNIVERSITY OF BONN]

HERE speaks the greatest man of letters of our time—in a ringing philippic against the Nazi way of life.

Thomas Mann was not seriously disturbed by the early threats and tempests of Adolf Hitler, and even as late as 1930 dismissed him as a figure that would soon pass from the scene.

But when the first wave of Nazi intolerance actually threatened to engulf Germany, he spoke out in no uncertain terms. As soon as the Nazis actually took over control of the government in 1933, he declared himself again, but the climax of indignation and inspired and disciplined wrath came at the beginning of 1937, when Thomas Mann, then living in temporary exile in Zurich, received a letter from the Dean of the Philosophical Faculty of the Frederick-William University at Bonn stating:

TO HERR THOMAS MANN, WRITER: By the request of the Rector of the University of Bonn, I must inform you that as a consequence of your loss of citizenship the Philosophical Faculty finds itself obliged to strike your name off its roll of honorary doctors. Your right to use this title is cancelled in accordance with Article VIII of the regulations concerning the conferring of degrees.

(signature illegible)

—DEAN

514

To this curt note, *Thomas Mann replied, addressing not only the Dean but the German people, in the letter that follows:*

"God help our darkened and desecrated country . . ."

To the Dean of the Philosophical Faculty
of the University of Bonn:

I have received the melancholy communication which you addressed to me on the nineteenth of December. Permit me to reply to it as follows:

The German universities share a heavy responsibility for all the present distresses which they called down upon their heads when they tragically misunderstood their historic hour and allowed their soil to nourish the ruthless forces which have devastated Germany morally, politically, and economically.

This responsibility of theirs long ago destroyed my pleasure in my academic honour and prevented me from making any use of it whatever. Moreover, I hold today an honorary degree of Doctor of Letters conferred upon me more recently by Harvard University. I cannot refrain from explaining to you the grounds upon which it was conferred. My diploma contains a sentence which, translated from the Latin, runs as follows: ". . . we the President and Fellows with the approval of the honourable Board of Overseers of the University in solemn session have designated and appointed as honorary Doctor of Letters Thomas Mann, famous author, who has interpreted life to many of our fellow-citizens and together with a very few contemporaries sustains the high dignity of German culture; and we have granted to him all the rights and privileges appertaining to this degree."

515

In such terms, so curiously contradictory to the current German view, do free and enlightened men across the ocean think of me—and, I may add, not only there. It would never have occurred to me to boast of the words I have quoted; but here and today I may, nay, I must repeat them.

If you, Herr Dean (I am ignorant of the procedure involved), have posted a copy of your communication to me on the bulletin board of your university, it would gratify me to have this reply of mine receive the same honour. Perhaps some member of the university, some student or professor, may be visited by a sudden fear, a swiftly suppressed and dismaying presentiment, on reading a document which gives him in his disgracefully enforced isolation and ignorance a brief revealing glimpse of the free world of the intellect that still exists outside.

Here I might close. And yet at this moment certain further explanations seem to me desirable or at least permissible. I made no statement when my loss of civil rights was announced, though I was more than once asked to do so. But I regard the academic divestment as a suitable occasion for a brief personal declaration. I would beg you, Herr Dean (I have not even the honour of knowing your name), to regard yourself as merely the chance recipient of a communication not designed for you in a personal sense.

I have spent four years in an exile which it would be euphemistic to call voluntary since if I had remained in Germany or gone back there I should probably not be alive today. In these four years the odd blunder committed by fortune when she put me in this situation has never once ceased to trouble me. I could never have dreamed, it could never have been prophesied of me at my cradle, that I should spend my later years as an émigré, expropriated, outlawed, and committed to inevitable political protest.

From the beginning of my intellectual life I had felt myself in happiest accord with the temper of my nation and at home in its intellectual traditions. I am better suited to represent those traditions than to become a martyr for them; far more fitted to add a little to the gaiety of the world than to foster conflict and hatred in it. Something very wrong must have happened to make my life take so false and unnatural a turn. I tried to check it, this very wrong thing, so far as my weak powers were able—and in so doing I called down on myself the fate which I must now learn to reconcile with a nature essentially foreign to it.

Certainly I challenged the wrath of these despots by remaining away and giving evidence of my irrepressible disgust. But it is not merely in the last four years that I have done so. I felt thus long before, and was driven to it because I saw—earlier than my now desperate fellow-countrymen—who and what would emerge from all this. But when Germany had actually fallen into those hands I thought to keep silent. I believed that by the sacrifice I had made I had earned the right to silence; that it would enable me to preserve something dear to my heart—the contact with my public within Germany. My books, I said to myself, are written for Germans, for them above all; the outside world and its sympathy have always been for me only a happy accident. They are—these books of mine—the product of a mutually nourishing bond between nation and author, and depend on conditions which I myself have helped to create in Germany. Such bonds as these are delicate and of high importance; they ought not to be rudely sundered by politics. Though there might be impatient ones at home who, muzzled themselves, would take ill the silence of a free man, I was still able to hope that the great majority of Germans would understand my reserve, perhaps even thank me for it.

These were my assumptions. They could not be carried out. I could not have lived or worked, I should have suffocated, had I not been able now and again to cleanse my heart, so to speak, to give from time to time free vent to my abysmal disgust at what was

517

happening at home—the contemptible words and still more contemptible deeds. Justly or not, my name had once and for all become connected for the world with the conception of a Germany which it loved and honoured. The disquieting challenge rang in my ears: that I and no other must in clear terms contradict the ugly falsification which this conception of Germany was now suffering. That challenge disturbed all the free-flowing creative fancies to which I would so gladly have yielded. It was a challenge hard to resist for one to whom it had always been given to express himself, to release himself through language, to whom experience had always been one with the purifying and preserving Word.

The mystery of the Word is great; the responsibility for it and its purity is of a symbolic and spiritual kind; it has not only an artistic but also a general ethical significance; it is responsibility itself, human responsibility quite simply, also the responsibility for one's own people, the duty of keeping pure its image in the sight of humanity. In the Word is involved the unity of humanity, the wholeness of the human problem, which permits nobody, today less than ever, to separate the intellectual and artistic from the political and social, and to isolate himself within the ivory tower of the "cultural" proper. This true totality is equated with humanity itself, and anyone—whoever he be—is making a criminal attack upon humanity when he undertakes to "totalize" a segment of human life—by which I mean politics, I mean the State.

A German author accustomed to this responsibility of the Word —a German whose patriotism, perhaps naively, expresses itself in a belief in the infinite moral significance of whatever happens in Germany—should he be silent, wholly silent, in the face of the inexpiable evil that is done daily in my country to bodies, souls, and minds, to right and truth, to men and mankind? And should he be silent in the face of the frightful danger to the whole continent presented by this soul-destroying regime, which exists in abysmal ignorance of the hour that has struck today in the world? It was not possible for me to be silent. And so, contrary to my intentions, came the utterances, the unavoidably compromising gestures which have now resulted in the absurd and deplorable business of my national excommunication. The mere knowledge of who these men are who happen to possess the pitiful outward power to deprive me of my German birthright is enough to make the act appear in all its absurdity. I, forsooth, am supposed to have dishonoured the Reich, Germany, in acknowledging that I am against *them!* They have the incredible effrontery to confuse themselves with Germany! When, after all, perhaps the moment is not far off when it will be of supreme importance to the German people not to be confused with them.

To what a pass, in less than four years, have they brought Germany! Ruined, sucked dry body and soul by armaments with which they threaten the whole world, holding up the whole world and hindering it in its real task of peace, loved by nobody, regarded with fear and cold aversion by all, it stands on the brink of economic disaster, while its "enemies" stretch out their hands in alarm to snatch back from the abyss so important a member of the future family of nations, to help it, if only it will come to its senses and try to understand the real needs of the world at this hour, instead of dreaming dreams about mythical "sacred necessities."

Yes, after all, it must be helped by those whom it hinders and menaces, in order that it may not drag down the rest of the continent with it and unleash the war upon which as the *ultima ratio* it keeps its eyes ever fixed. The mature and cultural states—by which I mean those which understand the fundamental fact that war is no longer permissible—treat this endangered and endangering country, or rather the impossible leaders into whose hands it has fallen, as doctors treat a sick man—with the utmost tact and caution, with inexhaustible if not very flattering patience. But it

519

thinks it must play politics—the politics of power and hegemony —with the doctors. That is an unequal game. If one side plays politics when the other no longer thinks of politics but of peace, then for a time the first side reaps certain advantages. Anachronistic ignorance of the fact that war is no longer permissible results for a while of course in "successes" against those who are aware of the truth. But woe to the people which, not knowing what way to turn, at last actually seeks its way out through the abomination of war, hated of God and man! Such a people will be lost. It will be so vanquished that it will never rise again.

The meaning and purpose of the National Socialist state is this alone and can be only this: to put the German people in readiness for the "coming war" by ruthless repression, elimination, extirpation of every stirring of opposition; to make of them an instrument of war, infinitely compliant, without a single critical thought, driven by a blind and fanatical ignorance. Any other meaning and purpose, any other excuse this system cannot have; all the sacrifices of freedom, justice, human happiness, including the secret and open crimes for which it has blithely been responsible, can be justified only by the end—absolute fitness for war. If the idea of war as an aim in itself disappeared, the system would mean nothing but the exploitation of the people; it would be utterly senseless and superfluous.

Truth to tell, it is both of these, senseless and superfluous, not only because war will not be permitted it but also because its leading idea, the absolute readiness for war, will result precisely in the opposite of what it is striving for. No other people on earth is today so utterly incapable of war, so little in condition to endure one. That Germany would have no allies, not a single one in the world, is the first consideration but the smallest. Germany would be forsaken—terrible of course even in her isolation—but the really frightful thing would be the fact that she had forsaken herself. Intellectually reduced and humbled, morally gutted, inwardly torn apart by her deep mistrust of her leaders and the mischief they have done her in these years, profoundly uneasy herself, ignorant of the future, of course, but full of forebodings of evil, she would go into war not in the condition of 1914 but, even physically, of 1917 or 1918. The ten per cent of direct beneficiaries of the system—half even of them fallen away—would not be enough to win a war in which the majority of the rest would only see the opportunity of shaking off the shameful oppression that has weighed upon them so long—a war, that is, which after the first inevitable defeat would turn into a civil war.

No, this war is impossible; Germany cannot wage it; and if its dictators are in their senses, then their assurances of readiness for peace are not tactical lies repeated with a wink at their partisans; they spring from a faint-hearted perception of just this impossibility.

But if war cannot and shall not be—then why these robbers and murderers? Why isolation, world hostility, lawlessness, intellectual interdict, cultural darkness, and every other evil? Why not rather Germany's voluntary return to the European system, her reconciliation with Europe, with all the inward accompaniments of freedom, justice, well-being, and human decency, and a jubilant welcome from the rest of the world? Why not? Only because a regime which, in word and deed, denies the rights of man, which wants above all else to remain in power, would stultify itself and be abolished if, since it cannot make war, it actually made peace! But is that a reason?

I had forgotten, Herr Dean, that I was still addressing you. Certainly I may console myself with the reflection that you long since ceased to read this letter, aghast at language which in Germany has long been unspoken, terrified because somebody dares use the German tongue with the ancient freedom. I have not spoken out of arrogant presumption, but out of a concern and a distress from which your usurpers did not release me when they decreed that I was no longer a German—a mental and spiritual distress from which for four years not an hour of my life has been free, and struggling with which I have had to accomplish my creative work day by day. The pressure was great. And as a man who out of diffidence in religious matters will seldom or never either by tongue or pen let the name of the Deity escape him, yet in moments of deep emotion cannot refrain, let me—since after all one cannot say everything—close this letter with the brief and fervent prayer: *God help our darkened and desecrated country and teach it to make its peace with the world and with itself!*

Thomas Mann

Küsnacht, Zurich, New Year's Day, 1937

SHORTLY *after this exchange of letters, Thomas Mann came to America to establish his permanent home. On April 14, 1937, Dorothy Thompson expressed the thought of "all sharers in the great Western passion: the love of freedom" when she said: "We are glad that you are here, Thomas Mann. No nation can exile you. Yours is a larger citizenship, in no mean country. Wherever men love reason, hate obscurantism, shun darkness, turn toward light, know gratitude, praise virtue, despise meanness, kindle to sheer beauty; wherever minds are sensitive, hearts generous and spirits free—there is your home. In welcoming you, a country but honors itself. And of your future in history we have no doubt. Generations from now men may speculate about your persecutors, however the circle turns. But of you they will say: His virtue was equal to his gifts. He served with humbleness a most exacting art and with nobility the loftiest human aims."*

The letter to the Dean of the Philosophical Faculty of the University

522

of Bonn aroused great attention in five continents, and, in the words of Oswald Garrison Villard was even "greedily read in Germany, read with danger."

Thomas Mann is now living in Princeton, New Jersey, not far from that other world-famous exile, Albert Einstein.

Acknowledgments

THE editor of this anthology is indebted to so many friends and colleagues and to so many authors and publishers for invaluable aid and ideas, and for generous co-operation in every stage of the preparation of this volume, over a period of many years, that he has found it necessary to set aside the following pages to enumerate their names.

Embarrassed by the wealth of material thus placed at his disposal, he has simply listed the names in alphabetical order, with a deep sense of obligation that can be suggested only faintly by what appeared to be a routine tabulation.

A few names, however, must in all fairness be singled out for special gratitude:

Marjorie Marks Jacobson, for her indefatigable and brilliant research work on the biographical material, and her general editorial assistance in the early stages of this book;

Ann Glenna Colligan, my first secretary, and Hazel Jacobson, my present one, for their tireless and incomparably dependable and resourceful secretarial and research work over a period of years (Miss Hazel Jacobson deserves special gratitude and commendation for her judgment and energy in co-ordinating and directing all the clerical and administrative activity on a complex and difficult job of manuscript preparation, checking, and filing);

Robert Josephy and T. T. Bevans, for typographical guidance of great value;

Wallace Brockway and Herbert Winer for editorial research,

bibliographical guidance, and exceptionally learned and indefatigable aid in the preparation and correction of the final manuscript and proofs;

Lt. Col. Ralph H. Isham, Dr. A. S. W. Rosenbach, and Thomas F. Madigan for making available many rare and priceless letters and useful facsimiles, in some cases never before generally published, including those of Voltaire, Boswell, Keats, Washington, Jefferson, and Poe;

Critchell Rimington, for his unstinted co-operation in citing and supplying many letters, and for most graciously turning over to me his own manuscript of an independently planned anthology in the same general field, thus enabling me to obtain several choice letters I would otherwise have missed;

The publishers listed below for permission to use the following letters, quoted from the books designated:

Elizabeth Barrett—Robert Browning, *The Letters of Robert and Elizabeth Barrett Browning*. Harper & Brothers, 1899. By permission of the United Features Syndicate.

Marie Bashkirtseff to Guy de Maupassant, *The Letters of Marie Bashkirtseff*, translated by Mary J. Serrano. Cassell Publishing Co., 1891.

P. T. Barnum to Ulysses S. Grant, *Barnum's Own Story*. The Viking Press, 1927.

Boswell to Temple, *Private Papers of James Boswell from Malahide Castle* (Isham Collection), 1928 (The Viking Press).

Joseph Conrad to Edward Garnett, *Letters from Joseph Conrad*, edited by Edward Garnett. The Bobbs-Merrill Co., 1928.

Pierre Curie to Marie Sklodovska, *Madame Curie*, by Eve Curie. Doubleday, Doran & Co., 1938.

Charles Darwin to A. R. Wallace, *The Life and Letters of Charles Darwin*. D. Appleton-Century Co., 1887.

Emily Dickinson to Colonel Thomas Wentworth Higginson, *The Life and Letters of Emily Dickinson*, by Martha Dickinson Bianchi. Houghton Mifflin Co., 1924.

Dostoevsky to His Brother Mihail, *Dostoevsky: His Life and Letters*, translated by Koteliansky and Murry. Alfred A. Knopf, 1923.

Ralph Waldo Emerson to Walt Whitman, *Adventures in Genius*, by Will Durant. Simon & Schuster, 1931.

Paul Gauguin—August Strindberg, *Paul Gauguin, His Life and Art*, by John Gould Fletcher. N. L. Brown, 1921.

William James to His Pupils, *The Letters of William James*, edited by Henry James. The Atlantic Monthly Press, 1920.

D. H. Lawrence to J. Middleton Murry, *The Letters of D. H. Lawrence*, edited by Aldous Huxley. The Viking Press, 1932.

Thomas Mann to Chancellor Bonn, *An Exchange of Letters*. Alfred A. Knopf, 1937.

Nadejda von Meck—Piotr Tchaikovsky, *Beloved Friend*, by Catherine Drinker Bowen and Barbara von Meck. Random House, 1938.

H. L. Mencken to Will Durant, *On the Meaning of Life*, by Will Durant. Ray Long & Richard B. Smith, 1932.

Friedrich Nietzsche to Richard Wagner, *The Nietzsche-Wagner Correspondence*, edited by Elizabeth Foerster-Nietzsche. Boni & Liveright, 1921.

Napoleon Letters, *Napoleon's Letters to Marie Louise*. Farrar & Rinehart, 1935.

Pliny to Emperor Trajan, *Private Letters, Pagan and Christian*, compiled by Dorothy Brooke. E. P. Dutton & Co., 1930.

Franz Schubert to King Francis II, *Franz Schubert's Letters and Other Writings*, edited by Otto Erich Deutsch. Faber & Gwyer, 1928.

Ellen Terry—George Bernard Shaw, *Ellen Terry and Bernard*

527

Shaw; A Correspondence, edited by Christopher St. John. G. P. Putnam's Sons, 1919.

Mark Twain to No. 1365, *Mark Twain's Letters*, arranged by Albert Bigelow Paine. Harper & Bros., 1917.

Bartolomeo Vanzetti to Dante Sacco, *The Letters of Sacco and Vanzetti*, edited by Marion Denman Frankfurter and Gardner Jackson, The Viking Press, 1928.

Voltaire to Boswell, *Private Papers of James Boswell from Malahide Castle* (Isham Collection), 1928 (The Viking Press).

Voltaire to Olympe Dunoyer, *Voltaire in His Letters*, by S. G. Tallentyre. G. P. Putnam's Sons, 1919.

Individuals—For their help and advice:

Frances Bender

Tom Torre Bevans

Martha Dickinson Bianchi

Wallace Brockway

Eleanor Burke

Henry Seidel Canby

Cass Canfield

George Carlin

Bennett Cerf

Helen Cohan

Ann G. Colligan

Will Durant

Max Eastman

Irwin Edman

Albert Einstein

Charles Evans

Clifton Fadiman

John Farrar

John Gould Fletcher

Mrs. Ossip Gabrilowitsch

Jack Goodman

Allen Grover

Harold Guinzburg

William Stanley Hall

William Randolph Hearst

Wilson Hicks

Quincy Howe

Colonel Ralph H. Isham

Hazel Jacobson

Marjorie Marks Jacobson

Henry James

Matthew Josephson

Malcolm Johnson

Robert Josephy

Alfred A. Knopf

Maria Leiper

Albert Rice Leventhal

Isaac Don Levine

Ephraim London
Thoms F. Madigan
Henry L. Mencken
Christopher Morley
Frank V. Morley
Laurence Pollinger
Critchell Rimington
Robert L. Ripley
Dr. A. S. W. Rosenbach
Max D. Schachtman
Barnet Schuster
Esther Schuster
Ray Schuster

George Bernard Shaw
Leon Shimkin
Richard L. Simon
Gerald B. Spiero
Philip Van Doren Stern
J. W. N. Sullivan
Cornelius Vanderbilt, Jr.
Carl Van Doren
Edward Weeks
Jerome Weidman
Walter Winchell
Herbert Winer

Publishing Firms—For permission to quote letters:

D. Appleton-Century Co.
The Bobbs-Merrill Co.
Cassell & Co.
Doubleday, Doran
E. P. Dutton & Co., Inc.
Faber & Faber, Ltd.
Farrar & Rinehart
Harper & Brothers
Houghton Mifflin Co.

Alfred A. Knopf, Inc.
Liveright
The Macmillan Co.
G. P. Putnam's Sons
Random House, Inc.
The Saturday Review of Literature
The Viking Press

In conclusion, I must record my gratitude and obligations to numerous earlier anthologists, scholars, and editors in the field of epistolary treasures, especially George Saintsbury, E. V. Lucas, Lord Birkenhead, and Robert Gentry; and to my friend and partner, Richard L. Simon, to my wife, and to my parents who have all gallantly aided, abetted, and encouraged me in this enterprise.

Every conscientious effort has been made to give due acknowledgment and full credit for copyrighted material, but if through

ACKNOWLEDGMENTS

any unwitting oversight some trespass has been committed, by quoting from secondary sources, forgiveness is sought in advance, apology is freely offered, and correction promised in any subsequent editions.

THE EDITOR

530

Index

Abbey, Richard, English tea merchant, friend of Keats, 245
in letter from Keats to his sister Fanny, 246

Abelard, Peter, French scholastic philosopher (1079-1142), 34-36, 60
letter from Heloise, 37-46
letter to Heloise, 47-59

Actors' Theatrical Fund, 306

Adam,
in letter from Spinoza to Albert Burgh, 120

Adams, John, second President of the U.S.A. (1735-1826), 167, 170, 177
in letter from Thomas Paine to George Washington, 180

Addison, Joseph, English essayist (1672-1719), 150

Adonais (Shelley), 242

Adonis, 242

Aeneid (Virgil), 32

Aeschylus, Greek dramatist (525-456 B.C.), 354

Age of Reason, The (Paine), 178

Agrippina II, Roman empress (15?-60), 20, 22
letter to Nero, 21-22

Alaric, King of the Visigoths (376?-410), 32

Alcott, A. Bronson, American philosopher (1799-1888), 269

Alexander the Great, King of Macedon (356-323 B.C.), 3-5, 6, 8, 10
in letter from Aurangzeb to Mullah Sahe, 99
in letter from Diogenes to Aristippus, 11-12

letter from Darius III, 5-6
letters to Darius III, 6-8, 9-10

Alexander I, Czar of Russia (1777-1825), 490

Alexander VI (Rodrigo Borgia), Pope (1431-1503), 61

Alexandra Fiedorovna, consort of Nicholas II of Russia (1872-1918), 485, 486, 489-490
letter to the Czar, 487-489

Alexeiev, Mikhail, Russian general (1857-1918),
in letter from Czarina Alexandra Fiedorovna to Czar Nicholas II, 488

Almayer's Folly (Conrad), 442

Alva, Fernando Álvarez de Toledo, Duke of (1508-1582),
in letter from Spinoza to Albert Burgh, 118

Amadis of Gaul, hero of a medieval cycle of chivalry,
in letter from Albert Burgh to Spinoza, 114

American Bible, An (Hubbard),
in letter from Vanzetti to Dante Sacco, 499

American Language, The (Mencken), 506

American Mercury, The, 506

American Review, The,
in letter from Edgar Allan Poe to George Eveleth, 294

American Revolution, 165, 166, 172, 223

Amundsen, Roald, Norwegian explorer (1872-1928), 456, 460

Andrew, John Albion, American statesman (1818-1867), 319

531

Billot, Jean Baptiste, French general,
in letter from Émile Zola to the President of the French Republic, 437

Biology,
in letter from John Stuart Mill to Herbert Spencer, 359

Bion, Greek pastoral poet (2nd century B.C.), 242

Birrell, Augustine, English lawyer, politician, and critic (1850-1933), 128

Birth of Tragedy out of the Spirit of Music, The (Nietzsche), 354

Bixby, Charles, Edward, George, Henry, and Oliver, sons of Mrs. Lydia Bixby, 321

Bixby, Lydia Parker (Mrs. Cromwell), 319-320, 321, 322
letter from Abraham Lincoln, 320-321

Blackstone, Sir William, English legist, author of famed *Commentaries* (1723-1780), 165

Blackwood's Magazine, 237, 243

Blanqui, Louis Auguste, French Socialist (1805-1881),
in letter from Leon Trotsky to Jules Guesde, 479

Blücher, Gebhard Leberecht von, Prussian field marshal (1742-1819), 207, 208

Blue Review, The, 471

Boisdeffre, Raoul François Charles le Mouton de, French general (1839-1919),
in letter from Émile Zola to the President of the French Republic, 437

Boleyn, Anne, second wife of Henry VIII (1507-1536), 76, 77, 80
letter from Henry VIII, 77
letter to Henry VIII, 78-80

Bolitho, William, English journalist (1890-1930), 500

Bonaparte, Louis Napoleon; see Napoleon III

Bonaparte, Napoleon; see Napoleon I

Bone, David, Scottish master mariner and author (1874-   ),
in letter from Christopher Morley to T. A. Daly, 504

Bonn, University of, 514, 515
letter from Thomas Mann, 515-522

Book of Revelation, 23

Books and Bidders (Rosenbach), 61

Bordman, Nelly,
in letter from Elizabeth Barrett Browning to her sisters, 287

Boswell, James, Scottish man of letters (1740-1795), 129, 134, 137-139, 148, 151, 152
letter from Voltaire, 152
letter to William Johnson Temple, 139-148

Boswell, Margaret (née Montgomerie), the biographer's wife and cousin (d. 1789), 148

Boswell, Miss; see Talbot de Malahide, Lady

Bourderon, M.,
in letter from Leon Trotsky to Jules Guesde, 480

Boutelle, Charles Addison, American congressman (1839-1901),
in letter from William Randolph Hearst to his father, 391-392

Bowen, Catherine Drinker, American author (1897-   ), 373

Bowers, H. R., Polar explorer (d. 1912), 456

Boyd, Mr.,
in letter from Elizabeth Barrett Browning to her sisters, 290

Bramante (real name, Donato d'Agnolo), Italian architect and painter (1444-1514), 72

Brawne, Fanny (later, Mrs. Louis Lindon), Keats' beloved, 243, 248-250, 252
letter from John Keats, 250-252

Braxton, Carter, one of the Signers (1736-1797),
in letter from Thomas Jefferson to William Fleming, 169

Brest-Litovsk, Treaty of, 483

Brett,
in letter from Sir Walter Raleigh to his wife, 83

545

in letter from Thomas Babington Macaulay to Henry S. Randall, 331
letter to William Fleming, 168-169
Jehan, Shah; see Shah Jehan
Jerome, Saint (Eusebius Sophronius Hieronymus), translator of the Bible into Latin (340-420), 26, 31-32, 33
letter to a friend, 32-33
Jesus Christ, 13, 20, 191
in letter from Abelard to Heloise, 57, 58
in letter from John Brown to his family, 336
in letter from Burgh to Spinoza, 109, 110, 113, 115, 116
in letter from Columbus to Gabriel Sanchez, 67
in letter from Pliny the Younger to Trajan, 25
in letter from Spinoza to Burgh, 118, 121
in letter from Stevenson to Rev. Dr. Hyde, 413
in letters of Saint Paul, 15, 16, 17, 18
Jew Süss (Feuchtwanger), 511
John the Baptist,
in letter from Robert Louis Stevenson to the Rev. Dr. Hyde, 412
John the Divine, Saint,
in letter from Spinoza to Albert Burgh, 118
John Mistletoe (Morley), 500
Johnson, Samuel, English lexicographer and man of letters (1709-1784), 125, 128-129, 131, 132-133, 134, 137, 138, 139, 148, 165
in letter from Disraeli to Thomas Carlyle, 369
letter to Lord Chesterfield, 129-131
letter to Mrs. Thrale, 133-134
Johnston, John D., Lincoln's stepbrother (1854-?), 311
letter from Abraham Lincoln, 311-313
Jonson, Ben, English dramatist (1573?-1637),
in letter from Rupert Brooke to Edward Marsh, 464
Josephine, Empress of the French (1763-1814), 192, 193-194, 195, 196, 197, 199, 202, 203, 204, 205, 208

letters from Napoleon, 194, 195-196, 197, 198, 202, 204
letter to Napoleon, 205-206
Julius II (Giuliano della Rovere), Pope (1443?-1513), 72, 74
in letter from Michelangelo to Maestro Giuliano, 73, 74
Jurgenson, Piotr Ivanovich, Russian musical publisher (1836-1904),
in letter from Tchaikovsky to Mme von Meck, 376

Kaiser Wilhelm Institute, Berlin, 454
Kamenev, Y. (né Lev Borisovich Rosenfeld), Soviet Russian leader (1883-1936),
in Lenin's Deathbed Testament, 494
Kansas-Nebraska Act, 314
in letter from Abraham Lincoln to Joshua F. Speed, 316
Kathleen (Morley), 500
Kaufmann,
in letter from Czarina Alexandra Fiedorovna to Czar Nicholas II, 488
Keats, Frances Mary ("Fanny"), the poet's sister (1803-1889), 243-244
letter from John Keats, 245-247
Keats, George, the poet's brother, businessman in America (1797-1841), 243, 244
in letter from Keats to his sister Fanny, 246, 247
Keats, Georgiana Wylie, wife of George Keats, 244
Keats, John, English poet (1795-1821), 237, 241-242, 243-245, 247, 248-250, 252-253
letter from Percy Bysshe Shelley, 238-239
letter to Fanny Brawne, 250-252
letter to Fanny Keats, 245-247
letter to Percy Bysshe Shelley, 240-241
Kelvin, William Thomson, Baron, British physicist (1824-1907), 420
Kenyon, John, Jamaica-born English poet and philanthropist (1784-1856),
in letter from Elizabeth Barrett to Robert Browning, 281-282
in letter from Elizabeth Barrett Browning to her sisters, 286-287

547

in letter from George Bernard Shaw
to Ellen Terry, 450

MacArthur, Charles, American author
and playwright (1895-   ), 418
Macaulay, Thomas Babington, Baron
Macaulay of Rothley, English historian, essayist, and statesman
(1800-1859), 150, 329-330, 333
letter to Henry S. Randall, 331-333
Madariaga, Salvador de, Spanish diplomat and man of letters (1886-
), 63
Mahler, Gustav, Bohemian composer and
conductor (1860-1911),
in letter from Feuchtwanger to Mr.
X, 512
Maikov, Apollon, Russian poet (1821-
1847),
in letter from Dostoevsky to his
brother, 301
Maikov, Nikolay Apollonovich, Russian
poet (1821-1897),
in letter from Dostoevsky to his
brother, 301
Maikova, Eugenia Petrovna,
in letter from Dostoevsky to his
brother, 301, 304
Maine, Anne Louise Bénédicte de Bour-
bon, Duchess du, French patroness
of arts and letters (1676-1753), 155
Makarov, A., Russian Minister of Interior from 1911 to 1913,
in letter from Czarina Alexandra Fiedorovna to Czar Nicholas II, 488
Malahide Castle, near Dublin, 137, 151
Malvy, Louis Jean, French politician
(1875-   ), 483
in letter from Leon Trotsky to Jules
Guesde, 475, 477, 480
Manet, Édouard, French impressionist
painter (1832-1883),
in letter from August Strindberg to
Paul Gauguin, 426
Mann, Thomas, German novelist living
in America (1875-   ), 514-515,
522-523
letter to the Dean of the Philosophical Faculty of the University of
Bonn, 515-522

Mansel, Henry Longueville, English
metaphysician (1820-1871),
in letter from Thomas Huxley to
Charles Kingsley, 342
Mansfield, Katherine (pen name of
Kathleen Beauchamp), English short-
story writer, wife of J. Middleton
Murry (1890-1923), 467, 471-472
in letter from D. H. Lawrence to
John Middleton Murry, 467-471
Mardonius, Persian general (c. 480 B.C.),
in letter from Alexander the Great to
Darius III, 9
Marie Antoinette, consort of Louis XVI
of France (1755-1793), 76
Marie Louise, second wife of Napoleon
I, afterwards Duchess of Parma
(1791-1847), 203, 206-208
letter from Napoleon, 207
Markham, Edwin, American poet (1852-
1940), 309-310
Martin, Mrs.,
in letter from Elizabeth Barrett
Browning to her sisters, 290
Marsh, Sir Edward Howard, English diplomat and writer (1872-   ),
letter from Rupert Brooke, 461-464
Marx, Karl, German socialist and journalist (1818-1883), 492
Mathews, Cornelius, American dramatist, editor, and poet (1817-1889),
in letter from Edgar Allan Poe to
George Eveleth, 295
Maupassant, Guy de, French short-story
writer and novelist (1850-1893),
379, 381, 383
letter from Marie Bashkirtseff, 380-
381
letter to Marie Bashkirtseff, 381-382
Meaning of Truth, The (William
James), 431
Meck, Barbara Karpoff von, granddaughter of Tchaikovsky's patron
(1889-   ), 373
Meck, Nadejda Philaretovna von, Russian millionaire, patron of music
(1831-1894), 373-374, 377-378
letter from Tchaikovsky, 376-377
letter to Tchaikovsky, 375-376

Tennyson, Alfred, First Baron, English poet laureate (1809-1892), 460
in letter from Rupert Brooke to Edward Marsh, 462
in letter from Disraeli to Thomas Carlyle, 369

Ten Thousand Letters of Charles Dickens, 306

Terra Nuova, Robert Falcon Scott's boat, 456

Terror, Reign of (French Revolution), 135, 136, 178, 185, 187

Terry, Ellen Alicia, English actress (1848-1928), 444-446, 448, 452
letter from George Bernard Shaw, 449-451
letter to George Bernard Shaw, 447-448

Tertullian (Quintus Septimius Florens Tertullianus), voluminous Christian apologist (160?-230?), 26-27

Thanatopsis (Bryant), 257

Thayer, Alexander Wheelock, American biographer of Beethoven (1817-1897), 210

Thayer, Webster, judge at the Sacco-Vanzetti trial, 499

Thomas, Albert, French politician (1878-),
in letter from Leon Trotsky to Jules Guesde, 477, 479, 481

Thompson, Dorothy (Mrs. Sinclair Lewis), American journalist (1894-), 522

Thompson, Francis, English poet (1859-1907), 229, 236, 237, 252

Thoreau, Henry David, American philosophical writer (1817-1862), 269-271, 273-274
letter to Ralph Waldo Emerson, 271-273

Thoughts on Religion and Evidences of Christianity (Pascal), 94

Thrale, Henry, brewer, first husband of Hester Lynch Piozzi (d. 1780), 132

Thrale, Hester Lynch, English bluestocking, friend of Dr. Johnson (1741-1821), 132-133, 134
letter from Dr. Johnson, 133-134

Three Hours for Lunch Club, 500

Throgmorton, Elizabeth; see Raleigh, Elizabeth, Lady

Thunder on the Left (Morley), 500

Tinker, Chauncey Brewster, American man of letters, educator (1876-), 138

"To a Skylark" (Shelley), 237

Todd, Mary; see Lincoln, Mary Todd

Tom Sawyer (Twain), 394, 395, 398
in letter from Mark Twain to No. 1365, 395-396

Tower of London, 77, 81, 85, 87, 89

Tractatus Theologico-Politicus (Spinoza); see *Treatise on Religion and the State, A* (Spinoza)

Trajan (Marcus Ulpius Nerva Trajanus), Roman emperor (52-117), 23, 26
letter from Pliny the Younger, 24-26

Treatise on Religion and the State, A (Spinoza), 106
in letter from Spinoza to Albert Burgh, 122

Treatise on the Gods: A Philosophic Study on Right and Wrong (Mencken), 510

Trepov, A. F., Russian statesman,
in letter from Czarina Alexandra Fiedorovna to Czar Nicholas II, 488

Tristan und Isolde (Wagner), 349, 352
in letter from Baron von Hornstein to Richard Wagner, 351

Triumph of Life, The (Shelley), 242

Trotsky, Leon (né Lev Davidovich Bronstein), Russian revolutionary (1877-1940), 473-474, 482-484, 485-486, 490, 491, 495
in Lenin's Deathbed Testament, 493, 494, 495
letter to Jules Guesde, 474-482

Trumbull, Jonathan, American statesman (1740-1809), 175

Turgeniev, Ivan, Russian novelist (1818-1883), 373

Twain, Mark (né Samuel Langhorne Clemens), American writer (1835-1910), 394-395, 398
letter to No. 1365, 395-398

Winslow, Gertrude L., woman who befriended Sacco and Vanzetti,
in letter from Vanzetti to Dante Sacco,
499
Wise, American politician,
in letter from William Randolph
Hearst to his father, 391-392
Witchcraft (Mathews),
in letter from Edgar Allan Poe to
George Eveleth, 295
Witte, Count Sergei Yulievich, Russian
statesman (1849-1915),
in letter from Czarina Alexandra Fiedorovna to Czar Nicholas II, 488
Woollcott, Alexander, American man of
letters (1887-   ), 418
Wordsworth, William, English poet
laureate (1770-1850), 236, 277
Work of Valerian Maikov, The,
in letter from Dostoevsky to his
brother, 304
World (London),
in letter from Dr. Johnson to Lord
Chesterfield, 129
World, The (New York),
in letter from William Randolph
Hearst to his father, 390, 391
World War, First, 439, 461, 485
Wyatt, Sir Thomas, English poet (1503?-
1542), 76

Yellow Book, The,
in letter from Leon Trotsky to Jules
Guesde, 479
Yussupov, Prince Felix, Russian con-
spirator (1887-   ), 490

Zélide, pen name of Isabella Agneta van
Serooskerken van Tuyll, later Mme
de Charrière, Dutch writer and bluestocking (1740-1805),
in letter from James Boswell to William Johnson Temple, 145-146
Zenobia, Queen of Palmyra (d. 295?),
28, 29-30
letter from Aurelian, 28
letter to Aurelian, 29
Zetkin, Klara Zundel, German Socialist
(1857-1933),
in letter from Leon Trotsky to Jules
Guesde, 481
Zinoviev, Gregor Evseievich, Russian
soviet leader (1883-1937),
in Lenin's Deathbed Testament, 494
Zola, Émile, French novelist (1840-
1902), 381, 435-436, 439, 440
letter to the President of the French
Republic, 436-438
Zu-ul-Kurnain; see Alexander the Great

A Representative Selection of Simon and Schuster Publications

HOW TO READ A BOOK by MORTIMER ADLER

AMERICAN WHITE PAPER by JOSEPH ALSOP and ROBERT KINTNER

THE BIBLE DESIGNED TO BE READ AS LIVING LITERATURE
edited by ERNEST SUTHERLAND BATES

MEN OF MATHEMATICS by E. T. BELL

KINGS ROW by HENRY BELLAMANN

MEN OF MUSIC by WALLACE BROCKWAY AND HERBERT WEINSTOCK

MEN OF ART and MODERN ART by THOMAS CRAVEN

A TREASURY OF AMERICAN PRINTS and A TREASURY OF ART MASTERPIECES
edited by THOMAS CRAVEN

THE ART OF THINKING by ABBÉ ERNEST DIMNET

THE STORY OF PHILOSOPHY, OUR ORIENTAL HERITAGE,
and THE LIFE OF GREECE by WILL DURANT

THE EVOLUTION OF PHYSICS by ALBERT EINSTEIN AND LEOPOLD INFELD

THE PULSE OF DEMOCRACY by GEORGE GALLUP and SAMUEL FORBES RAE

WITH MALICE TOWARD SOME by MARGARET HALSEY

I BELIEVE: THE PERSONAL PHILOSOPHIES OF CERTAIN EMINENT
MEN AND WOMEN OF OUR TIME edited by CLIFTON FADIMAN

NOW IN NOVEMBER by JOSEPHINE JOHNSON

MATHEMATICS AND THE IMAGINATION by EDWARD KASNER and JAMES NEWMAN

A TREASURY OF THE THEATRE by BURNS MANTLE and JOHN GASSNER

NIJINSKY by ROMOLA NIJINSKY

WOLF SOLENT and OTHER NOVELS by JOHN COWPER POWYS

EYES ON THE WORLD: A PHOTOGRAPHIC RECORD OF HISTORY
IN THE MAKING by M. LINCOLN SCHUSTER

THE FIRST WORLD WAR: A PHOTOGRAPHIC HISTORY
edited by LAURENCE STALLINGS

HISTORY OF THE RUSSIAN REVOLUTION by LEON TROTSKY

VAN LOON'S GEOGRAPHY and THE ARTS
by HENDRIK WILLEM VAN LOON

from THE INNER SANCTUM of
SIMON and SCHUSTER
PUBLISHERS · 1230 SIXTH AVENUE
ROCKEFELLER CENTER · NEW YORK CITY